*Mr. Shuter, Mr. Quick and Mrs. Green in " She Stoops to Conquer."*

THE HARVARD CLASSICS
EDITED BY CHARLES W ELIOT LL D

# MODERN ENGLISH DRAMA

## DRYDEN · SHERIDAN · GOLDSMITH
## SHELLEY · BROWNING · BYRON

WITH INTRODUCTIONS
AND ILLUSTRATIONS

"DR ELIOT'S FIVE-FOOT SHELF OF BOOKS"

P F COLLIER & SON
NEW YORK

Designed, Printed, and Bound at
The Collier Press, New York

# CONTENTS

## INTRODUCTORY NOTE

THE age of Elizabeth, memorable for so many reasons in the history of England, was especially brilliant in literature, and, within literature, in the drama. With some falling off in spontaneity, the impulse to great dramatic production lasted till the Long Parliament closed the theaters in 1642; and when they were reopened at the Restoration, in 1660, the stage only too faithfully reflected the debased moral tone of the court society of Charles II.

John Dryden (1631-1700), the great representative figure in the literature of the latter part of the seventeenth century, exemplifies in his work most of the main tendencies of the time. He came into notice with a poem on the death of Cromwell in 1658, and two years later was composing couplets expressing his loyalty to the returned king. He married Lady Elizabeth Howard, the daughter of a royalist house, and for practically all the rest of his life remained an adherent of the Tory Party. In 1663 he began writing for the stage, and during the next thirty years he attempted nearly all the current forms of drama. His "Annus Mirabilis" (1666), celebrating the English naval victories over the Dutch, brought him in 1670 the Poet Laureateship. He had, meantime, begun the writing of those admirable critical essays, represented in the present series by his Preface to the "Fables" and his Dedication to the translation of Virgil. In these he shows himself not only a critic of sound and penetrating judgment, but the first master of modern English prose style.

With "Absalom and Achitophel," a satire on the Whig leader, Shaftesbury, Dryden entered a new phase, and achieved what is regarded as "the finest of all political satires." This was followed by "The Medal," again directed against the Whigs, and this by "Mac Flecknoe," a fierce attack on his enemy and rival Shadwell. The Government rewarded his services by a lucrative appointment.

After triumphing in the three fields of drama, criticism, and satire, Dryden appears next as a religious poet in his "Religio Laici," an exposition of the doctrines of the Church of England from a layman's point of view. In the same year that the Catholic James II. ascended the throne, Dryden joined the Roman Church, and two years later defended his new religion in "The

3

Hind and the Panther," an allegorical debate between two animals standing respectively for Catholicism and Anglicanism.

The Revolution of 1688 put an end to Dryden's prosperity; and after a short return to dramatic composition, he turned to translation as a means of supporting himself. He had already done something in this line; and after a series of translations from Juvenal, Persius, and Ovid, he undertook, at the age of sixty-three, the enormous task of turning the entire works of Virgil into English verse. How he succeeded in this, readers of the "Æneid" in a companion volume of these classics can judge for themselves. Dryden's production closes with the collection of narrative poems called "Fables," published in 1700, in which year he died and was buried in the Poet's Corner in Westminster Abbey.

Dryden lived in an age of reaction against excessive religious idealism, and both his character and his works are marked by the somewhat unheroic traits of such a period. But he was, on the whole, an honest man, open-minded, genial, candid, and modest; the wielder of a style, both in verse and prose, unmatched for clearness, vigor, and sanity.

Three types of comedy appeared in England in the time of Dryden—the comedy of humors, the comedy of intrigue, and the comedy of manners—and in all he did work that classed him with the ablest of his contemporaries. He developed the somewhat bombastic type of drama known as the heroic play, and brought it to its height in his "Conquest of Granada"; then, becoming dissatisfied with this form, he cultivated the French classic tragedy on the model of Racine. This he modified by combining with the regularity of the French treatment of dramatic action a richness of characterization in which he showed himself a disciple of Shakespeare, and of this mixed type his best example is "All for Love." Here he has the daring to challenge comparison with his master, and the greatest testimony to his achievement is the fact that, as Professor Noyes has said, "fresh from Shakespeare's 'Antony and Cleopatra,' we can still read with intense pleasure Dryden's version of the story."

# DEDICATION

To the Right Honourable, THOMAS, EARL OF DANBY, VISCOUNT LATIMER. and BARON OSBORNE of Kiveton, in Yorkshire; Lord High Treasurer of England, one of His Majesty's Most Honourable Privy Council, and Knight of the Most Noble Order of the Garter.

MY LORD,

THE gratitude of poets is so troublesome a virtue to great men, that you are often in danger of your own benefits: for you are threatened with some epistle, and not suffered to do good in quiet, or to compound for their silence whom you have obliged. Yet, I confess, I neither am or ought to be surprised at this indulgence; for your lordship has the same right to favour poetry, which the great and noble have ever had—

*Carmen amat, quisquis carmine digna gerit.*

There is somewhat of a tie in nature betwixt those who are born for worthy actions, and those who can transmit them to posterity; and though ours be much the inferior part, it comes at least within the verge of alliance; nor are we unprofitable members of the commonwealth, when we animate others to those virtues, which we copy and describe from you.

It is indeed their interest, who endeavour the subversion of governments, to discourage poets and historians; for the best which can happen to them, is to be forgotten. But such who, under kings, are the fathers of their country, and by a just and prudent ordering of affairs preserve it, have the same reason to cherish the chroniclers of their actions, as they have to lay up in safety the deeds and evidences of their estates; for such records are their undoubted titles to the love and reverence of after ages. Your lordship's administration has already taken up a considerable part of the English annals; and many of its

5

most happy years are owing to it. His Majesty, the most knowing judge of men, and the best master, has acknowledged the ease and benefit he receives in the incomes of his treasury, which you found not only disordered, but exhausted. All things were in the confusion of a chaos, without form or method, if not reduced beyond it, even to annihilation; so that you had not only to separate the jarring elements, but (if that boldness of expression might be allowed me) to create them. Your enemies had so embroiled the management of your office, that they looked on your advancement as the instrument of your ruin. And as if the clogging of the revenue, and the confusion of accounts, which you found in your entrance, were not sufficient, they added their own weight of malice to the public calamity, by forestalling the credit which should cure it. Your friends on the other side were only capable of pitying, but not of aiding you; no further help or counsel was remaining to you, but what was founded on yourself; and that indeed was your security; for your diligence, your constancy, and your prudence, wrought most surely within, when they were not disturbed by any outward motion. The highest virtue is best to be trusted with itself; for assistance only can be given by a genius superior to that which it assists; and it is the noblest kind of debt, when we are only obliged to God and nature. This then, my lord, is your just commendation, and that you have wrought out yourself a way to glory, by those very means that were designed for your destruction: You have not only restored but advanced the revenues of your master, without grievance to the subject; and, as if that were little yet, the debts of the exchequer, which lay heaviest both on the crown, and on private persons, have by your conduct been established in a certainty of satisfaction. An action so much the more great and honourable, because the case was without the ordinary relief of laws; above the hopes of the afflicted and beyond the narrowness of the treasury to redress, had it been managed by a less able hand. It is certainly the happiest, and most unenvied part of all your fortune, to do good to many, while you do injury to none; to receive at once the prayers of the subject, and the praises of the prince; and, by the care of your conduct, to give him means of exerting the chiefest (if any be the chiefest) of his royal virtues, his distributive justice to the deserving, and his bounty and compassion to the wanting.

The disposition of princes towards their people cannot be better discovered than in the choice of their ministers; who, like the animal spirits betwixt the soul and body, participate somewhat of both natures, and make the communication which is betwixt them. A king, who is just and moderate in his nature, who rules according to the laws, whom God has made happy by forming the temper of his soul to the constitution of his government, and who makes us happy, by assuming over us no other sovereignty than that wherein our welfare and liberty consists; a prince, I say, of so excellent a character, and so suitable to the wishes of all good men, could not better have conveyed himself into his people's apprehensions, than in your lordship's person; who so lively express the same virtues, that you seem not so much a copy, as an emanation of him. Moderation is doubtless an establishment of greatness; but there is a steadiness of temper which is likewise requisite in a minister of state; so equal a mixture of both virtues, that he may stand like an isthmus betwixt the two encroaching seas of arbitrary power, and lawless anarchy. The undertaking would be difficult to any but an extraordinary genius, to stand at the line, and to divide the limits; to pay what is due to the great representative of the nation, and neither to enhance, nor to yield up, the undoubted prerogatives of the crown. These, my lord, are the proper virtues of a noble Englishman, as indeed they are properly English virtues; no people in the world being capable of using them, but we who have the happiness to be born under so equal, and so well-poised a government;—a government which has all the advantages of liberty beyond a commonwealth, and all the marks of kingly sovereignty, without the danger of a tyranny. Both my nature, as I am an Englishman, and my reason, as I am a man, have bred in me a loathing to that specious name of a republic; that mock appearance of a liberty, where all who have not part in the government, are slaves; and slaves they are of a viler note, than such as are subjects to an absolute dominion. For no Christian monarchy is so absolute, but it is circumscribed with laws; but when the executive power is in the law-makers, there is no further check upon them; and the people must suffer without a remedy, because they are oppressed by their representatives. If I must serve, the number of my masters, who were born my equals, would but add to the ignominy of my bondage. The nature of our government, above all others, is exactly suited both to the situation of our country, and the temper of the natives; an island being more proper for commerce and for defence, than for extending its dominions on the Continent; for what the valour of its inhabitants might gain, by reason of its remoteness, and the casualties of the seas, it could not so easily preserve: And, therefore, neither the arbitrary power of One, in a monarchy, nor of Many, in a commonwealth, could make us greater than we are. It is true, that vaster and more frequent taxes might be gathered, when the consent of the people was not asked or needed; but this were only by conquering abroad, to be poor at home; and the examples of our neighbours teach us, that they are not always the happiest subjects, whose kings extend their dominions farthest. Since therefore we cannot win by an offensive war, at least, a land war, the model of our government seems naturally contrived for the defensive part; and the consent of a people is easily obtained to contribute to that power which must protect it. *Felices nimium, bona si sua nôrint, Angligenæ!* And yet there are not wanting malcontents among us, who, surfeiting themselves on too much happiness, would persuade the people that they might be happier by a change. It was indeed the policy of their old forefather, when himself was fallen from the station of glory, to seduce mankind into the same rebellion with him, by telling him he might yet be freer than he was; that is more free than his nature would allow, or, if I may so say, than God could make him. We have already all the liberty which free-born subjects can enjoy, and all beyond it is but licence. But if it be liberty of conscience which they pretend, the moderation of our church is such, that its practice extends not to the severity of persecution; and its discipline is withal so easy, that it allows more freedom to dissenters than any of the sects would allow to it. In the meantime, what right can be pretended by these men to attempt innovation in church or state? Who made them the trustees, or to speak a little nearer their own language, the keepers of the liberty of England? If their call be extraordinary, let them convince us by working miracles; for ordinary vocation they can have none, to disturb the government under which they were born, and which protects them. He who has often changed his party, and always has made his interest the rule of it, gives little evidence of his sincerity for the public good; it is manifest he changes but for himself, and takes the people for tools to work his fortune. Yet the experience of all ages might let him know, that they who trouble the waters first, have seldom the benefit of the fishing; as they who began the late rebellion enjoyed not the fruit of their undertaking, but were crushed themselves by the usurpation of their own instrument. Neither is it enough for them to answer, that they only intend a reformation of the government, but not the subversion of it: on such pretence all insurrections have been founded; it is striking at the root of power, which is obedience. Every remonstrance of private men has the seed of treason in it; and discourses, which are couched in ambiguous terms, are therefore the more dangerous, because they do all the mischief of open sedition, yet are safe from the punishment of the laws. These, my lord, are considerations, which I should not pass so lightly over, had I room to manage them as they deserve; for no man can be so inconsiderable in a nation, as not to have a share in the welfare of it; and if he be a true Englishman, he must at the same time be fired with indignation, and revenge himself as he can on the disturbers of his country. And to whom could I more fitly apply myself than to your lordship, who have not only an inborn, but an hereditary loyalty? The memorable constancy and sufferings of your father, almost to the ruin of his estate, for the royal cause, were an earnest of that which such a parent and such an institution would produce in the person of a son. But so unhappy an occasion of manifesting your own zeal, in suffering for his present majesty, the providence of God, and the prudence of your administration, will, I hope, prevent; that, as your father's fortune waited on the unhappiness of his sovereign, so your own may participate of the better fate which attends his son. The relation which you have by alliance to the noble family of your lady, serves to confirm to you both this happy augury. For what can deserve a greater place in the English chronicle, than the loyalty and courage, the actions and death, of the general of an army, fighting for his prince and country? The honour and gallantry of the Earl of Lindsey is so illustrious a subject, that it is fit to adorn an heroic poem; for he was the protomartyr of the cause, and the type of his unfortunate royal master.

Yet after all, my lord, if I may speak my thoughts, you are

happy rather to us than to yourself; for the multiplicity, the cares, and the vexations of your employment, have betrayed you from yourself, and given you up into the possession of the public. You are robbed of your privacy and friends, and scarce any hour of your life you can call your own. Those, who envy your fortune, if they wanted not good-nature, might more justly pity it; and when they see you watched by a crowd of suitors, whose importunity it is impossible to avoid, would conclude, with reason, that you have lost much more in true content, than you have gained by dignity; and that a private gentleman is better attended by a single servant, than your lordship with so clamorous a train. Pardon me, my lord, if I speak like a philosopher on this subject; the fortune which makes a man uneasy, cannot make him happy; and a wise man must think himself uneasy, when few of his actions are in his choice.

This last consideration has brought me to another, and a very seasonable one for your relief; which is, that while I pity your want of leisure, I have impertinently detained you so long a time. I have put off my own business, which was my dedication, till it is so late, that I am now ashamed to begin it; and therefore I will say nothing of the poem, which I present to you, because I know not if you are like to have an hour, which, with a good conscience, you may throw away in perusing it; and for the author, I have only to beg the continuance of your protection to him, who is,

My Lord,

> Your Lordship's most obliged,
> > Most humble, and
> > > Most obedient, servant,
> > > > JOHN DRYDEN.

# PREFACE

THE death of Antony and Cleopatra is a subject which has
been treated by the greatest wits of our nation, after Shakespeare; and by all so variously, that their example has given
me the confidence to try myself in this bow of Ulysses amongst
the crowd of suitors, and, withal, to take my own measures, in
aiming at the mark. I doubt not but the same motive has prevailed with all of us in this attempt; I mean the excellency of
the moral: For the chief persons represented were famous
patterns of unlawful love; and their end accordingly was unfortunate. All reasonable men have long since concluded, that the
hero of the poem ought not to be a character of perfect virtue,
for then he could not, without injustice, be made unhappy; nor
yet altogether wicked, because he could not then be pitied. I have
therefore steered the middle course; and have drawn the character of Antony as favourably as Plutarch, Appian, and Dion
Cassius would give me leave; the like I have observed in Cleopatra. That which is wanting to work up the pity to a greater
height, was not afforded me by the story; for the crimes of
love, which they both committed, were not occasioned by any
necessity, or fatal ignorance, but were wholly voluntary; since
our passions are, or ought to be, within our power. The fabric
of the play is regular enough, as to the inferior parts of it;
and the unities of time, place, and action, more exactly observed,
than perhaps the English theatre requires. Particularly, the
action is so much one, that it is the only one of the kind without
episode, or underplot; every scene in the tragedy conducing to
the main design, and every act concluding with a turn of it.
The greatest error in the contrivance seems to be in the person
of Octavia; for, though I might use the privilege of a poet, to
introduce her into Alexandria, yet I had not enough considered,
that the compassion she moved to herself and children was destructive to that which I reserved for Antony and Cleopatra;

whose mutual love being founded upon vice, must lessen the favour of the audience to them, when virtue and innocence were oppressed by it. And, though I justified Antony in some measure, by making Octavia's departure to proceed wholly from herself; yet the force of the first machine still remained; and the dividing of pity, like the cutting of a river into many channels, abated the strength of the natural stream. But this is an objection which none of my critics have urged against me; and therefore I might have let it pass, if I could have resolved to have been partial to myself. The faults my enemies have found are rather cavils concerning little and not essential decencies; which a master of the ceremonies may decide betwixt us. The French poets, I confess, are strict observers of these punctilios: They would not, for example, have suffered Cleopatra and Octavia to have met; or, if they had met, there must have only passed betwixt them some cold civilities, but no eagerness of repartee, for fear of offending against the greatness of their characters, and the modesty of their sex. This objection I foresaw, and at the same time contemned; for I judged it both natural and probable, that Octavia, proud of her new-gained conquest, would search out Cleopatra to triumph over her; and that Cleopatra, thus attacked, was not of a spirit to shun the encounter: And it is not unlikely, that two exasperated rivals should use such satire as I have put into their mouths; for, after all, though the one were a Roman, and the other a queen, they were both women. It is true, some actions, though natural, are not fit to be represented; and broad obscenities in words ought in good manners to be avoided: expressions therefore are a modest clothing of our thoughts, as breeches and petticoats are of our bodies. If I have kept myself within the bounds of modesty, all beyond, it is but nicety and affectation; which is no more but modesty depraved into a vice. They betray themselves who are too quick of apprehension in such cases, and leave all reasonable men to imagine worse of them, than of the poet.

Honest Montaigne goes yet further: *Nous ne sommes que cérémonie; la cérémonie nous emporte, et laissons la substance des choses. Nous nous tenons aux branches, et abandonnons le tronc et le corps. Nous avons appris aux dames de rougir, oyans seulement nommer ce qu'elles ne craignent aucunement à faire: Nous n'osons appeller à droit nos membres, et ne craig-*

*nons pas de les employer à toute sorte de débauche. La céré-
monie nous defend d'exprimer par paroles les choses licites et
naturelles, et nous l'en croyons; la raison nous défend de n'en
faire point d'illicites et mauvaises, et personne ne l'en croit.*
My comfort is, that by this opinion my enemies are but sucking
critics, who would fain be nibbling ere their teeth are come.

Yet, in this nicety of manners does the excellency of French
poetry consist. Their heroes are the most civil people breathing;
but their good breeding seldom extends to a word of sense; all
their wit is in their ceremony; they want the genius which ani-
mates our stage; and therefore it is but necessary, when they
cannot please, that they should take care not to offend. But as
the civilest man in the company is commonly the dullest, so these
authors, while they are afraid to make you laugh or cry, out of
pure good manners make you sleep. They are so careful not
to exasperate a critic, that they never leave him any work; so
busy with the broom, and make so clean a riddance that there is
little left either for censure or for praise: For no part of a
poem is worth our discommending, where the whole is insipid;
as when we have once tasted of palled wine, we stay not to
examine it glass by glass. But while they affect to shine in
trifles, they are often careless in essentials. Thus, their Hippolytus is so scrupulous in point of decency, that he will rather
expose himself to death, than accuse his stepmother to his
father; and my critics I am sure will commend him for it. But
we of grosser apprehensions are apt to think that this excess of
generosity is not practicable, but with fools and madmen. This
was good manners with a vengeance; and the audience is like
to be much concerned at the misfortunes of this admirable hero.
But take Hippolytus out of his poetic fit, and I suppose he
would think it a wiser part to set the saddle on the right horse,
and choose rather to live with the reputation of a plain-spoken,
honest man, than to die with the infamy of an incestuous villain.
In the meantime we may take notice, that where the poet ought
to have preserved the character as it was delivered to us by
antiquity, when he should have given us the picture of a rough
young man, of the Amazonian strain, a jolly huntsman, and both
by his profession and his early rising a mortal enemy to love,
he has chosen to give him the turn of gallantry, sent him to travel
from Athens to Paris, taught him to make love, and transformed

the Hippolytus of Euripides into Monsieur Hippolyte. I should
not have troubled myself thus far with French poets, but that I
find our *Chedreux* critics wholly form their judgments by them.
But for my part, I desire to be tried by the laws of my own
country; for it seems unjust to me, that the French should prescribe here, till they have conquered. Our little sonneteers,
who follow them, have too narrow souls to judge of poetry.
Poets themselves are the most proper, though I conclude not the
only critics. But till some genius, as universal as Aristotle,
shall arise, one who can penetrate into all arts and sciences, without the practice of them, I shall think it reasonable, that the
judgment of an artificer in his own art should be preferable
to the opinion of another man; at least where he is not bribed
by interest, or prejudiced by malice. And this, I suppose, is
manifest by plain inductions: For, first, the crowd cannot be
presumed to have more than a gross instinct of what pleases or
displeases them: Every man will grant me this; but then, by a
particular kindness to himself, he draws his own stake first, and
will be distinguished from the multitude, of which other men
may think him one. But, if I come closer to those who are
allowed for witty men, either by the advantage of their quality,
or by common fame, and affirm that neither are they qualified
to decide sovereignly concerning poetry, I shall yet have a strong
party of my opinion; for most of them severally will exclude
the rest, either from the number of witty men, or at least of
able judges. But here again they are all indulgent to themselves; and every one who believes himself a wit, that is, every
man, will pretend at the same time to a right of judging. But
to press it yet further, there are many witty men, but few poets;
neither have all poets a taste of tragedy. And this is the rock
on which they are daily splitting. Poetry, which is a picture of
nature, must generally please; but it is not to be understood that
all parts of it must please every man; therefore is not tragedy
to be judged by a witty man, whose taste is only confined to
comedy. Nor is every man, who loves tragedy, a sufficient judge
of it; he must understand the excellences of it too, or he will
only prove a blind admirer, not a critic. From hence it comes
that so many satires on poets, and censures of their writings,
fly abroad. Men of pleasant conversation (at least esteemed
so), and endued with a trifling kind of fancy, perhaps helped out

with some smattering of Latin, are ambitious to distinguish
themselves from the herd of gentlemen, by their poetry—

> *Rarus enim fermè sensus communis in illâ*
> *Fortunâ.*

And is not this a wretched affectation, not to be contented
with what fortune has done for them, and sit down quietly with
their estates, but they must call their wits in question, and
needlessly expose their nakedness to public view? Not considering that they are not to expect the same approbation from sober
men, which they have found from their flatterers after the third
bottle. If a little glittering in discourse has passed them on
us for witty men, where was the necessity of undeceiving the
world? Would a man who has an ill title to an estate, but yet
is in possession of it; would he bring it of his own accord, to
be tried at Westminster? We who write, if we want the talent,
yet have the excuse that we do it for a poor subsistence; but
what can be urged in their defence, who, not having the vocation
of poverty to scribble, out of mere wantonness take pains to
make themselves ridiculous? Horace was certainly in the right,
where he said, "That no man is satisfied with his own condition."
A poet is not pleased, because he is not rich; and the rich are dis-
contented, because the poets will not admit them of their number.
Thus the case is hard with writers: If they succeed not, they
must starve; and if they do, some malicious satire is prepared to
level them, for daring to please without their leave. But while
they are so eager to destroy the fame of others, their ambition is
manifest in their concernment; some poem of their own is to be
produced, and the slaves are to be laid flat with their faces on the
ground, that the monarch may appear in the greater majesty.

Dionysius and Nero had the same longings, but with all their
power they could never bring their business well about. 'Tis
true, they proclaimed themselves poets by sound of trumpet; and
poets they were, upon pain of death to any man who durst call
them otherwise. The audience had a fine time on't, you may
imagine; they sat in a bodily fear, and looked as demurely as
they could: for it was a hanging matter to laugh unseasonably;
and the tyrants were suspicious, as they had reason, that their
subjects had them in the wind; so, every man, in his own
defence, set as good a face upon the business as he could. It

was known beforehand that the monarchs were to be crowned laureates; but when the show was over, and an honest man was suffered to depart quietly, he took out his laughter which he had stifled, with a firm resolution never more to see an emperor's play, though he had been ten years a-making it. In the meantime the true poets were they who made the best markets: for they had wit enough to yield the prize with a good grace, and not contend with him who had thirty legions. They were sure to be rewarded, if they confessed themselves bad writers, and that was somewhat better than to be martyrs for their reputation. Lucan's example was enough to teach them manners; and after he was put to death, for overcoming Nero, the emperor carried it without dispute for the best poet in his dominions. No man was ambitious of that grinning honour; for if he heard the malicious trumpeter proclaiming his name before his betters, he knew there was but one way with him. Mæcenas took another course, and we know he was more than a great man, for he was witty too: But finding himself far gone in poetry, which Seneca assures us was not his talent, he thought it his best way to be well with Virgil and with Horace; that at least he might be a poet at the second hand; and we see how happily it has succeeded with him; for his own bad poetry is forgotten, and their panegyrics of him still remain. But they who should be our patrons are for no such expensive ways to fame; they have much of the poetry of Mæcenas, but little of his liberality. They are for prosecuting Horace and Virgil, in the persons of their successors; for such is every man who has any part of their soul and fire, though in a less degree. Some of their little zanies yet go further; for they are persecutors even of Horace himself, as far as they are able, by their ignorant and vile imitations of him; by making an unjust use of his authority, and turning his artillery against his friends. But how would he disdain to be copied by such hands! I dare answer for him, he would be more uneasy in their company, than he was with Crispinus, their forefather, in the Holy Way; and would no more have allowed them a place amongst the critics, than he would Demetrius the mimic, and Tigellius the buffoon;

> ————— *Demetri, teque, Tigelli,*
> *Discipulorum inter jubeo plorare cathedras.*

With what scorn would he look down on such miserable translators, who make doggerel of his Latin, mistake his meaning, misapply his censures, and often contradict their own? He is fixed as a landmark to set out the bounds of poetry—

————— *Saxum antiquum, ingens,—*
*Limes agro positus, litem ut discerneret arvis.*

But other arms than theirs, and other sinews are required, to raise the weight of such an author; and when they would toss him against enemies—

*Genua labant, gelidus concrevit frigore sanguis.*
*Tum lapis ipse viri, vacuum per inane volatus,*
*Nec spatium evasit totum, nec pertulit ictum.*

For my part, I would wish no other revenge, either for myself, or the rest of the poets, from this rhyming judge of the twelvepenny gallery, this legitimate son of Sternhold, than that he would subscribe his name to his censure, or (not to tax him beyond his learning) set his mark: For, should he own himself publicly, and come from behind the lion's skin, they whom he condemns would be thankful to him, they whom he praises would choose to be condemned; and the magistrates, whom he has elected, would modestly withdraw from their employment, to avoid the scandal of his nomination. The sharpness of his satire, next to himself, falls most heavily on his friends, and they ought never to forgive him for commending them perpetually the wrong way, and sometimes by contraries. If he have a friend, whose hastiness in writing is his greatest fault, Horace would have taught him to have minced the matter, and to have called it readiness of thought, and a flowing fancy; for friendship will allow a man to christen an imperfection by the name of some neighbour virtue—

*Vellem in amicitiâ sic erraremus; et isti*
*Errori nomen virtus posuisset honestum.*

But he would never have allowed him to have called a slow man hasty, or a hasty writer a slow drudge, as Juvenal explains it—

————— *Canibus pigris, scabieque vetustâ*
*Lævibus, et siccæ lambentibus ora lucernæ,*
*Nomen erit, Pardus, Tigris, Leo; si quid adhuc est*
*Quod fremit in terris violentius.*

Yet Lucretius laughs at a foolish lover, even for excusing the imperfections of his mistress—

> *Nigra* μελίχροος *est, immunda et fœtida* ἄκοσμος
> *Balba loqui non quit,* τραυλίζει; *muta pudens est,* etc.

But to drive it *ad Æthiopem cygnum* is not to be endured. I leave him to interpret this by the benefit of his French version on the other side, and without further considering him, than I have the rest of my illiterate censors, whom I have disdained to answer, because they are not qualified for judges. It remains that I acquaint the reader, that I have endeavoured in this play to follow the practice of the ancients, who, as Mr Rymer has judiciously observed, are and ought to be our masters. Horace likewise gives it for a rule in his art of poetry—

> ———— *Vos exemplaria Græca*
> *Nocturnâ versate manu, versate diurnâ.*

Yet, though their models are regular, they are too little for English tragedy; which requires to be built in a larger compass. I could give an instance in the *Oedipus Tyrannus,* which was the masterpiece of Sophocles; but I reserve it for a more fit occasion, which I hope to have hereafter. In my style, I have professed to imitate the divine Shakespeare; which that I might perform more freely, I have disencumbered myself from rhyme. Not that I condemn my former way, but that this is more proper to my present purpose. I hope I need not to explain myself, that I have not copied my author servilely: Words and phrases must of necessity receive a change in succeeding ages; but it is almost a miracle that much of his language remains so pure; and that he who began dramatic poetry amongst us, untaught by any, and as Ben Jonson tells us, without learning, should by the force of his own genius perform so much, that in a manner he has left no praise for any who come after him. The occasion is fair, and the subject would be pleasant to handle the difference of styles betwixt him and Fletcher, and wherein, and how far they are both to be imitated. But since I must not be over-confident of my own performance after him, it will be prudence in me to be silent. Yet, I hope, I may affirm, and without vanity, that, by imitating him, I have excelled myself throughout the play; and particularly, that I prefer the scene betwixt Antony and Ventidius in the first act, to anything which I have written in this kind.

# PROLOGUE

WHAT flocks of critics hover here to-day,
As vultures wait on armies for their prey,
All gaping for the carcase of a play!
With croaking notes they bode some dire event,
And follow dying poets by the scent.
Ours gives himself for gone; y' have watched your time:
He fights this day unarmed,—without his rhyme;—
And brings a tale which often has been told;
As sad as Dido's; and almost as old.
His hero, whom you wits his bully call,
Bates of his mettle, and scarce rants at all;
He's somewhat lewd; but a well-meaning mind;
Weeps much; fights little; but is wond'rous kind.
In short, a pattern, and companion fit,
For all the keeping Tonies of the pit.
I could name more: a wife, and mistress too;
Both (to be plain) too good for most of you:
The wife well-natured, and the mistress true.

  Now, poets, if your fame has been his care,
Allow him all the candour you can spare.
A brave man scorns to quarrel once a day;
Like Hectors in at every petty fray.
Let those find fault whose wit's so very small,
They've need to show that they can think at all;
Errors, like straws, upon the surface flow;
He who would search for pearls, must dive below.
Fops may have leave to level all they can;
As pigmies would be glad to lop a man.
Half-wits are fleas; so little and so light,
We scarce could know they live, but that they bite.
But, as the rich, when tired with daily feasts,
For change, become their next poor tenant's guests:

Drink hearty draughts of ale from plain brown bowls,
And snatch the homely rasher from the coals:
So you, retiring from much better cheer,
For once, may venture to do penance here.
And since that plenteous autumn now is past,
Whose grapes and peaches have indulged your taste,
Take in good part, from our poor poet's board,
Such rivelled fruits as winter can afford.

# ALL FOR LOVE

OR

# THE WORLD WELL LOST

## A TRAGEDY

### DRAMATIS PERSONÆ

| | |
|---|---|
| MARK ANTONY. | ALEXAS, the Queen's Eunuch. |
| VENTIDIUS, his General. | SERAPION, Priest of Isis. |
| DOLABELLA, his Friend. | MYRIS, another Priest. |

Servants to Antony.

| | | |
|---|---|---|
| CLEOPATRA, Queen of Egypt. | CHARMION, | Cleopatra's Maids. |
| OCTAVIA, Antony's Wife. | IRAS, | |

Antony's two little Daughters.

SCENE.—ALEXANDRIA.

## ACT I

### SCENE I.—*The Temple of Isis*

*Enter* SERAPION, MYRIS, Priests of Isis

*Serapion*

PORTENTS and prodigies have grown so frequent,
That they have lost their name. Our fruitful Nile
Flowed ere the wonted season, with a torrent
So unexpected, and so wondrous fierce,
That the wild deluge overtook the haste
Even of the hinds that watched it: Men and beasts
Were borne above the tops of trees, that grew
On the utmost margin of the water-mark.
Then, with so swift an ebb the flood drove backward,
It slipt from underneath the scaly herd:
Here monstrous phocæ panted on the shore;
Forsaken dolphins there with their broad tails,
Lay lashing the departing waves: hard by them,

Sea horses floundering in the slimy mud,
Tossed up their heads, and dashed the ooze about them.


*Enter* ALEXAS *behind them*

MYR. Avert these omens, Heaven!

SERAP. Last night, between the hours of twelve and one,
In a lone aisle of the temple while I walked,
A whirlwind rose, that, with a violent blast,
Shook all the dome: the doors around me clapt;
The iron wicket, that defends the vault,
Where the long race of Ptolemies is laid,
Burst open, and disclosed the mighty dead.
From out each monument, in order placed,
An armed ghost starts up: the boy-king last
Reared his inglorious head. A peal of groans
Then followed, and a lamentable voice
Cried, Egypt is no more! My blood ran back,
My shaking knees against each other knocked;
On the cold pavement down I fell entranced,
And so unfinished left the horrid scene.

ALEX. And dreamed you this? or did invent the story,

[*Showing himself.*

To frighten our Egyptian boys withal,
And train them up, betimes, in fear of priesthood?

SERAP. My lord, I saw you not,
Nor meant my words should reach your ears; but what
I uttered was most true.

ALEX. A foolish dream,
Bred from the fumes of indigested feasts,
And holy luxury.

SERAP. I know my duty:
This goes no further.

ALEX. 'Tis not fit it should;
Nor would the times now bear it, were it true.
All southern, from yon hills, the Roman camp
Hangs o'er us black and threatening like a storm
Just breaking on our heads.

SERAP. Our faint Egyptians pray for Antony;
But in their servile hearts they own Octavius.

Myr. Why then does Antony dream out his hours,
And tempts not fortune for a noble day,
Which might redeem what Actium lost?

Alex. He thinks 'tis past recovery.

Serap. Yet the foe
Seems not to press the siege.

Alex. Oh, there's the wonder.
Mæcenas and Agrippa, who can most
With Cæsar, are his foes. His wife Octavia,
Driven from his house, solicits her revenge;
And Dolabella, who was once his friend,
Upon some private grudge, now seeks his ruin:
Yet still war seems on either side to sleep.

Serap. 'Tis strange that Antony, for some days past,
Has not beheld the face of Cleopatra;
But here, in Isis' temple, lives retired,
And makes his heart a prey to black despair.

Alex. 'Tis true; and we much fear he hopes by absence
To cure his mind of love.

Serap. If he be vanquished,
Or make his peace, Egypt is doomed to be
A Roman province; and our plenteous harvests
Must then redeem the scarceness of their soil.
While Antony stood firm, our Alexandria
Rivalled proud Rome (dominion's other seat),
And fortune striding, like a vast Colossus,
Could fix an equal foot of empire here.

Alex. Had I my wish, these tyrants of all nature,
Who lord it o'er mankind, should perish,—perish,
Each by the other's sword; But, since our will
Is lamely followed by our power, we must
Depend on one; with him to rise or fall.

Serap. How stands the queen affected?

Alex. Oh, she dotes,
She dotes, Serapion, on this vanquished man,
And winds herself about his mighty ruins;
Whom would she yet forsake, yet yield him up,
This hunted prey, to his pursuer's hands,
She might preserve us all: but 'tis in vain—
This changes my designs, this blasts my counsels,

And makes me use all means to keep him here.
Whom I could wish divided from her arms,
Far as the earth's deep centre.  Well, you know
The state of things; no more of your ill omens
And black prognostics; labour to confirm
The people's hearts.


*Enter* VENTIDIUS, *talking aside with a*
Gentleman *of* ANTONY's

SERAP. These Romans will o'erhear us.
But who's that stranger?  By his warlike port,
His fierce demeanour, and erected look,
He's of no vulgar note.
    ALEX. Oh, 'tis Ventidius,
Our emperor's great lieutenant in the East,
Who first showed Rome that Parthia could be conquered.
When Antony returned from Syria last,
He left this man to guard the Roman frontiers.
    SERAP. You seem to know him well.
    ALEX. Too well.  I saw him at Cilicia first,
When Cleopatra there met Antony:
A mortal foe he was to us, and Egypt.
But,—let me witness to the worth I hate,—
A braver Roman never drew a sword;
Firm to his prince, but as a friend, not slave,
He ne'er was of his pleasures; but presides
O'er all his cooler hours, and morning counsels:
In short the plainness, fierceness, rugged virtue,
Of an old true-stampt Roman lives in him.
His coming bodes I know not what of ill
To our affairs.  Withdraw to mark him better;
And I'll acquaint you why I sought you here,
And what's our present work.
    [*They withdraw to a corner of the stage; and* VEN-
        TIDIUS, *with the other, comes forward to the front.*
    VENT. Not see him; say you?
I say, I must, and will.
    GENT. He has commanded,
On pain of death, none should approach his presence.

Vent. I bring him news will raise his drooping spirits,
Give him new life.

Gent. He sees not Cleopatra.

Vent. Would he had never seen her!

Gent. He eats not, drinks not, sleeps not, has no use
Of anything, but thought; or if he talks,
'Tis to himself, and then 'tis perfect raving:
Then he defies the world, and bids it pass,
Sometimes he gnaws his lips, and curses loud
The boy Octavius; then he draws his mouth
Into a scornful smile, and cries, " Take all,
The world's not worth my care."

Vent. Just, just his nature.
Virtue's his path; but sometimes 'tis too narrow
For his vast soul; and then he starts out wide,
And bounds into a vice, that bears him far
From his first course, and plunges him in ills:
But, when his danger makes him find his faults,
Quick to observe, and full of sharp remorse,
He censures eagerly his own misdeeds,
Judging himself with malice to himself,
And not forgiving what as man he did,
Because his other parts are more than man.—
He must not thus be lost.

[Alexas *and the Priests come forward.*

Alex. You have your full instructions, now advance,
Proclaim your orders loudly.

Serap. Romans, Egyptians, hear the queen's command.
Thus Cleopatra bids: Let labour cease;
To pomp and triumphs give this happy day,
That gave the world a lord: 'tis Antony's.
Live, Antony; and Cleopatra live!
Be this the general voice sent up to heaven,
And every public place repeat this echo.

Vent. Fine pageantry!                               [*Aside*

Serap. Set out before your doors
The images of all your sleeping fathers,
With laurels crowned; with laurels wreath your posts,
And strew with flowers the pavement; let the priests
Do present sacrifice; pour out the wine,

And call the gods to join with you in gladness.

VENT. Curse on the tongue that bids this general joy!
Can they be friends of Antony, who revel
When Antony's in danger?  Hide, for shame,
You Romans, your great grandsires' images,
For fear their souls should animate their marbles,
To blush at their degenerate progeny.

ALEX. A love, which knows no bounds, to Antony,
Would mark the day with honours, when all heaven
Laboured for him, when each propitious star
Stood wakeful in his orb, to watch that hour
And shed his better influence.  Her own birthday
Our queen neglected like a vulgar fate,
That passed obscurely by.

VENT. Would it had slept,
Divided far from his; till some remote
And future age had called it out, to ruin
Some other prince, not him!

ALEX. Your emperor,
Though grown unkind, would be more gentle, than
To upbraid my queen for loving him too well.

VENT. Does the mute sacrifice upbraid the priest!
He knows him not his executioner.
Oh, she has decked his ruin with her love,
Led him in golden bands to gaudy slaughter,
And made perdition pleasing: She has left him
The blank of what he was.
I tell thee, eunuch, she has quite unmanned him.
Can any Roman see, and know him now,
Thus altered from the lord of half mankind,
Unbent, unsinewed, made a woman's toy,
Shrunk from the vast extent of all his honours,
And crampt within a corner of the world?
O Antony!
Thou bravest soldier, and thou best of friends!
Bounteous as nature; next to nature's God!
Couldst thou but make new worlds, so wouldst thou give
    them,
As bounty were thy being! rough in battle,
As the first Romans when they went to war;

Yet after victory more pitiful
Than all their praying virgins left at home!
   ALEX. Would you could add, to those more shining
      virtues,
His truth to her who loves him.
   VENT. Would I could not!
But wherefore waste I precious hours with thee!
Thou art her darling mischief, her chief engine,
Antony's other fate. Go, tell thy queen,
Ventidius is arrived, to end her charms.
Let your Egyptian timbrels play alone,
Nor mix effeminate sounds with Roman trumpets,
You dare not fight for Antony; **go** pray
And keep your cowards' holiday in temples.
                    *[Exeunt* ALEXAS, SERAPION.

     *Re-enter the* Gentleman of M. ANTONY

   2 GENT. The emperor approaches, and commands,
On pain of death, that none presume to stay.
   1 GENT. I dare not disobey him.
                    *[Going out with the other.*
   VENT. Well, I dare.
But I'll observe him first unseen, and find
Which way his humour drives: The rest I'll venture.
                    *[Withdraws.*

   *Enter* ANTONY, *walking with a disturbed motion*
         *before he speaks*

   ANT. They tell me, 'tis my birthday, and I'll keep it
With double pomp of sadness.
'Tis what the day deserves, which gave me breath.
Why was I raised the meteor of the world,
Hung in the skies, and blazing as I travelled,
'Till all my fires were spent; and then cast downward,
To be trod out by Cæsar?
   VENT. [*aside*]. On my soul,
'Tis mournful, wondrous mournful!
   ANT. Count thy gains.
Now, Antony, wouldst thou be born for this?
Glutton of fortune, thy devouring youth

Has starved thy wanting age.

VENT. How sorrow shakes him!    *[Aside.*

So, now the tempest tears him up by the roots,
And on the ground extends the noble ruin.

     *[ANTONY having thrown himself down.*

Lie there, thou shadow of an emperor;
The place thou pressest on thy mother earth
Is all thy empire now: now it contains thee;
Some few days hence, and then 'twill be too large,
When thou'rt contracted in thy narrow urn,
Shrunk to a few ashes; then Octavia
(For Cleopatra will not live to see it),
Octavia then will have thee all her own,
And bear thee in her widowed hand to Cæsar;
Cæsar will weep, the crocodile will weep,
To see his rival of the universe
Lie still and peaceful there. I'll think no more on't.

 ANT. Give me some music, look that it be sad.
I'll soothe my melancholy, till I swell,
And burst myself with sighing.—  *[Soft music.*
'Tis somewhat to my humour; stay, I fancy
I'm now turned wild, a commoner of nature;
Of all forsaken, and forsaking all;
Live in a shady forest's sylvan scene,
Stretched at my length beneath some blasted oak,
I lean my head upon the mossy bark,
And look just of a piece as I grew from it;
My uncombed locks, matted like mistletoe,
Hang o'er my hoary face; a murm'ring brook
Runs at my foot.

 VENT. Methinks I fancy
Myself there too.

 ANT. The herd come jumping by me,
And fearless, quench their thirst, while I look on,
And take me for their fellow-citizen.
More of this image, more; it lulls my thoughts.

      *[Soft music again.*

 VENT. I must disturb him; I can hold no longer.

      *[Stands before him.*

 ANT. [*starting up*]. Art thou Ventidius?

VENT. Are you Antony?
I'm liker what I was, than you to him
I left you last.
   ANT. I'm angry.
   VENT. So am I.
   ANT. I would be private: leave me.
   VENT. Sir, I love you,
And therefore will not leave you.
   ANT. Will not leave me!
Where have you learnt that answer? Who am I?
   VENT. My emperor; the man I love next Heaven:
If I said more, I think 'twere scarce a sin:
You're all that's good, and god-like.
   ANT. All that's wretched.
You will not leave me then?
   VENT. 'Twas too presuming
To say I would not; but I dare not leave you:
And, 'tis unkind in you to chide me hence
So soon, when I so far have come to see you.
   ANT. Now thou hast seen me, art thou satisfied?
For, if a friend, thou hast beheld enough;
And, if a foe, too much.
   VENT. Look, emperor, this is no common dew.

                               *[Weeping.*

I have not wept this forty years; but now
My mother comes afresh into my eyes;
I cannot help her softness.
   ANT. By heavens, he weeps! poor good old man, he
      weeps!
The big round drops course one another down
The furrows of his cheeks.—Stop them, Ventidius,
Or I shall blush to death, they set my shame,
That caused them, full before me.
   VENT. I'll do my best.
   ANT. Sure there's contagion in the tears of friends:
See, I have caught it too. Believe me, 'tis not
For my own griefs, but thine.—Nay, father!
   VENT. Emperor.
   ANT. Emperor! Why, that's the style of victory;
The conqu'ring soldier, red with unfelt wounds,

Salutes his general so; but never more
Shall that sound reach my ears.

VENT. I warrant you.

ANT. Actium, Actium! Oh!—

VENT. It sits too near you.

ANT. Here, here it lies a lump of lead by day,
And, in my short, distracted, nightly slumbers,
The hag that rides my dreams.—

VENT. Out with it; give it vent.

ANT. Urge not my shame.

I lost a battle,—

VENT. So has Julius done.

ANT. Thou favour'st me, and speak'st not half thou
        think'st;

For Julius fought it out, and lost it fairly.
But Antony—

VENT. Nay, stop not.

ANT. Antony—

Well, thou wilt have it,—like a coward, fled,
Fled while his soldiers fought; fled first, Ventidius.
Thou long'st to curse me, and I give thee leave.
I know thou cam'st prepared to rail.

VENT. I did.

ANT. I'll help thee.—I have been a man, Ventidius.

VENT. Yes, and a brave one! but—

ANT. I know thy meaning.

But I have lost my reason, have disgraced
The name of soldier, with inglorious ease.
In the full vintage of my flowing honours,
Sat still, and saw it prest by other hands.
Fortune came smiling to my youth, and wooed it,
And purple greatness met my ripened years.
When first I came to empire, I was borne
On tides of people, crowding to my triumphs;
The wish of nations, and the willing world
Received me as its pledge of future peace;
I was so great, so happy, so beloved,
Fate could not ruin me; till I took pains,
And worked against my fortune, chid her from me,
And turned her loose; yet still she came again.

My careless days, and my luxurious nights,
At length have wearied her, and now she's gone,
Gone, gone, divorced for ever. Help me, soldier,
To curse this madman, this industrious fool,
Who laboured to be wretched: Pr'ythee, curse me.

VENT. No.

ANT. Why?

VENT. You are too sensible already
Of what you've done, too conscious of your failings;
And, like a scorpion, whipt by others first
To fury, sting yourself in mad revenge.
I would bring balm, and pour it in your wounds,
Cure your distempered mind, and heal your fortunes.

ANT. I know thou would'st.

VENT. I will.

ANT. Ha, ha, ha, ha!

VENT. You laugh.

ANT. I do, to see officious love.
Give cordials to the dead.

VENT. You would be lost, then?

ANT. I am.

VENT. I say you are not. Try your fortune.

ANT. I have, to the utmost. Dost thou think me
    desperate,
Without just cause? No, when I found all lost
Beyond repair, I hid me from the world,
And learnt to scorn it here; which now I do
So heartily, I think it is not worth
The cost of keeping.

VENT. Cæsar thinks not so;
He'll thank you for the gift he could not take.
You would be killed like Tully, would you? do,
Hold out your throat to Cæsar, and die tamely.

ANT. No, I can kill myself; and so resolve.

VENT. I can die with you too, when time shall serve;
But fortune calls upon us now to live,
To fight, to conquer.

ANT. Sure thou dream'st, Ventidius.

VENT. No; 'tis you dream; you sleep away your
    hours

In desperate sloth, miscalled philosophy.
Up, up, for honour's sake; twelve legions wait you,
And long to call you chief: By painful journeys
I led them, patient both of heat and hunger,
Down from the Parthian marches to the Nile.
'Twill do you good to see their sunburnt faces,
Their scarred cheeks, and chopt hands: there's virtue in
        them.
They'll sell those mangled limbs at dearer rates
Than yon trim bands can buy.
    ANT.  Where left you them?
    VENT.  I said in Lower Syria.
    ANT.  Bring them hither;
There may be life in these.
    VENT.  They will not come.
    ANT.  Why didst thou mock my hopes with promised
        aids,
To double my despair?  They're mutinous.
    VENT.  Most firm and loyal.
    ANT.  Yet they will not march
To succour me.  O trifler!
    VENT.  They petition
You would make haste to head them.
    ANT.  I'm besieged.
    VENT.  There's but one way shut up: How came I hither?
    ANT.  I will not stir.
    VENT.  They would perhaps desire
A better reason.
    ANT.  I have never used
My soldiers to demand a reason of
My actions.  Why did they refuse to march?
    VENT.  They said they would not fight for Cleopatra.
    ANT.  What was't they said?
    VENT.  They said they would not fight for Cleopatra.
Why should they fight indeed, to make her conquer,
And make you more a slave? to gain you kingdoms,
Which, for a kiss, at your next midnight feast,
You'll sell to her?  Then she new-names her jewels,
And calls this diamond such or such a tax;
Each pendant in her ear shall be a province.

ANT. Ventidius, I allow your tongue free licence
On all my other faults; but, on your life,
No word of Cleopatra: she deserves
More worlds than I can lose.

VENT. Behold, you Powers,
To whom you have intrusted humankind!
See Europe, Afric, Asia, put in balance,
And all weighed down by one light, worthless woman!
I think the gods are Antonies, and give,
Like prodigals, this nether world away
To none but wasteful hands.

ANT. You grow presumptuous.

VENT. I take the privilege of plain love to speak.

ANT. Plain love! plain arrogance, plain insolence!
Thy men are cowards; thou, an envious traitor;
Who, under seeming honesty, hast vented
The burden of thy rank, o'erflowing gall.
O that thou wert my equal; great in arms
As the first Cæsar was, that I might kill thee
Without a stain to honour!

VENT. You may kill me;
You have done more already,—called me traitor.

ANT. Art thou not one?

VENT. For showing you yourself,
Which none else durst have done? but had I been
That name, which I disdain to speak again,
I needed not have sought your abject fortunes,
Come to partake your fate, to die with you.
What hindered me to have led my conquering eagles
To fill Octavius' bands? I could have been
A traitor then, a glorious, happy traitor,
And not have been so called.

ANT. Forgive me, soldier;
I've been too passionate.

VENT. You thought me false;
Thought my old age betrayed you: Kill me, sir,
Pray, kill me; yet you need not, your unkindness
Has left your sword no work.

ANT. I did not think so;
I said it in my rage: Pr'ythee, forgive me.

Why didst thou tempt my anger, by discovery
Of what I would not hear?
 VENT. No prince but you
Could merit that sincerity I used,
Nor durst another man have ventured it;
But you, ere love misled your wandering eyes,
Were sure the chief and best of human race,
Framed in the very pride and boast of nature;
So perfect, that the gods, who formed you, wondered
At their own skill, and cried—A lucky hit
Has mended our design. Their envy hindered,
Else you had been immortal, and a pattern,
When Heaven would work for ostentation's sake
To copy out again.
 ANT. But Cleopatra—
Go on; for I can bear it now.
 VENT. No more.
 ANT. Thou dar'st not trust my passion, but thou may'st;
Thou only lov'st, the rest have flattered me.
 VENT. Heaven's blessing on your heart for that kind
  word!
May I believe you love me? Speak again.
 ANT. Indeed I do. Speak this, and this, and this.
           [*Hugging him.*
Thy praises were unjust; but, I'll deserve them,
And yet mend all. Do with me what thou wilt;
Lead me to victory! thou know'st the way.
 VENT. And, will you leave this—
 ANT. Pr'ythee, do not curse her,
And I will leave her; though, Heaven knows, I love
Beyond life, conquest, empire, all, but honour;
But I will leave her.
 VENT. That's my royal master;
And, shall we fight?
 ANT. I warrant thee, old soldier.
Thou shalt behold me once again in iron;
And at the head of our old troops, that beat
The Parthians, cry aloud—Come, follow me!
 VENT. Oh, now I hear my emperor! in that word
Octavius fell. Gods, let me see that day,

And, if I have ten years behind, take all:
I'll thank you for the exchange.
    ANT. O Cleopatra!
    VENT. Again?
    ANT. I've done: In that last sigh she went.
Cæsar shall know what 'tis to force a lover
From all he holds most dear.
    VENT. Methinks, you breathe
Another soul: Your looks are more divine;
You speak a hero, and you move a god.
    ANT. Oh, thou hast fired me; my soul's up in arms,
And mans each part about me: Once again,
That noble eagerness of fight has seized me;
That eagerness with which I darted upward
To Cassius' camp: In vain the steepy hill
Opposed my way; in vain a war of spears
Sung round my head, and planted on my shield;
I won the trenches, while my foremost men
Lagged on the plain below.
    VENT. Ye gods, ye gods,
For such another honour!
    ANT. Come on, my soldier!
Our hearts and arms are still the same: I long
Once more to meet our foes; that thou and I,
Like Time and Death, marching before our troops,
May taste fate to them; mow them out a passage,
And, entering where the foremost squadrons yield,
Begin the noble harvest of the field.    [*Exeunt.*

## ACT II

### SCENE I

#### *Enter* CLEOPATRA, IRAS, *and* ALEXAS

    CLEO. What shall I do, or whither shall I turn?
        Ventidius has o'ercome, and he will go.
    ALEX. He goes to fight for you.
    CLEO. Then he would see me, ere he went to fight:
Flatter me not: If once he goes, he's lost.

And all my hopes destroyed.

    ALEX.  Does this weak passion
Become a mighty queen?

    CLEO.  I am no queen:
Is this to be a queen, to be besieged
By yon insulting Roman, and to wait
Each hour the victor's chain? These ills are small:
For Antony is lost, and I can mourn
For nothing else but him. Now come, Octavius,
I have no more to lose! prepare thy bands;
I'm fit to be a captive: Antony
Has taught my mind the fortune of a slave.

    IRAS.  Call reason to assist you.

    CLEO.  I have none,
And none would have: My love's a noble madness,
Which shows the cause deserved it. Moderate sorrow
Fits vulgar love, and for a vulgar man:
But I have loved with such transcendent passion,
I soared, at first, quite out of reason's view,
And now am lost above it. No, I'm proud
'Tis thus: Would Antony could see me now
Think you he would not sigh, though he must leave me?
Sure he would sigh; for he is noble-natured,
And bears a tender heart: I know him well.
Ah, no, I know him not; I knew him once,
But now 'tis past.

    IRAS.  Let it be past with you:
Forget him, madam.

    CLEO.  Never, never, Iras.
He once was mine; and once, though now 'tis gone,
Leaves a faint image of possession still.

    ALEX.  Think him inconstant, cruel, and ungrateful.

    CLEO.  I cannot: If I could, those thoughts were vain.
Faithless, ungrateful, cruel, though he be,
I still must love him.

*Enter* CHARMION

Now, what news, my Charmion?
Will he be kind? and will he not forsake me?
Am I to live, or die?—nay, do I live?

Or am I dead? for when he gave his answer,
Fate took the word, and then I lived or died.

    CHAR.  I found him, madam—

    CLEO.  A long speech preparing?
If thou bring'st comfort, haste, and give it me,
For never was more need.

    IRAS.  I know he loves you.

    CLEO.  Had he been kind, her eyes had told me so,
Before her tongue could speak it: Now she studies,
To soften what he said; but give me death,
Just as he sent it, Charmion, undisguised,
And in the words he spoke.

    CHAR.  I found him, then,
Encompassed round, I think, with iron statues;
So mute, so motionless his soldiers stood,
While awfully he cast his eyes about,
And every leader's hopes or fears surveyed:
Methought he looked resolved, and yet not pleased.
When he beheld me struggling in the crowd,
He blushed, and bade make way.

    ALEX.  There's comfort yet.

    CHAR.  Ventidius fixed his eyes upon my passage
Severely, as he meant to frown me back,
And sullenly gave place: I told my message,
Just as you gave it, broken and disordered;
I numbered in it all your sighs and tears,
And while I moved your pitiful request,
That you but only begged a last farewell,
He fetched an inward groan; and every time
I named you, sighed, as if his heart were breaking,
But, shunned my eyes, and guiltily looked down:
He seemed not now that awful Antony,
Who shook an armed assembly with his nod;
But, making show as he would rub his eyes,
Disguised and blotted out a falling tear.

    CLEO.  Did he then weep? And was I worth a
      tear?
If what thou hast to say be not as pleasing,
Tell me no more, but let me die contented.

    CHAR.  He bid me say,—He knew himself so well,

He could deny you nothing, if he saw you;
And therefore—

　CLEO.　Thou wouldst say, he would not see me?

　CHAR.　And therefore begged you not to use a power,
Which he could ill resist; yet he should ever
Respect you, as he ought.

　CLEO.　Is that a word
For Antony to use to Cleopatra?
O that faint word, *respect!* how I disdain it!
Disdain myself, for loving after it!
He should have kept that word for cold Octavia.
Respect is for a wife: Am I that thing,
That dull, insipid lump, without desires,
And without power to give them?

　ALEX.　You misjudge;
You see through love, and that deludes your sight;
As, what is straight, seems crooked through the water:
But I, who bear my reason undisturbed,
Can see this Antony, this dreaded man,
A fearful slave, who fain would run away,
And shuns his master's eyes: If you pursue him,
My life on't, he still drags a chain along.
That needs must clog his flight.

　CLEO.　Could I believe thee!—

　ALEX.　By every circumstance I know he loves.
True, he's hard prest, by interest and by honour;
Yet he but doubts, and parleys, and casts out
Many a long look for succour.

　CLEO.　He sends word,
He fears to see my face.

　ALEX.　And would you more?
He shows his weakness who declines the combat,
And you must urge your fortune. Could he speak
More plainly? To my ears, the message sounds—
Come to my rescue, Cleopatra, come;
Come, free me from Ventidius; from my tyrant:
See me, and give me a pretence to leave him!—
I hear his trumpets. This way he must pass.
Please you, retire a while; I'll work him first,
That he may bend more easy.

CLEO. You shall rule me;
But all, I fear, in vain.     [*Exit with* CHARMION *and* IRAS.
ALEX. I fear so too;
Though I concealed my thoughts, to make her bold;
But 'tis our utmost means, and fate befriend it!
                                        [*Withdraws.*

*Enter* Lictors *with Fasces; one bearing the Eagle; then*
*enter* ANTONY *with* VENTIDIUS, *followed by other*
Commanders

ANT. Octavius is the minion of blind chance,
But holds from virtue nothing.
VENT. Has he courage?
ANT. But just enough to season him from coward.
Oh, 'tis the coldest youth upon a charge,
The most deliberate fighter! if he ventures
(As in Illyria once, they say, he did,
To storm a town), 'tis when he cannot choose;
When all the world have fixt their eyes upon him;
And then he lives on that for seven years after;
But, at a close revenge he never fails.
VENT. I heard you challenged him.
ANT. I did, Ventidius.
What think'st thou was his answer? 'Twas so tame!—
He said, he had more ways than one to die;
I had not.
VENT. Poor!
ANT. He has more ways than one;
But he would choose them all before that one.
VENT. He first would choose an ague, or a fever.
ANT. No; it must be an ague, not a fever;
He has not warmth enough to die by that.
VENT. Or old age and a bed.
ANT. Ay, there's his choice,
He would live, like a lamp, to the last wink,
And crawl the utmost verge of life.
O Hercules! Why should a man like this,
Who dares not trust his fate for one great action,
Be all the care of Heaven? Why should he lord it

O'er fourscore thousand men, of whom each one
Is braver than himself?
    VENT.  You conquered for him:
Philippi knows it; there you shared with him
That empire, which your sword made all your own.
    ANT.  Fool that I was, upon my eagle's wings
I bore this wren, till I was tired with soaring,
And now he mounts above me.
Good heavens, is this,—is this the man who braves
      me?
Who bids my age make way? Drives me before him,
To the world's ridge, and sweeps me off like rubbish?
    VENT.  Sir, we lose time; the troops are mounted all.
    ANT.  Then give the word to march:
I long to leave this prison of a town,
To join thy legions; and, in open field,
Once more to show my face. Lead, my deliverer.


*Enter* ALEXAS

    ALEX.  Great emperor,
In mighty arms renowned above mankind,
But, in soft pity to the opprest, a god;
This message sends the mournful Cleopatra
To her departing lord.
    VENT.  Smooth sycophant!
    ALEX.  A thousand wishes, and ten thousand prayers,
Millions of blessings wait you to the wars;
Millions of sighs and tears she sends you too,
And would have sent
As many dear embraces to your arms,
As many parting kisses to your lips;
But those, she fears, have wearied you already.
    VENT. [*aside*].  False crocodile!
    ALEX.  And yet she begs not now, you would not leave
      her;
That were a wish too mighty for her hopes,
Too presuming
For her low fortune, and your ebbing love;
That were a wish for her more prosperous days,

Her blooming beauty, and your growing kindness.

    ANT. [*aside*]. Well, I must man it out:—What would
      the queen?

    ALEX. First, to these noble warriors, who attend
Your daring courage in the chase of fame,—
Too daring, and too dangerous for her quiet,—
She humbly recommends all she holds dear,
All her own cares and fears,—the care of you.

    VENT. Yes, witness Actium.

    ANT. Let him speak, Ventidius.

    ALEX. You, when his matchless valour bears him
      forward,
With ardour too heroic, on his foes,
Fall down, as she would do, before his feet;
Lie in his way, and stop the paths of death:
Tell him, this god is not invulnerable;
That absent Cleopatra bleeds in him;
And, that you may remember her petition,
She begs you wear these trifles, as a pawn,
Which, at your wished return, she will redeem
               [*Gives jewels to the Commanders.*
With all the wealth of Egypt:
This to the great Ventidius she presents,
Whom she can never count her enemy,
Because he loves her lord.

    VENT. Tell her, I'll none on't;
I'm not ashamed of honest poverty;
Not all the diamonds of the east can bribe
Ventidius from his faith. I hope to see
These and the rest of all her sparkling store,
Where they shall more deservingly be placed,

    ANT. And who must wear them then?

    VENT. The wronged Octavia.

    ANT. You might have spared that word.

    VENT. And he that bribe.

    ANT. But have I no remembrance?

    ALEX. Yes, a dear one;
Your slave the queen—

    ANT. My mistress.

    ALEX. Then your mistress;

Your mistress would, she says, have sent her soul,
But that you had long since; she humbly begs
This ruby bracelet, set with bleeding hearts,
The emblems of her own, may bind your arm.

        *[Presenting a bracelet.*

 VENT. Now, my best lord,—in honour's name, I ask
   you,
For manhood's sake, and for your own dear safety,—
Touch not these poisoned gifts,
Infected by the sender; touch them not;
Myriads of bluest plagues lie underneath them,
And more than aconite has dipt the silk.

 ANT. Nay, now you grow too cynical, Ventidius:
A lady's favours may be worn with honour.
What, to refuse her bracelet! On my soul,
When I lie pensive in my tent alone,
'Twill pass the wakeful hours of winter nights,
To tell these pretty beads upon my arm,
To count for every one a soft embrace,
A melting kiss at such and such a time:
And now and then the fury of her love,
When——And what harm's in this?

 ALEX. None, none, my lord,
But what's to her, that now 'tis past for ever.

 ANT. [*going to tie it*]. We soldiers are so awkward—
   help me tie it.

 ALEX. In faith, my lord, we courtiers too are awkward
In these affairs: so are all men indeed:
Even I, who am not one. But shall I speak?

 ANT. Yes, freely.

 ALEX. Then, my lord, fair hands alone
Are fit to tie it; she, who sent it can.

 VENT. Hell, death! this eunuch pander ruins you.
You will not see her?

     *[ALEXAS whispers an Attendant, who goes out.*

 ANT. But to take my leave.

 VENT. Then I have washed an Æthiop. You're
   undone;
Y' are in the toils; y' are taken; y' are destroyed:
Her eyes do Cæsar's work.

ANT. You fear too soon.
I'm constant to myself: I know my strength;
And yet she shall not think me barbarous neither,
Born in the depths of Afric: I am a Roman,
Bred in the rules of soft humanity.
A guest, and kindly used, should bid farewell.
VENT. You do not know
How weak you are to her, how much an infant:
You are not proof against a smile, or glance;
A sigh will quite disarm you.
ANT. See, she comes!
Now you shall find your error.—Gods, I thank you:
I formed the danger greater than it was,
And now 'tis near, 'tis lessened.
VENT. Mark the end yet.

*Enter* CLEOPATRA, CHARMION, *and* IRAS

ANT. Well, madam, we are met.
CLEO. Is this a meeting?
Then, we must part?
ANT. We must.
CLEO. Who says we must?
ANT. Our own hard fates.
CLEO. We make those fates ourselves.
ANT. Yes, we have made them; we have loved each
other,
Into our mutual ruin.
CLEO. The gods have seen my joys with envious eyes;
I have no friends in heaven; and all the world,
As 'twere the business of mankind to part us,
Is armed against my love: even you yourself
Join with the rest; you, you are armed against me.
ANT. I will be justified in all I do
To late posterity, and therefore hear me.
If I mix a lie
With any truth, reproach me freely with it;
Else, favour me with silence.
CLEO. You command me,
And I am dumb.

VENT. I like this well; he shows authority.

ANT. That I derive my ruin
From you alone——

CLEO. O heavens! I ruin you!

ANT. You promised me your silence, and you break it
Ere I have scarce begun.

CLEO. Well, I obey you.

ANT. When I beheld you first, it was in Egypt.
Ere Cæsar saw your eyes, you gave me love,
And were too young to know it; that I settled
Your father in his throne, was for your sake;
I left the acknowledgment for time to ripen.
Cæsar stept in, and, with a greedy hand,
Plucked the green fruit, ere the first blush of red,
Yet cleaving to the bough. He was my lord,
And was, beside, too great for me to rival;
But, I deserved you first, though he enjoyed you.
When, after, I beheld you in Cilicia,
An enemy to Rome, I pardoned you.

CLEO. I cleared myself——

ANT. Again you break your promise.
I loved you still, and took your weak excuses,
Took you into my bosom, stained by Cæsar,
And not half mine: I went to Egypt with you,
And hid me from the business of the world,
Shut out inquiring nations from my sight,
To give whole years to you.

VENT. Yes, to your shame be't spoken.    [*Aside.*

ANT. How I loved.
Witness, ye days and nights, and all ye hours,
That danced away with down upon your feet,
As all your business were to count my passion!
One day passed by, and nothing saw but love;
Another came, and still 'twas only love:
The suns were wearied out with looking on,
And I untired with loving.
I saw you every day, and all the day;
And every day was still but as the first,
So eager was I still to see you more.

VENT. 'Tis all too true.

ANT. Fulvia, my wife, grew jealous,
(As she indeed had reason) raised a war
In Italy, to call me back.
    VENT. But yet
You went not.
    ANT. While within your arms I lay,
The world fell mouldering from my hands each hour,
And left me scarce a grasp—I thank your love for't.
    VENT. Well pushed: that last was home.
    CLEO. Yet may I speak?
    ANT. If I have urged a falsehood, yes; else, not.
Your silence says, I have not.  Fulvia died,
(Pardon, you gods, with my unkindness died);
To set the world at peace, I took Octavia,
This Cæsar's sister; in her pride of youth,
And flower of beauty, did I wed that lady,
Whom blushing I must praise, because I left her.
You called; my love obeyed the fatal summons:
This raised the Roman arms; the cause was yours.
I would have fought by land, where I was stronger;
You hindered it: yet, when I fought at sea,
Forsook me fighting; and (O stain to honour!
O lasting shame!) I knew not that I fled;
But fled to follow you.
    VENT. What haste she made to hoist her purple sails!
And, to appear magnificent in flight,
Drew half our strength away.
    ANT. All this you caused.
And, would you multiply more ruins on me?
This honest man, my best, my only friend,
Has gathered up the shipwreck of my fortunes;
Twelve legions I have left, my last recruits.
And you have watched the news, and bring your eyes
    To seize them too.  If you have aught to answer,
Now speak, you have free leave.
    ALEX. [*aside*]. She stands confounded:
Despair is in her eyes.
    VENT. Now lay a sigh in the way to stop his passage:
Prepare a tear, and bid it for his legions;
'Tis like they shall be sold.

CLEO. How shall I plead my cause, when you, my judge,
Already have condemned me? Shall I bring
The love you bore me for my advocate?
That now is turned against me, that destroys me;
For love, once past, is, at the best, forgotten;
But oftener sours to hate: 'twill please my lord
To ruin me, and therefore I'll be guilty.
But, could I once have thought it would have pleased
      you,
That you would pry, with narrow searching eyes,
Into my faults, severe to my destruction,
And watching all advantages with care,
That serve to make me wretched? Speak, my lord,
For I end here. Though I deserved this usage,
Was it like you to give it?

ANT. Oh, you wrong me,
To think I sought this parting, or desired
To accuse you more than what will clear myself,
And justify this breach.

CLEO. Thus low I thank you;
And, since my innocence will not offend,
I shall not blush to own it.

VENT. After this,
I think she'll blush at nothing.

CLEO. You seem grieved
(And therein you are kind) that Cæsar first
Enjoyed my love, though you deserved it better:
I grieve for that, my lord, much more than you;
For, had I first been yours, it would have saved
My second choice: I never had been his,
And ne'er had been but yours. But Cæsar first,
You say, possessed my love. Not so, my lord:
He first possessed my person; you, my love:
Cæsar loved me; but I loved Antony.
If I endured him after, 'twas because
I judged it due to the first name of men;
And, half constrained, I gave, as to a tyrant,
What he would take by force.

VENT. O Syren! Syren!
Yet grant that all the love she boasts were true,

Has she not ruined you? I still urge that,
The fatal consequence.

CLEO. The consequence indeed—
For I dare challenge him, my greatest foe,
To say it was designed: 'tis true, I loved you,
And kept you far from an uneasy wife,—
Such Fulvia was.
Yes, but he'll say, you left Octavia for me;—
And, can you blame me to receive that love,
Which quitted such desert, for worthless me?
How often have I wished some other Cæsar,
Great as the first, and as the second young,
Would court my love, to be refused for you!

VENT. Words, words; but Actium, sir; remember
Actium.

CLEO. Even there, I dare his malice. True, I counselled
To fight at sea; but I betrayed you not.
I fled, but not to the enemy. 'Twas fear;
Would I had been a man, not to have feared!
For none would then have envied me your friendship,
Who envy me your love.

ANT. We are both unhappy:
If nothing else, yet our ill fortune parts us.
Speak; would you have me perish by my stay?

CLEO. If, as a friend, you ask my judgment, go;
If, as a lover, stay. If you must perish—
'Tis a hard word—but stay.

VENT. See now the effects of her so boasted love!
She strives to drag you down to ruin with her;
But, could she 'scape without you, oh, how soon
Would she let go her hold, and haste to shore,
And never look behind!

CLEO. Then judge my love by this.
[*Giving* ANTONY *a writing.*
Could I have borne
A life or death, a happiness or woe,
From yours divided, this had given me means.

ANT. By Hercules, the writing of Octavius!
I know it well: 'tis that proscribing hand,
Young as it was, that led the way to mine,

And left me but the second place in murder.—
See, see, Ventidius! here he offers Egypt,
And joins all Syria to it, as a present;
So, in requital, she forsake my fortunes,
And join her arms with his.

    CLEO. And yet you leave me!
You leave me, Antony; and yet I love you,
Indeed I do: I have refused a kingdom;
That is a trifle;
For I could part with life, with anything,
But only you. Oh, let me die but with you!
Is that a hard request?

    ANT. Next living with you,
'Tis all that Heaven can give.

    ALEX. He melts; we conquer.       [*Aside.*

    CLEO. No; you shall go: your interest calls you hence;
Yes; your dear interest pulls too strong, for these
Weak arms to hold you here.     [*Takes his hand.*
Go; leave me, soldier
(For you're no more a lover): leave me dying:
Push me, all pale and panting, from your bosom,
And, when your march begins, let one run after,
Breathless almost for joy, and cry—She's dead.
The soldiers shout; you then, perhaps, may sigh,
And muster all your Roman gravity:
Ventidius chides; and straight your brow clears up,
As I had never been.

    ANT. Gods, 'tis too much; too much for man to bear.

    CLEO. What is't for me then,
A weak, forsaken woman, and a lover?—
Here let me breathe my last: envy me not
This minute in your arms: I'll die apace,
As fast as e'er I can, and end your trouble.

    ANT. Die! rather let me perish; loosened nature
Leap from its hinges, sink the props of heaven,
And fall the skies, to crush the nether world!
My eyes, my soul, my all!     [*Embraces her.*

    VENT. And what's this toy,
In balance with your fortune, honour, fame?

    ANT. What is't, Ventidius?—it outweighs them all;

Why, we have more than conquered Cæsar now:
My queen's not only innocent, but loves me.
This, this is she, who drags me down to ruin!
" But, could she 'scape without me, with what haste
Would she let slip her hold, and make to shore,
And never look behind ! "
Down on thy knees, blasphemer as thou art,
And ask forgiveness of wronged innocence.

    VENT. I'll rather die, than take it. Will you go?

    ANT. Go! whither? Go from all that's excellent?
Faith, honour, virtue, all good things forbid,
That I should go from her, who sets my love
Above the price of kingdoms ! Give, you gods,
Give to your boy, your Cæsar,
This rattle of a globe to play withal,
This gewgaw world, and put him cheaply off:
I'll not be pleased with less than Cleopatra.

    CLEO. She's wholly yours. My heart's so full of joy,
That I shall do some wild extravagance
Of love, in public; and the foolish world,
Which knows not tenderness, will think me mad.

    VENT. O women! women! women! all the gods
Have not such power of doing good to man,
As you of doing harm.                 [*Exit.*

    ANT. Our men are armed:—
Unbar the gate that looks to Cæsar's camp:
I would revenge the treachery he meant me;
And long security makes conquest easy.
I'm eager to return before I go;
For, all the pleasures I have known beat thick
On my remembrance.—How I long for night!
That both the sweets of mutual love may try,
And triumph once o'er Cæsar ere we die.     [*Exeunt.*

## ACT III

### Scene I

*At one door enter* Cleopatra, Charmion, Iras, *and* Alexas,
*a Train of* Egyptians: *at the other* Antony *and* Romans.
*The entrance on both sides is prepared by music; the
trumpets first sounding on* Antony's *part: then answered by timbrels, etc., on* Cleopatra's. Charmion
*and* Iras *hold a laurel wreath betwixt them. A Dance
of* Egyptians. *After the ceremony,* Cleopatra *crowns*
Antony

Ant. I thought how those white arms would fold me in,
And strain me close, and melt me into love;
So pleased with that sweet image, I sprung forwards,
And added all my strength to every blow.
　　Cleo. Come to me, come, my soldier, to my arms!
You've been too long away from my embraces;
But, when I have you fast, and all my own,
With broken murmurs, and with amorous sighs,
I'll say, you were unkind, and punish you,
And mark you red with many an eager kiss.
　　Ant. My brighter Venus!
　　Cleo. O my greater Mars!
　　Ant. Thou join'st us well, my love!
Suppose me come from the Phlegræan plains,
Where gasping giants lay, cleft by my sword,
And mountain-tops paired off each other blow,
To bury those I slew. Receive me, goddess!
Let Cæsar spread his subtle nets; like Vulcan,
In thy embraces I would be beheld
By heaven and earth at once;
And make their envy what they meant their sport
Let those, who took us, blush; I would love on,
With awful state, regardless of their frowns,
As their superior gods.
There's no satiety of love in thee:
Enjoyed, thou still art new; perpetual spring
Is in thy arms; the ripened fruit but falls,

And blossoms rise to fill its empty place;
And I grow rich by giving.


*Enter* VENTIDIUS, *and stands apart.*

ALEX. Oh, now the danger's past, your general comes!
He joins not in your joys, nor minds your triumphs;
But, with contracted brows, looks frowning on,
As envying your success.

ANT. Now, on my soul, he loves me; truly loves me:
He never flattered me in any vice,
But awes me with his virtue: even this minute,
Methinks, he has a right of chiding me.
Lead to the temple: I'll avoid his presence;
It checks too strong upon me.      [*Exeunt the rest.*
     [*As* ANTONY *is going,* VENTIDIUS *pulls him by*
         *the robe.*

VENT. Emperor!
ANT. 'Tis the old argument; I pr'ythee, spare me.
     [*Looking back.*

VENT. But this one hearing, emperor.
ANT. Let go
My robe; or, by my father Hercules—
VENT. By Hercules' father, that's yet greater,
I bring you somewhat you would wish to know.
ANT. Thou see'st we are observed; attend me here,
And I'll return.      [*Exit.*
VENT. I am waning in his favour, yet I love him;
I love this man, who runs to meet his ruin;
And sure the gods, like me, are fond of him:
His virtues lie so mingled with his crimes,
As would confound their choice to punish one,
And not reward the other.


*Enter* ANTONY.

ANT. We can conquer,
You see, without your aid.
We have dislodged their troops;
They look on us at distance, and, like curs

Scaped from the lion's paws, they bay far off,
And lick their wounds, and faintly threaten war.
Five thousand Romans, with their faces upward,
Lie breathless on the plain.

    VENT. 'Tis well; and he,
Who lost them, could have spared ten thousand more.
Yet if, by this advantage, you could gain
An easier peace, while Cæsar doubts the chance
Of arms—

    ANT. Oh, think not on't, Ventidius!
The boy pursues my ruin, he'll no peace;
His malice is considerate in advantage.
Oh, he's the coolest murderer! so staunch,
He kills, and keeps his temper.

    VENT. Have you no friend
In all his army, who has power to move him?
Mæcenas, or Agrippa, might do much.

    ANT. They're both too deep in Cæsar's interests.
We'll work it out by dint of sword, or perish.

    VENT. Fain I would find some other.

    ANT. Thank thy love.
Some four or five such victories as this
Will save thy further pains.

    VENT. Expect no more; Cæsar is on his guard:
I know, sir, you have conquered against odds;
But still you draw supplies from one poor town,
And of Egyptians: he has all the world,
And, at his beck, nations come pouring in,
To fill the gaps you make. Pray, think again.

    ANT. Why dost thou drive me from myself, to search
For foreign aids?—to hunt my memory,
And range all o'er a waste and barren place,
To find a friend? The wretched have no friends.
Yet I had one, the bravest youth of Rome,
Whom Cæsar loves beyond the love of women:
He could resolve his mind, as fire does wax,
From that hard rugged image melt him down,
And mould him in what softer form he pleased.

    VENT. Him would I see; that man, of all the world;
Just such a one we want.

ANT. He loved me too;
I was his soul; he lived not but in me:
We were so closed within each other's breasts,
The rivets were not found, that joined us first.
That does not reach us yet: we were so mixt,
As meeting streams, both to ourselves were lost;
We were one mass; we could not give or take,
But from the same; for he was I, I he.

VENT. He moves as I would wish him.          [*Aside.*

ANT. After this,
I need not tell his name;—'twas Dolabella.

VENT. He's now in Cæsar's camp.

ANT. No matter where,
Since he's no longer mine. He took unkindly,
That I forbade him Cleopatra's sight,
Because I feared he loved her: he confessed,
He had a warmth, which, for my sake, he stifled;
For 'twere impossible that two, so one,
Should not have loved the same. When he departed,
He took no leave; and that confirmed my thoughts.

VENT. It argues, that he loved you more than her,
Else he had stayed; but he perceived you jealous,
And would not grieve his friend: I know he loves you.

ANT. I should have seen him, then, ere now.

VENT. Perhaps
He has thus long been labouring for your peace.

ANT. Would he were here!

VENT. Would you believe he loved you?
I read your answer in your eyes, you would.
Not to conceal it longer, he has sent
A messenger from Cæsar's camp, with letters.

ANT. Let him appear.

VENT. I'll bring him instantly.

          [*Exit* VENTIDIUS, *and re-enters immediately with*
                              DOLABELLA.

ANT. 'Tis he himself! himself, by holy friendship!
                    [*Runs to embrace him.*
Art thou returned at last, my better half?
Come, give me all myself!
Let me not live,

If the young bridegroom, longing for his night,
Was ever half so fond.

DOLA. I must be silent, for my soul is busy
About a nobler work: she's new come home,
Like a long-absent man, and wanders o'er
Each room, a stranger to her own, to look
If all be safe.

ANT. Thou hast what's left of me;
For I am now so sunk from what I was,
Thou find'st me at my lowest water-mark.
The rivers that ran in, and raised my fortunes,
Are all dried up, or take another course:
What I have left is from my native spring;
I've still a heart that swells, in scorn of fate,
And lifts me to my banks.

DOLA. Still you are lord of all the world to me.

ANT. Why, then I yet am so; for thou art all.
If I had any joy when thou wert absent,
I grudged it to myself; methought I robbed
Thee of thy part. But, O my Dolabella!
Thou hast beheld me other than I am.
Hast thou not seen my morning chambers filled
With sceptred slaves, who waited to salute me?
With eastern monarchs, who forgot the sun,
To worship my uprising?—menial kings
Ran coursing up and down my palace-yard,
Stood silent in my presence, watched my eyes,
And, at my least command, all started out,
Like racers to the goal.

DOLA. Slaves to your fortune.

ANT. Fortune is Cæsar's now; and what am I?

VENT. What you have made yourself; I will not
flatter.

ANT. Is this friendly done?

DOLA. Yes; when his end is so, I must join with him;
Indeed I must, and yet you must not chide;
Why am I else your friend?

ANT. Take heed, young man,
How thou upbraid'st my love: The queen has eyes,
And thou too hast a soul. Canst thou remember.

When, swelled with hatred, thou beheld'st her first,
As accessary to thy brother's death?

DOLA. Spare my remembrance; 'twas a guilty day,
And still the blush hangs here.

ANT. To clear herself,
For sending him no aid, she came from Egypt.
Her galley down the silver Cydnus rowed,
The tackling silk, the streamers waved with gold;
The gentle winds were lodged in purple sails:
Her nymphs, like Nereids, round her couch were placed;
Where she, another sea-born Venus, lay.

DOLA. No more; I would not hear it.

ANT. Oh, you must!
She lay, and leant her cheek upon her hand,
And cast a look so languishingly sweet,
As if, secure of all beholders' hearts,
Neglecting, she could take them: boys, like Cupids,
Stood fanning, with their painted wings, the winds.
That played about her face. But if she smiled
A darting glory seemed to blaze abroau,
That men's desiring eyes were never wearied,
But hung upon the object: To soft flutes
The silver oars kept time; and while they played,
The hearing gave new pleasure to the sight;
And both to thought. 'Twas heaven, or somewhat more;
For she so charmed all hearts, that gazing crowds
Stood panting on the shore, and wanted breath
To give their welcome voice.
Then, Dolabella, where was then thy soul?
Was not thy fury quite disarmed with wonder?
Didst thou not shrink behind me from those eyes
And whisper in my ear—Oh, tell her not
That I accused her with my brother's death?

DOLA. And should my weakness be a plea for yours?
Mine was an age when love might be excused,
When kindly warmth, and when my springing youth
Made it a debt to nature. Yours—

VENT. Speak boldly.
Yours, he would say, in your declining age,
When no more heat was left but what you forced,

When all the sap was needful for the trunk,
When it went down, then you constrained the course,
And robbed from nature, to supply desire;
In you (I would not use so harsh a word)
'Tis but plain dotage.

ANT. Ha!

DOLA. 'Twas urged too home.—
But yet the loss was private, that I made;
'Twas but myself I lost: I lost no legions;
I had no world to lose, no people's love.

ANT. This from a friend?

DOLA. Yes, Antony, a true one;
A friend so tender, that each word I speak
Stabs my own heart, before it reach your ear.
Oh, judge me not less kind, because I chide!
To Cæsar I excuse you.

ANT. O ye gods!
Have I then lived to be excused to Cæsar?

DOLA. As to your equal.

ANT. Well, he's but my equal:
While I wear this he never shall be more.

DOLA. I bring conditions from him.

ANT. Are they noble?
Methinks thou shouldst not bring them else; yet he
Is full of deep dissembling; knows no honour
Divided from his interest. Fate mistook him;
For nature meant him for an usurer:
He's fit indeed to buy, not conquer kingdoms.

VENT. Then, granting this,
What power was theirs, who wrought so hard a temper
To honourable terms?

ANT. It was my Dolabella, or some god.

DOLA. Nor I, nor yet Mæcenas, nor Agrippa:
They were your enemies; and I, a friend,
Too weak alone; yet 'twas a Roman's deed.

ANT. 'Twas like a Roman done: show me that man,
Who has preserved my life, my love, my honour;
Let me but see his face.

VENT. That task is mine,
And, Heaven, thou know'st how pleasing. [*Exit* VENT.

DOLA. You'll remember
To whom you stand obliged?
    ANT. When I forget it
Be thou unkind, and that's my greatest curse.
My queen shall thank him too,
    DOLA. I fear she will not.
    ANT. But she shall do it: The queen, my Dolabella!
Hast thou not still some grudgings of thy fever?
    DOLA. I would not see her lost.
    ANT. When I forsake her,
Leave me my better stars! for she has truth
Beyond her beauty.  Cæsar tempted her,
At no less price than kingdoms, to betray me;
But she resisted all: and yet thou chidest me
For loving her too well.  Could I do so?
    DOLA. Yes; there's my reason.


*Re-enter* VENTIDIUS, *with* OCTAVIA, *leading*
        ANTONY's *two little* Daughters

    ANT. Where?—Octavia there!        [*Starting back.*
    VENT. What, is she poison to you?—a disease?
Look on her, view her well, and those she brings:
Are they all strangers to your eyes? has nature
No secret call, no whisper they are yours?
    DOLA. For shame, my lord, if not for love, receive them
With kinder eyes.  If you confess a man,
Meet them, embrace them, bid them welcome to you.
Your arms should open, even without your knowledge,
To clasp them in; your feet should turn to wings,
To bear you to them; and your eyes dart out
And aim a kiss, ere you could reach the lips.
    ANT. I stood amazed, to think how they came hither.
    VENT. I sent for them; I brought them in unknown
To Cleopatra's guards.
    DOLA. Yet, are you cold?
    OCTAV. Thus long I have attended for my welcome;
Which, as a stranger, sure I might expect.
Who am I?
    ANT. Cæsar's sister.

OCTAV. That's unkind.
Had I been nothing more than Cæsar's sister,
Know, I had still remained in Cæsar's camp:
But your Octavia, your much injured wife,
Though banished from your bed, driven from your house,
In spite of Cæsar's sister, still is yours.
'Tis true, I have a heart disdains your coldness,
And prompts me not to seek what you should offer;
But a wife's virtue still surmounts that pride.
I come to claim you as my own; to show
My duty first; to ask, nay beg, your kindness:
Your hand, my lord; 'tis mine, and I will have it.

                                                   [*Taking his hand.*

   VENT. Do, take it; thou deserv'st it.
   DOLA. On my soul,
And so she does: she's neither too submissive,
Nor yet too haughty; but so just a mean
Shows, as it ought, a wife and Roman too.
   ANT. I fear, Octavia, you have begged my life.
   OCTAV. Begged it, my lord?
   ANT. Yes, begged it, my ambassadress;
Poorly and basely begged it of your brother.
   OCTAV. Poorly and basely I could never beg:
Nor could my brother grant.
   ANT. Shall I, who, to my kneeling slave, could say,
Rise up, and be a king; shall I fall down
And cry,—Forgive me, Cæsar! Shall I set
A man, my equal, in the place of Jove,
As he could give me being? No; that word,
Forgive, would choke me up,
And die upon my tongue.
   DOLA. You shall not need it.
   ANT. I will not need it. Come, you've all betrayed
      me,—
My friend too!—to receive some vile conditions.
My wife has bought me, with her prayers and tears;
And now I must become her branded slave.
In every peevish mood, she will upbraid
The life she gave: if I but look awry,
She cries—I'll tell my brother.

OCTAV. My hard fortune
Subjects me still to your unkind mistakes.
But the conditions I have brought are such,
You need not blush to take: I love your honour,
Because 'tis mine; it never shall be said,
Octavia's husband was her brother's slave.
Sir, you are free; free, even from her you loathe;
For, though my brother bargains for your love,
Makes me the price and cement of your peace,
I have a soul like yours; I cannot take
Your love as alms, nor beg what I deserve.
I'll tell my brother we are reconciled;
He shall draw back his troops, and you shall march
To rule the East: I may be dropt at Athens;
No matter where. I never will complain,
But only keep the barren name of wife,
And rid you of the trouble.

    VENT. Was ever such a strife of sullen
       honour!
Both scorn to be obliged.
    DOLA. Oh, she has touched him in the ten-
       derest part;
See how he reddens with despite and shame,    *Apart.*
To be outdone in generosity!
    VENT. See how he winks! how he dries up a
       tear,
That fain would fall!
    ANT. Octavia, I have heard you, and must praise
The greatness of your soul;
But cannot yield to what you have proposed:
For I can ne'er be conquered but by love;
And you do all for duty. You would free me,
And would be dropt at Athens; was't not so?
    OCTAV. It was, my lord.
    ANT. Then I must be obliged
To one who loves me not; who, to herself,
May call me thankless and ungrateful man:—
I'll not endure it; no.
    VENT. I am glad it pinches there.      *[Aside.*
    OCTAV. Would you triumph o'er poor Octavia's virtue?

That pride was all I had to bear me up;
That you might think you owed me for your life,
And owed it to my duty, not my love.
I have been injured, and my haughty soul
Could brook but ill the man who slights my bed.

    ANT. Therefore you love me not.

    OCTAV. Therefore, my lord,
I should not love you.

    ANT. Therefore you would leave me?

    OCTAV. And therefore I should leave you—if I
      could.

    DOLA. Her soul's too great, after such injuries,
To say she loves; and yet she lets you see it.
Her modesty and silence plead her cause.

    ANT. O Dolabella, which way shall I turn?
I find a secret yielding in my soul;
But Cleopatra, who would die with me,
Must she be left? Pity pleads for Octavia;
But does it not plead more for Cleopatra?

    VENT. Justice and pity both plead for Octavia;
For Cleopatra, neither.
One would be ruined with you; but she first
Had ruined you: The other, you have ruined,
And yet she would preserve you.
In everything their merits are unequal.

    ANT. O my distracted soul!

    OCTAV. Sweet Heaven compose it!—
Come, come, my lord, if I can pardon you,
Methinks you should accept it. Look on these;
Are they not yours? or stand they thus neglected,
As they are mine? Go to him, children, go;
Kneel to him, take him by the hand, speak to
    him;
For you may speak, and he may own you too,
Without a blush; and so he cannot all
His children: go, I say, and pull him to me,
And pull him to yourselves, from that bad woman.
You, Agrippina, hang upon his arms;
And you, Antonia, clasp about his waist:
If he will shake you off, if he will dash you

Against the pavement, you must bear it, children;
For you are mine, and I was born to suffer.

> *[Here the* Children *go to him, etc.*

VENT. Was ever sight so moving?—Emperor!

DOLA. Friend!

OCTAV. Husband!

BOTH CHILD. Father!

ANT. I am vanquished: take me,
Octavia; take me, children; share me all.

> *[Embracing them.*

I've been a thriftless debtor to your loves,
And run out much, in riot, from your stock;
But all shall be amended.

OCTAV. O blest hour!

DOLA. O happy change!

VENT. My joy stops at my tongue;
But it has found two channels here for one,
And bubbles out above.

ANT. [*to* OCTAV.]. This is thy triumph; lead me where
  thou wilt;
Even to thy brother's camp.

OCTAV. All there are yours.


> *Enter* ALEXAS *hastily*

ALEX. The queen, my mistress, sir, and yours—

ANT. 'Tis past.—
Octavia, you shall stay this night: To-morrow,
Cæsar and we are one.

> *[Exit leading* OCTAVIA; DOLABELLA *and the*
> Children *follow.*

VENT. There's news for you; run, my officious eunuch,
Be sure to be the first; haste forward:
Haste, my dear eunuch, haste,                    *[Exit.*

ALEX. This downright fighting fool, this thick-skulled
  hero,
This blunt, unthinking instrument of death,
With plain dull virtue has outgone my wit.
Pleasure forsook my earliest infancy;
The luxury of others robbed my cradle,

And ravished thence the promise of a man.
Cast out from nature, disinherited
Of what her meanest children claim by kind,
Yet greatness kept me from contempt: that's gone.
Had Cleopatra followed my advice,
Then he had been betrayed who now forsakes.
She dies for love; but she has known its joys:
Gods, is this just, that I, who know no joys,
Must die, because she loves?

 

    *Enter* CLEOPATRA, CHARMION, IRAS, *and Train*

O madam, I have seen what blasts my eyes!
Octavia's here.
    CLEO. Peace with that raven's note.
I know it too; and now am in
The pangs of death.
    ALEX. You are no more a queen;
Egypt is lost.
    CLEO. What tell'st thou me of Egypt?
My life, my soul is lost! Octavia has him!—
O fatal name to Cleopatra's love!
My kisses, my embraces now are hers;
While I—But thou hast seen my rival; speak,
Does she deserve this blessing? Is she fair?
Bright as a goddess? and is all perfection
Confined to her? It is. Poor I was made
Of that coarse matter, which, when she was finished,
The gods threw by for rubbish.
    ALEX. She is indeed a very miracle.
    CLEO. Death to my hopes, a miracle!
    ALEX. A miracle;               *[Bowing.*
I mean of goodness; for in beauty, madam,
You make all wonders cease.
    CLEO. I was too rash:
Take this in part of recompense. But, oh!
                      *[Giving a ring.*
I fear thou flatterest me.
    CHAR. She comes! she's here!
    IRAS. Fly, madam, Cæsar's sister!

CLEO. Were she the sister of the thunderer Jove,
And bore her brother's lightning in her eyes,
Thus would I face my rival.

> [*Meets* OCTAVIA *with* VENTIDIUS. OCTAVIA
> *bears up to her. Their Trains come up on
> either side.*

OCTAV. I need not ask if you are Cleopatra;
Your haughty carriage—
CLEO. Shows I am a queen:
Nor need I ask you, who you are.
OCTAV. A Roman:
A name, that makes and can unmake a queen.
CLEO. Your lord, the man who serves me, is a Roman.
OCTAV. He was a Roman, till he lost that name,
To be a slave in Egypt; but I come
To free him thence.
CLEO. Peace, peace, my lover's Juno.
When he grew weary of that household clog,
He chose my easier bonds.
OCTAV. I wonder not
Your bonds are easy: you have long been practised
In that lascivious art: He's not the first
For whom you spread your snares: Let Cæsar witness.
CLEO. I loved not Cæsar; 'twas but gratitude
I paid his love: The worst your malice can,
Is but to say the greatest of mankind
Has been my slave. The next, but far above him
In my esteem, is he whom law calls yours,
But whom his love made mine.
OCTAV. I would view nearer. [*Coming up close to her.*
That face, which has so long usurped my right,
To find the inevitable charms, that catch
Mankind so sure, that ruined my dear lord.
CLEO. Oh, you do well to search; for had you known
But half these charms, you had not lost his heart.
OCTAV. Far be their knowledge from a Roman lady,
Far from a modest wife! Shame of our sex,
Dost thou not blush to own those black endearments,
That make sin pleasing?
CLEO. You may blush, who want them.

If bounteous nature, if indulgent Heaven
Have given me charms to please the bravest man,
Should I not thank them?  Should I be ashamed,
And not be proud?  I am, that he has loved me;
And, when I love not him, Heaven change this face
For one like that.

  OCTAV. Thou lov'st him not so well.

  CLEO. I love him better, and deserve him more.

  OCTAV. You do not; cannot: You have been his
   ruin.

Who made him cheap at Rome, but Cleopatra?
Who made him scorned abroad, but Cleopatra?
At Actium, who betrayed him? Cleopatra.
Who made his children orphans, and poor me
A wretched widow? only Cleopatra.

  CLEO. Yet she, who loves him best, is Cleopatra.
If you have suffered, I have suffered more.
You bear the specious title of a wife,
To gild your cause, and draw the pitying world
To favour it: the world condemns poor me.
For I have lost my honour, lost my fame,
And stained the glory of my royal house,
And all to bear the branded name of mistress.
There wants but life, and that too I would lose
For him I love.

  OCTAV. Be't so, then; take thy wish.

           *[Exit with her Train.*

  CLEO. And 'tis my wish,
Now he is lost for whom alone I lived.
My sight grows dim, and every object dances,
And swims before me, in the maze of death.
My spirits, while they were opposed, kept up;
They could not sink beneath a rival's scorn!
But now she's gone, they faint.

  ALEX. Mine have had leisure
To recollect their strength, and furnish counsel,
To ruin her, who else must ruin you.

  CLEO. Vain promiser!
Lead me, my Charmion; nay, your hand too, Iras.
My grief has weight enough to sink you both.

Conduct me to some solitary chamber,
And draw the curtains round;
Then leave me to myself, to take alone
My fill of grief:
 There I till death will his unkindness weep;
 As harmless infants moan themselves asleep. [*Exeunt.*

## ACT IV

### Scene i

#### *Enter* Antony *and* Dolabella

Dola. Why would you shift it from yourself on me?
Can you not tell her, you must part?
 Ant. I cannot.
I could pull out an eye, and bid it go,
And t'other should not weep. O Dolabella,
How many deaths are in this word, *Depart!*
I dare not trust my tongue to tell her so:
One look of hers would thaw me into tears,
And I should melt, till I were lost again.
 Dola. Then let Ventidius;
He's rough by nature.
 Ant. Oh, he'll speak too harshly;
He'll kill her with the news: Thou, only thou.
 Dola. Nature has cast me in so soft a mould,
That but to hear a story, feigned for pleasure,
Of some sad lover's death, moistens my eyes,
And robs me of my manhood. I should speak
So faintly, with such fear to grieve her heart,
She'd not believe it earnest.
 Ant. Therefore,—therefore
Thou only, thou art fit: Think thyself me;
And when thou speak'st (but let it first be long),
Take off the edge from every sharper sound,
And let our parting be as gently made,
As other loves begin: Wilt thou do this?
 Dola. What you have said so sinks into my soul,
That, if I must speak, I shall speak just so.

ANT. I leave you then to your sad task: Farewell.
I sent her word to meet you.

*[Goes to the door, and comes back.*

I forgot;
Let her be told, I'll make her peace with mine,
Her crown and dignity shall be preserved,
If I have power with Cæsar.—Oh, be sure
To think on that.

DOLA. Fear not, I will remember.

*[ANTONY goes again to the door, and comes back.*

ANT. And tell her, too, how much I was constrained;
I did not this, but with extremest force.
Desire her not to hate my memory,
For I still cherish hers:—insist on that.

DOLA. Trust me. I'll not forget it.

ANT. Then that's all.

*[Goes out, and returns again.*

Wilt thou forgive my fondness this once more?
Tell her, though we shall never meet again,
If I should hear she took another love,
The news would break my heart.—Now I must go;
For every time I have returned, I feel
My soul more tender; and my next command
Would be, to bid her stay, and ruin both.      *[Exit.*

DOLA. Men are but children of a larger growth;
Our appetites as apt to change as theirs,
And full as craving too, and full as vain;
And yet the soul, shut up in her dark room,
Viewing so clear abroad, at home sees nothing:
But, like a mole in earth, busy and blind,
Works all her folly up, and casts it outward
To the world's open view: Thus I discovered,
And blamed the love of ruined Antony:
Yet wish that I were he, to be so ruined.


*Enter* VENTIDIUS *above*

VENT. Alone, and talking to himself? concerned too?
Perhaps my guess is right; he loved her once,
And may pursue it still.

DOLA. O friendship! friendship!
Ill canst thou answer this; and reason, worse:
Unfaithful in the attempt; hopeless to win;
And if I win, undone: mere madness all.
And yet the occasion's fair. What injury
To him, to wear the robe which he throws by!
VENT. None, none at all. This happens as I wish,
To ruin her yet more with Antony.

*Enter* CLEOPATRA *talking with* ALEXAS;
CHARMION, IRAS *on the other side.*

DOLA. She comes! What charms have sorrow on that
face!
Sorrow seems pleased to dwell with so much sweetness;
Yet, now and then, a melancholy smile
Breaks loose, like lightning in a winter's night,
And shows a moment's day.
VENT. If she should love him too! her eunuch there?
That porc'pisce bodes ill weather. Draw, draw nearer,
Sweet devil, that I may hear.
ALEX. Believe me; try
[DOLABELLA *goes over to* CHARMION *and* IRAS;
*seems to talk with them.*
To make him jealous; jealousy is like
A polished glass held to the lips when life's in doubt;
If there be breath, 'twill catch the damp, and show it.
CLEO. I grant you, jealousy's a proof of love,
But 'tis a weak and unavailing medicine;
It puts out the disease, and makes it show,
But has no power to cure.
ALEX. 'Tis your last remedy, and strongest too:
And then this Dolabella, who so fit
To practise on? He's handsome, valiant, young,
And looks as he were laid for nature's bait,
To catch weak women's eyes.
He stands already more than half suspected
Of loving you: the least kind word or glance,
You give this youth, will kindle him with love:
Then, like a burning vessel set adrift,

You'll send him down amain before the wind,
To fire the heart of jealous Antony.

CLEO. Can I do this? Ah, no, my love's so true,
That I can neither hide it where it is,
Nor show it where it is not. Nature meant me
A wife; a silly, harmless, household dove,
Fond without art, and kind without deceit;
But Fortune, that has made a mistress of me,
Has thrust me out to the wide world, unfurnished
Of falsehood to be happy.

ALEX. Force yourself.
The event will be, your lover will return,
Doubly desirous to possess the good
Which once he feared to lose.

CLEO. I must attempt it;
But oh, with what regret!

> [*Exit* ALEXAS. *She comes up to* DOLABELLA.

VENT. So, now the scene draws near; they're in my
reach.

CLEO. [*to* DOL.] Discoursing with my women! might
not I
Share in your entertainment?

CHAR. You have been
The subject of it, madam.

CLEO. How! and how?

IRAS. Such praises of your beauty!

CLEO. Mere poetry.
Your Roman wits, your Gallus and Tibullus,
Have taught you this from Cytheris and Delia.

DOLA. Those Roman wits have never been in Egypt;
Cytheris and Delia else had been unsung:
I, who have seen—had I been born a poet,
Should choose a nobler name.

CLEO. You flatter me.
But, 'tis your nation's vice: All of your country
Are flatterers, and all false. Your friend's like you.
I'm sure, he sent you not to speak these words.

DOLA. No, madam; yet he sent me—

CLEO. Well, he sent you—

DOLA. Of a less pleasing errand.

Cleo. How less pleasing?
Less to yourself, or me?

Dola. Madam, to both;
For you must mourn, and I must grieve to cause it.

Cleo. You, Charmion, and your fellow, stand at
  distance.—
Hold up, my spirits. [*Aside*.]—Well, now your mournful matter;
For I'm prepared, perhaps can guess it too.

Dola. I wish you would; for 'tis a thankless office,
To tell ill news: And I, of all your sex,
Most fear displeasing you.

Cleo. Of all your sex,
I soonest could forgive you, if you should.

Vent. Most delicate advances! Women! women!
Dear, damned, inconstant sex!

Cleo. In the first place,
I am to be forsaken; is't not so?

Dola. I wish I could not answer to that question.

Cleo. Then pass it o'er, because it troubles you:
I should have been more grieved another time.
Next I'm to lose my kingdom—Farewell, Egypt!
Yet, is there any more?

Dola. Madam, I fear
Your too deep sense of grief has turned your reason.

Cleo. No, no, I'm not run mad; I can bear fortune:
And love may be expelled by other love,
As poisons are by poisons.

Dola. You o'erjoy me, madam,
To find your griefs so moderately borne.
You've heard the worst; all are not false like him.

Cleo. No; Heaven forbid they should.

Dola. Some men are constant.

Cleo. And constancy deserves reward, that's certain.

Dola. Deserves it not; but give it leave to hope.

Vent. I'll swear, thou hast my leave. I have enough:
But how to manage this! Well, I'll consider.    [*Exit*.

Dola. I came prepared
To tell you heavy news; news, which I thought
Would fright the blood from your pale cheeks to hear:

But you have met it with a cheerfulness,
That makes my task more easy: and my tongue,
Which on another's message was employed,
Would gladly speak its own.
    CLEO. Hold, Dolabella.
First tell me, were you chosen by my lord?
Or sought you this employment?
    DOLA. He picked me out; and, as his bosom friend,
He charged me with his words.
    CLEO. The message then
I know was tender, and each accent smooth,
To mollify that rugged word, *Depart*.
    DOLA. Oh, you mistake: He chose the harshest words;
With fiery eyes, and contracted brows,
He coined his face in the severest stamp;
And fury shook his fabric, like an earthquake;
He heaved for vent, and burst like bellowing Ætna,
In sounds scarce human—" Hence away for ever,
Let her begone, the blot of my renown,
And bane of all my hopes!"
           [*All the time of this speech,* CLEOPATRA *seems
               more and more concerned, till she sinks quite
               down.*
"Let her be driven, as far as men can think,
From man's commerce! she'll poison to the centre."
    CLEO. Oh, I can bear no more!
    DOLA. Help, help!—O wretch! O cursed, cursed
          wretch!
What have I done!
    CHAR. Help, chafe her temples, Iras.
    IRAS. Bend, bend her forward quickly.
    CHAR. Heaven be praised,
She comes again.
    CLEO. Oh, let him not approach me.
Why have you brought me back to this loathed being;
The abode of falsehood, violated vows,
And injured love? For pity, let me go;
For, if there be a place of long repose,
I'm sure I want it. My disdainful lord
Can never break that quiet; nor awake

The sleeping soul, with hollowing in my tomb
Such words as fright her hence.—Unkind, unkind!
  DOLA. Believe me, 'tis against myself I speak;
                              *[Kneeling.*

That sure desires belief; I injured him:
My friend ne'er spoke those words. Oh, had you seen
How often he came back, and every time
With something more obliging and more kind,
To add to what he said; what dear farewells;
How almost vanquished by his love he parted,
And leaned to what unwillingly he left!
I, traitor as I was, for love of you
(But what can you not do, who made me false?)
I forged that lie; for whose forgiveness kneels
This self-accused, self-punished criminal.
  CLEO. With how much ease believe we what we wish!
Rise, Dolabella; if you have been guilty,
I have contributed, and too much love
Has made me guilty too.
The advance of kindness, which I made, was feigned,
To call back fleeting love by jealousy;
But 'twould not last. Oh, rather let me lose,
Than so ignobly trifle with his heart.
  DOLA. I find your breast fenced round from human reach,
Transparent as a rock of solid crystal;
Seen through, but never pierced. My friend, my friend,
What endless treasure hast thou thrown away;
And scattered, like an infant, in the ocean,
Vain sums of wealth, which none can gather thence!
  CLEO. Could you not beg
An hour's admittance to his private ear?
Like one, who wanders through long barren wilds
And yet foreknows no hospitable inn
Is near to succour hunger, eats his fill,
Before his painful march;
So would I feed a while my famished eyes
Before we part; for I have far to go,
If death be far, and never must return.

VENTIDIUS *with* OCTAVIA, *behind*

VENT. From hence you may discover—oh, sweet, sweet!
Would you indeed? The pretty hand in earnest?

DOLA. I will, for this reward. [*Takes her hand.*
Draw it not back.
'Tis all I e'er will beg.

VENT. They turn upon us.

OCTAV. What quick eyes has guilt!

VENT. Seem not to have observed them, and go on.
[*They enter.*

DOLA. Saw you the emperor, Ventidius?

· VENT. No.
I sought him; but I heard that he was private,
None with him but Hipparchus, his freedman.

DOLA. Know you his business?

VENT. Giving him instructions,
And letters to his brother Cæsar.

DOLA. Well,
He must be found.
[*Exeunt* DOLABELLA *and* CLEOPATRA.

OCTAV. Most glorious impudence!

VENT. She looked, methought,
As she would say—Take your old man, Octavia;
Thank you, I'm better here.—
Well, but what use
Make we of this discovery?

OCTAV. Let it die.

VENT. I pity Dolabella; but she's dangerous:
Her eyes have power beyond Thessalian charms,
To draw the moon from heaven; for eloquence,
The sea-green Syrens taught her voice their flattery;
And, while she speaks, night steals upon the day,
Unmarked of those that hear. Then she's so charming,
Age buds at sight of her, and swells to youth:
The holy priests gaze on her when she smiles;
And with heaved hands, forgetting gravity,
They bless her wanton eyes: Even I, who hate her,
With a malignant joy behold such beauty;
And, while I curse, desire it. Antony

Must needs have some remains of passion still,
Which may ferment into a worse relapse,
If now not fully cured. I know, this minute,
With Cæsar he's endeavouring her peace.

OCTAV. You have prevailed:—But for a further purpose
[*Walks off*.
I'll prove how he will relish this discovery.
What, make a strumpet's peace! it swells my heart:
It must not, shall not be.

VENT. His guards appear.
Let me begin, and you shall second me.

*Enter* ANTONY

ANT. Octavia, I was looking you, my love:
What, are your letters ready? I have given
My last instructions.

OCTAV. Mine, my lord, are written

ANT. Ventidius. [*Drawing him aside.*

VENT. My lord?

ANT. A word in private.—
When saw you Dolabella?

VENT. Now, my lord,
He parted hence; and Cleopatra with him.

ANT. Speak softly.—'Twas by my command he went,
To bear my last farewell.

VENT. It looked indeed [*Aloud.*
Like your farewell.

ANT. More softly.—My farewell?
What secret meaning have you in those words
Of—My farewell? He did it by my order.

VENT. Then he obeyed your order. I suppose
[*Aloud.*
You bid him do it with all gentleness,
All kindness, and all—love.

ANT. How she mourned,
The poor forsaken creature!

VENT. She took it as she ought; she bore your parting
As she did Cæsar's, as she would another's,
Were a new love to come.

ANT. Thou dost belie her; [*Aloud.*
Most basely, and maliciously belie her.

VENT. I thought not to displease you; I have done.

OCTAV. You seemed disturbed, my lord.    [*Coming up.*

ANT. A very trifle.

Retire, my love.

VENT. It was indeed a trifle.

He sent—

ANT. No more.    Look how thou disobey'st me;

[*Angrily.*

Thy life shall answer it.

OCTAV. Then 'tis no trifle.

VENT. [*to* OCTAV.] 'Tis less; a very nothing: You too
    saw it,

As well as I, and therefore 'tis no secret.

ANT. She saw it!

VENT. Yes:  She saw young Dolabella—

ANT. Young Dolabella!

VENT. Young, I think him young,

And handsome too; and so do others think him.

But what of that?  He went by your command,

Indeed 'tis probable, with some kind message;

For she received it graciously; she smiled;

And then he grew familiar with her hand,

Squeezed it, and worried it with ravenous kisses;

She blushed, and sighed, and smiled, and blushed again;

At last she took occasion to talk softly,

And brought her cheek up close, and leaned on his;

At which, he whispered kisses back on hers;

And then she cried aloud—That constancy

Should be rewarded.

OCTAV. This I saw and heard.

ANT. What woman was it, whom you heard and saw
So playful with my friend?

Not Cleopatra?

VENT. Even she, my lord.

ANT. My Cleopatra?

VENT. Your Cleopatra;

Dolabella's Cleopatra; every man's Cleopatra.

ANT. Thou liest.

VENT. I do not lie, my lord.

Is this so strange?  Should mistresses be left,

And not provide against a time of change?
You know she's not much used to lonely nights.

ANT. I'll think no more on't.
I know 'tis false, and see the plot betwixt you.—
You needed not have gone this way, Octavia.
What harms it you that Cleopatra's just?
She's mine no more. I see, and I forgive:
Urge it no further, love.

OCTAV. Are you concerned,
That she's found false?

ANT. I should be, were it so;
For, though 'tis past, I would not that the world
Should tax my former choice, that I loved one
Of so light note; but I forgive you both.

VENT. What has my age deserved, that you should think
I would abuse your ears with perjury?
If Heaven be true, she's false.

ANT. Though heaven and earth
Should witness it, I'll not believe her tainted.

VENT. I'll bring you, then, a witness
From hell, to prove her so.—Nay, go not back;

[*Seeing* ALEXAS *just entering, and starting back.*
For stay you must and shall.

ALEX. What means my lord?

VENT. To make you do what most you hate,—speak
truth.
You are of Cleopatra's private counsel,
Of her bed-counsel, her lascivious hours;
Are conscious of each nightly change she makes,
And watch her, as Chaldæans do the moon,
Can tell what signs she passes through, what day.

ALEX. My noble lord!

VENT. My most illustrious pander,
No fine set speech, no cadence, no turned periods,
But a plain homespun truth, is what I ask.
I did, myself, o'erhear your queen make love
To Dolabella. Speak; for I will know,
By your confession, what more passed betwixt them;
How near the business draws to your employment;
And when the happy hour.

ANT. Speak truth, Alexas; whether it offend
Or please Ventidius, care not: Justify
Thy injured queen from malice: Dare his worst.

OCTAV. [*aside*]. See how he gives him courage! how
he fears
To find her false! and shuts his eyes to truth,
Willing to be misled!

ALEX. As far as love may plead for woman's frailty,
Urged by desert and greatness of the lover,
So far, divine Octavia, may my queen
Stand even excused to you for loving him
Who is your lord: so far, from brave Ventidius,
May her past actions hope a fair report.

ANT. 'Tis well, and truly spoken: mark, Ventidius.

ALEX. To you, most noble emperor, her strong passion
Stands not excused, but wholly justified.
Her beauty's charms alone, without her crown,
From Ind and Meroe drew the distant vows
Of sighing kings; and at her feet were laid
The sceptres of the earth, exposed on heaps,
To choose where she would reign:
She thought a Roman only could deserve her,
And, of all Romans, only Antony;
And, to be less than wife to you, disdained
Their lawful passion.

ANT. 'Tis but truth.

ALEX. And yet, though love, and your unmatched desert,
Have drawn her from the due regard of honour,
At last Heaven opened her unwilling eyes
To see the wrongs she offered fair Octavia,
Whose holy bed she lawlessly usurped.
The sad effects of this improsperous war
Confirmed those pious thoughts.

VENT. [*aside*]. Oh, wheel you there?
Observe him now; the man begins to mend,
And talk substantial reason.—Fear not, eunuch;
The emperor has given thee leave to speak.

ALEX. Else had I never dared to offend his ears
With what the last necessity has urged
On my forsaken mistress; yet I must not

Presume to say, her heart is wholly altered.

ANT. No, dare not for thy life, I charge thee dare not
Pronounce that fatal word!

OCTAV. Must I bear this? Good Heaven, afford me
    patience.                                     [*Aside.*

VENT. On, sweet eunuch; my dear half-man, proceed.

ALEX. Yet Dolabella
Has loved her long; he, next my god-like lord,
Deserves her best; and should she meet his passion,
Rejected, as she is, by him she loved——

ANT. Hence from my sight! for I can bear no more:
Let furies drag thee quick to hell; let all
The longer damned have rest; each torturing hand
Do thou employ, till Cleopatra comes;
Then join thou too, and help to torture her!

                [*Exit* ALEXAS, *thrust out by* ANTONY.

OCTAV. 'Tis not well.
Indeed, my lord, 'tis much unkind to me,
To show this passion, this extreme concernment,
For an abandoned, faithless prostitute.

ANT. Octavia, leave me; I am much disordered:
Leave me, I say.

OCTAV. My lord!

ANT. I bid you leave me.

VENT. Obey him, madam: best withdraw a while,
And see how this will work.

OCTAV. Wherein have I offended you, my lord,
That I am bid to leave you? Am I false,
Or infamous? Am I a Cleopatra?
Were I she,
Base as she is, you would not bid me leave you;
But hang upon my neck, take slight excuses,
And fawn upon my falsehood.

ANT. 'Tis too much.
Too much, Octavia; I am pressed with sorrows
Too heavy to be borne; and you add more:
I would retire, and recollect what's left
Of man within, to aid me.

OCTAV. You would mourn,
In private, for your love, who has betrayed you.

You did but half return to me: your kindness
Lingered behind with her. I hear, my lord,
You make conditions for her,
And would include her treaty. Wondrous proofs
Of love to me!

ANT. Are you my friend, Ventidius?
Or are you turned a Dolabella too,
And let this fury loose?

VENT. Oh, be advised,
Sweet madam, and retire.

OCTAV. Yes, I will go; but never to return.
You shall no more be haunted with this Fury.
My lord, my lord, love will not always last,
When urged with long unkindness and disdain:
Take her again, whom you prefer to me;
She stays but to be called. Poor cozened man!
Let a feigned parting give her back your heart,
Which a feigned love first got; for injured me,
Though my just sense of wrongs forbid my stay,
My duty shall be yours.
To the dear pledges of our former love
My tenderness and care shall be transferred,
And they shall cheer, by turns, my widowed nights:
So, take my last farewell; for I despair
To have you whole, and scorn to take you half. [Exit.

VENT. I combat Heaven, which blasts my best designs;
My last attempt must be to win her back;
But oh! I fear in vain.                    [Exit.

ANT. Why was I framed with this plain, honest heart,
Which knows not to disguise its griefs and weakness,
But bears its workings outward to the world?
I should have kept the mighty anguish in,
And forced a smile at Cleopatra's falsehood:
Octavia had believed it, and had stayed.
But I am made a shallow-forded stream,
Seen to the bottom: all my clearness scorned,
And all my faults exposed.—See where he comes,

*Enter* DOLABELLA

Who has profaned the sacred name of friend,
And worn it into vileness!
With how secure a brow, and specious form,
He gilds the secret villain!    Sure that face
Was meant for honesty; but Heaven mismatched it,
And furnished treason out with nature's pomp,
To make its work more easy.
   DOLA.  O my friend!
   ANT.  Well, Dolabella, you performed my message?
   DOLA.  I did, unwillingly.
   ANT.  Unwillingly?
Was it so hard for you to bear our parting?
You should have wished it.
   DOLA.  Why?
   ANT.  Because you love me.
And she received my message with as true,
With as unfeigned a sorrow as you brought it?
   DOLA.  She loves you, even to madness.
   ANT.  Oh, I know it.
You, Dolabella, do not better know
How much she loves me.  And should I
Forsake this beauty?  This all-perfect creature?
   DOLA.  I could not, were she mine.
   ANT.  And yet you first
Persuaded me: How come you altered since?
   DOLA.  I said at first I was not fit to go:
I could not hear her sighs, and see her tears,
But pity must prevail: And so, perhaps,
It may again with you; for I have promised,
That she should take her last farewell: And, see,
She comes to claim my word.


*Enter* CLEOPATRA

   ANT.  False Dolabella!
   DOLA.  What's false, my lord?
   ANT.  Why, Dolabella's false,
And Cleopatra's false; both false and faithless.

Draw near, you well-joined wickedness, you serpents,
Whom I have in my kindly bosom warmed,
Till I am stung to death.

DOLA. My lord, have I
Deserved to be thus used?

CLEO. Can Heaven prepare
A newer torment? Can it find a curse
Beyond our separation?

ANT. Yes, if fate
Be just, much greater: Heaven should be ingenious
In punishing such crimes. The rolling stone,
And gnawing vulture, were slight pains, invented
When Jove was young, and no examples known
Of mighty ills; but you have ripened sin,
To such a monstrous growth, 'twill pose the gods
To find an equal torture. Two, two such!—
Oh, there's no further name,—two such! to me,
To me, who locked my soul within your breasts,
Had no desires, no joys, no life, but you;
When half the globe was mine, I gave it you
In dowry with my heart; I had no use,
No fruit of all, but you: A friend and mistress
Was what the world could give. O Cleopatra!
O Dolabella! how could you betray
This tender heart, which with an infant fondness
Lay lulled betwixt your bosoms, and there slept,
Secure of injured faith?

DOLA. If she has wronged you,
Heaven, hell, and you revenge it.

ANT. If she has wronged me!
Thou wouldst evade thy part of guilt; but swear
Thou lov'st not her.

DOLA. Not so as I love you.

ANT. Not so? Swear, swear, I say, thou dost not love
her.

DOLA. No more than friendship will allow.

ANT. No more?
Friendship allows thee nothing: Thou art perjured—
And yet thou didst not swear thou lov'st her not;
But not so much, no more. O trifling hypocrite,

Who dar'st not own to her, thou dost not love,
Nor own to me, thou dost! Ventidius heard it;
Octavia saw it.

CLEO. They are enemies.

ANT. Alexas is not so: He, he confessed it;
He, who, next hell, best knew it, he avowed it.
Why do I seek a proof beyond yourself?

[*To* DOLABELLA.

You, whom I sent to bear my last farewell,
Returned, to plead her stay.

DOLA. What shall I answer?
If to have loved be guilt, then I have sinned;
But if to have repented of that love
Can wash away my crime, I have repented.
Yet, if I have offended past forgiveness,
Let not her suffer: She is innocent.

CLEO. Ah, what will not a woman do, who loves?
What means will she refuse, to keep that heart,
Where all her joys are placed? 'Twas I encouraged,
'Twas I blew up the fire that scorched his soul,
To make you jealous, and by that regain you.
But all in vain; I could not counterfeit:
In spite of all the dams my love broke o'er,
And drowned my heart again: fate took the occasion;
And thus one minute's feigning has destroyed
My whole life's truth.

ANT. Thin cobweb arts of falsehood;
Seen, and broke through at first.

DOLA. Forgive your mistress.

CLEO. Forgive your friend.

ANT. You have convinced yourselves.
You plead each other's cause: What witness have you,
That you but meant to raise my jealousy?

CLEO. Ourselves, and Heaven.

ANT. Guilt witnesses for guilt. Hence, love and
friendship!
You have no longer place in human breasts,
These two have driven you out: Avoid my sight!
I would not kill the man whom I have loved,
And cannot hurt the woman; but avoid me:

I do not know how long I can be tame;
For, if I stay one minute more, to think
How I am wronged, my justice and revenge
Will cry so loud within me, that my pity
Will not be heard for either.

 Dola. Heaven has but
Our sorrow for our sins; and then delights
To pardon erring man: Sweet mercy seems
Its darling attribute, which limits justice;
As if there were degrees in infinite,
And infinite would rather want perfection
Than punish to extent.

 Ant. I can forgive
A foe; but not a mistress and a friend.
Treason is there in its most horrid shape,
Where trust is greatest; and the soul resigned,
Is stabbed by its own guards: I'll hear no more;
Hence from my sight for ever!

 Cleo. How? for ever!
I cannot go one moment from your sight,
And must I go for ever?
My joys, my only joys, are centred here:
What place have I to go to? My own kingdom?
That I have lost for you: Or to the Romans?
They hate me for your sake: Or must I wander
The wide world o'er, a helpless, banished woman,
Banished for love of you; banished from you?
Ay, there's the banishment! Oh, hear me; hear me,
With strictest justice: For I beg no favour;
And if I have offended you, then kill me,
But do not banish me.

 Ant. I must not hear you.
I have a fool within me takes your part;
But honour stops my ears.

 Cleo. For pity hear me!
Would you cast off a slave who followed you?
Who crouched beneath your spurn?—He has no
  pity!
See, if he gives one tear to my departure;
One look, one kind farewell: O iron heart!

Let all the gods look down, and judge betwixt us,
If he did ever love!

ANT. No more: Alexas!

DOLA. A perjured villain!

ANT. [*to* CLEO.]. Your Alexas; yours.

CLEO. Oh, 'twas his plot; his ruinous design,
To engage you in my love by jealousy.
Hear him; confront him with me; let him speak.

ANT. I have; I have.

CLEO. And if he clear me not—

ANT. Your creature! one, who hangs upon your smiles!
Watches your eye, to say or to unsay,
Whate'er you please! I am not to be moved.

CLEO. Then must we part? Farewell, my cruel lord!
The appearance is against me; and I go,
Unjustified, for ever from your sight.
How I have loved, you know; how yet I love,
My only comfort is, I know myself:
I love you more, even now you are unkind,
Then when you loved me most; so well, so truly
I'll never strive against it; but die pleased,
To think you once were mine.

ANT. Good heaven, they weep at parting!
Must I weep too? that calls them innocent.
I must not weep; and yet I must, to think
That I must not forgive.—
Live, but live wretched; 'tis but just you should,
Who made me so: Live from each other's sight:
Let me not hear you meet. Set all the earth,
And all the seas, betwixt your sundered loves:
View nothing common but the sun and skies.
Now, all take several ways;

And each your own sad fate, with mine, deplore;
That you were false, and I could trust no more.

[*Exeunt severally.*

## ACT V

### SCENE I

*Enter* CLEOPATRA, CHARMION, *and* IRAS

CHAR. Be juster, Heaven; such virtue punished thus,
Will make us think that chance rules all above,
And shuffles, with a random hand, the lots,
Which man is forced to draw.

CLEO. I could tear out these eyes, that gained his heart,
And had not power to keep it. O the curse
Of doting on, even when I find it dotage!
Bear witness, gods, you heard him bid me go;
You, whom he mocked with imprecating vows
Of promised faith!—I'll die; I will not bear it.
You may hold me—

    *[She pulls out her dagger, and they hold her.*
But I can keep my breath; I can die inward,
And choke this love.

### Enter ALEXAS

IRAS. Help, O Alexas, help!
The queen grows desperate; her soul struggles in her
With all the agonies of love and rage,
And strives to force its passage.

CLEO. Let me go.
Art thou there, traitor!—O,
O for a little breath, to vent my rage,
Give, give me way, and let me loose upon him.

ALEX. Yes, I deserve it, for my ill-timed truth.
Was it for me to prop
The ruins of a falling majesty?
To place myself beneath the mighty flaw,
Thus to be crushed, and pounded into atoms,
By its o'erwhelming weight? 'Tis too presuming
For subjects to preserve that wilful power,
Which courts its own destruction.

CLEO. I would reason

More calmly with you.  Did not you o'errule,
And force my plain, direct, and open love,
Into these crooked paths of jealousy?
Now, what's the event?  Octavia is removed;
But Cleopatra's banished.  Thou, thou villain,
Hast pushed my boat to open sea; to prove,
At my sad cost, if thou canst steer it back.
It cannot be; I'm lost too far; I'm ruined:
Hence, thou impostor, traitor, monster, devil!—
I can no more: Thou, and my griefs, have sunk
Me down so low, that I want voice to curse thee.

   ALEX.  Suppose some shipwrecked seaman near the
      shore,
Dropping and faint, with climbing up the cliff,
If, from above, some charitable hand
Pull him to safety, hazarding himself,
To draw the other's weight; would he look back,
And curse him for his pains?  The case is yours;
But one step more, and you have gained the height.

   CLEO.  Sunk, never more to rise.

   ALEX.  Octavia's gone, and Dolabella banished.
Believe me, madam, Antony is yours.
His heart was never lost, but started off
To jealousy, love's last retreat and covert;
Where it lies hid in shades, watchful in silence,
And listening for the sound that calls it back.
Some other, any man ('tis so advanced),
May perfect this unfinished work, which I
(Unhappy only to myself) have left
So easy to his hand.

   CLEO.  Look well thou do't; else—

   ALEX.  Else, what your silence threatens.—Antony
Is mounted up the Pharos; from whose turret,
He stands surveying our Egyptian galleys,
Engaged with Cæsar's fleet.  Now death or conquest!
If the first happen, fate acquits my promise;
If we o'ercome, the conqueror is yours.

                     *[A distant shout within.*

   CHAR.  Have comfort, madam: Did you mark that
      shout?              *[Second shout nearer.*

IRAS.   Hark! they redouble it.

ALEX.   'Tis from the port.

The loudness shows it near: Good news, kind heavens!

CLEO.   Osiris make it so!

*Enter* SERAPION

SERAP.   Where, where's the queen?

ALEX.   How frightfully the holy coward stares

As if not yet recovered of the assault,

When all his gods, and, what's more dear to him,

His offerings, were at stake.

SERAP.   O horror, horror!

Egypt has been; our latest hour has come:

The queen of nations, from her ancient seat,

Is sunk for ever in the dark abyss:

Time has unrolled her glories to the last,

And now closed up the volume.

CLEO.   Be more plain:

Say, whence thou comest; though fate is in thy face,

Which from thy haggard eyes looks wildly out,

And threatens ere thou speakest.

SERAP.   I came from Pharos;

From viewing (spare me, and imagine it)

Our land's last hope, your navy—

CLEO.   Vanquished?

SERAP.   No:

They fought not.

CLEO.   Then they fled.

SERAP.   Nor that. I saw,

With Antony, your well-appointed fleet

Row out; and thrice he waved his hand on high,

And thrice with cheerful cries they shouted back:

'Twas then false Fortune, like a fawning strumpet,

About to leave the bankrupt prodigal,

With a dissembled smile would kiss at parting,

And flatter to the last; the well-timed oars,

Now dipt from every bank, now smoothly run

To meet the foe; and soon indeed they met,

But not as foes. In few, we saw their caps

On either side thrown up; the Egyptian galleys,
Received like friends, passed through, and fell behind
The Roman rear: And now, they all come forward,
And ride within the port.

CLEO. Enough, Serapion:
I've heard my doom.—This needed not, you gods:
When I lost Antony, your work was done;
'Tis but superfluous malice.—Where's my lord?
How bears he this last blow?

SERAP. His fury cannot be expressed by words:
Thrice he attempted headlong to have fallen
Full on his foes, and aimed at Cæsar's galley:
Withheld, he raves on you; cries,—He's betrayed.
Should he now find you—

ALEX. Shun him; seek your safety,
Till you can clear your innocence.

CLEO. I'll stay.

ALEX. You must not; haste you to your monument,
While I make speed to Cæsar.

CLEO. Cæsar! No,
I have no business with him.

ALEX. I can work him
To spare your life, and let this madman perish.

CLEO. Base fawning wretch! wouldst thou betray him
     too?
Hence from my sight! I will not hear a traitor;
'Twas thy design brought all this ruin on us.—
Serapion, thou art honest; counsel me:
But haste, each moment's precious.

SERAP. Retire; you must not yet see Antony.
He who began this mischief,
'Tis just he tempt the danger; let him clear you:
And, since he offered you his servile tongue,
To gain a poor precarious life from Cæsar,
Let him expose that fawning eloquence,
And speak to Antony.

ALEX. O heavens! I dare not;
I meet my certain death.

CLEO. Slave, thou deservest it.—
Not that I fear my lord, will I avoid him;

I know him noble: when he banished me,
And thought me false, he scorned to take my life;
But I'll be justified, and then die with him.

    ALEX.  O pity me, and let me follow you.

    CLEO.  To death, if thou stir hence.  Speak, if thou
       canst,
Now for thy life, which basely thou wouldst save;
While mine I prize at—this!  Come, good Serapion.

    [*Exeunt* CLEOPATRA, SERAPION, CHARMION, *and* IRAS.

    ALEX.  O that I less could fear to lose this being,
Which, like a snowball in my coward hand,
The more 'tis grasped, the faster melts away.
Poor reason! what a wretched aid art thou!
For still, in spite of thee,
These two long lovers, soul and body, dread
Their final separation.  Let me think:
What can I say, to save myself from death?
No matter what becomes of Cleopatra.

    ANT.  Which way? where?           [*Within.*

    VENT.  This leads to the monument.    [*Within.*

    ALEX.  Ah me! I hear him; yet I'm unprepared:
My gift of lying's gone;
And this court-devil, which I so oft have raised,
Forsakes me at my need.  I dare not stay;
Yet cannot far go hence.           [*Exit.*


*Enter* ANTONY *and* VENTIDIUS

    ANT.  O happy Cæsar! thou hast men to lead:
Think not 'tis thou hast conquered Antony;
But Rome has conquered Egypt.  I'm betrayed.

    VENT.  Curse on this treacherous train!
Their soil and heaven infect them all with baseness:
And their young souls come tainted to the world
With the first breath they draw.

    ANT.  The original villain sure no god created;
He was a bastard of the sun, by Nile,
Aped into man; with all his mother's mud
Crusted about his soul.

    VENT.  The nation is

One universal traitor; and their queen
The very spirit and extract of them all.

  Ant.  Is there yet left
A possibility of aid from valour?
Is there one god unsworn to my destruction?
The least unmortgaged hope? for, if there be,
Methinks I cannot fall beneath the fate
Of such a boy as Cæsar.
The world's one half is yet in Antony;
And from each limb of it, that's hewed away,
The soul comes back to me.

  Vent.  There yet remain
Three legions in the town. The last assault
Lopt off the rest; if death be your design,—
As I must wish it now,—these are sufficient
To make a heap about us of dead foes,
An honest pile for burial.

  Ant.  They are enough.
We'll not divide our stars; but, side by side,
Fight emulous, and with malicious eyes
Survey each other's acts: So every death
Thou giv'st, I'll take on me, as a just debt,
And pay thee back a soul.

  Vent.  Now you shall see I love you. Not a word
Of chiding more. By my few hours of life,
I am so pleased with this brave Roman fate,
That I would not be Cæsar, to outlive you.
When we put off this flesh, and mount together,
I shall be shown to all the ethereal crowd,—
Lo, this is he who died with Antony!

  Ant.  Who knows, but we may pierce through all their
      troops,
And reach my veterans yet? 'tis worth the 'tempting,
To o'erleap this gulf of fate,
And leave our wandering destinies behind.


*Enter* Alexas, *trembling*

  Vent.  See, see, that villain!
See Cleopatra stamped upon that face,
With all her cunning, all her arts of falsehood!

How she looks out through those dissembling eyes!
How he sets his countenance for deceit,
And promises a lie, before he speaks!
Let me despatch him first.          *[Drawing.*

   Alex. O spare me, spare me!
   Ant. Hold; he's not worth your killing.—On thy
      life,
Which thou may'st keep, because I scorn to take it,
No syllable to justify thy queen;
Save thy base tongue its office.
   Alex. Sir, she is gone.
Where she shall never be molested more
By love, or you.
   Ant. Fled to her Dolabella!
Die, traitor! I revoke my promise! die!
                      *[Going to kill him.*

   Alex. O hold! she is not fled.
   Ant. She is: my eyes
Are open to her falsehood; my whole life
Has been a golden dream of love and friendship;
But, now I wake, I'm like a merchant, roused
From soft repose, to see his vessel sinking,
And all his wealth cast over. Ungrateful woman!
Who followed me, but as the swallow summer,
Hatching her young ones in my kindly beams,
Singing her flatteries to my morning wake:
But, now my winter comes, she spreads her wings,
And seeks the spring of Cæsar.
   Alex. Think not so;
Her fortunes have, in all things, mixed with yours.
Had she betrayed her naval force to Rome,
How easily might she have gone to Cæsar,
Secure by such a bribe!
   Vent. She sent it first,
To be more welcome after.
   Ant. 'Tis too plain;
Else would she have appeared, to clear herself.
   Alex. Too fatally she has: she could not bear
To be accused by you; but shut herself
Within her monument; looked down and sighed;

While, from her unchanged face, the silent tears
Dropt, as they had not leave, but stole their parting.
Some indistinguished words she only murmured;
At last, she raised her eyes; and, with such looks
As dying Lucrece cast—

ANT.  My heart forebodes—

VENT.  All for the best:—Go on.

ALEX.  She snatched her poniard,
And, ere we could prevent the fatal blow,
Plunged it within her breast; then turned to me:
Go, bear my lord, said she, my last farewell;
And ask him, if he yet suspect my faith.
More she was saying, but death rushed betwixt.
She half pronounced your name with her last breath,
And buried half within her.

VENT.  Heaven be praised!

ANT.  Then art thou innocent, my poor dear love,
And art thou dead?
O those two words! their sound should be divided:
Hadst thou been false, and died; or hadst thou lived,
And hadst been true—But innocence and death!
This shows not well above.  Then what am I,
The murderer of this truth, this innocence!
Thoughts cannot form themselves in words so horrid
As can express my guilt!

VENT.  Is't come to this?  The gods have been too
        gracious;
And thus you thank them for it!

ANT. [to ALEX.].  Why stayest thou here?
Is it for thee to spy upon my soul,
And see its inward mourning?  Get thee hence;
Thou art not worthy to behold, what now
Becomes a Roman emperor to perform.

ALEX.  He loves her still:
His grief betrays it.  Good! the joy to find
She's yet alive, completes the reconcilement.
I've saved myself, and her.  But, oh! the Romans!
Fate comes too fast upon my wit,
Hunts me too hard, and meets me at each double.
                                [*Aside. Exit.*

VENT.  Would she had died a little sooner, though!
Before Octavia went, you might have treated:
Now 'twill look tame, and would not be received.
Come, rouse yourself, and let's die warm together.

ANT.  I will not fight: there's no more work for war.
The business of my angry hours is done.

VENT.  Cæsar is at your gates.

ANT.  Why, let him enter;
He's welcome now.

VENT.  What lethargy has crept into your soul?

ANT.  'Tis but a scorn of life, and just desire
To free myself from bondage.

VENT.  Do it bravely.

ANT.  I will; but not by fighting.  O Ventidius!
What should I fight for now?—my queen is dead.
I was but great for her; my power, my empire,
Were but my merchandise to buy her love;
And conquered kings, my factors.  Now she's dead,
Let Cæsar take the world,—
An empty circle, since the jewel's gone
Which made it worth my strife: my being's nauseous;
For all the bribes of life are gone away.

VENT.  Would you be taken?

ANT.  Yes, I would be taken;
But, as a Roman ought,—dead, my Ventidius:
For I'll convey my soul from Cæsar's reach,
And lay down life myself.  'Tis time the world
Should have a lord, and know whom to obey.
We two have kept its homage in suspense,
And bent the globe, on whose each side we trod,
Till it was dented inwards.  Let him walk
Alone upon't: I'm weary of my part.
My torch is out; and the world stands before me,
Like a black desert at the approach of night:
I'll lay me down, and stray no farther on.

VENT.  I could be grieved,
But that I'll not outlive you: choose your death;
For, I have seen him in such various shapes,
I care not which I take: I'm only troubled,
The life I bear is worn to such a rag,

'Tis scarce worth giving.  I could wish, indeed,
We threw it from us with a better grace;
That, like two lions taken in the toils,
We might at last thrust out our paws, and wound
The hunters that inclose us.

    ANT.  I have thought on it.
Ventidius, you must live.

    VENT.  I must not, sir.

    ANT.  Wilt thou not live, to speak some good of me?
To stand by my fair fame, and guard the approaches
From the ill tongues of men?

    VENT.  Who shall guard mine,
For living after you?

    ANT.  Say, I command it.

    VENT.  If we die well, our deaths will speak themselves
And need no living witness.

    ANT.  Thou hast loved me,
And fain I would reward thee.  I must die;
Kill me, and take the merit of my death,
To make thee friends with Cæsar.

    VENT.  Thank your kindness.
You said I loved you; and in recompense,
You bid me turn a traitor: Did I think
You would have used me thus?—that I should die
With a hard thought of you?

    ANT.  Forgive me, Roman.
Since I have heard of Cleopatra's death,
My reason bears no rule upon my tongue,
But lets my thoughts break all at random out.
I've thought better; do not deny me twice.

    VENT.  By Heaven I will not.
Let it not be to outlive you.

    ANT.  Kill me first,
And then die thou; for 'tis but just thou serve
Thy friend, before thyself.

    VENT.  Give me your hand.
We soon shall meet again.  Now, farewell, emperor!—
                        [*Embrace.*

Methinks that word's too cold to be my last:
Since death sweeps all distinctions, farewell, friend!

That's all—
I will not make a business of a trifle;
And yet I cannot look on you, and kill you;
Pray turn your face.

    ANT. I do: strike home, be sure.

    VENT. Home as my sword will reach.

[Kills himself.

    ANT. Oh, thou mistak'st;
That wound was not of thine; give it me back:
Thou robb'st me of my death.

    VENT. I do indeed;
But think 'tis the first time I e'er deceived you,
If that may plead my pardon.—And you, gods,
Forgive me, if you will; for I die perjured,
Rather than kill my friend.         [Dies.

    ANT. Farewell! Ever my leader, even in death!
My queen and thou have got the start of me,
And I'm the lag of honour.—Gone so soon?
Is Death no more? he used him carelessly,
With a familiar kindness: ere he knocked,
Ran to the door, and took him in his arms,
As who should say—You're welcome at all hours,
A friend need give no warning. Books had spoiled him;
For all the learned are cowards by profession.
'Tis not worth
My further thought; for death, for aught I know,
Is but to think no more. Here's to be satisfied.

[Falls on his sword.

I've missed my heart. O unperforming hand!
Thou never couldst have erred in a worse time.
My fortune jades me to the last; and death,
Like a great man, takes state, and makes me wait
For my admittance.—     [Trampling within.
Some, perhaps, from Cæsar:
If he should find me living, and suspect
That I played booty with my life! I'll mend
My work, ere they can reach me.

[Rises upon his knees.

*Enter* CLEOPATRA, CHARMION, *and* IRAS

CLEO. Where is my lord? where is he?

CHAR. There he lies,
And dead Ventidius by him.

CLEO. My tears were prophets; I am come too late.
O that accursed Alexas! [*Runs to him.*

ANT. Art thou living?
Or am I dead before I knew, and thou
The first kind ghost that meets me?

CLEO. Help me seat him.
Send quickly, send for help!

[*They place him in a chair.*

ANT. I am answered.
We live both. Sit thee down, my Cleopatra:
I'll make the most I can of life, to stay
A moment more with thee.

CLEO. How is it with you?

ANT. 'Tis as with a man
Removing in a hurry; all packed up,
But one dear jewel that his haste forgot;
And he, for that, returns upon the spur:
So I come back for thee.

CLEO. Too long, ye heavens, you have been cruel to me:
Now show your mended faith, and give me back
His fleeting life!

ANT. It will not be, my love;
I keep my soul by force.
Say but, thou art not false.

CLEO. 'Tis now too late
To say I'm true: I'll prove it, and die with you.
Unknown to me, Alexas feigned my death:
Which, when I knew, I hasted to prevent
This fatal consequence. My fleet betrayed
Both you and me.

ANT. And Dolabella—

CLEO. Scarce
Esteemed before he loved; but hated now.

ANT. Enough: my life's not long enough for more.
Thou say'st, thou wilt come after: I believe thee;

For I can now believe whate'er thou sayest,
That we may part more kindly.

    CLEO. I will come:
Doubt not, my life, I'll come, and quickly too:
Cæsar shall triumph o'er no part of thee.

    ANT. But grieve not, while thou stayest,
My last disastrous times:
Think we have had a clear and glorious day
And Heaven did kindly to delay the storm,
Just till our close of evening. Ten years' love,
And not a moment lost, but all improved
To the utmost joys,—what ages have we lived?
And now to die each other's; and, so dying,
While hand in hand we walk in groves below,
Whole troops of lovers' ghosts shall flock about us,
And all the train be ours.

    CLEO. Your words are like the notes of dying swans,
Too sweet to last. Were there so many hours
For your unkindness, and not one for love?

    ANT. No, not a minute.—This one kiss—more worth
Than all I leave to Cæsar.               [*Dies.*

    CLEO. O tell me so again,
And take ten thousand kisses for that word.
My lord, my lord! speak, if you yet have being;
Sign to me, if you cannot speak; or cast
One look! Do anything that shows you live.

    IRAS. He's gone too far to hear you;
And this you see, a lump of senseless clay,
The leavings of a soul.

    CHAR. Remember, madam,
He charged you not to grieve.

    CLEO. And I'll obey him.
I have not loved a Roman, not to know
What should become his wife; his wife, my Charmion!
For 'tis to that high title I aspire;
And now I'll not die less. Let dull Octavia
Survive, to mourn him dead: My nobler fate
Shall knit our spousals with a tie, too strong
For Roman laws to break.

    IRAS. Will you then die?

CLEO. Why shouldst thou make that question?

IRAS. Cæsar is merciful.

CLEO. Let him be so
To those that want his mercy: My poor lord
Made no such covenant with him, to spare me
When he was dead. Yield me to Cæsar's pride?
What! to be led in triumph through the streets,
A spectacle to base plebeian eyes;
While some dejected friend of Antony's,
Close in a corner, shakes his head, and mutters
A secret curse on her who ruined him!
I'll none of that.

CHAR. Whatever you resolve,
I'll follow, even to death.

IRAS. I only feared
For you; but more should fear to live without you.

CLEO. Why, now, 'tis as it should be. Quick, my
friends,
Despatch; ere this, the town's in Cæsar's hands:
My lord looks down concerned, and fears my stay,
Lest I should be surprised;
Keep him not waiting for his love too long.
You, Charmion, bring my crown and richest jewels;
With them, the wreath of victory I made
(Vain augury!) for him, who now lies dead:
You, Iras, bring the cure of all our ills.

IRAS. The aspics, madam?

CLEO. Must I bid you twice?

[*Exit* CHARMION *and* IRAS.

'Tis sweet to die, when they would force life on me,
To rush into the dark abode of death,
And seize him first; if he be like my love,
He is not frightful, sure.
We're now alone, in secrecy and silence;
And is not this like lovers? I may kiss
These pale, cold lips; Octavia does not see me:
And, oh! 'tis better far to have him thus,
Than see him in her arms.—Oh, welcome, welcome!

*Enter* CHARMION *and* IRAS

CHAR. What must be done?

CLEO. Short ceremony, friends;
But yet it must be decent. First, this laurel
Shall crown my hero's head: he fell not basely,
Nor left his shield behind him.—Only thou
Couldst triumph o'er thyself; and thou alone
Wert worthy so to triumph.

CHAR. To what end
These ensigns of your pomp and royalty?

CLEO. Dull, that thou art! why 'tis to meet my love;
As when I saw him first, on Cydnus' bank,
All sparkling, like a goddess: so adorned,
I'll find him once again; my second spousals
Shall match my first in glory. Haste, haste, both,
And dress the bride of Antony.

CHAR. 'Tis done.

CLEO. Now seat me by my lord. I claim this place,
For I must conquer Cæsar too, like him,
And win my share of the world.—Hail, you dear relics
Of my immortal love!
O let no impious hand remove you hence:
But rest for ever here! Let Egypt give
His death that peace, which it denied his life.—
Reach me the casket.

IRAS. Underneath the fruit
The aspic lies.

CLEO. Welcome, thou kind deceiver!

[*Putting aside the leaves.*

Thou best of thieves: who, with an easy key,
Dost open life, and, unperceived by us,
Even steal us from ourselves; discharging so
Death's dreadful office, better than himself;
Touching our limbs so gently into slumber,
That Death stands by, deceived by his own image,
And thinks himself but sleep.

SERAP. The queen, where is she? [*Within.*
The town is yielded, Cæsar's at the gates.

CLEO. He comes too late to invade the rights of death!

Haste, bare my arm, and rouse the serpent's fury.

*[Holds out her arm, and draws it back.*

Coward flesh,
Wouldst thou conspire with Cæsar to betray me,
As thou wert none of mine? I'll force thee to it,
And not be sent by him,
But bring, myself, my soul to Antony.

*[Turns aside, and then shows her arm bloody.*

Take hence; the work is done.

SERAP. Break ope the door,             *[Within.*
And guard the traitor well.

CHAR. The next is ours.

IRAS. Now, Charmion, to be worthy
Of our great queen and mistress.

*[They apply the aspics.*

CLEO. Already, death, I feel thee in my veins:
I go with such a will to find my lord,
That we shall quickly meet.
A heavy numbness creeps through every limb,
And now 'tis at my head: My eyelids fall,
And my dear love is vanquished in a mist.
Where shall I find him, where? O turn me to him,
And lay me on his breast!—Cæsar, thy worst;
Now part us, if thou canst.           *[Dies.*

*[IRAS sinks down at her feet, and dies; CHARMION
stands behind her chair, as dressing her head.*


*Enter* SERAPION, *two* Priests, ALEXAS *bound,* Egyptians

PRIEST. Behold, Serapion,
What havoc death has made!

SERAP. 'Twas what I feared.—
Charmion, is this well done?

CHAR. Yes, 'tis well done, and like a queen, the last
Of her great race: I follow her.    *[Sinks down: dies.*

ALEX. 'Tis true,
She has done well: Much better thus to die,
Than live to make a holiday in Rome.

SERAP. See how the lovers sit in state together,
As they were giving laws to half mankind!

The impression of a smile, left in her face,
Shows she died pleased with him for whom she lived,
And went to charm him in another world.
Cæsar's just entering: grief has now no leisure.
Secure that villain, as our pledge of safety,
To grace the imperial triumph.—Sleep, blest pair,
Secure from human chance, long ages out,
While all the storms of fate fly o'er your tomb;
  And fame to late posterity shall tell,
  No lovers lived so great, or died so well.    [*Exeunt.*

# EPILOGUE

POETS, like disputants, when reasons fail,
Have one sure refuge left—and that's to rail.
Fop, coxcomb, fool, are thundered through the pit;
And this is all their equipage of wit.
We wonder how the devil this difference grows
Betwixt our fools in verse, and yours in prose:
For, 'faith, the quarrel rightly understood,
'Tis civil war with their own flesh and blood.
The threadbare author hates the gaudy coat;
And swears at the gilt coach, but swears afoot:
For 'tis observed of every scribbling man,
He grows a fop as fast as e'er he can;
Prunes up, and asks his oracle, the glass,
If pink or purple best become his face.
For our poor wretch, he neither rails nor prays;
Nor likes your wit just as you like his plays;
He has not yet so much of Mr Bayes.
He does his best; and if he cannot please,
Would quietly sue out his *writ of ease*.
Yet, if he might his own grand jury call,
By the fair sex he begs to stand or fall.
Let Cæsar's power the men's ambition move,
But grace you him who lost the world for love!
   Yet if some antiquated lady say,
The last age is not copied in his play;
Heaven help the man who for that face must drudge,
Which only has the wrinkles of a judge.
Let not the young and beauteous join with those;
For should you raise such numerous hosts of foes,
Young wits and sparks he to his aid must call;
'Tis more than one man's work to please you all.

# THE SCHOOL FOR SCANDAL

BY

RICHARD BRINSLEY SHERIDAN

# INTRODUCTORY NOTE

RICHARD BRINSLEY SHERIDAN, *statesman and dramatist, was born in Dublin on Oct. 30, 1751. He belonged to a highly talented family, his grandfather, Thomas Sheridan, being a prominent Jacobite and a historian, and his father, also Thomas Sheridan, a distinguished actor, theatrical manager, and author.*

*Sheridan was educated for the bar, but the success of his comedy, "The Rivals," led him into close relations with the theatre. "The Rivals" was followed by "St. Patrick's Day," a farce; "The Duenna," a comic opera; "A Trip to Scarborough," an adaptation from Vanbrugh; "The School for Scandal" (1777); and a patriotic melodrama, "Pizarro." He was manager of Drury Lane Theatre, which he twice had a chief part in rebuilding; and though he had periods of marked prosperity in his management, and exercised a powerful influence on the stage history of his time, his theatrical activities frequently involved him in grave financial difficulties.*

*In 1780 Sheridan entered Parliament, and for over thirty years he took a highly distinguished part in politics. He held cabinet office a number of times, and was regarded as the most brilliant and effective orator of his day. His most famous speeches dealt with the prosecution of Warren Hastings; the French Revolution, in connection with which he urged the policy of letting the French manage their own government, but of resisting their attempts to spread their principles by conquest; the war with the American colonies, by his opposition to which he earned the gratitude of Congress; and the liberty of the press, of which he was an uncompromising champion. Throughout his career he was an honest and intrepid advocate of liberal ideas.*

*In "The School for Scandal" Sheridan carried the comedy of manners to the highest point it has reached in England. In the permanence of its hold on the public it is surpassed only by the plays of Shakespeare; and in characters like Joseph Surface, Sir Peter, and Lady Teazle, and in the scandal scene and the auction scene the author added to the lasting glories of the English stage.*

*Sheridan died in 1816, and was buried with great pomp in Westminster Abbey.*

# A PORTRAIT

## ADDRESSED TO MRS CREWE, WITH THE COMEDY OF THE SCHOOL FOR SCANDAL

### BY R. B. SHERIDAN, ESQ.

TELL me, ye prim adepts in Scandal's school,
Who rail by precept, and detract by rule,
Lives there no character, so tried, so known,
So decked with grace, and so unlike your own,
That even you assist her fame to raise,
Approve by envy, and by silence praise!
Attend!—a model shall attract your view—
Daughters of calumny, I summon you!
You shall decide if this a portrait prove,
Or fond creation of the Muse and Love.
Attend, ye virgin critics, shrewd and sage,
Ye matron censors of this childish age,
Whose peering eye and wrinkled front declare
A fixed antipathy to young and fair;
By cunning, cautious; or by nature, cold,
In maiden madness, virulently bold!—
Attend, ye skilled to coin the precious tale,
Creating proof, where inuendos fail!
Whose practised memories, cruelly exact,
Omit no circumstance, except the fact!—
Attend, all ye who boast,—or old or young,—
The living libel of a slanderous tongue!
So shall my theme as far contrasted be,
As saints by fiends, or hymns by calumny.
Come, gentle Amoret (for 'neath that name
In worthier verse is sung thy beauty's fame);
Come— for but thee who seeks the Muse? and while
Celestial blushes check thy conscious smile,
With timid grace, and hesitating eye,

The perfect model, which I boast, supply:—
Vain Muse! couldst thou the humblest sketch create
Of her, or slightest charm couldst imitate—
Could thy blest strain in kindred colours trace
The faintest wonder of her form and face—
Poets would study the immortal line,
And Reynolds own his art subdued by thine;
That art, which well might added lustre give
To Nature's best, and Heaven's superlative:
On Granby's cheek might bid new glories rise,
Or point a purer beam from Devon's eyes!
Hard is the task to shape that beauty's praise,
Whose judgment scorns the homage flattery pays!
But praising Amoret we cannot err,
No tongue o'ervalues Heaven, or flatters her!
Yet she by Fate's perverseness—she alone
Would doubt our truth, nor deem such praise her own.
Adorning fashion, unadorned by dress,
Simple from taste, and not from carelessness;
Discreet in gesture, in deportment mild,
Not stiff with prudence, nor uncouthly wild:
No state has Amoret; no studied mien;
She frowns no goddess, and she moves no queen.
The softer charm that in her manner lies
Is framed to captivate, yet not surprise;
It justly suits the expression of her face,—
'Tis less than dignity, and more than grace!
On her pure cheek the native hue is such,
That, formed by Heaven to be admired so much,
The hand divine, with a less partial care,
Might well have fixed a fainter crimson there,
And bade the gentle inmate of her breast—
Inshrinèd Modesty—supply the rest.
But who the peril of her lips shall paint?
Strip them of smiles—still, still all words are faint.
But moving Love himself appears to teach
Their action, though denied to rule her speech;
And thou who seest her speak, and dost not hear,
Mourn not her distant accents 'scape thine ear;
Viewing those lips, thou still may'st make pretence

To judge of what she says, and swear 'tis sense:
Clothed with such grace, with such expression fraught,
They move in meaning, and they pause in thought!
But dost thou farther watch, with charmed surprise,
The mild irresolution of her eyes,
Curious to mark how frequent they repose,
In brief eclipse and momentary close—
Ah! seest thou not an ambushed Cupid there,
Too timorous of his charge, with jealous care
Veils and unveils those beams of heavenly light,
Too full, too fatal else, for mortal sight?
Nor yet, such pleasing vengeance fond to meet,
In pardoning dimples hope a safe retreat.
What though her peaceful breast should ne'er allow
Subduing frowns to arm her altered brow,
By Love, I swear, and by his gentle wiles,
More fatal still the mercy of her smiles!
Thus lovely, thus adorned, possessing all
Of bright or fair that can to woman fall,
The height of vanity might well be thought
Prerogative in her, and Nature's fault.
Yet gentle Amoret, in mind supreme
As well as charms, rejects the vainer theme;
And, half mistrustful of her beauty's store,
She barbs with wit those darts too keen before:—
Read in all knowledge that her sex should reach,
Though Greville, or the Muse, should deign to teach,
Fond to improve, nor timorous to discern
How far it is a woman's grace to learn;
In Millar's dialect she would not prove
Apollo's priestess, but Apollo's love,
Graced by those signs which truth delights to own,
The timid blush, and mild submitted tone:
Whate'er she says, though sense appear throughout,
Displays the tender hue of female doubt;
Decked with that charm, how lovely wit appears,
How graceful science, when that robe she wears!
Such too her talents, and her bent of mind,
As speak a sprightly heart by thought refined:
A taste for mirth, by contemplation schooled,

A turn for ridicule, by candour ruled,
A scorn of folly, which she tries to hide;
An awe of talent, which she owns with pride!
　　Peace, idle Muse! no more thy strain prolong,
But yield a theme, thy warmest praises wrong;
Just to her merit, though thou canst not raise
Thy feeble verse, behold th' acknowledged praise
Has spread conviction through the envious train,
And cast a fatal gloom o'er Scandal's reign!
And lo! each pallid hag, with blistered tongue.
Mutters assent to all thy zeal has sung—
Owns all the colours just—the outline true;
Thee my inspirer, and my model—CREWE!

# PROLOGUE

## WRITTEN BY MR. GARRICK

A School for Scandal! tell me, I beseech you,
Needs there a school this modish art to teach you?
No need of lessons now, the knowing think;
We might as well be taught to eat and drink.
Caused by a dearth of scandal, should the vapours
Distress our fair ones—let them read the papers;
Their powerful mixtures such disorders hit;
Crave what you will—there's *quantum sufficit*.
"Lord!" cries my Lady Wormwood (who loves tattle,
And puts much salt and pepper in her prattle),
Just risen at noon, all night at cards when threshing
Strong tea and scandal—"Bless me, how refreshing!
Give me the papers, Lisp—how bold and free!          [*Sips.*
*Last night Lord L.* [*Sips*] *was caught with Lady D.*
For aching heads what charming sal volatile!          [*Sips.*
*If Mrs B. will still continue flirting,*
*We hope she'll* DRAW, *or we'll* UNDRAW *the curtain.*
Fine satire, poz—in public all abuse it,
But, by ourselves [*Sips*], our praise we can't refuse it.
Now, Lisp, read you—there, at that dash and star:"
"Yes, ma'am—*A certain lord had best beware,*
*Who lives not twenty miles from Grosvenor Square;*
*For, should he Lady W. find willing,*
*Wormwood is bitter"*——"Oh! that's me! the villain!
Throw it behind the fire, and never more
Let that vile paper come within my door."
Thus at our friends we laugh, who feel the dart;
To reach our feelings, we ourselves must smart.
Is our young bard so young, to think that he
Can stop the full spring-tide of calumny?
Knows he the world so little, and its trade?

Alas! the devil's sooner raised than laid.
So strong, so swift, the monster there's no gagging:
Cut Scandal's head off, still the tongue is wagging.
Proud of your smiles once lavishly bestowed,
Again our young Don Quixote takes the road:
To show his gratitude he draws his pen,
And seeks this hydra, Scandal, in his den.
For your applause all perils fie would through—
He'll fight—that's write—a cavalliero true,
Till every drop of blood—that's ink—is spilt for you.

# THE SCHOOL FOR SCANDAL

## DRAMATIS PERSONÆ

AS ORIGINALLY ACTED AT DRURY-LANE THEATRE IN 1777

| | |
|---|---|
| SIR PETER TEAZLE . . . . . | Mr King |
| SIR OLIVER SURFACE . . . . | Mr Yates |
| SIR HARRY BUMPER . . . . | Mr Gawdry |
| SIR BENJAMIN BACKBITE . . . | Mr Dodd |
| JOSEPH SURFACE . . . . . | Mr Palmer |
| CHARLES SURFACE . . . . . | Mr Smith |
| CARELESS . . . . . . | Mr Farren |
| SNAKE . . . . . . . | Mr Packer |
| CRABTREE . . . . . . | Mr Parsons |
| ROWLEY . . . . . . | Mr Aickin |
| MOSES . . . . . . . | Mr Baddeley |
| TRIP . . . . . . . | Mr Lamask |
| LADY TEAZLE . . . . . | Mrs Abington |
| LADY SNEERWELL . . . . . | Miss Sherry |
| MRS CANDOUR . . . . . | Miss Pope |
| MARIA . . . . . . . | Miss P. Hopkins |

Gentlemen, Maid, and Servants

SCENE: *London*

## ACT FIRST

### SCENE I.—LADY SNEERWELL'S *Dressing-room.*

LADY SNEERWELL *discovered at her toilet;* SNAKE *drinking chocolate.*

*Lady Sneerwell*

THE paragraphs, you say, Mr Snake, were all inserted?
SNAKE. They were, madam; and, as I copied them myself in a feigned hand, there can be no suspicion whence they came.

LADY SNEER. Did you circulate the report of Lady Brittle's intrigue with Captain Boastall?

SNAKE. That's in as fine a train as your ladyship could wish. In the common course of things, I think it must reach

111

Mrs Clackitt's ears within four-and-twenty hours; and then, you know, the business is as good as done.

LADY SNEER. Why, truly, Mrs Clackitt has a very pretty talent, and a great deal of industry.

SNAKE. True, madam, and has been tolerably successful in her day. To my knowledge, she has been the cause of six matches being broken off, and three sons being disinherited; of four forced elopements, and as many close confinements; nine separate maintenances, and two divorces. Nay, I have more than once traced her causing a *tête-à-tête* in the " Town and County Magazine," when the parties, perhaps, had never seen each other's face before in the course of their lives.

LADY SNEER. She certainly has talents, but her manner is gross.

SNAKE. 'Tis very true. She generally designs well, has a free tongue and a bold invention; but her colouring is too dark, and her outlines often extravagant. She wants that delicacy of tint, and mellowness of sneer, which distinguish your ladyship's scandal.

LADY SNEER. You are partial, Snake.

SNAKE. Not in the least; everybody allows that Lady Sneerwell can do more with a word or look than many can with the most laboured detail, even when they happen to have a little truth on their side to support it.

LADY SNEER. Yes, my dear Snake; and I am no hypocrite to deny the satisfaction I reap from the success of my efforts. Wounded myself, in the early part of my life, by the envenomed tongue of slander, I confess I have since known no pleasure equal to the reducing others to the level of my own reputation.

SNAKE. Nothing can be more natural. But, Lady Sneerwell, there is one affair in which you have lately employed me, wherein, I confess, I am at a loss to guess your motives.

LADY SNEER. I conceive you mean with respect to my neighbour, Sir Peter Teazle, and his family?

SNAKE. I do. Here are two young men, to whom Sir Peter has acted as a kind of guardian since their father's death; the eldest possessing the most amiable character, and universally well spoken of—the youngest, the most dissipated and extravagant young fellow in the kingdom, without friends or character; the former an avowed admirer of your ladyship, and apparently your favourite; the latter attached to Maria, Sir Peter's ward, and confessedly beloved by her. Now, on the face of these circumstances, it is utterly unaccountable to me, why you, the widow of a city knight, with a good jointure, should not close with the passion of a man of such character and expectations as Mr Surface; and more so why you should be so uncommonly earnest to destroy the mutual attachment subsisting between his brother Charles and Maria.

LADY SNEER. Then, at once to unravel this mystery, I must inform you that love has no share whatever in the intercourse between Mr Surface and me.

SNAKE. No!

LADY SNEER. His real attachment is to Maria, or her fortune; but, finding in his brother a favoured rival, he has been obliged to mask his pretensions, and profit by my assistance.

SNAKE. Yet still I am more puzzled why you should interest yourself in his success.

LADY SNEER. Heavens! how dull you are! Cannot you surmise the weakness which I hitherto, through shame, have concealed even from you? Must I confess that Charles—that libertine, that extravagant, that bankrupt in fortune and reputation—that he it is for whom I am thus anxious and malicious, and to gain whom I would sacrifice every thing?

SNAKE. Now, indeed, your conduct appears consistent: but how came you and Mr Surface so confidential?

LADY SNEER. For our mutual interest. I have found him out a long time since. I know him to be artful, selfish, and malicious—in short, a sentimental knave; while with Sir Peter, and indeed with all his acquaintance, he passes for a youthful miracle of prudence, good sense, and benevolence.

SNAKE. Yes; yet Sir Peter vows he has not his equal in England; and, above all, he praises him as a man of sentiment.

LADY SNEER. True; and with the assistance of his sentiment and hypocrisy he has brought Sir Peter entirely into his interest with regard to Maria; while poor Charles has no friend in the house—though, I fear, he has a powerful one in Maria's heart, against whom we must direct our schemes.

*Enter* SERVANT

SER. Mr Surface.

LADY SNEER. Show him up. [*Exit Servant.*] He generally calls about this time. I don't wonder at people giving him to me for a lover.

*Enter* JOSEPH SURFACE

JOS. SURF. My dear Lady Sneerwell, how do you do today? Mr Snake, your most obedient.

LADY SNEER. Snake has just been rallying me on our mutual attachment, but I have informed him of our real views. You know how useful he has been to us; and, believe me, the confidence is not ill-placed.

JOS. SURF. Madam, it is impossible for me to suspect a man of Mr Snake's sensibility and discernment.

LADY SNEER. Well, well, no compliments now; but tell me when you saw your mistress, Maria—or, what is more material to me, your brother.

JOS. SURF. I have not seen either since I left you; but I can inform you that they never meet. Some of your stories have taken a good effect on Maria.

LADY SNEER. Ah, my dear Snake! the merit of this belongs to you. But do your brother's distresses increase?

JOS. SURF. Every hour. I am told he has had another execution in the house yesterday. In short, his dissipation and extravagance exceed any thing I have ever heard of.

LADY SNEER. Poor Charles!

JOS. SURF. True, madam; notwithstanding his vices, one can't help feeling for him. Poor Charles! I'm sure I wish it were in my power to be of any essential service to him; for the man who does not share in the distresses of a brother, even though merited by his own misconduct, deserves—

LADY SNEER. O Lud! you are going to be moral, and forget that you are among friends.

JOS. SURF. Egad, that's true! I'll keep that sentiment till I see Sir Peter. However, it is certainly a charity to rescue Maria from such a libertine, who if he is to be reclaimed, can be so only by a person of your ladyship's superior accomplishments and understanding.

SNAKE. I believe, Lady Sneerwell, here's company coming: I'll go and copy the letter I mentioned to you. Mr Surface, your most obedient.

JOS. SURF. Sir, your very devoted.—[*Exit* SNAKE.] Lady Sneerwell, I am very sorry you have put any farther confidence in that fellow.

LADY SNEER. Why so?

JOS. SURF. I have lately detected him in frequent conference with old Rowley, who was formerly my father's steward, and has never, you know, been a friend of mine.

LADY SNEER. And do you think he would betray us?

JOS. SURF. Nothing more likely; take my word for't, Lady Sneerwell, that fellow hasn't virtue enough to be faithful even to his own villany. Ah, Maria!

*Enter* MARIA

LADY SNEER. Maria, my dear, how do you do? What's the matter?

MAR. Oh! there's that disagreeable lover of mine, Sir Benjamin Backbite, has just called at my guardian's, with his odious uncle, Crabtree; so I slipped out, and ran hither to avoid them.

LADY SNEER. Is that all?

JOS. SURF. If my brother Charles had been of the party, madam, perhaps you would not have been so much alarmed.

LADY SNEER. Nay, now you are severe; for I dare swear the truth of the matter is, Maria heard you were here. But, my dear, what has Sir Benjamin done, that you should avoid him so?

MAR. Oh, he has done nothing—but 'tis for what he has said: his conversation is a perpetual libel on all his acquaintance.

JOS. SURF. Ay, and the worst of it is, there is no advantage in not knowing him; for he'll abuse a stranger just as soon as his best friend: and his uncle's as bad.

LADY SNEER. Nay, but we should make allowance; Sir Benjamin is a wit and a poet.

MAR. For my part, I own, madam, wit loses its respect with me, when I see it in company with malice. What do you think, Mr Surface?

JOS. SURF. Certainly, madam; to smile at the jest which plants a thorn in another's breast is to become a principal in the mischief.

LADY SNEER. Psha! there's no possibility of being witty without a little ill nature: the malice of a good thing is the barb that makes it stick. What's your opinion, Mr Surface?

JOS. SURF. To be sure, madam; that conversation, where the spirit of raillery is suppressed, will ever appear tedious and insipid.

MAR. Well, I'll not debate how far scandal may be allowable; but in a man, I am sure, it is always contemptible. We have pride, envy, rivalship, and a thousand motives to depreciate each other; but the male slanderer must have the cowardice of a woman before he can traduce one.

### Re-enter SERVANT

SER. Madam, Mrs Candour is below, and, if your ladyship's at leisure, will leave her carriage.

LADY SNEER. Beg her to walk in.—[Exit SERVANT.] Now, Maria, here is a character to your taste; for, though Mrs Candour is a little talkative, every body allows her to be the best natured and best sort of woman.

MAR. Yes, with a very gross affectation of good nature and benevolence, she does more mischief than the direct malice of old Crabtree.

JOS. SURF. I' faith that's true, Lady Sneerwell: whenever I hear the current running against the characters of my friends, I never think them in such danger as when Candour undertakes their defence.

LADY SNEER. Hush!—here she is!

### Enter MRS CANDOUR

MRS CAN. My dear Lady Sneerwell, how have you been this century?—Mr Surface, what news do you hear?—though indeed it is no matter, for I think one hears nothing else but scandal.

Jos. Surf. Just so, indeed, ma'am.

Mrs Can. Oh, Maria! child,—what, is the whole affair off between you and Charles? His extravagance, I presume —the town talks of nothing else.

Mar. I am very sorry, ma'am, the town has so little to do.

Mrs Can. True, true, child: but there's no stopping people's tongues. I own I was hurt to hear it, as I indeed was to learn, from the same quarter, that your guardian, Sir Peter, and Lady Teazle have not agreed lately as well as could be wished.

Mar. 'Tis strangely impertinent for people to busy themselves so.

Mrs Can. Very true, child: but what's to be done? People will talk—there's no preventing it. Why, it was but yesterday I was told that Miss Gadabout had eloped with Sir Filigree Flirt. But, Lord! there's no minding what one hears; though, to be sure, I had this from very good authority.

Mar. Such reports are highly scandalous.

Mrs Can. So they are, child—shameful, shameful! But the world is so censorious, no character escapes. Lord, now who would have suspected your friend, Miss Prim, of an indiscretion? Yet such is the ill nature of people, that they say her uncle stopped her last week, just as she was stepping into the York Mail with her dancing-master.

Mar. I'll answer for 't there are no grounds for that report.

Mrs Can. Ah, no foundation in the world, I dare swear; no more, probably, than for the story circulated last month, of Mrs Festino's affair with Colonel Cassino—though, to be sure, that matter was never rightly cleared up.

Jos. Surf. The licence of invention some people take is monstrous indeed.

Mar. 'Tis so; but, in my opinion, those who report such things are equally culpable.

Mrs Can. To be sure they are; tale-bearers are as bad as the tale-makers—'tis an old observation, and a very true one: but what's to be done, as I said before? how will you prevent people from talking? To-day, Mrs Clackitt assured me, Mr and Mrs Honeymoon were at last become mere man and wife, like the rest of their acquaintance. She likewise hinted that a certain widow, in the next street, had got rid of her dropsy and recovered her shape in a most surprising manner. And at the same time Miss Tattle, who was by, affirmed that Lord Buffalo had discovered his lady at a house of no extraordinary fame; and that Sir Harry Bouquet and Tom Saunter were to measure swords on a similar provocation. But, Lord, do you think I would report these things! No, no! tale-bearers, as I said before, are just as bad as the tale-makers.

Jos. SURF. Ah! Mrs Candour, if every body had your forbearance and good nature!

MRS CAN. I confess, Mr Surface, I cannot bear to hear people attacked behind their backs; and when ugly circumstances come out against our acquaintance, I own I always love to think the best. By the by, I hope 'tis not true that your brother is absolutely ruined?

Jos. SURF. I am afraid his circumstances are very bad indeed, ma'am.

MRS CAN. Ah! I heard so—but you must tell him to keep up his spirits; every body almost is in the same way: Lord Spindle, Sir Thomas Splint, Captain Quinze, and Mr Nickit —all up, I hear, within this week; so, if Charles is undone, he'll find half his acquaintance ruined too, and that, you know, is a consolation.

Jos. SURF. Doubtless, ma'am—a very great one.

### Re-enter SERVANT

SER. Mr Crabtree and Sir Benjamin Backbite.    [*Exit.*

LADY SNEER. So, Maria, you see your lover pursues you; positively you sha'n't escape.

### Enter CRABTREE *and* SIR BENJAMIN BACKBITE

CRAB. Lady Sneerwell, I kiss your hand. Mrs Candour, I don't believe you are acquainted with my nephew, Sir Benjamin Backbite? Egad, ma'am, he has a pretty wit, and is a pretty poet too. Isn't he, Lady Sneerwell?

SIR BEN. Oh, fie, uncle!

CRAB. Nay, egad it's true; I back him at a rebus or a charade against the best rhymer in the kingdom. Has your ladyship heard the epigram he wrote last week on Lady Frizzle's feather catching fire?—Do, Benjamin, repeat it, or the charade you made last night extempore at Mrs Drozie's conversazione. Come, now, your first is the name of a fish, your second a great naval commander, and—

SIR BEN. Uncle, now—pr'thee—

CRAB. I'faith, ma'am, 'twould surprise you to hear how ready he is at all these sorts of things.

LADY SNEER. I wonder, Sir Benjamin, you never publish any thing.

SIR BEN. To say truth, ma'am, 'tis very vulgar to print; and as my little productions are mostly satires and lampoons on particular people, I find they circulate more by giving copies in confidence to the friends of the parties. However, I have some love elegies, which, when favoured with this lady's smiles, I mean to give the public. [*Pointing to* MARIA.

CRAB. [*To* MARIA.] 'Fore heaven, ma'am, they'll immortalize you!—you will be handed down to posterity, like Petrarch's Laura, or Waller's Sacharissa.

SIR BEN. [*To* MARIA.] Yes, madam, I think you will like them, when you shall see them on a beautiful quarto page, where a neat rivulet of text shall meander through a meadow of margin. 'Fore Gad they will be the most elegant things of their kind!

CRAB. But, ladies, that's true—have you heard the news?

MRS CAN. What, sir, do you mean the report of—

CRAB. No, ma'am, that's not it.—Miss Nicely is going to be married to her own footman.

MR CAN. Impossible!

CRAB. Ask Sir Benjamin.

SIR BEN. 'Tis very true, ma'am: every thing is fixed, and the wedding liveries bespoke.

CRAB. Yes—and they do say there were pressing reasons for it.

LADY SNEER. Why, I have heard something of this before.

MRS CAN. It can't be—and I wonder any one should believe such a story of so prudent a lady as Miss Nicely.

SIR BEN. O Lud! ma'am, that's the very reason 'twas believed at once. She has always been so cautious and so reserved, that every body was sure there was some reason for it at bottom.

Mrs Can. Why, to be sure, a tale of scandal is as fatal to the credit of a prudent lady of her stamp as a fever is generally to those of the strongest constitutions. But there is a sort of puny sickly reputation, that is always ailing, yet will outlive the robuster characters of a hundred prudes.

Sir Ben. True, madam, there are valetudinarians in reputation as well as constitution, who, being conscious of their weak part, avoid the least breath of air, and supply their want of stamina by care and circumspection.

Mrs Can. Well, but this may be all a mistake. You know, Sir Benjamin, very trifling circumstances often give rise to the most injurious tales.

Crab. That they do, I'll be sworn, ma'am. Did you ever hear how Miss Piper came to lose her lover and her character last summer at Tunbridge?—Sir Benjamin, you remember it?

Sir Ben. Oh, to be sure!—the most whimsical circumstance.

Lady Sneer. How was it, pray?

Crab. Why, one evening, at Mrs Ponto's assembly, the conversation happened to turn on the breeding Nova Scotia sheep in this country. Says a young lady in company, " I have known instances of it; for Miss Letitia Piper, a first cousin of mine, had a Nova Scotia sheep that produced her twins." " What! " cries the Lady Dowager Dundizzy (who you know is as deaf as a post), " has Miss Piper had twins? " This mistake, as you may imagine, threw the whole company into a fit of laughter. However, 'twas the next morning everywhere reported, and in a few days believed by the whole town, that Miss Letitia Piper had actually been brought to bed of a fine boy and a girl: and in less than a week there were some people who could name the father, and the farm-house where the babies were put to nurse.

Lady Sneer. Strange, indeed!

Crab. Matter of fact, I assure you. O Lud! Mr Surface, pray is it true that your uncle, Sir Oliver, is coming home?

Jos. Surf. Not that I know of, indeed, sir.

Crab. He has been in the East Indies a long time. You can scarcely remember him, I believe? Sad comfort, whenever he returns, to hear how your brother has gone on!

Jos. Surf. Charles has been imprudent, sir, to be sure; but I hope no busy people have already prejudiced Sir Oliver against him. He may reform.

Sir Ben. To be sure he may: for my part, I never believed him to be so utterly void of principle as people say; and, though he has lost all his friends, I am told nobody is better spoken of by the Jews.

Crab. That's true, egad, nephew. If the Old Jewry was a ward, I believe Charles would be an alderman: no man more popular there, 'fore Gad! I hear he pays as many annuities as the Irish tontine; and that, whenever he is sick, they have prayers for the recovery of his health in all the synagogues.

Sir Ben. Yet no man lives in greater splendour. They tell me, when he entertains his friends he will sit down to dinner with a dozen of his own securities; have a score of tradesmen waiting in the antechamber, and an officer behind every guest's chair.

Jos. Surf. This may be entertainment to you, gentlemen, but you pay very little regard to the feelings of a brother.

Mar. [*Aside.*] Their malice is intolerable!—[*Aloud.*] Lady Sneerwell, I must wish you a good morning: I'm not very well.          [*Exit.*

Mrs. Can. O dear! she changes colour very much.

Lady Sneer. Do, Mrs. Candour, follow her: she may want your assistance.

Mrs. Can. That I will, with all my soul, ma'am.—Poor dear girl, who knows what her situation may be!     [*Exit.*

Lady Sneer. 'Twas nothing but that she could not bear to hear Charles reflected on, notwithstanding their difference.

Sir Ben. The young lady's *penchant* is obvious.

Crab. But, Benjamin, you must not give up the pursuit for that: follow her, and put her into good humour. Repeat her some of your own verses. Come, I'll assist you.

Sir Ben. Mr. Surface, I did not mean to hurt you; but depend on't your brother is utterly undone.

CRAB. O Lud, ay! undone as ever man was—can't raise a guinea!

SIR BEN. And everything sold, I'm told, that was movable.

CRAB. I have seen one that was at his house. Not a thing left but some empty bottles that were overlooked, and the family pictures, which I believe are framed in the wainscots.

SIR BEN. And I'm very sorry also to hear some bad stories against him. [Going.

CRAB. Oh, he has done many mean things, that's certain.

SIR BEN. But, however, as he's your brother—
[Going.

CRAB. We'll tell you all another opportunity.
[Exeunt CRABTREE and SIR BENJAMIN.

LADY SNEER. Ha! ha! 'tis very hard for them to leave a subject they have not quite run down.

JOS. SURF. And I believe the abuse was no more acceptable to your ladyship than Maria.

LADY SNEER. I doubt her affections are farther engaged than we imagine. But the family are to be here this evening, so you may as well dine where you are, and we shall have an opportunity of observing farther; in the meantime, I'll go and plot mischief, and you shall study sentiment.
[Exeunt.

SCENE II.—*A Room in* SIR PETER TEAZLE'S *House*

*Enter* SIR PETER TEAZLE

SIR PET. When an old bachelor marries a young wife, what is he to expect? 'Tis now six months since Lady Teazle made me the happiest of men—and I have been the most miserable dog ever since! We tiffed a little going to church, and fairly quarrelled before the bell had done ringing. I was more than once nearly choked with gall during the honeymoon, and had lost all comfort in life before my friends had done wishing me joy. Yet I chose with caution—a girl bred wholly in the country, who never knew luxury beyond one silk gown, nor dissipation above the annual gala of a race ball. Yet she now plays her part in all the extravagant fopperies of fashion and the

town, with as ready a grace as if she never had seen a bush
or a grass-plot out of Grosvenor Square! I am sneered
at by all my acquaintance, and paragraphed in the newspapers. She dissipates my fortune, and contradicts all my
humours; yet the worst of it is, I doubt I love her, or
I should never bear all this. However, I'll never be weak
enough to own it.

*Enter* ROWLEY

Row. Oh! Sir Peter, your servant: how is it with you, sir?

SIR PET. Very bad, Master Rowley, very bad. I meet
with nothing but crosses and vexations.

Row. What can have happened since yesterday?

SIR PET. A good question to a married man!

Row. Nay, I'm sure, Sir Peter, your lady can't be the
cause of your uneasiness.

SIR PET. Why, has any body told you she was dead?

Row. Come, come, Sir Peter, you love her, notwithstanding your tempers don't exactly agree.

SIR PET. But the fault is entirely hers, Master Rowley.
I am, myself, the sweetest-tempered man alive, and hate a
teasing temper; and so I tell her a hundred times a day.

Row. Indeed!

SIR PET. Ay; and what is very extraordinary, in all our
disputes she is always in the wrong! But Lady Sneerwell,
and the set she meets at her house, encourage the perverseness of her disposition. Then, to complete my vexation,
Maria, my ward, whom I ought to have the power of a
father over, is determined to turn rebel too, and absolutely
refuses the man whom I have long resolved on for her
husband; meaning, I suppose, to bestow herself on his
profligate brother.

Row. You know, Sir Peter, I have always taken the liberty
to differ with you on the subject of these two young gentlemen. I only wish you may not be deceived in your opinion
of the elder. For Charles, my life on't! he will retrieve his
errors yet. Their worthy father, once my honoured master,
was, at his years, nearly as wild a spark; yet, when he died,
he did not leave a more benevolent heart to lament his loss.

SIR PET. You are wrong, Master Rowley. On their

father's death, you know, I acted as a kind of guardian to them both, till their uncle Sir Oliver's liberality gave them an early independence.  Of course, no person could have more opportunities of judging of their hearts, and I was never mistaken in my life.  Joseph is indeed a model for the young men of the age.  He is a man of sentiment, and acts up to the sentiments he professes; but for the other, take my word for't, if he had any grain of virtue by descent, he has dissipated it with the rest of his inheritance.  Ah! my old friend, Sir Oliver, will be deeply mortified when he finds how part of his bounty has been misapplied.

Row. I am sorry to find you so violent against the young man, because this may be the most critical period of his fortune.  I came hither with news that will surprise you.

Sir Pet. What! let me hear.

Row. Sir Oliver is arrived, and at this moment in town.

Sir Pet. How! you astonish me!  I thought you did not expect him this month.

Row. I did not: but his passage has been remarkably quick.

Sir Pet. Egad, I shall rejoice to see my old friend.  'Tis sixteen years since we met.  We have had many a day together:—but does he still enjoin us not to inform his nephews of his arrival?

Row. Most strictly.  He means, before it is known, to make some trial of their dispositions.

Sir Pet. Ah! there needs no art to discover their merits— however, he shall have his way; but, pray, does he know I am married?

Row. Yes, and will soon wish you joy.

Sir Pet. What, as we drink health to a friend in a consumption!  Ah! Oliver will laugh at me.  We used to rail at matrimony together, but he has been steady to his text.  Well, he must be soon at my house, though—I'll instantly give orders for his reception.  But, Master Rowley, don't drop a word that Lady Teazle and I ever disagree.

Row. By no means.

Sir Pet. For I should never be able to stand Noll's jokes; so I'll have him think, Lord forgive me! that we are a very happy couple.

Row. I understand you:—but then you must be very careful not to differ while he is in the house with you.

Sir Pet. Egad, and so we must—and that's impossible. Ah! Master Rowley, when an old bachelor marries a young wife, he deserves—no—the crime carries its punishment along with it.

## ACT SECOND

### Scene I.—*A Room in* Sir Peter Teazle's *House*

#### *Enter* Sir Peter *and* Lady Teazle

Sir Pet. Lady Teazle, Lady Teazle, I'll not bear it!

Lady Teazle. Sir Peter, Sir Peter, you may bear it or not, as you please; but I ought to have my own way in every thing, and, what's more, I will too. What! though I was educated in the country, I know very well that women of fashion in London are accountable to nobody after they are married.

Sir Pet. Very well, ma'am, very well; so a husband is to have no influence, no authority?

Lady Teaz. Authority! No, to be sure: if you wanted authority over me, you should have adopted me, and not married me: I'm sure you were old enough.

Sir Pet. Old enough!—ay, there it is. Well, well, Lady Teazle, though my life may be made unhappy by your temper, I'll not be ruined by your extravagance!

Lady Teaz. My extravagance! I'm sure I'm not more extravagant than a woman of fashion ought to be.

Sir Pet. No, no, madam, you shall throw away no more sums on such unmeaning luxury. 'Slife! to spend as much to furnish your dressing-room with flowers in winter as would suffice to turn the Pantheon into a greenhouse, and give a *fête champêtre* ^t Christmas.

Lady Teaz. And am I to blame, Sir Peter, because flowers are dear in cold weather? You should find fault with the climate, and not with me. For my part, I'm sure I wish it was spring all the year round, and that roses grew under our feet!

Sir Pet. Oons! madam—if you had been born to this, I

shouldn't wonder at you talking thus; but you forget what your situation was when I married you.

LADY TEAZ. No, no, I don't; 'twas a very disagreeable one, or I should never have married you.

SIR PET. Yes, yes, madam, you were then in somewhat a humbler style—the daughter of a plain country squire. Recollect, Lady Teazle, when I saw you first sitting at your tambour, in a pretty figured linen gown, with a bunch of keys at your side, your hair combed smooth over a roll, and your apartment hung round with fruits in worsted, of your own working.

LADY TEAZ. Oh, yes! I remember it very well, and a curious life I led. My daily occupation to inspect the dairy, superintend the poultry, make extracts from the family receipt-book, and comb my aunt Deborah's lapdog.

SIR PET. Yes, yes, ma'am, 'twas so indeed.

LADY TEAZ. And then you know, my evening amusements! To draw patterns for ruffles, which I had not materials to make up; to play Pope Joan with the curate; to read a sermon to my aunt; or to be stuck down to an old spinet to strum my father to sleep after a fox-chase.

SIR PET. I am glad you have so good a memory. Yes, madam, these were the recreations I took you from! but now you must have your coach—*vis-à-vis*—and three powdered footmen before your chair; and, in the summer, a pair of white cats to draw you to Kensington Gardens. No recollection, I suppose, when you were content to ride double, behind the butler, on a docked coach-horse.

LADY TEAZ. No—I swear I never did that: I deny the butler and the coach-horse.

SIR PET. This, madam, was your situation; and what have I done for you? I have made you a woman of fashion, of fortune, of rank—in short, I have made you my wife.

LADY TEAZ. Well, then, and there is but one thing more you can make me to add to the obligation, this is—

SIR PET. My widow, I suppose?

LADY TEAZ. Hem! hem!

SIR PET. I thank you, madam—but don't flatter yourself, for, though your ill conduct may disturb my peace of mind, it shall never break my heart, I promise you: however, I am equally obliged to you for the hint.

LADY TEAZ. Then why will you endeavour to make yourself so disagreeable to me, and thwart me in every little elegant expense?

SIR PET. 'Slife, madam, I say, had you any of these little elegant expenses when you married me?

LADY TEAZ. Lud, Sir Peter! would you have me be out of the fashion?

SIR PET. The fashion, indeed! what had you to do with the fashion before you married me?

LADY TEAZ. For my part, I should think you would like to have your wife thought a woman of taste.

SIR PET. Ay—there again—taste! Zounds! madam, you had no taste when you married me!

LADY TEAZ. That's very true, indeed, Sir Peter! and, after having married you, I should never pretend to taste again, I allow. But now, Sir Peter, since we have finished our daily jangle, I presume I may go to my engagement at Lady Sneerwell's.

SIR PET. Ay, there's another precious circumstance—a charming set of acquaintance you have made there!

LADY TEAZ. Nay, Sir Peter, they are all people of rank and fortune, and remarkably tenacious of reputation.

SIR PET. Yes, egad, they are tenacious of reputation with a vengeance; for they don't choose anybody should have a character but themselves! Such a crew! Ah! many a wretch has rid on a hurdle who has done less mischief than these utterers of forged tales, coiners of scandal, and clippers of reputation.

LADY TEAZ. What, would you restrain the freedom of speech?

SIR PET. Ah! they have made you just as bad as any one of the society.

LADY TEAZ. Why, I believe I do bear a part with a miserable grace.

SIR PET. Grace indeed!

LADY TEAZ. But I vow I bear no malice against the people I abuse: when I say an ill-natured thing, 'tis out of pure good humour; and I take it for granted

they deal exactly in the same manner with me. But, Sir
Peter, you know you promised to come to Lady Sneerwell's
too.

SIR PET. Well, well, I'll call in, just to look after my
own character.

LADY TEAZ. Then, indeed, you must make haste after me,
or you'll be too late. So goodbye to ye.            [*Exit.*

SIR PET. So—I have gained much by my intended expostulation! Yet with what a charming air she contradicts
every thing I say, and how pleasantly she shows her contempt
for my authority! Well, though I can't make her love
me, there is great satisfaction in quarrelling with her; and I
think she never appears to such advantage as when she
is doing every thing in her power to plague me.     [*Exit.*


SCENE II.—*A Room in* LADY SNEERWELL'S *House*

LADY SNEERWELL, MRS CANDOUR, CRABTREE, SIR BEN-
    JAMIN BACKBITE, *and* JOSEPH SURFACE, *discovered*

LADY SNEER. Nay, positively, we will hear it.

JOS. SURF. Yes, yes, the epigram, by all means.

SIR BEN. O plague on't, uncle! 'tis mere nonsense.

CRAB. No, no; 'fore Gad, very clever for an extempore!

SIR BEN. But, ladies, you should be acquainted with the
circumstance. You must know, that one day last week, as
Lady Betty Curricle was taking the dust in Hyde Park, in
a sort of duodecimo phaeton, she desired me to write
some verses on her ponies; upon which, I took out my
pocket-book, and in a moment produced the following:—

> Sure never were seen two such beautiful ponies;
> Other horses are clowns, but these macaronies:
> To give them this title I'm sure can't be wrong,
> Their legs are so slim, and their tails are so long.

CRAB. There, ladies, done in the smack of a whip, and on
horseback too.

JOS. SURF. A very Phœbus, mounted—indeed, Sir Benjamin!

SIR BEN. Oh dear, sir! trifles—trifles.

*Enter* LADY TEAZLE *and* MARIA

MRS CAN. I must have a copy.

LADY SNEER. Lady Teazle, I hope we shall see Sir Peter?

LADY TEAZ. I believe he'll wait on your ladyship presently.

LADY SNEER. Maria, my love, you look grave. Come, you shall sit down to piquet with Mr Surface.

MAR. I take very little pleasure in cards—however, I'll do as your ladyship pleases.

LADY TEAZ. I am surprised Mr Surface should sit down with her; I thought he would have embraced this opportunity of speaking to me before Sir Peter came.          [*Aside.*

MRS CAN. Now, I'll die, but you are so scandalous, I'll forswear your society.

LADY TEAZ. What's the matter, Mrs Candour?

MRS CAN. They'll not allow our friend Miss Vermilion to be handsome.

LADY SNEER. Oh, surely she is a pretty woman.

CRAB. I am very glad you think so, ma'am.

MRS CAN. She has a charming fresh colour.

LADY TEAZ. Yes, when it is fresh put on.

MRS CAN. Oh, fie! I'll swear her colour is natural: I have seen it come and go!

LADY TEAZ. I dare swear you have, ma'am: it goes off at night, and comes again in the morning.

SIR BEN. True, ma'am, it not only comes and goes; but, what's more, egad, her maid can fetch and carry it!

MRS CAN. Ha! ha! ha! how I hate to hear you talk so! But surely, now, her sister is, or was, very handsome.

CRAB. Who? Mrs. Evergreen? O Lord! she's six-and-fifty if she's an hour!

MRS CAN. Now positively you wrong her; fifty-two or fifty-three is the utmost—and I don't think she looks more.

SIR BEN. Ah! there's no judging by her looks, unless one could see her face.

LADY SNEER. Well, well, if Mrs. Evergreen does take some pains to repair the ravages of time, you must allow she effects it with great ingenuity; and surely that's better than the careless manner in which the widow Ochre caulks her wrinkles.

SIR BEN. Nay, now, Lady Sneerwell, you are severe

upon the widow. Come, come, 'tis not that she paints so ill—but, when she has finished her face, she joins it on so badly to her neck, that she looks like a mended statue, in which the connoisseur may see at once that the head is modern, though the trunk's antique.

CRAB. Ha! ha! ha! Well said, nephew!

MRS CAN. Ha! ha! ha! Well, you make me laugh; but I vow I hate you for it. What do you think of Miss Simper?

SIR BEN. Why, she has very pretty teeth.

LADY TEAZ. Yes; and on that account, when she is neither speaking nor laughing (which very seldom happens), she never absolutely shuts her mouth, but leaves it always a-jar, as it were—thus.                    [Shows her teeth.

MRS CAN. How can you be so ill-natured?

LADY TEAZ. Nay, I allow even that's better than the pains Mrs Prim takes to conceal her losses in front. She draws her mouth till it positively resembles the aperture of a poor's-box, and all her words appear to slide out edgewise, as it were— thus: How do you do, madam? Yes, madam.        [Mimics.

LADY SNEER. Very well, Lady Teazle; I see you can be a little severe.

LADY TEAZ. In defence of a friend it is but justice. But here comes Sir Peter to spoil our pleasantry.


*Enter* SIR PETER TEAZLE

SIR PET. Ladies, your most obedient.—[*Aside.*] Mercy on me, here is the whole set! a character dead at every word, I suppose.

MRS CAN. I am rejoiced you are come, Sir Peter. They have been so censorious—and Lady Teazle as bad as any one.

SIR PET. That must be very distressing to you, indeed, Mrs Candour.

MRS CAN. Oh, they will allow good qualities to nobody; not even good nature to our friend Mrs Pursy.

LADY TEAZ. What, the fat dowager who was at Mrs Quadrille's last night?

MRS CAN. Nay, her bulk is her misfortune; and, when she takes so much pains to get rid of it, you ought not to reflect on her.

LADY SNEER. That's very true, indeed.

LADY TEAZ. Yes, I know she almost lives on acids and small whey; laces herself by pulleys; and often, in the hottest noon in summer, you may see her on a little squat pony, with her hair plaited up behind like a drummer's and puffing round the Ring on a full trot.

MRS CAN. I thank you, Lady Teazle, for defending her.

SIR PET. Yes, a good defence, truly.

MRS CAN. Truly, Lady Teazle is as censorious as Miss Sallow.

CRAB. Yes, and she is a curious being to pretend to be censorious—an awkward gawky, without any one good point under heaven.

MRS CAN. Positively you shall not be so very severe. Miss Sallow is a near relation of mine by marriage, and, as for her person, great allowance is to be made; for, let me tell you, a woman labours under many disadvantages who tries to pass for a girl of six-and-thirty.

LADY SNEER. Though, surely, she is handsome still—and for the weakness in her eyes, considering how much she reads by candlelight, it is not to be wondered at.

MRS CAN. True, and then as to her manner; upon my word I think it is particularly graceful, considering she never had the least education: for you know her mother was a Welsh milliner, and her father a sugar-baker at Bristol.

SIR BEN. Ah! you are both of you too good-natured!

SIR PET. Yes, damned good-natured! This their own relation! mercy on me!                              [*Aside.*

MRS CAN. For my part, I own I cannot bear to hear a friend ill spoken of.

SIR PET. No, to be sure!

SIR BEN. Oh! you are of a moral turn. Mrs Candour and I can sit for an hour and hear Lady Stucco talk sentiment.

LADY TEAZ. Nay, I vow Lady Stucco is very well with the dessert after dinner; for she's just like the French fruit one cracks for mottoes—made up of paint and proverb.

MRS CAN. Well, I will never join in ridiculing a friend; and so I constantly tell my cousin Ogle, and you all know what pretensions she has to be critical on beauty.

CRAB. Oh, to be sure! she has herself the oddest countenance that ever was seen; 'tis a collection of features from all the different countries of the globe.

SIR BEN. So she has, indeed—an Irish front—

CRAB. Caledonian locks—

SIR BEN. Dutch nose—

CRAB. Austrian lips—

SIR BEN. Complexion of a Spaniard—

CRAB. And teeth *à la Chinoise*—

SIR BEN. In short, her face resembles a *table d'hôte* at Spa—where no two guests are of a nation—

CRAB. Or a congress at the close of a general war—wherein all the members, even to her eyes, appear to have a different interest, and her nose and chin are the only parties likely to join issue.

MRS CAN. Ha! ha! ha!

SIR PET. Mercy on my life!—a person they dine with twice a week!                    [*Aside.*

MRS CAN. Nay, but I vow you shall not carry the laugh off so—for give me leave to say, that Mrs Ogle—

SIR PET. Madam, madam, I beg your pardon—there's no stopping these good gentlemen's tongues. But when I tell you, Mrs Candour, that the lady they are abusing is a particular friend of mine, I hope you'll not take her part.

LADY SNEER. Ha! ha! ha! well said, Sir Peter! but you are a cruel creature—too phlegmatic yourself for a jest, and too peevish to allow wit in others.

SIR PET. Ah, madam, true wit is more nearly allied to good nature than your ladyship is aware of.

LADY TEAZ. True, Sir Peter: I believe they are so near akin that they can never be united.

SIR BEN. Or rather, suppose them man and wife, because one seldom sees them together.

LADY TEAZ. But Sir Peter is such an enemy to scandal, I believe he would have it put down by parliament.

SIR PET. 'Fore heaven, madam, if they were to consider the sporting with reputation of as much importance as poaching on manors, and pass an act for the preservation of fame, as well as game, I believe many would thank them for the bill.

LADY SNEER. O Lud! Sir Peter; would you deprive us of our privileges?

SIR PET. Ay, madam; and then no person should be permitted to kill characters and run down reputations, but qualified old maids and disappointed widows.

LADY SNEER. Go, you monster!

MRS. CAN. But surely, you would not be quite so severe on those who only report what they hear?

SIR PET. Yes, madam, I would have law merchant for them too; and in all cases of slander currency, whenever the drawer of the lie was not to be found, the injured parties should have a right to come on any of the indorsers.

CRAB. Well, for my part, I believe there never was a scandalous tale without some foundation.

LADY SNEER. Come, ladies, shall we sit down to cards in the next room?

*Enter* SERVANT, *who whispers* SIR PETER

SIR PET. I'll be with them directly.—[*Exit* SERVANT.] I'll get away unperceived.                    [*Aside.*

LADY SNEER. Sir Peter, you are not going to leave us?

SIR PET. Your ladyship must excuse me; I'm called away by particular business. But I leave my character behind me.                                        [*Exit.*

SIR BEN. Well—certainly, Lady Teazle, that lord of yours is a strange being: I could tell you some stories of him would make you laugh heartily if he were not your husband.

LADY TEAZ. Oh, pray don't mind that; come, do let's hear them.    [*Exeunt all but* JOSEPH SURFACE *and* MARIA.

JOS. SURF. Maria, I see you have no satisfaction in this society.

MAR. How is it possible I should? If to raise malicious smiles at the infirmities or misfortunes of those who have never injured us be the province of wit or humour, Heaven grant me a double portion of dulness!

JOS. SURF. Yet they appear more ill-natured than they are; they have no malice at heart.

MAR. Then is their conduct still more contemptible; for, in my opinion, nothing could excuse the intemperance of their tongues but a natural and uncontrollable bitterness of mind.

Jos. Surf. Undoubtedly, madam; and it has always been a sentiment of mine, that to propagate a malicious truth wantonly is more despicable than to falsify from revenge. But can you, Maria, feel thus for others, and be unkind to me alone? Is hope to be denied the tenderest passion?

Mar. Why will you distress me by renewing this subject?

Jos. Surf. Ah, Maria! you would not treat me thus, and oppose your guardian, Sir Peter's will, but that I see that profligate Charles is still a favoured rival.

Mar. Ungenerously urged! But, whatever my sentiments are for that unfortunate young man, be assured I shall not feel more bound to give him up, because his distresses have lost him the regard even of a brother.

Jos. Surf. Nay, but, Maria, do not leave me with a frown: by all that is honest, I swear—                              [*Kneels.*

### Re-enter Lady Teazle *behind*

'Aside.] Gad's life, here's Lady Teazle.—[*Aloud to* Maria.] You must not—no, you shall not—for, though I have the greatest regard for Lady Teazle—

Mar. Lady Teazle!

Jos. Surf. Yet were Sir Peter to suspect—

Lady Teaz. [*Coming forward.*] What is this, pray? Does he take her for me?—Child, you are wanted in the next room.—[*Exit* Maria.] What is all this, pray?

Jos. Surf. Oh, the most unlucky circumstance in nature! Maria has somehow suspected the tender concern I have for your happiness, and threatened to acquaint Sir Peter with her suspicions, and I was just endeavouring to reason with her when you came in.

Lady Teaz. Indeed! but you seemed to adopt a very tender mode of reasoning—do you usually argue on your knees?

Jos. Surf. Oh, she's a child, and I thought a little bombast —But, Lady Teazle, when are you to give me your judgment on my library, as you promised?

Lady Teaz. No, no; I begin to think it would be imprudent, and you know I admit you as a lover no farther than fashion requires.

Jos. Surf. True—a mere Platonic cicisbeo, what every wife is entitled to.

Lady Teaz. Certainly, one must not be out of the fashion. However, I have so many of my country prejudices left, that, though Sir Peter's ill humour may vex me ever so, it never shall provoke me to—

Jos. Surf. The only revenge in your power. Well, I applaud your moderation.

Lady Teaz. Go—you are an insinuating wretch! But we shall be missed—let us join the company.

Jos Surf. But we had best not return together.

Lady Teaz. Well, don't stay; for Maria sha'n't come to hear any more of your reasoning, I promise you.    [*Exit.*

Jos. Surf. A curious dilemma, truly, my politics have run me into! I wanted, at first, only to ingratiate myself with Lady Teazle, that she might not be my enemy with Maria; and I have, I don't know how, become her serious lover. Sincerely I begin to wish I had never made such a point of gaining so very good a character, for it has led me into so many cursed rogueries that I doubt I shall be exposed at last.
    [*Exit.*

Scene III.—*A Room in* Sir Peter Teazle's *House*

*Enter* Sir Oliver Surface *and* Rowley

Sir Oliv. Ha! ha! ha! so my old friend is married, hey? —a young wife out of the country. Ha! ha! ha! that he should have stood bluff to old bachelor so long, and sink into a husband at last!

Row. But you must not rally him on the subject, Sir Oliver; 'tis a tender point, I assure you, though he has been married only seven months.

Sir Oliv. Then he has been just half a year on the stool of repentance!—Poor Peter! But you say he has entirely given up Charles—never sees him, hey?

Row. His prejudice against him is astonishing, and I am sure greatly increased by a jealousy of him with Lady Teazle, which he has industriously been led into by a scandalous society in the neighbourhood, who have contributed not a little to Charles's ill name. Whereas the truth is, I believe, if the lady is partial to either of them, his brother is the favourite.

SIR OLIV. Ay, I know there are a set of malicious, prating, prudent gossips, both male and female, who murder characters to kill time, and will rob a young fellow of his good name before he has years to know the value of it. But I am not to be prejudiced against my nephew by such, I promise you! No, no: if Charles has done nothing false or mean, I shall compound for his extravagance.

Row. Then, my life on't, you will reclaim him. Ah, sir, it gives me new life to find that your heart is not turned against him, and that the son of my good old master has one friend, however, left.

SIR OLIV. What! shall I forget, Master Rowley, when I was at his years myself? Egad, my brother and I were neither of us very prudent youths; and yet, I believe, you have not seen many better men than your old master was?

Row. Sir, 'tis this reflection gives me assurance that Charles may yet be a credit to his family. But here comes Sir Peter.

SIR OLIV. Egad, so he does! Mercy on me! he's greatly altered, and seems to have a settled married look! One may read husband in his face at this distance!

*Enter* SIR PETER TEAZLE

SIR PET. Ha! Sir Oliver—my old friend! Welcome to England a thousand times!

SIR OLIV. Thank you, thank you, Sir Peter! and i' faith I am glad to find you well, believe me!

SIR PET. Oh! 'tis a long time since we met—fifteen years, I doubt, Sir Oliver, and many a cross accident in the time.

SIR OLIV. Ay, I have had my share. But what! I find you are married, hey, my old boy? Well, well, it can't be helped; and so—I wish you joy with all my heart!

SIR PET. Thank you, thank you, Sir Oliver.—Yes, I have entered into—the happy state; but we'll not talk of that now.

SIR OLIV. True, true, Sir Peter; old friends should not begin on grievances at first meeting. No, no, no.

Row. [*Aside to* SIR OLIVER.] Take care, pray, sir.

Sir Oliv. Well, so one of my nephews is a wild rogue, hey?

Sir Pet. Wild! Ah! my old friend, I grieve for your disappointment there; he's a lost young man, indeed. However, his brother will make you amends; Joseph is, indeed, what a youth should be—every body in the world speaks well of him.

Sir Oliv. I am sorry to hear it; he has too good a character to be an honest fellow. Every body speaks well of him! Psha! then he has bowed as low to knaves and fools as to the honest dignity of genius and virtue.

Sir Pet. What, Sir Oliver! do you blame him for not making enemies?

Sir Oliv. Yes, if he has merit enough to deserve them.

Sir Pet. Well, well—you'll be convinced when you know him. 'Tis edification to hear him converse; he professes the noblest sentiments.

Sir Oliv. Oh, plague of his sentiments! If he salutes me with a scrap of morality in his mouth, I shall be sick directly. But, however, don't mistake me, Sir Peter; I don't mean to defend Charles's errors: but, before I form my judgment of either of them, I intend to make a trial of their hearts; and my friend Rowley and I have planned something for the purpose.

Row. And Sir Peter shall own for once he has been mistaken.

Sir Pet. Oh, my life on Joseph's honour!

Sir Oliv. Well—come, give us a bottle of good wine, and we'll drink the lads' health, and tell you our scheme.

Sir Pet. *Allons,* then!

Sir Oliv. And don't, Sir Peter, be so severe against your old friend's son. Odds my life! I am not sorry that he has run out of the course a little: for my part, I hate to see prudence clinging to the green suckers of youth; 'tis like ivy round a sapling, and spoils the growth of the tree.

[*Exeunt.*

## ACT THIRD

SCENE I.—*A Room in* SIR PETER TEAZLE'S *House*

*Enter* SIR PETER TEAZLE, SIR OLIVER SURFACE, *and* ROWLEY

SIR PET. Well, then, we will see this fellow first, and have our wine afterwards. But how is this, Master Rowley? I don't see the jest of your scheme.

Row. Why, sir, this Mr Stanley, whom I was speaking of, is nearly related to them by their mother. He was once a merchant in Dublin, but has been ruined by a series of undeserved misfortunes. He has applied, by letter, since his confinement, both to Mr Surface and Charles: from the former he has received nothing but evasive promises of future service, while Charles has done all that his extravagance has left him power to do; and he is, at this time, endeavouring to raise a sum of money, part of which, in the midst of his own distresses, I know he intends for the service of poor Stanley.

SIR OLIV. Ah! he is my brother's son.

SIR PET. Well, but how is Sir Oliver personally to—

Row. Why, sir, I will inform Charles and his brother that Stanley has obtained permission to apply personally to his friends; and, as they have neither of them ever seen him, let Sir Oliver assume his character, and he will have a fair opportunity of judging, at least, of the benevolence of their dispositions: and believe me, sir, you will find in the youngest brother one who, in the midst of folly and dissipation, has still, as our immortal bard expresses it,—

> "a heart to pity, and a hand,
> Open as day, for melting charity."

SIR PET. Psha! What signifies his having an open hand or purse either, when he has nothing left to give? Well, well, make the trial, if you please. But where is the fellow whom you brought for Sir Oliver to examine, relative to Charles's affairs?

Row. Below, waiting his commands, and no one can give him better intelligence.—This, Sir Oliver, is a friendly Jew,

who, to do him justice, has done every thing in his power
to bring your nephew to a proper sense of his extravagance.

SIR PET. Pray let us have him in.

Row. Desire Mr Moses to walk up stairs.

*[Calls to* SERVANT.

SIR PET. But, pray, why should you suppose he will speak
the truth?

Row. Oh, I have convinced him that he has no chance
of recovering certain sums advanced to Charles but through
the bounty of Sir Oliver, who he knows is arrived; so that
you may depend on his fidelity to his own interests. I have
another evidence in my power, one Snake, whom I have
detected in a matter little short of forgery, and shall shortly
produce to remove some of your prejudices, Sir Peter, relative to Charles and Lady Teazle.

SIR PET. I have heard too much on that subject.

Row. Here comes the honest Israelite.

*Enter* MOSES

—This is Sir Oliver.

SIR OLIV. Sir, I understand you have lately had great
dealings with my nephew Charles?

Mos. Yes, Sir Oliver, I have done all I could for him;
but he was ruined before he came to me for assistance.

SIR OLIV. That was unlucky, truly; for you have had
no opportunity of showing your talents.

Mos. None at all; I hadn't the pleasure of knowing his
distresses till he was some thousands worse than nothing.

SIR OLIV. Unfortunate, indeed! But I suppose you have
done all in your power for him, honest Moses?

Mos. Yes, he knows that. This very evening I was to
have brought him a gentleman from the city, who does not
know him, and will, I believe, advance him some money.

SIR PET. What, one Charles has never had money from
before?

Mos. Yes, Mr Premium, of Crutched Friars, formerly
a broker.

SIR PET. Egad, Sir Oliver, a thought strikes me!—Charles,
you say, does not know Mr Premium?

Mos. Not at all.

Sir Pet. Now then, Sir Oliver, you may have a better opportunity of satisfying yourself than by an old romancing tale of a poor relation: go with my friend Moses, and represent Premium, and then, I'll answer for it, you'll see your nephew in all his glory.

Sir Oliv. Egad, I like this idea better than the other, and I may visit Joseph afterwards as old Stanley.

Sir Pet. True—so you may.

Row. Well, this is taking Charles rather at a disadvantage, to be sure. However, Moses, you understand Sir Peter, and will be faithful?

Mos. You may depend upon me.—[Looks at his watch.] This is near the time I was to have gone.

Sir Oliv. I'll accompany you as soon as you please, Moses —But hold! I have forgot one thing—how the plague shall I be able to pass for a Jew?

Mos. There's no need—the principal is Christian.

Sir Oliv. Is he? I'm very sorry to hear it. But, then again, ain't I rather too smartly dressed to look like a money lender?

Sir Pet. Not at all; 'twould not be out of character, if you went in your own carriage—would it, Moses?

Mos. Not in the least.

Sir Oliv. Well, but how must I talk; there's certainly some cant of usury and mode of treating that I ought to know?

Sir Pet. Oh, there's not much to learn. The great point, as I take it, is to be exorbitant enough in your demands. Hey, Moses?

Mos. Yes, that's a very great point.

Sir Oliv. I'll answer for't I'll not be wanting in that. I'll ask him eight or ten per cent. on the loan, at least.

Mos. If you ask him no more than that, you'll be discovered immediately.

Sir Oliv. Hey! what, the plague! how much then?

Mos. That depends upon the circumstances. If he appears not very anxious for the supply, you should require only forty or fifty per cent.; but if you find him in great distress, and want the moneys very bad, you may ask double.

Sir Pet. A good honest trade you're learning, Sir Oliver!

Sir Oliv. Truly, I think so—and not unprofitable.

Mos. Then, you know, you haven't the moneys yourself, but are forced to borrow them for him of a friend.

Sir Oliv. Oh! I borrow it of a friend, do I?

Mos. And your friend is an unconscionable dog: but you can't help that.

Sir Oliv. My friend an unconscionable dog, is he?

Mos. Yes, and he himself has not the moneys by him, but is forced to sell stock at a great loss.

Sir Oliv. He is forced to sell stock at a great loss, is he? Well, that's very kind of him.

Sir Pet. I' faith, Sir Oliver—Mr Premium, I mean— you'll soon be master of the trade. But, Moses! would not you have him run out a little against the Annuity Bill? That would be in character, I should think.

Mos. Very much.

Row. And lament that a young man now must be at years of discretion before he is suffered to ruin himself?

Mos. Ay, great pity!

Sir Pet. And abuse the public for allowing merit to an act whose only object is to snatch misfortune and impru- dence from the rapacious gripe of usury, and give the minor a chance of inheriting his estate without being undone by coming into possession.

Sir Oliv. So, so—Moses shall give me farther instruc- tions as we go together.

Sir Pet. You will not have much time, for your nephew lives hard by.

Sir Oliv. Oh, never fear! my tutor appears so able, that though Charles lived in the next street, it must be my own fault if I am not a complete rogue before I turn the corner.                    [*Exit with* Moses.

Sir Pet. So, now, I think Sir Oliver will be convinced: you are partial, Rowley, and would have prepared Charles for the other plot.

Row. No, upon my word, Sir Peter.

Sir Pet. Well, go bring me this Snake, and I'll hear what he has to say presently. I see Maria, and want to speak with her.—[*Exit* Rowley.] I should be glad to be convinced my suspicions of Lady Teazle and Charles were unjust. I have never yet opened my mind on this subject to my friend Joseph—I am determined I will do it—he will give me his opinion sincerely.

*Enter* MARIA

So, child, has Mr Surface returned with you?

MAR. No, sir; he was engaged.

SIR PET. Well, Maria, do you not reflect, the more you converse with that amiable young man, what return his partiality for you deserves?

MAR. Indeed, Sir Peter, your frequent importunity on this subject distresses me extremely—you compel me to declare, that I know no man who has ever paid me a particular attention whom I would not prefer to Mr Surface.

SIR PET. So—here's perverseness! No, no, Maria, 'tis Charles only whom you would prefer. 'Tis evident his vices and follies have won your heart.

MAR. This is unkind, sir. You know I have obeyed you in neither seeing nor corresponding with him: I have heard enough to convince me that he is unworthy my regard. Yet I cannot think it culpable, if while my understanding severely condemns his vices, my heart suggests some pity for his distresses.

SIR PET. Well, well, pity him as much as you please; but give your heart and hand to a worthier object.

MAR. Never to his brother!

SIR PET. Go, perverse and obstinate! But take care, madam; you have never yet known what the authority of a guardian is: don't compel me to inform you of it.

MAR. I can only say, you shall not have just reason. 'Tis true, by my father's will, I am for a short period bound to regard you as his substitute; but must cease to think you so, when you would compel me to be miserable.

[*Exit.*

SIR PET. Was ever man so crossed as I am, every thing conspiring to fret me! I had not been involved in matrimony a fortnight, before her father, a hale and hearty man, died, on purpose, I believe, for the pleasure of plaguing me with the care of his daughter.—[LADY TEAZLE *sings without.*] But here comes my helpmate! She appears in great good humour. How happy I should be if I could tease her into loving me, though but a little!

### *Enter* LADY TEAZLE

LADY TEAZLE. Lud! Sir Peter, I hope you haven't been quarrelling with Maria? It is not using me well to be ill-humoured when I am not by.

SIR PET. Ah, Lady Teazle, you might have the power to make me good humoured at all times.

LADY TEAZ. I am sure I wish I had; for I want you to be in a charming sweet temper at this moment. Do be good humoured now, and let me have two hundred pounds, will you?

SIR PET. Two hundred pounds; what, ain't I to be in a good humour without paying for it! But speak to me thus, and i' faith there's nothing I could refuse you. You shall have it; but seal me a bond for the repayment.

LADY TEAZ. Oh, no—there—my note of hand will do as well.                    [*Offering her hand.*

SIR PET. And you shall no longer reproach me with not giving you an independent settlement. I mean shortly to surprise you: but shall we always live thus, hey?

LADY TEAZ. If you please. I'm sure I don't care how soon we leave off quarrelling, provided you'll own you were tired first.

SIR PET. Well—then let our future contest be, who shall be most obliging.

LADY TEAZ. I assure you, Sir Peter, good nature becomes you. You look now as you did before we were married, when you used to walk with me under the elms, and tell me stories of what a gallant you were in your youth, and chuck me under the chin, you would; and asked me if I thought I could love an old fellow, who would deny me nothing—didn't you?

SIR PET. Yes, yes, and you were as kind and attentive—

LADY TEAZ. Ay, so I was, and would always take your

part, when my acquaintance used to abuse you, and turn you into ridicule.

Sir Pet. Indeed!

Lady Teaz. Ay, and when my cousin Sophy has called you a stiff, peevish old bachelor, and laughed at me for thinking of marrying one who might be my father, I have always defended you, and said, I didn't think you so ugly by any means.

Sir Pet. Thank you.

Lady Teaz. And I dared say you'd make a very good sort of a husband.

Sir Pet. And you prophesied right; and we shall now be the happiest couple—

Lady Teaz. And never differ again?

Sir Pet. No, never!—though at the same time, indeed, my dear Lady Teazle, you must watch your temper very seriously; for in all our little quarrels, my dear, if you recollect, my love, you always began first.

Lady Teaz. I beg your pardon, my dear Sir Peter: indeed, you always gave the provocation.

Sir Pet. Now see, my angel! take care—contradicting isn't the way to keep friends.

Lady Teaz. Then don't you begin it, my love!

Sir Pet. There, now! you—you are going on. You don't perceive, my life, that you are just doing the very thing which you know always makes me angry.

Lady Teaz. Nay, you know, if you will be angry without any reason, my dear—

Sir Pet. There! now you want to quarrel again.

Lady Teaz. No, I'm sure I don't: but, if you will be so peevish—

Sir Pet. There now! who begins first?

Lady Teaz. Why, you, to be sure. I said nothing—but there's no bearing your temper.

Sir Pet. No, no, madam: the fault's in your own temper.

Lady Teaz. Ay, you are just what my cousin Sophy said you would be.

Sir Pet. Your cousin Sophy is a forward, impertinent gipsy.

LADY TEAZ. You are a great bear, I'm sure, to abuse my relations.

SIR PET. Now may all the plagues of marriage be doubled on me, if ever I try to be friends with you any more!

LADY TEAZ. So much the better.

SIR PET. No, no, madam: 'tis evident you never cared a pin for me, and I was a madman to marry you—a pert, rural coquette, that had refused half the honest squires in the neighbourhood!

LADY TEAZ. And I am sure I was a fool to marry you—an old dangling bachelor, who was single at fifty, only because he never could meet with any one who would have him.

SIR PET. Ay, ay, madam; but you were pleased enough to listen to me: you never had such an offer before.

LADY TEAZ. No! didn't I refuse Sir Tivy Terrier, who every body said would have been a better match? for his estate is just as good as yours, and he has broke his neck since we have been married.

SIR PET. I have done with you, madam! You are an unfeeling, ungrateful—but there's an end of everything. I believe you capable of everything that is bad. Yes, madam, I now believe the reports relative to you and Charles, madam. Yes, madam, you and Charles are, not without grounds—

LADY TEAZ. Take care, Sir Peter! you had better not insinuate any such thing! I'll not be suspected without cause, I promise you.

SIR PET. Very well, madam! very well! A separate maintenance as soon as you please. Yes, madam, or a divorce! I'll make an example of myself for the benefit of all old bachelors. Let us separate, madam.

LADY TEAZ. Agreed! agreed! And now, my dear Sir Peter, we are of a mind once more, we may be the happiest couple, and never differ again, you know: ha! ha! ha! Well, you are going to be in a passion, I see, and I shall only interrupt you—so, bye! bye!          [Exit.

SIR PET. Plagues and tortures! can't I make her angry either! Oh, I am the most miserable fellow! But I'll not bear her presuming to keep her temper: no! she may break my heart, but she shan't keep her temper.          [Exit.

SCENE II.—*A Room in* CHARLES SURFACE'S *House*

*Enter* TRIP, MOSES, *and* SIR OLIVER SURFACE

TRIP. Here, Master Moses! if you'll stay a moment I'll try whether—what's the gentleman's name?

SIR OLIV. Mr Moses, what is my name? [*Aside to* MOSES.

MOS. Mr Premium.

TRIP. Premium—very well. [*Exit taking snuff.*

SIR OLIV. To judge by the servants, one wouldn't believe the master was ruined. But what!—sure, this was my brother's house?

MOS. Yes, sir; Mr Charles bought it of Mr Joseph, with the furniture, pictures, &c., just as the old gentleman left it. Sir Peter thought it a piece of extravagance in him.

SIR OLIV. In my mind, the other's economy in selling it to him was more reprehensible by half.

*Re-enter* TRIP

TRIP. My master says you must wait, gentlemen: he has company, and can't speak with you yet.

SIR OLIV. If he knew who it was wanted to see him, perhaps he would not send such a message.

TRIP. Yes, yes, sir; he knows you are here—I did not forget little Premium: no, no, no.

SIR OLIV. Very well; and I pray, sir, what may be your name?

TRIP. Trip, sir; my name is Trip, at your service.

SIR OLIV. Well, then, Mr Trip, you have a pleasant sort of place here, I guess?

TRIP. Why, yes—here are three or four of us pass our time agreeably enough; but then our wages are sometimes a little in arrear—and not very great either—but fifty pounds a year, and find our own bags and bouquets.

SIR OLIV. Bags and bouquets! halters and bastinadoes!

[*Aside.*

TRIP. And *à propos,* Moses, have you been able to get me that little bill discounted?

SIR OLIV. Wants to raise money too!—mercy on me! Has

his distresses too, I warrant, like a lord, and affects creditors and duns.   [*Aside.*

Mos. 'Twas not to be done, indeed, Mr Trip.

TRIP. Good lack, you surprise me! My friend Brush has indorsed it, and I thought when he put his name at the back of a bill 'twas the same as cash.

Mos. No, 'twouldn't do.

TRIP. A small sum—but twenty pounds. Hark'ee, Moses, do you think you couldn't get it me by way of annuity?

SIR OLIV. An annuity! ha! ha! a footman raise money by way of annuity. Well done, luxury, egad!   [*Aside.*

Mos. Well, but you must insure your place.

TRIP. Oh, with all my heart! I'll insure my place, and my life too, if you please.

SIR OLIV. It's more than I would your neck.   [*Aside.*

Mos. But is there nothing you could deposit?

TRIP. Why, nothing capital of my master's wardrobe has dropped lately; but I could give you a mortgage on some of his winter clothes, with equity of redemption before November—or you shall have the reversion of the French velvet, or a post-obit on the blue and silver;—these, I should think, Moses, with a few pair of point ruffles, as a collateral security —hey, my little fellow?

Mos. Well, well.   [*Bell rings.*

TRIP. Egad, I heard the bell. I believe, gentlemen, I can now introduce you. Don't forget the annuity, little Moses! This way, gentlemen, I'll insure my place, you know.

SIR OLIV. [*Aside.*] If the man be a shadow of the master, this is the temple of dissipation indeed!   [*Exeunt.*

SCENE III.—*Another Room in the same*

CHARLES SURFACE, SIR HARRY BUMPER, CARELESS, *and* Gentlemen, *discovered drinking*

CHAS. SURF. 'Fore heaven, 'tis true!—there's the great degeneracy of the age. Many of our acquaintance have taste, spirit, and politeness; but, plague on 't, they won't drink.

CARE. It is so, indeed, Charles! they give into all the substantial luxuries of the table, and abstain from nothing but

**wine** and wit.  Oh, certainly society suffers by it intolerably!
for now, instead of the social spirit of raillery that used to
mantle over a glass of bright Burgundy, their conversation
is become just like the Spa-water they drink, which has all the
pertness and flatulency of champagne, without its spirit or
flavour.

1 GENT.  But what are they to do who love play better than
wine?

CARE.  True! there's Sir Harry diets himself for gaming,
and is now under a hazard regimen.

CHAS. SURF.  Then he'll have the worst of it.  What! you
wouldn't train a horse for the course by keeping him from
corn?  For my part, egad, I am never so successful as when
I am a little merry: let me throw on a bottle of champagne,
and I never lose.

ALL.  Hey, what?

CARE.  At least I never feel my losses, which is exactly the
same thing.

2 GENT.  Ay, that I believe.

CHAS. SURF.  And then, what man can pretend to be a be-
liever in love, who is an abjurer of wine?  'Tis the test by
which the lover knows his own heart.  Fill a dozen bumpers
to a dozen beauties, and she that floats at the top is the maid
that has bewitched you.

CARE.  Now then, Charles, be honest, and give us your real
favourite.

CHAS. SURF.  Why, I have withheld her only in compassion
to you.  If I toast her, you must give a round of her peers,
which is impossible—on earth.

CARE.  Oh! then we'll find some canonised vestals or
heathen goddesses that will do, I warrant.

CHAS. SURF.  Here, then, bumpers, you rogues! bumpers!
Maria! Maria!—

SIR HAR.  Maria who?

CHAS. SURF.  Oh, damn the surname!—'tis too formal to
be registered in Love's calendar—Maria!

ALL.  Maria!

CHAS. SURF.  But now, Sir Harry, beware, we must have
beauty superlative.

CARE.  Nay, never study, Sir Harry: we'll stand to the

toast, though your mistress should want an eye, and you know you have a song will excuse you.

SIR HAR. Egad, so I have! and I'll give him the song instead of the lady.                                    [*Sings.*

> Here's to the maiden of bashful fifteen;
>    Here's to the widow of fifty;
> Here's to the flaunting extravagant quean,
>    And here's to the housewife that's thrifty.

*Chorus.* Let the toast pass,—
>    Drink to the lass,
> I'll warrant she'll prove an excuse for the glass.

> Here's to the charmer whose dimples we prize;
>    Now to the maid who has none, sir:
> Here's to the girl with a pair of blue eyes,
>    And here's to the nymph with but one, sir.

*Chorus.* Let the toast pass, &c.

> Here's to the maid with a bosom of snow:
>    Now to her that's as brown as a berry:
> Here's to the wife with a face full of woe,
>    And now to the damsel that's merry.

*Chorus.* Let the toast pass, &c.

> For let 'em be clumsy, or let 'em be slim,
>    Young or ancient, I care not a feather;
> So fill a pint bumper quite up to the brim,
> So fill up your glasses, nay, fill to the brim,
>    And let us e'en toast them together.

*Chorus.* Let the toast pass, &c.

ALL. Bravo! bravo!


*Enter* TRIP, *and whispers* CHARLES SURFACE

CHAS. SURF. Gentlemen, you must excuse me a little.— Careless, take the chair, will you?

CARE. Nay, pr'ythee, Charles, what now? This is one of your peerless beauties, I suppose, has dropped in by chance?

CHAS. SURF. No, faith! To tell you the truth, 'tis a Jew and a broker, who are come by appointment.

CARE. Oh, damn it! let's have the Jew in.

1 GENT. Ay, and the broker too, by all means.

2 GENT. Yes, yes, the Jew and the broker.

CHAS. SURF. Egad, with all my heart!—Trip, bid the gentlemen walk in.—[*Exit* TRIP.] Though there's one of them a stranger, I can tell you.

CARE. Charles, let us give them some generous Burgundy, and perhaps they'll grow conscientious.

CHAS. SURF. Oh, hang 'em, no! wine does but draw forth a man's natural qualities; and to make them drink would only be to whet their knavery.


*Re-enter* TRIP, *with* SIR OLIVER SURFACE *and* MOSES

CHAS. SURF. So, honest Moses; walk in, pray, Mr Premium—that's the gentleman's name, isn't it, Moses?

MOS. Yes, sir.

CHAS. SURF. Set chairs, Trip.—Sit down, Mr Premium.—Glasses, Trip.—[TRIP *gives chairs and glasses, and exit.*] Sit down, Moses.—Come, Mr Premium, I'll give you a sentiment; here's *Success to usury!*—Moses, fill the gentleman a bumper.

MOS. Success to usury!                              [*Drinks.*

CARE. Right, Moses—usury is prudence and industry, and deserves to succeed.

SIR OLIV. Then here's—All the success it deserves!

[*Drinks.*

CARE. No, no, that won't do! Mr Premium, you have demurred at the toast, and must drink it in a pint bumper.

1 GENT. A pint bumper, at least.

MOS. Oh, pray, sir, consider—Mr Premium's a gentleman.

CARE. And therefore loves good wine.

2 GENT. Give Moses a quart glass—this is mutiny, and a high contempt for the chair.

CARE. Here, now for 't! I'll see justice done to the last drop of my bottle.

SIR OLIV. Nay, pray, gentlemen—I did not expect this usage.

CHAS. SURF. No, hang it, you shan't; Mr Premium's a stranger.

Sir. Oliv. Odd! I wish I was well out of their company.
                                                    [*Aside.*

Care. Plague on 'em then! if they won't drink, we'll not sit down with them. Come, Harry, the dice are in the next room.—Charles, you'll join us when you have finished your business with the gentlemen?

Chas. Surf. I will! I will!—[*Exeunt* Sir Harry Bumper *and* Gentlemen; Careless *following.*] Careless!

Care. [*Returning.*] Well!

Chas. Surf. Perhaps I may want you.

Care. Oh, you know I am always ready: word, note, or bond, 'tis all the same to me.                    [*Exit.*

Mos. Sir, this is Mr Premium, a gentleman of the strictest honour and secrecy; and always performs what he undertakes. Mr Premium, this is—

Chas. Surf. Psha! have done. Sir, my friend Moses is a very honest fellow, but a little slow at expression: he'll be an hour giving us our titles. Mr. Premium, the plain state of the matter is this: I am an extravagant young fellow who wants to borrow money; you I take to be a prudent old fellow, who have got money to lend. I am blockhead enough to give fifty per cent, sooner than not have it; and you, I presume, are rogue enough to take a hundred if you can get it. Now, sir, you see we are acquainted at once, and may proceed to business without further ceremony.

Sir Oliv. Exceeding frank, upon my word. I see, sir, you are not a man of many compliments.

Chas. Surf. Oh, no, sir! plain dealing in business I always think best.

Sir Oliv. Sir, I like you better for it. However, you are mistaken in one thing; I have no money to lend, but I believe I could procure some of a friend; but then he's an unconscionable dog. Isn't he, Moses? And must sell stock to accommodate you. Mustn't he, Moses?

Mos. Yes, indeed! You know I always speak the truth, and scorn to tell a lie!

Chas. Surf. Right. People that speak truth generally do. But these are trifles, Mr Premium. What! I know money isn't to be bought without paying for 't!

SIR OLIV. Well, but what security could you give? You have no land, I suppose?

CHAS. SURF. Not a mole-hill, nor a twig, but what's in the bough-pots out of the window!

SIR OLIV. Nor any stock, I presume?

CHAS. SURF. Nothing but live stock—and that's only a few pointers and ponies. But pray, Mr Premium, are you acquainted at all with any of my connexions?

SIR OLIV. Why, to say truth, I am.

CHAS. SURF. Then you must know that I have a devilish rich uncle in the East Indies, Sir Oliver Surface, from whom I have the greatest expectations?

SIR OLIV. That you have a wealthy uncle, I have heard; but how your expectations will turn out is more, I believe, than you can tell.

CHAS. SURF. Oh, no!—there can be no doubt. They tell me I'm a prodigious favourite, and that he talks of leaving me every thing.

SIR OLIV. Indeed! this is the first I've heard of it.

CHAS. SURF. Yes, yes, 'tis just so. Moses knows 'tis true; don't you, Moses?

MOS. Oh, yes! I'll swear to't.

SIR OLIV. Egad, they'll persuade me presently I'm at Bengal.                                                    [Aside.

CHAS. SURF. Now I propose, Mr Premium, if it's agreeable to you, a post-obit on Sir Oliver's life: though at the same time the old fellow has been so liberal to me, that I give you my word, I should be very sorry to hear that any thing had happened to him.

SIR OLIV. Not more than I should, I assure you. But the bond you mention happens to be just the worst security you could offer me—for I might live to a hundred and never see the principal.

CHAS. SURF. Oh, yes, you would! the moment Sir Oliver dies, you know, you would come on me for the money.

SIR OLIV. Then I believe I should be the most unwelcome dun you ever had in your life.

CHAS. SURF. What! I suppose you're afraid that Sir Oliver is too good a life?

SIR OLIV. No, indeed I am not; though I have heard he

is as hale and healthy as any man of his years in Christendom.

CHAS. SURF. There again, now, you are misinformed. No, no, the climate has hurt him considerably, poor uncle Oliver. Yes, yes, he breaks apace, I'm told—and is so much altered lately that his nearest relations would not know him.

SIR OLIV. No! Ha! ha! ha! so much altered lately that his nearest relations would not know him! Ha! ha! ha! egad —ha! ha! ha!

CHAS. SURF. Ha! ha!—you're glad to hear that, little Premium?

SIR OLIV. No, no, I'm not.

CHAS. SURF. Yes, yes, you are—ha! ha! ha!—you know that mends your chance.

SIR OLIV. But I'm told Sir Oliver is coming over; nay, some say he is actually arrived.

CHAS. SURF. Psha! sure I must know better than you whether he's come or not. No, no, rely on't he's at this moment at Calcutta. Isn't he, Moses?

MOS. Oh, yes, certainly.

SIR OLIV. Very true, as you say, you must know better than I, though I have it from pretty good authority. Haven't I, Moses?

MOS. Yes, most undoubted!

SIR OLIV. But, sir, as I understand you want a few hundreds immediately, is there nothing you could dispose of?

CHAS. SURF. How do you mean?

SIR OLIV. For instance, now, I have heard that your father left behind him a great quantity of massy old plate.

CHAS. SURF. O Lud! that's gone long ago. Moses can tell you how better than I can.

SIR OLIV. [Aside.] Good lack! all the family race-cups and corporation-bowls!—[Aloud.] Then it was also supposed that his library was one of the most valuable and compact.

CHAS. SURF. Yes, yes, so it was—vastly too much so for a private gentleman. For my part, I was always of a communicative disposition, so I thought it a shame to keep so much knowledge to myself.

Sir Oliv. [*Aside.*] Mercy upon me! learning that had run in the family like an heir-loom!—[*Aloud.*] Pray, what are become of the books?

Chas. Surf. You must inquire of the auctioneer, Master Premium, for I don't believe even Moses can direct you.

Mos. I know nothing of books.

Sir Oliv. So, so, nothing of the family property left, I suppose?

Chas. Surf. Not much, indeed; unless you have a mind to the family pictures. I have got a room full of ancestors above; and if you have a taste for old paintings, egad, you shall have 'em a bargain!

Sir Oliv. Hey! what the devil! sure, you wouldn't sell your forefathers, would you?

Chas. Surf. Every man of them, to the best bidder.

Sir Oliv. What! your great-uncles and aunts?

Chas. Surf. Ay, and my great-grandfathers and grand-mothers too.

Sir Oliv. [*Aside.*] Now I give him up!—[*Aloud.*] What the plague, have you no bowels for your own kindred? Odds life! do you take me for Shylock in the play, that you would raise money of me on your own flesh and blood?

Chas. Surf. Nay, my little broker, don't be angry: what need you care, if you have your money's worth?

Sir Oliv. Well, I'll be the purchaser: I think I can dispose of the family canvas.—[*Aside.*] Oh, I'll never forgive him this! never!

*Re-enter* Careless

Care. Come, Charles, what keeps you?

Chas. Surf. I can't come yet. I'faith, we are going to have a sale above stairs; here's little Premium will buy all my ancestors!

Care. Oh, burn your ancestors!

Chas. Surf. No, he may do that afterwards, if he pleases. Stay, Careless, we want you: egad, you shall be auctioneer—so come along with us.

Care. Oh, have with you, if that's the case. I can handle a hammer as well as a dice-box! Going! going!

Sir Oliv. Oh, the profligates! [*Aside.*

CHAS. SURF. Come, Moses, you shall be appraiser, if we want one. Gad's life, little Premium, you don't seem to like the business?

SIR OLIV. Oh yes, I do, vastly! Ha! ha! ha! yes, yes, I think it a rare joke to sell one's family by auction—ha! ha!—[*Aside.*] Oh, the prodigal!

CHAS. SURF. To be sure! when a man wants money, where the plague should he get assistance, if he can't make free with his own relations!

SIR OLIV. I'll never forgive him; never! never! [*Exeunt.*

## ACT FOURTH

SCENE I.—*A Picture Room in* CHARLES SURFACE'S *House*

*Enter* CHARLES SURFACE, SIR OLIVER SURFACE, MOSES, *and* CARELESS

CHAS. SURFACE. Walk in, gentlemen, pray walk in;— here they are, the family of the Surfaces, up to the Conquest.

SIR OLIV. And, in my opinion, a goodly collection.

CHAS. SURF. Ay, ay, these are done in the true spirit of portrait-painting; no *volontière grace* or expression. Not like the works of your modern Raphaels, who give you the strongest resemblance, yet contrive to make your portrait independent of you; so that you may sink the original and not hurt the picture. No, no; the merit of these is the inveterate likeness—all stiff and awkward as the originals, and like nothing in human nature besides.

SIR OLIV. Ah! we shall never see such figures of men again.

CHAS. SURF. I hope not. Well, you see, Master Premium, what a domestic character I am; here I sit of an evening surrounded by my family. But come, get to your pulpit, Mr Auctioneer; here's an old gouty chair of my grandfather's will answer the purpose.

CARE. Ay, ay, this will do. But, Charles, I haven't a hammer; and what's an auctioneer without his hammer?

CHAS. SURF. Egad, that's true. What parchment have

we here? Oh, our genealogy in full. [*Taking pedigree down.*] Here, Careless, you shall have no common bit of mahogany, here's the family tree for you, you rogue! This shall be your hammer, and now you may knock down my ancestors with their own pedigree.

SIR OLIV. What an unnatural rogue!—an *ex post facto* parricide!                                              [*Aside.*

CARE. Yes, yes, here's a list of your generation indeed; faith, Charles, this is the most convenient thing you could have found for the business, for 'twill not only serve as a hammer, but a catalogue into the bargain. Come, begin— A-going, a-going, a-going!

CHAS. SURF. Bravo, Careless! Well, here's my great-uncle, Sir Richard Raveline, a marvellous good general in his day, I assure you. He served in all the Duke of Marlborough's wars, and got that cut over his eye at the battle of Malplaquet. What say you, Mr Premium? look at him— there's a hero! not cut out of his feathers, as your modern clipped captains are, but enveloped in wig and regimentals, as a general should be. What do you bid?

SIR OLIV. [*Aside to* MOSES.] Bid him speak.

MOS. Mr Premium would have you speak.

CHAS. SURF. Why, then, he shall have him for ten pounds, and I'm sure that's not dear for a staff-officer.

SIR OLIV. [*Aside.*] Heaven deliver me! his famous uncle Richard for ten pounds!—[*Aloud.*] Very well, sir, I take him at that.

CHAS. SURF. Careless, knock down my uncle Richard.— Here, now, is a maiden sister of his, my great-aunt Deborah, done by Kneller, in his best manner and esteemed a very formidable likeness. There she is, you see, a shepherdess feeding her flock. You shall have her for five pounds ten— the sheep are worth the money.

SIR OLIV. [*Aside.*] Ah! poor Deborah! a woman who set such a value on herself!—[*Aloud.*] Five pounds ten— she's mine.

CHAS. SURF. Knock down my aunt Deborah! Here, now, are two that were a sort of cousins of theirs.—You see, Moses, these pictures were done some time ago, when beaux wore wigs, and the ladies their own hair.

SIR OLIV. Yes, truly, head-dresses appear to have been a little lower in those days.

CHAS. SURF. Well, take that couple for the same.

MOS. 'Tis a good bargain.

CHAS. SURF. Careless!—This, now, is a grandfather of my mother's, a learned judge, well known on the western circuit.—What do you rate him at, Moses?

MOS. Four guineas.

CHAS. SURF. Four guineas! Gad's life, you don't bid me the price of his wig.—Mr Premium, you have more respect for the woolsack; do let us knock his lordship down at fifteen.

SIR OLIV. By all means.

CARE. Gone!

CHAS. SURF. And there are two brothers of his, William and Walter Blunt, Esquires, both members of parliament, and noted speakers; and, what's very extraordinary, I believe, this is the first time they were ever bought or sold.

SIR OLIV. That is very extraordinary, indeed! I'll take them at your own price, for the honour of parliament.

CARE. Well said, little Premium! I'll knock them down at forty.

CHAS. SURF. Here's a jolly fellow—I don't know what relation, but he was mayor of Norwich: take him at eight pounds.

SIR OLIV. No, no; six pounds will do for the mayor.

CHAS. SURF. Come, make it guineas, and I'll throw you the two alderman there into the bargain.

SIR OLIV. They're mine.

CHAS. SURF. Careless, knock down the mayor and aldermen. But, plague on't! we shall be all day retailing in this manner; do let us deal wholesale: what say you, little Premium? Give me three hundred pounds for the rest of the family in the lump.

CARE. Ay, ay, that will be the best way.

SIR OLIV. Well, well, any thing to accommodate you; they are mine. But there is one portrait which you have always passed over.

CARE. What, that ill-looking little fellow over the settee.

SIR OLIV. Yes, sir, I mean that; though I don't think him so ill-looking a little fellow, by any means.

CHAS. SURF. What, that? Oh; that's my uncle Oliver! 'twas done before he went to India.

CARE. Your uncle Oliver! Gad, then you'll never be friends, Charles. That, now, to me, is as stern a looking rogue as ever I saw; an unforgiving eye, and a damned disinheriting countenance! an inveterate knave, depend on't. Don't you think so, little Premium?

SIR OLIV. Upon my soul, sir, I do not; I think it is as honest a looking face as any in the room, dead or alive. But I suppose uncle Oliver goes with the rest of the lumber?

CHAS. SURF. No, hang it! I'll not part with poor Noll. The old fellow has been very good to me, and, egad, I'll keep his picture while I've a room to put it in.

SIR OLIV. [Aside.] The rogue's my nephew after all!—[Aloud.] But, sir, I have somehow taken a fancy to that picture.

CHAS. SURF. I'm sorry for't, for you certainly will not have it. Oons, haven't you got enough of them?

SIR OLIV. [Aside.] I forgive him every thing!—[Aloud.] But, sir, when I take a whim in my head, I don't value money. I'll give you as much for that as for all the rest.

CHAS. SURF. Don't tease me, master broker; I tell you I'll not part with it, and there's an end of it.

SIR OLIV. [Aside.] How like his father the dog is!—[Aloud.] Well, well, I have done.—[Aside.] I did not perceive it before, but I think I never saw such a striking resemblance.—[Aloud.] Here is a draft for your sum.

CHAS. SURF. Why, 'tis for eight hundred pounds!

SIR. OLIV. You will not let Sir Oliver go?

CHAS. SURF. Zounds! no! I tell you, once more.

SIR OLIV. Then never mind the difference, we'll balance that another time. But give me your hand on the bargain; you are an honest fellow, Charles—I beg pardon, sir, for being so free.—Come, Moses.

CHAS. SURF. Egad, this is a whimsical old fellow!—But hark'ee, Premium, you'll prepare lodgings for these gentlemen.

SIR OLIV. Yes, yes, I'll send for them in a day or two.

CHAS. SURF. But hold; do now send a genteel conveyance for them, for, I assure you, they were most of them used to ride in their own carriages.

SIR OLIV. I will, I will—for all but Oliver.

CHAS. SURF. Ay, all but the little nabob.

SIR OLIV. You're fixed on that?

CHAS. SURF. Peremptorily.

SIR OLIV. [*Aside.*] A dear extravagant rogue!—[*Aloud.*] Good day!—Come, Moses.—[*Aside.*] Let me hear now who dares call him profligate.      [*Exit with* MOSES.

CARE. Why, this is the oddest genius of the sort I ever met with!

CHAS. SURF. Egad, he's the prince of brokers, I think. I wonder how the devil Moses got acquainted with so honest a fellow.—Ha! here's Rowley.—Do, Careless, say I'll join the company in a few moments.

CARE. I will—but don't let that old blockhead persuade you to squander any of that money on old musty debts, or any such nonsense; for tradesmen, Charles, are the most exorbitant fellows.

CHAS. SURF. Very true, and paying them is only encouraging them.

CARE. Nothing else.

CHAS. SURF. Ay, ay, never fear.—[*Exit* CARELESS.] So! this was an odd old fellow, indeed. Let me see, two-thirds of these five hundred and thirty odd pounds are mine by right. 'Fore heaven! I find one's ancestors are more valuable relations than I took them for!—Ladies and gentlemen, your most obedient and very grateful servant.

[*Bows ceremoniously to the pictures.*

*Enter* ROWLEY

Ha! old Rowley! egad, you are just come in time to take leave of your old acquaintance.

ROW. Yes, I heard they were a-going. But I wonder you can have such spirits under so many distresses.

CHAS. SURF. Why, there's the point! my distresses are so many, that I can't afford to part with my spirits; but I shall be rich and splenetic, all in good time. However, I suppose you are surprised that I am not more sorrowful at parting with so many near relations; to be sure, 'tis very affecting, but you see they never move a muscle, so why should I?

Row. There's no making you serious a moment.

CHAS. SURF. Yes, faith, I am so now. Here, my honest Rowley, here, get me this changed directly, and take a hundred pounds of it immediately to old Stanley.

Row. A hundred pounds! Consider only—

CHAS. SURF. Gad's life, don't talk about it! poor Stanley's wants are pressing, and, if you don't make haste, we shall have some one call that has a better right to the money.

Row. Ah! there's the point! I never will cease dunning you with the old proverb—

CHAS. SURF. *Be just before you're generous.*—Why, so I would if I could; but Justice is an old, hobbling beldame, and I can't get her to keep pace with Generosity, for the soul of me.

Row. Yet, Charles, believe me, one hour's reflection—

CHAS. SURF. Ay, ay, it's very true; but, hark'ee, Rowley, while I have, by Heaven I'll give; so, damn your economy! and now for hazard.

SCENE II.—*Another room in the same*

*Enter* SIR OLIVER SURFACE *and* MOSES

Mos. Well, sir, I think, as Sir Peter said, you have seen Mr. Charles in high glory; 'tis great pity he's so extravagant.

SIR OLIV. True, but he would not sell my picture.

Mos. And loves wine and women so much.

SIR OLIV. But he would not sell my picture.

Mos. And games so deep.

SIR OLIV. But he would not sell my picture. Oh, here's Rowley.

*Enter* ROWLEY

Row. So, Sir Oliver, I find you have made a purchase—

SIR OLIV. Yes, yes, our young rake has parted with his ancestors like old tapestry.

Row. And here has he commissioned me to redeliver you

part of the purchase money—I mean, though, in your necessitous character of old Stanley.

Mos. Ah! there is the pity of all; he is so damned charitable.

Row. And I left a hosier and two tailors in the hall, who, I'm sure, won't be paid, and this hundred would satisfy them.

Sir Oliv. Well, well, I'll pay his debts, and his benevolence too. But now I am no more a broker, and you shall introduce me to the elder brother as old Stanley.

Row. Not yet awhile; Sir Peter, I know, means to call there about this time.

*Enter* Trip

Trip. Oh, gentlemen, I beg pardon for not showing you out; this way—Moses, a word.          [*Exit with* Moses.

Sir Oliv. There's a fellow for you! Would you believe it, that puppy intercepted the Jew on our coming, and wanted to raise money before he got to his master!

Row. Indeed!

Sir Oliv. Yes, they are now planning an annuity business. Ah, Master Rowley, in my days servants were content with the follies of their masters, when they were worn a little threadbare; but now they have their vices, like their birthday clothes, with the gloss on.          [*Exeunt.*

Scene III.—*A Library in* Joseph Surface's *House*

*Enter* Joseph Surface *and* Servant

Jos. Surf. No letter from Lady Teazle?

Ser. No, sir.

Jos. Surf. [*Aside.*] I am surprised she has not sent, if she is prevented from coming. Sir Peter certainly does not suspect me. Yet I wish I may not lose the heiress, through the scrape I have drawn myself into with the wife; however, Charles's imprudence and bad character are great points in my favour.          [*Knocking without.*

Ser. Sir, I believe that must be Lady Teazle.

Jos. Surf. Hold! See whether it is or not, before you go

to the door: I have a particular message for you if it should be my brother.

SER. 'Tis her ladyship, sir; she always leaves her chair at the milliner's in the next street.

JOS. SURF. Stay, stay; draw that screen before the window —that will do;—my opposite neighbour is a maiden lady of so curious a temper—[SERVANT *draws the screen, and exit.*] I have a difficult hand to play in this affair. Lady Teazle has lately suspected my views on Maria; but she must by no means be let into that secret,—at least, till I have her more in my power.

#### *Enter* LADY TEAZLE

LADY TEAZ. What, sentiment in soliloquy now? Have you been very impatient? O Lud! don't pretend to look grave. I vow I couldn't come before.

JOS. SURF. O madam, punctuality is a species of constancy very unfashionable in a lady of quality.

[*Places chairs, and sits after* LADY TEAZLE *is seated.*

LADY TEAZ. Upon my word, you ought to pity me. Do you know Sir Peter is grown so ill-natured to me of late, and so jealous of Charles too—that's the best of the story, isn't it?

JOS. SURF. I am glad my scandalous friends keep that up.

[*Aside.*

LADY TEAZ. I am sure I wish he would let Maria marry him, and then perhaps he would be convinced; don't you, Mr. Surface?

JOS. SURF. [*Aside.*] Indeed I do not.—[*Aloud.*] Oh, certainly I do! for then my dear Lady Teazle would also be convinced how wrong her suspicions were of my having any design on the silly girl.

LADY TEAZ. Well, well, I'm inclined to believe you. But isn't it provoking, to have the most ill-natured things said of one? And there's my friend Lady Sneerwell has circulated I don't know how many scandalous tales of me, and all without any foundation too; that's what vexes me.

JOS. SURF. Ay, madam, to be sure, that is the provoking circumstance—without foundation; yes, yes, there's the mortification, indeed; for when a scandalous story is believed against one, there certainly is no comfort like the consciousness of having deserved it.

LADY TEAZ. No, to be sure, then I'd forgive their malice; but to attack me, who am really so innocent, and who never say an ill-natured thing of any body—that is, of any friend; and then Sir Peter, too, to have him so peevish, and so suspicious, when I know the integrity of my own heart—indeed 'tis monstrous!

JOS. SURF. But, my dear Lady Teazle, 'tis your own fault if you suffer it. When a husband entertains a groundless suspicion of his wife, and withdraws his confidence from her, the original compact is broken, and she owes it to the honour of her sex to endeavour to outwit him.

LADY TEAZ. Indeed! So that, if he suspects me without cause, it follows, that the best way of curing his jealousy is to give him reason for't?

JOS. SURF. Undoubtedly—for your husband should never be deceived in you: and in that case it becomes you to be frail in compliment to his discernment.

LADY TEAZ. To be sure, what you say is very reasonable, and when the consciousness of my innocence—

JOS. SURF. Ah, my dear madam, there is the great mistake! 'tis this very conscious innocence that is of the greatest prejudice to you. What is it makes you negligent of forms, and careless of the world's opinion? why, the consciousness of your own innocence. What makes you thoughtless in your conduct, and apt to run into a thousand little imprudences? why, the consciousness of your own innocence. What makes you impatient of Sir Peter's temper, and outrageous at his suspicions? why, the consciousness of your innocence.

LADY TEAZ. 'Tis very true!

JOS. SURF. Now, my dear Lady Teazle, if you would but once make a trifling *faux pas,* you can't conceive how cautious you would grow, and how ready to humour and agree with your husband.

LADY TEAZ. Do you think so?

JOS. SURF. Oh, I am sure on't; and then you would find all scandal would cease at once, for—in short, your character at present is like a person in a plethora, absolutely dying from too much health.

LADY TEAZ. So, so; then I perceive your prescription is, that I must sin in my own defence, and part with my virtue to preserve my reputation?

JOS. SURF. Exactly so, upon my credit, ma'am.

LADY TEAZ. Well, certainly this is the oddest doctrine, and the newest receipt for avoiding calumny!

JOS. SURF. An infallible one, believe me. Prudence, like experience, must be paid for.

LADY TEAZ. Why, if my understanding were once convinced—

JOS. SURF. Oh, certainly, madam, your understanding should be convinced. Yes, yes—Heaven forbid I should persuade you to do any thing you thought wrong. No, no, I have too much honour to desire it.

LADY TEAZ. Don't you think we may as well leave honour out of the argument? [*Rises.*

JOS. SURF. Ah, the ill effects of your country education, I see, still remain with you.

LADY TEAZ. I doubt they do indeed; and I will fairly own to you, that if I could be persuaded to do wrong, it would be by Sir Peter's ill usage sooner than your honourable logic, after all.

JOS. SURF. Then, by this hand, which he is unworthy of— [*Taking her hand.*


### Re-enter SERVANT

'Sdeath, you blockhead—what do you want?

SER. I beg your pardon, sir, but I thought you would not choose Sir Peter to come up without announcing him.

JOS. SURF. Sir Peter!—Oons—the devil!

LADY TEAZ. Sir Peter! O Lud! I'm ruined! I'm ruined!

SER. Sir, 'twasn't I let him in.

LADY TEAZ. Oh! I'm quite undone! What will become of me? Now, Mr Logic—Oh! mercy, sir, he's on the stairs— I'll get behind here—and if ever I'm so imprudent again—
[*Goes behind the screen.*

JOS. SURF. Give me that book.
[*Sits down.* SERVANT *pretends to adjust his chair.*

*Enter* Sir Peter Teazle

Sir Pet. Ay, ever improving himself—Mr Surface, Mr Surface—                    [*Pats* Joseph *on the shoulder.*

Jos. Surf. Oh, my dear Sir Peter, I beg your pardon.— [*Gaping, throws away the book.*] I have been dozing over a stupid book. Well, I am much obliged to you for this call. You haven't been here, I believe, since I fitted up this room. Books, you know, are the only things I am a coxcomb in.

Sir Pet. 'Tis very neat indeed. Well, well, that's proper; and you can make even your screen a source of knowledge— hung, I perceive, with maps.

Jos. Surf. Oh, yes, I find great use in that screen.

Sir Pet. I dare say you must, certainly, when you want to find any thing in a hurry.

Jos. Surf. Ay, or to hide any thing in a hurry either.
                                                              [*Aside.*

Sir Pet. Well, I have a little private business—

Jos. Surf. You need not stay.            [*To* Servant.

Ser. No, sir.                                    [*Exit.*

Jos. Surf. Here's a chair, Sir Peter—I beg—

Sir Pet. Well, now we are alone, there is a subject, my dear friend, on which I wish to unburden my mind to you— a point of the greatest moment to my peace; in short, my good friend, Lady Teazle's conduct of late has made me very unhappy.

Jos. Surf. Indeed! I am very sorry to hear it.

Sir Pet. 'Tis but too plain she has not the least regard for me; but, what's worse, I have pretty good authority to suppose she has formed an attachment to another.

Jos. Surf. Indeed! you astonish me!

Sir Pet. Yes! and, between ourselves, I think I've discovered the person.

Jos. Surf. How! you alarm me exceedingly.

Sir Pet. Ay, my dear friend, I knew you would sympathise with me!

Jos. Surf. Yes, believe me, Sir Peter, such a discovery would hurt me just as much as it would you.

Sir Pet. I am convinced of it. Ah! it is a happiness to

have a friend whom we can trust even with one's family secrets. But have you no guess who I mean?

Jos. Surf. I haven't the most distant idea. It can't be Sir Benjamin Backbite!

Sir Pet. Oh, no! What say you to Charles?

Jos. Surf. My brother! impossible!

Sir Pet. Oh, my dear friend, the goodness of your own heart misleads you. You judge of others by yourself.

Jos. Surf. Certainly, Sir Peter, the heart that is conscious of its own integrity is ever slow to credit another's treachery.

Sir Pet. True; but your brother has no sentiment—you never hear him talk so.

Jos. Surf. Yet I can't but think Lady Teazle herself has too much principle.

Sir Pet. Ay; but what is principle against the flattery of a handsome, lively young fellow?

Jos. Surf. That's very true.

Sir Pet. And then, you know, the difference of our ages makes it very improbable that she should have any great affection for me; and if she were to be frail, and I were to make it public, why the town would only laugh at me, the foolish old bachelor, who had married a girl.

Jos. Surf. That's true, to be sure—they would laugh.

Sir Pet. Laugh! ay, and make ballads, and paragraphs, and the devil knows what of me.

Jos. Surf. No, you must never make it public.

Sir Pet. But then again—that the nephew of my old friend, Sir Oliver, should be the person to attempt such a wrong, hurts me more nearly.

Jos. Surf. Ay, there's the point. When ingratitude barbs the dart of injury, the wound has double danger in it.

Sir Pet. Ay—I, that was, in a manner, left his guardian; in whose house he had been so often entertained; who never in my life denied him—my advice!

Jos. Surf. Oh, 'tis not to be credited! There may be a man capable of such baseness, to be sure; but, for my part, till you can give me positive proofs, I cannot but doubt it. However, if it should be proved on him, he is no longer a brother of mine—I disclaim kindred with him: for the man who can break the laws of hospitality, and tempt the wife of his friend, deserves to be branded as the pest of society.

SIR PET. What a difference there is between you! What noble sentiments!

JOS. SURF. Yet I cannot suspect Lady Teazle's honour.

SIR PET. I am sure I wish to think well of her, and to remove all ground of quarrel between us. She has lately reproached me more than once with having made no settlement on her; and, in our last quarrel, she almost hinted that she should not break her heart if I was dead. Now, as we seem to differ in our ideas of expense, I have resolved she shall have her own way, and be her own mistress in that respect for the future; and, if I were to die, she will find I have not been inattentive to her interest while living. Here, my friend, are the drafts of two deeds, which I wish to have your opinion on. By one, she will enjoy eight hundred a year independent while I live; and, by the other, the bulk of my fortune at my death.

JOS. SURF. This conduct, Sir Peter, is indeed truly generous.—[*Aside.*] I wish it may not corrupt my pupil.

SIR PET. Yes, I am determined she shall have no cause to complain, though I would not have her acquainted with the latter instance of my affection yet awhile.

JOS. SURF. Nor I, if I could help it. [*Aside.*

SIR PET. And now, my dear friend, if you please, we will talk over the situation of your hopes with Maria.

JOS. SURF. [*Softly.*] Oh, no, Sir Peter; another time, if you please.

SIR PET. I am sensibly chagrined at the little progress you seem to make in her affections.

JOS. SURF. [*Softly.*] I beg you will not mention it. What are my disappointments when your happiness is in debate!— [*Aside.*] 'Sdeath, I shall be ruined every way!

SIR PET. And though you are averse to my acquainting Lady Teazle with your passion, I'm sure she's not your enemy in the affair.

JOS. SURF. Pray, Sir Peter, now oblige me. I am really too much affected by the subject we have been speaking of to bestow a thought on my own concerns. The man who is entrusted with his friend's distresses can never—

*Re-enter* SERVANT

Well, sir?

SER. Your brother, sir, is speaking to a gentleman in the street, and says he knows you are within.

Jos. SURF. 'Sdeath, blockhead, I'm not within—I'm out for the day.

SIR PET. Stay—hold—a thought has struck me:—you shall be at home.

Jos. SURF. Well, well, let him come up.—[*Exit* SERVANT.] He'll interrupt Sir Peter, however. [*Aside.*

SIR PET. Now, my good friend, oblige me, I entreat you. Before Charles comes, let me conceal myself somewhere, then do you tax him on the point we have been talking, and his answer may satisfy me at once.

Jos. SURF. Oh, fie, Sir Peter! would you have me join in so mean a trick?—to trepan my brother too?

SIR PET. Nay, you tell me you are sure he is innocent; if so you do him the greatest service by giving him an opportunity to clear himself, and you will set my heart at rest. Come, you shall not refuse me: [*Going up.*] here, behind the screen will be—Hey! what the devil! there seems to be one listener here already—I'll swear I saw a petticoat!

Jos. SURF. Ha! ha! ha! Well, this is ridiculous enough. I'll tell you, Sir Peter, though I hold a man of intrigue to be a most despicable character, yet, you know, it does not follow that one is to be an absolute Joseph either! Hark'ee, 'tis a little French milliner, a silly rogue that plagues me; and having some character to lose, on your coming, sir, she ran behind the screen.

SIR PET. Ah, Joseph! Joseph! Did I ever think that you —But, egad, she has overheard all I have been saying of my wife.

Jos. SURF. Oh, 'twill never go any farther, you may depend upon it!

SIR PET. No! then, faith, let her hear it out.—Here's a closet will do as well.

Jos. SURF. Well, go in there.

SIR PET. Sly rogue! sly rogue! [*Goes into the closet.*

Jos. Surf. A narrow escape, indeed! and a curious situation I'm in, to part man and wife in this manner.

Lady Teaz. [*Peeping.*] Couldn't I steal off?

Jos. Surf. Keep close, my angel!

Sir Pet. [*Peeping.*] Joseph, tax him home.

Jos. Surf. Back, my dear friend!

Lady Teaz. [*Peeping.*] Couldn't you lock Sir Peter in?

Jos. Surf. Be still, my life!

Sir Pet. [*Peeping.*] You're sure the little milliner won't blab?

Jos. Surf. In, in, my dear Sir Peter!—'Fore Gad, I wish I had a key to the door.

*Enter* Charles Surface

Chas. Surf. Holla! brother, what has been the matter? Your fellow would not let me up at first. What! have you had a Jew or a wench with you?

Jos. Surf. Neither, brother, I assure you.

Chas. Surf. But what has made Sir Peter steal off? I thought he had been with you.

Jos. Surf. He was, brother; but, hearing you were coming, he did not choose to stay.

Chas. Surf. What! was the old gentleman afraid I wanted to borrow money of him?

Jos. Surf. No, sir; but I am sorry to find, Charles, you have lately given that worthy man grounds for great uneasiness.

Chas. Surf. Yes, they tell me I do that to a great many worthy men. But how so, pray?

Jos. Surf. To be plain with you, brother, he thinks you are endeavouring to gain Lady Teazle's affections from him.

Chas. Surf. Who, I? O Lud! not I, upon my word.—Ha! ha! ha! so the old fellow has found out that he has got a young wife, has he?—or, what is worse, Lady Teazle has found out she has an old husband?

Jos. Surf. This is no subject to jest on, brother. He who can laugh—

Chas. Surf. True, true, as you were going to say—then, seriously, I never had the least idea of what you charge me with, upon my honour.

Jos. Surf. Well, it will give Sir Peter great satisfaction to
hear this.                                    [*Raising his voice.*

Chas. Surf. To be sure, I once thought the lady seemed to
have taken a fancy to me; but, upon my soul, I never gave
her the least encouragement. Besides, you know my attachment to Maria.

Jos. Surf. But sure, brother, even if Lady Teazle had betrayed the fondest partiality for you—

Chas. Surf. Why, look'ee, Joseph, I hope I shall never
deliberately do a dishonourable action; but if a pretty
woman was purposely to throw herself in my way—and that
pretty woman married to a man old enough to be her
father—

Jos. Surf. Well!

Chas. Surf. Why, I believe I should be obliged to—

Jos. Surf. What?

Chas. Surf. To borrow a little of your morality, that's all.
But, brother, do you know now that you surprise me exceedingly, by naming me with Lady Teazle; for, i' faith, I always
understood you were her favourite.

Jos. Surf. Oh, for shame, Charles! This retort is foolish.

Chas. Surf. Nay, I swear I have seen you exchange such
significant glances—

Jos. Surf. Nay, nay, sir, this is no jest.

Chas. Surf. Egad, I'm serious! Don't you remember one
day, when I called here—

Jos. Surf. Nay, pr'ythee, Charles—

Chas. Surf. And found you together—

Jos. Surf. Zounds, sir, I insist—

Chas. Surf. And another time when your servant—

Jos. Surf. Brother, brother, a word with you!—[*Aside.*]
Gad, I must stop him.

Chas. Surf. Informed, I say, that—

Jos. Surf. Hush! I beg your pardon, but Sir Peter has
overheard all we have been saying. I knew you would clear
yourself, or I should not have consented.

Chas. Surf. How, Sir Peter! Where is he?

Jos. Surf. Softly, there!                    [*Points to the closet.*

Chas. Surf. Oh, 'fore Heaven, I'll have him out. Sir
Peter, come forth!

Jos. Surf.  No, no—

Chas. Surf.  I say, Sir Peter, come into court.—[*Pulls in Sir Peter.*] What! my old guardian!—What! turn inquisitor, and take evidence incog.?  Oh, fie!  Oh, fie!

Sir Pet.  Give me your hand, Charles—I believe I have suspected you wrongfully; but you mustn't be angry with Joseph—'twas my plan!

Chas. Surf.  Indeed!

Sir Pet.  But I acquit you.  I promise you I don't think near so ill of you as I did: what I have heard has given me great satisfaction.

Chas. Surf.  Egad, then, 'twas lucky you didn't hear any more.  Wasn't it, Joseph?

Sir Pet.  Ah! you would have retorted on him.

Chas. Surf.  Ah, ay, that was a joke.

Sir Pet.  Yes, yes, I know his honour too well.

Chas. Surf.  But you might as well have suspected him as me in this matter, for all that.  Mightn't he, Joseph?

Sir Pet.  Well, well, I believe you.

Jos. Surf.  Would they were both out of the room.  [*Aside.*

Sir Pet.  And in future, perhaps, we may not be such strangers.

*Re-enter* Servant, *and whispers* Joseph Surface

Ser.  Lady Sneerwell is below, and says she will come up.

Jos. Surf.  Lady Sneerwell!  Gad's life! she must not come here.  [*Exit* Servant.]  Gentlemen, I beg pardon—I must wait on you down stairs: here is a person come on particular business.

Chas. Surf.  Well, you can see him in another room.  Sir Peter and I have not met a long time, and I have something to say to him.

Jos. Surf.  [*Aside.*]  They must not be left together.— [*Aloud.*]  I'll send Lady Sneerwell away, and return directly. —[*Aside to* Sir Peter.]  Sir Peter, not a word of the French milliner.

Sir Pet.  [*Aside to* Joseph Surface.]  I! not for the world! —[*Exit* Joseph Surface.]  Ah, Charles, if you associated more with your brother, one might indeed hope for your reformation. He is a man of sentiment. Well, there is nothing in the world so noble as a man of sentiment.

CHAS. SURF. Psha! he is too moral by half; and so apprehensive of his good name, as he calls it, that I suppose he would as soon let a priest into his house as a wench.

SIR PET. No, no,—come, come,—you wrong him. No, no! Joseph is no rake, but he is no such saint either, in that respect.—[*Aside.*] I have a great mind to tell him—we should have such a laugh at Joseph.

CHAS. SURF. Oh, hang him! he's a very anchorite, a young hermit!

SIR PET. Hark'ee—you must not abuse him: he may chance to hear of it again, I promise you.

CHAS. SURF. Why, you won't tell him?

SIR PET. No—but—this way. [*Aside.*] Egad, I'll tell him. —[*Aloud*] Hark'ee—have you a mind to have a good laugh at Joseph?

CHAS. SURF. I should like it of all things.

SIR PET. Then, i' faith, we will! I'll be quit with him for discovering me. He had a girl with him when I called.

[*Whispers.*

CHAS. SURF. What! Joseph? you jest.

SIR PET. Hush!—a little French milliner—and the best of the jest is—she's in the room now.

CHAS. SURF. The devil she is!

SIR PET. Hush! I tell you.      [*Points to the screen.*

CHAS. SURF. Behind the screen! 'Slife, let's unveil her!

SIR PET. No, no, he's coming:—you sha'n't, indeed!

CHAS. SURF. Oh, egad, we'll have a peep at the little milliner!

SIR PET. Not for the world!—Joseph will never forgive me.

CHAS. SURF. I'll stand by you—

SIR PET. Odds, here he is!

[CHARLES SURFACE *throws down the screen.*


*Re-enter* JOSEPH SURFACE

CHAS. SURF. Lady Teazle, by all that's wonderful.

SIR PET. Lady Teazle, by all that's damnable!

CHAS. SURF. Sir Peter, this is one of the smartest French milliners I ever saw. Egad, you seem all to have been diverting yourselves here at hide and seek, and I don't see who is out of the secret. Shall I beg your ladyship to inform me? Not a word!—Brother, will you be pleased to explain this matter? What! is Morality dumb too?—Sir Peter, though I found you in the dark, perhaps you are not so now! All mute!—Well—though I can make nothing of the affair, I suppose you perfectly understand one another; so I'll leave you to yourselves.—[*Going.*] Brother, I'm sorry to find you have given that worthy man grounds for so much uneasiness. —Sir Peter! there's nothing in the world so noble as a man of sentiment! [*Exit.*

JOS. SURF. Sir Peter—notwithstanding—I confess—that appearances are against me—if you will afford me your patience—I make no doubt—but I shall explain every thing to your satisfaction.

SIR PET. If you please, sir.

JOS. SURF. The fact is, sir, that Lady Teazle, knowing my pretensions to your ward Maria—I say, sir, Lady Teazle, being apprehensive of the jealousy of your temper—and knowing my friendship to the family—she, sir, I say—called here—in order that—I might explain these pretensions—but on your coming—being apprehensive—as I said—of your jealousy—she withdrew—and this, you may depend on it, is the whole truth of the matter.

SIR PET. A very clear account, upon my word; and I dare swear the lady will vouch for every article of it.

LADY TEAZ. For not one word of it, Sir Peter!

SIR PET. How! don't you think it worth while to agree in the lie?

LADY TEAZ. There is not one syllable of truth in what that gentleman has told you.

SIR PET. I believe you, upon my soul, ma'am!

JOS. SURF. [*Aside to* LADY TEAZLE.] 'Sdeath, madam, will you betray me?

LADY TEAZ. Good Mr Hypocrite, by your leave, I'll speak for myself.

SIR PET. Ay, let her alone, sir; you'll find she'll make out a better story than you, without prompting.

LADY TEAZ. Hear me, Sir Peter!—I came here on no matter relating to your ward, and even ignorant of this gentleman's pretensions to her. But I came, seduced by his insidious arguments, at least to listen to his pretended passion, if not to sacrifice your honour to his baseness.

SIR PET. Now, I believe the truth is coming, indeed!

JOS. SURF. The woman's mad!

LADY TEAZ. No, sir; she has recovered her senses and your own arts have furnished her with the means.—Sir Peter, I do not expect you to credit me—but the tenderness you expressed for me, when I am sure you could not think I was a witness to it, has so penetrated to my heart, that had I left the place without the shame of this discovery, my future life should have spoken the sincerity of my gratitude. As for that smooth-tongued hypocrite, who would have seduced the wife of his too credulous friend, while he affected honourable addresses to his ward—I behold him now in a light so truly despicable, that I shall never again respect myself for having listened to him.                              [*Exit.*

JOS. SURF. Notwithstanding all this, Sir Peter, Heaven knows—

SIR PET. That you are a villain! and so I leave you to your conscience.

JOS. SURF. You are too rash, Sir Peter; you shall hear me. The man who shuts out conviction by refusing to—

SIR PET. Oh, damn your sentiments!

[*Exeunt* SIR PETER *and* JOSEPH SURFACE, *talking.*

## ACT FIFTH

### SCENE I.—*The Library in* JOSEPH SURFACE'S *House*

#### *Enter* JOSEPH SURFACE *and* Servant

JOS. SURF. Mr Stanley! and why should you think I would see him? you must know he comes to ask something.

SER. Sir, I should not have let him in, but that Mr Rowley came to the door with him.

JOS. SURF. Psha! blockhead! to suppose that I should now be in a temper to receive visits from poor relations!—Well, why don't you show the fellow up?

SER. I will, sir.—Why, sir, it was not my fault that Sir Peter discovered my lady—

JOS. SURF. Go, fool!—[*Exit* SERVANT.] Sure Fortune never played a man of my policy such a trick before! My character with Sir Peter, my hopes with Maria, destroyed in a moment! I'm in a rare humour to listen to other people's distresses! I sha'n't be able to bestow even a benevolent sentiment on Stanley.—So! here he comes, and Rowley with him. I must try to recover myself, and put a little charity into my face, however. [*Exit.*

*Enter* SIR OLIVER SURFACE *and* ROWLEY

SIR OLIV. What! does he avoid us? That was he, was it not?

ROW. It was, sir. But I doubt you are come a little too abruptly. His nerves are so weak, that the sight of a poor relation may be too much for him. I should have gone first to break it to him.

SIR OLIV. Oh, plague of his nerves! Yet this is he whom Sir Peter extols as a man of the most benevolent way of thinking!

ROW. As to his way of thinking, I cannot pretend to decide; for, to do him justice, he appears to have as much speculative benevolence as any private gentleman in the kingdom, though he is seldom so sensual as to indulge himself in the exercise of it.

SIR OLIV. Yet he has a string of charitable sentiments at his fingers' ends.

ROW. Or, rather, at his tongue's end, Sir Oliver; for I believe there is no sentiment he has such faith in as that *Charity begins at home.*

SIR OLIV. And his, I presume, is of that domestic sort which never stirs abroad at all.

ROW. I doubt you'll find it so; but he's coming. I mustn't seem to interrupt you; and you know, immediately as you leave him, I come in to announce your arrival in your real character.

SIR OLIV. True; and afterwards you'll meet me at Sir Peter's.

Row. Without losing a moment.　　　　　[*Exit.*

Sir Oliv. I don't like the complaisance of his features.


*Re-enter* Joseph Surface

Jos. Surf. Sir, I beg you ten thousand pardons for keeping you a moment waiting.— Mr Stanley, I presume.

Sir Oliv. At your service.

Jos. Surf. Sir, I beg you will do me the honour to sit down—I entreat you, sir.

Sir Oliv. Dear sir—there's no occasion.—[*Aside.*] Too civil by half!

Jos. Surf. I have not the pleasure of knowing you, Mr Stanley; but I am extremely happy to see you look so well. You were nearly related to my mother, I think, Mr Stanley?

Sir Oliv. I was, sir; so nearly that my present poverty, I fear, may do discredit to her wealthy children, else I should not have presumed to trouble you.

Jos. Surf. Dear sir, there needs no apology;—he that is in distress, though a stranger, has a right to claim kindred with the wealthy. I am sure I wish I was one of that class, and had it in my power to offer you even a small relief.

Sir Oliv. If your uncle, Sir Oliver, were here, I should have a friend.

Jos. Surf. I wish he was, sir, with all my heart; you should not want an advocate with him, believe me, sir.

Sir Oliv. I should not need one—my distresses would recommend me. But I imagined his bounty would enable you to become the agent of his charity.

Jos. Surf. My dear sir, you were strangely misinformed. Sir Oliver is a worthy man, a very worthy man; but avarice, Mr Stanley, is the vice of age. I will tell you, my good sir, in confidence, what he has done for me has been a mere nothing; though people, I know, have thought otherwise, and for my part, I never chose to contradict the report.

SIR OLIV. What! has he never transmitted you bullion —rupees—pagodas?

JOS. SURF. Oh, dear sir, nothing of the kind! No, no; a few presents now and then—china, shawls, congou tea, avadavats and Indian crackers—little more, believe me.

SIR OLIV. Here's gratitude for twelve thousand pounds! —Avadavats and Indian crackers!          [*Aside.*

JOS. SURF. Then, my dear sir, you have heard, I doubt not, of the extravagance of my brother: there are very few would credit what I have done for that unfortunate young man.

SIR OLIV. Not I, for one!          [*Aside.*

JOS. SURF. The sums I have lent him! Indeed I have been exceedingly to blame; it was an amiable weakness; however, I don't pretend to defend it—and now I feel it doubly culpable, since it has deprived me of the pleasure of serving you, Mr. Stanley, as my heart dictates.

SIR OLIV. [*Aside.*] Dissembler!—[*Aloud.*] Then, sir, you can't assist me?

JOS. SURF. At present, it grieves me to say, I cannot; but, whenever I have the ability, you may depend upon hearing from me.

SIR OLIV. I am extremely sorry—

JOS. SURF. Not more than I, believe me; to pity, without the power to relieve, is still more painful than to ask and be denied.

SIR OLIV. Kind sir, your most obedient humble servant.

JOS. SURF. You leave me deeply affected, Mr. Stanley. —William, be ready to open the door.          [*Calls to* SERVANT.

SIR OLIV. Oh, dear sir, no ceremony.

JOS. SURF. Your very obedient.

SIR OLIV. Your most obsequious.

JOS. SURF. You may depend upon hearing from me, whenever I can be of service.

SIR OLIV. Sweet sir, you are too good!

JOS. SURF. In the meantime I wish you health and spirits.

SIR OLIV. Your ever grateful and perpetual humble servant.

JOS. SURF. Sir, yours as sincerely.

SIR OLIV. [*Aside.*] Now I am satisfied.     [*Exit.*

JOS. SURF. This is one bad effect of a good character; it invites application from the unfortunate, and there needs no small degree of address to gain the reputation of benevolence without incurring the expense. The silver ore of pure charity is an expensive article in the catalogue of a man's good qualities; whereas the sentimental French plate I use instead of it makes just as good a show, and pays no tax.

*Re-enter* ROWLEY

ROW. Mr Surface, your servant: I was apprehensive of interrupting you, though my business demands immediate attention, as this note will inform you.

JOS. SURF. Always happy to see Mr Rowley,—a rascal. —[*Aside. Reads the letter.*] Sir Oliver Surface!—My uncle arrived!

ROW. He is, indeed: we have just parted—quite well, after a speedy voyage, and impatient to embrace his worthy nephew.

JOS. SURF. I am astonished!—William! stop Mr Stanley, if he's not gone.     [*Calls to* SERVANT.

ROW. Oh! he's out of reach, I believe.

JOS. SURF. Why did you not let me know this when you came in together?

ROW. I thought you had particular business. But I must be gone to inform your brother, and appoint him here to meet your uncle. He will be with you in a quarter of an hour.

JOS. SURF. So he says. Well, I am strangely overjoyed at his coming.—[*Aside.*] Never, to be sure, was anything so damned unlucky!

ROW. You will be delighted to see how well he looks.

JOS. SURF. Oh! I'm overjoyed to hear it.—[*Aside.*] Just at this time!

ROW. I'll tell him how impatiently you expect him.

JOS. SURF. Do, do; pray give my best duty and affection. Indeed, I cannot express the sensations I feel at the thought of seeing him.—[*Exit* ROWLEY.] Certainly his coming just at this time is the cruellest piece of ill fortune.     [*Exit.*

SCENE II.—*A Room in* SIR PETER TEAZLE'S *House*

### *Enter* MRS CANDOUR *and* Maid

MAID. Indeed, ma'am, my lady will see nobody at present.

MRS CAN. Did you tell her it was her friend Mrs Candour?

MAID. Yes, ma'am; but she begs you will excuse her.

MRS CAN. Do go again; I shall be glad to see her, if it be only for a moment, for I am sure she must be in great distress.—[*Exit* MAID.] Dear heart, how provoking! I'm not mistress of half the circumstances! We shall have the whole affair in the newspapers, with the names of the parties at length, before I have dropped the story at a dozen houses.

### *Enter* SIR BENJAMIN BACKBITE

Oh, dear Sir Benjamin! you have heard, I suppose—

SIR BEN. Of Lady Teazle and Mr Surface—

MRS CAN. And Sir Peter's discovery—

SIR BEN. Oh, the strangest piece of business, to be sure!

MRS CAN. Well, I never was so surprised in my life. I am so sorry for all parties, indeed.

SIR BEN. Now, I don't pity Sir Peter at all: he was so extravagantly partial to Mr Surface.

MRS CAN. Mr Surface! Why, 'twas with Charles Lady Teazle was detected.

SIR BEN. No, no, I tell you: Mr Surface is the gallant.

MRS CAN. No such thing! Charles is the man. 'Twas Mr Surface brought Sir Peter on purpose to discover them.

SIR BEN. I tell you I had it from one—

MRS CAN. And I have it from one—

SIR BEN. Who had it from one, who had it—

MRS CAN. From one immediately. But here comes Lady Sneerwell; perhaps she knows the whole affair.

### *Enter* LADY SNEERWELL

LADY SNEER. So, my dear Mrs Candour, here's a sad affair of our friend Lady Teazle!

Mrs Can. Ay, my dear friend, who would have thought—

Lady Sneer. Well, there is no trusting appearances; though, indeed, she was always too lively for me.

Mrs Can. To be sure, her manners were a little too free; but then she was so young!

Lady Sneer. And had, indeed, some good qualities.

Mrs Can. So she had, indeed. But have you heard the particulars?

Lady Sneer. No; but every body says that Mr Surface—

Sir Ben. Ay, there; I told you Mr Surface was the man.

Mrs Can. No, no: indeed the assignation was with Charles.

Lady Sneer. With Charles! You alarm me, Mrs Candour!

Mrs Can. Yes, yes; he was the lover. Mr Surface, to do him justice, was only the informer.

Sir Ben. Well, I'll not dispute with you, Mrs Candour; but, be it which it may, I hope that Sir Peter's wound will not—

Mrs Can. Sir Peter's wound! Oh, mercy! I didn't hear a word of their fighting.

Lady Sneer. Nor I, a syllable.

Sir Ben. No! what, no mention of the duel?

Mrs Can. Not a word.

Sir Ben. Oh, yes: they fought before they left the room.

Lady Sneer. Pray, let us hear.

Mrs Can. Ay, do oblige us with the duel.

Sir Ben. Sir, says Sir Peter, immediately after the discovery, *you are a most ungrateful fellow.*

Mrs Can. Ay, to Charles—

Sir Ben. No, no—to Mr Surface—*a most ungrateful fellow; and old as I am, sir,* says he, *I insist on immediate satisfaction.*

Mrs Can. Ay, that must have been to Charles; for 'tis very unlikely Mr Surface should fight in his own house.

Sir Ben. Gad's life, ma'am, not at all—*giving me immediate satisfaction.*—On this, ma'am, Lady Teazle, seeing Sir Peter in such danger, ran out of the room in strong hysterics, and Charles after her, calling out for hartshorn and water; then, madam, they began to fight with swords—

*Enter* CRABTREE

CRAB. With pistols, nephew, pistols! I have it from undoubted authority.

MRS CAN. Oh, Mr Crabtree, then it is all true!

CRAB. Too true, indeed, madam, and Sir Peter is dangerously wounded—

SIR BEN. By a thrust in segoon quite through his left side—

CRAB. By a bullet lodged in the thorax.

MRS CAN. Mercy on me! Poor Sir Peter!

CRAB. Yes, madam; though Charles would have avoided the matter, if he could.

MRS CAN. I told you who it was; I knew Charles was the person.

SIR BEN. My uncle, I see, knows nothing of the matter.

CRAB. But Sir Peter taxed him with basest ingratitude—

SIR BEN. That I told you, you know—

CRAB. Do, nephew, let me speak!—and insisted on immediate—

SIR BEN. Just as I said—

CRAB. Odds life, nephew, allow others to know something too! A pair of pistols lay on the bureau (for Mr Surface, it seems, had come home the night before late from Salthill, where he had been to see the Montem with a friend, who has a son at Eton), so, unluckily, the pistols were left charged.

SIR BEN. I heard nothing of this.

CRAB. Sir Peter forced Charles to take one, and they fired, it seems, pretty nearly together. Charles's shot took effect, as I tell you, and Sir Peter's missed; but, what is very extraordinary, the ball struck against a little bronze Shakespeare that stood over the fire place, grazed out of the window at a right angle, and wounded the postman, who was just coming to the door with a double letter from Northamptonshire.

SIR BEN. My uncle's account is more circumstantial, I confess; but I believe mine is the true one, for all that.

LADY SNEER. [*Aside.*] I am more interested in this affair than they imagine, and must have better information.   [*Exit.*

SIR BEN. Ah! Lady Sneerwell's alarm is very easily accounted for.

CRAB. Yes, yes, they certainly do say—but that's neither here nor there.

MRS CAN. But, pray, where is Sir Peter at present?

CRAB. Oh! they brought him home, and he is now in the house, though the servants are ordered to deny him.

MRS CAN. I believe so, and Lady Teazle, I suppose, attending him.

CRAB. Yes, yes; and I saw one of the faculty enter just before me.

SIR BEN. Hey! who comes here?

CRAB. Oh, this is he: the physician, depend on't.

MRS CAN. Oh, certainly! it must be the physician; and now we shall know.

*Enter* SIR OLIVER SURFACE

CRAB. Well, doctor, what hopes?

MRS CAN. Ay, doctor, how's your patient?

SIR BEN. Now, doctor, isn't it a wound with a small-sword?

CRAB. A bullet lodged in the thorax, for a hundred!

SIR OLIV. Doctor! a wound with a small-sword! and a bullet in the thorax!—Oons! are you mad, good people?

SIR BEN. Perhaps, sir, you are not a doctor?

SIR OLIV. Truly, I am to thank you for my degree, if I am.

CRAB. Only a friend of Sir Peter's, then, I presume. But, sir, you must have heard of his accident?

SIR OLIV. Not a word!

CRAB. Not of his being dangerously wounded?

SIR OLIV. The devil he is!

SIR BEN. Run through the body—

CRAB. Shot in the breast—

SIR BEN. By one Mr Surface—

CRAB. Ay, the younger.

SIR OLIV. Hey! what the plague! you seem to differ strangely in your accounts: however, you agree that Sir Peter is dangerously wounded.

SIR BEN. Oh, yes, we agree in that.

CRAB. Yes, yes, I believe there can be no doubt of that.

SIR OLIV. Then, upon my word, for a person in that situation, he is the most imprudent man alive; for here he comes, walking as if nothing at all was the matter.

### *Enter* SIR PETER TEAZLE

Odds heart, Sir Peter! you are come in good time, I promise you; for we had just given you over!

SIR BEN. [*Aside to* CRABTREE.] Egad, uncle, this is the most sudden recovery!

SIR OLIV. Why, man! what do you out of bed with a small-sword through your body, and a bullet lodged in your thorax?

SIR PET. A small-sword and a bullet!

SIR OLIV. Ay; these gentlemen would have killed you without law or physic, and wanted to dub me a doctor, to make me an accomplice.

SIR PET. Why, what is all this?

SIR BEN. We rejoice, Sir Peter, that the story of the duel is not true, and are sincerely sorry for your other misfortune.

SIR PET. So, so; all over the town already!      [*Aside.*

CRAB. Though, Sir Peter, you were certainly vastly to blame to marry at your years.

SIR PET. Sir, what business is that of yours?

MRS CAN. Though, indeed, as Sir Peter made so good a husband, he's very much to be pitied.

SIR PET. Plague on your pity, ma'am! I desire none of it.

SIR BEN. However, Sir Peter, you must not mind the laughing and jests you will meet with on the occasion.

SIR PET. Sir, sir! I desire to be master in my own house.

CRAB. 'Tis no uncommon case, that's one comfort.

SIR PET. I insist on being left to myself: without ceremony, I insist on your leaving my house directly!

MRS CAN. Well, well, we are going; and depend on't, we'll make the best report of it we can.      [*Exit.*

SIR PET. Leave my house!

CRAB. And tell how hardly you've been treated.      [*Exit.*

SIR PET. Leave my house!

SIR BEN. And how patiently you bear it.          [*Exit.*

SIR PET. Fiends! vipers! furies! Oh! that their own venom would choke them!

SIR OLIV. They are very provoking indeed, Sir Peter.

*Enter* ROWLEY

ROW. I heard high words: what has ruffled you, sir?

SIR PET. Psha! what signifies asking? Do I ever pass a day without my vexations?

ROW. Well, I'm not inquisitive.

SIR OLIV. Well, Sir Peter, I have seen both my nephews in the manner we proposed.

SIR PET. A precious couple they are!

ROW. Yes, and Sir Oliver is convinced that your judgment was right, Sir Peter.

SIR OLIV. Yes, I find Joseph is indeed the man, after all.

ROW. Ay, as Sir Peter says, he is a man of sentiment.

SIR OLIV. And acts up to the sentiments he professes.

ROW. It certainly is edification to hear him talk.

SIR OLIV. Oh, he's a model for the young men of the age!—but how's this, Sir Peter? you don't join us in your friend Joseph's praise, as I expected.

SIR PET. Sir Oliver, we live in a damned wicked world, and the fewer we praise the better.

ROW. What! do you say so, Sir Peter, who were never mistaken in your life?

SIR PET. Psha! plague on you both! I see by your sneering you have heard the whole affair. I shall go mad among you!

ROW. Then, to fret you no longer, Sir Peter, we are indeed acquainted with it all. I met Lady Teazle coming from Mr Surface's so humbled, that she deigned to request me to be her advocate with you.

SIR PET. And does Sir Oliver know all this?

SIR OLIV. Every circumstance.

SIR PET. What, of the closet and the screen, hey?

SIR OLIV. Yes, yes, and the little French milliner. Oh, I have been vastly diverted with the story! ha! ha! ha!

SIR PET. 'Twas very pleasant.

SIR OLIV. I never laughed more in my life, I assure you: ah! ah! ah!

SIR PET. Oh, vastly diverting! ha! ha! ha!

Row. To be sure, Joseph with his sentiments! ha! ha! ha?

SIR PET. Yes, yes, his sentiments! ha! ha! ha! Hypocritical villain!

SIR OLIV. Ay, and that rogue Charles to pull Sir Peter out of the closet: ha! ha! ha!

SIR PET. Ha! ha! 'twas devilish entertaining, to be sure!

SIR OLIV. Ha! ha! ha! Egad, Sir Peter, I should like to have seen your face when the screen was thrown down: ha! ha!

SIR PET. Yes, yes, my face when the screen was thrown down: ha! ha! ha! Oh, I must never show my head again!

SIR OLIV. But come, come, it isn't fair to laugh at you neither, my old friend; though, upon my soul, I can't help it.

SIR PET. Oh, pray don't restrain your mirth on my account: it does not hurt me at all! I laugh at the whole affair myself. Yes, yes, I think being a standing jest for all one's acquaintance a very happy situation. Oh, yes, and then of a morning to read the paragraphs about Mr S——, Lady T——, and Sir P——, will be so entertaining!

Row. Without affectation, Sir Peter, you may despise the ridicule of fools. But I see Lady Teazle going towards the next room; I am sure you must desire a reconciliation as earnestly as she does.

SIR OLIV. Perhaps my being here prevents her coming to you. Well, I'll leave honest Rowley to mediate between you; but he must bring you all presently to Mr Surface's, where I am now returning, if not to reclaim a libertine, at least to expose hypocrisy.

SIR PET. I'll be present at your discovering yourself there with all my heart; though 'tis a vile unlucky place for discoveries.

Row. We'll follow.          [*Exit* SIR OLIVER SURFACE.

SIR PET. She is not coming here, you see, Rowley.

Row. No, but she has left the door of that room open, you perceive. See, she is in tears.

SIR PET. Certainly a little mortification appears very becoming in a wife. Don't you think it will do her good to let her pine a little?

Row. Oh, this is ungenerous in you!

Sir Pet. Well, I know not what to think. You remember the letter I found of hers evidently intended for Charles?

Row. A mere forgery, Sir Peter! laid in your way on purpose. This is one of the points which I intend Snake shall give you conviction of.

Sir Pet. I wish I were once satisfied of that. She looks this way. What a remarkably elegant turn of the head she has! Rowley, I'll go to her.

Row. Certainly.

Sir Pet. Though, when it is known that we are reconciled, people will laugh at me ten times more.

Row. Let them laugh, and retort their malice only by showing them you are happy in spite of it.

Sir Pet. I' faith, so I will! and, if I'm not mistaken, we may yet be the happiest couple in the country.

Row. Nay, Sir Peter, he who once lays aside suspicion—

Sir Pet. Hold, Master Rowley! if you have any regard for me, never let me hear you utter any thing like a sentiment: I have had enough of them to serve me the rest of my life. [Exeunt.

Scene III.—*The Library of* Joseph Surface's *House*

*Enter* Joseph Surface *and* Lady Sneerwell

Lady Sneer. Impossible! Will not Sir Peter immediately be reconciled to Charles, and of course no longer oppose his union with Maria? The thought is distraction to me.

Jos. Surf. Can passion furnish a remedy?

Lady Sneer. No, nor cunning either. Oh, I was a fool, an idiot, to league with such a blunderer!

Jos. Surf. Sure, Lady Sneerwell, I am the greatest sufferer; yet you see I bear the accident with calmness.

Lady Sneer. Because the disappointment doesn't reach your heart; your interest only attached you to Maria. Had you felt for her what I have for that ungrateful libertine, neither your temper nor hypocrisy could prevent your showing the sharpness of your vexation.

JOS. SURF. But why should your reproaches fall on me for this disappointment?

LADY SNEER. Are you not the cause of it? Had you not a sufficient field for your roguery in imposing upon Sir Peter, and supplanting your brother, but you must endeavour to seduce his wife? I hate such an avarice of crimes; 'tis an unfair monopoly, and never prospers.

JOS. SURF. Well, I admit I have been to blame. I confess I deviated from the direct road of wrong, but I don't think we're so totally defeated neither.

LADY SNEER. No!

JOS. SURF. You tell me you have made a trial of Snake since we met, and that you still believe him faithful to us?

LADY SNEER. I do believe so.

JOS. SURF. And that he has undertaken, should it be necessary, to swear and prove, that Charles is at this time contracted by vows and honour to your ladyship, which some of his former letters to you will serve to support?

LADY SNEER. This, indeed, might have assisted.

JOS. SURF. Come, come; it is not too late yet.—[*Knocking at the door.*] But hark! this is probably my uncle, Sir Oliver: retire to that room; we'll consult farther when he is gone.

LADY SNEER. Well, but if he should find you out too?

JOS. SURF. Oh, I have no fear of that. Sir Peter will hold his tongue for his own credit's sake—and you may depend on it I shall soon discover Sir Oliver's weak side!

LADY SNEER. I have no diffidence of your abilities: only be constant to one roguery at a time.

JOS. SURF. I will, I will!—[*Exit* LADY SNEERWELL.] So! 'tis confounded hard, after such bad fortune, to be baited by one's confederate in evil. Well, at all events, my character is so much better than Charles's, that I certainly—hey! —what—this is not Sir Oliver, but old Stanley again. Plague on't that he should return to tease me just now! I shall have Sir Oliver come and find him here—and—

*Enter* Sir Oliver Surface

Gad's life, Mr. Stanley, why have you come back to plague me at this time? You must not stay now, upon my word.

Sir Oliv. Sir, I hear your uncle Oliver is expected here, and though he has been so penurious to you, I'll try what he'll do for me.

Jos. Surf. Sir, 'tis impossible for you to stay now, so I must beg—Come any other time, and I promise you, you shall be assisted.

Sir Oliv. No: Sir Oliver and I must be acquainted.

Jos. Surf. Zounds, sir! then I insist on your quitting the room directly.

Sir Oliv. Nay, sir—

Jos. Surf. Sir, I insist on't!—Here, William! show this gentleman out. Since you compel me, sir, not one moment— this is such insolence.            [*Going to push him out.*


*Enter* Charles Surface

Chas. Surf. Heyday! what's the matter now? What the devil, have you got hold of my little broker here? Zounds, brother, don't hurt little Premium. What's the matter, my little fellow?

Jos. Surf. So! he has been with you too, has he?

Chas. Surf. To be sure, he has. Why, he's as honest a little—But sure, Joseph, you have not been borrowing money too, have you?

Jos Surf. Borrowing! no!. But, brother, you know we expect Sir Oliver here every—

Chas. Surf. O Gad, that's true! Noll mustn't find the little broker here, to be sure.

Jos. Surf. Yet Mr Stanley insists—

Chas. Surf. Stanley! why his name's Premium.

Jos. Surf. No, sir, Stanley.

Chas. Surf. No, no, Premium.

Jos. Surf. Well, no matter which—but—

Chas. Surf. Ay, ay, Stanley or Premium, 'tis the same thing, as you say; for I suppose he goes by half a hundred names, besides A. B. at the coffee-house.            [*Knocking.*

Jos. Surf. 'Sdeath! here's Sir Oliver at the door.—Now I beg, Mr Stanley—

Chas. Surf. Ay, ay, and I beg, Mr Premium—

Sir Oliv. Gentlemen—

Jos. Surf. Sir, by Heaven you shall go!

Chas. Surf. Ay, out with him, certainly!

Sir Oliv. This violence—

Jos. Surf. Sir, 'tis your own fault.

Chas. Surf. Out with him, to be sure.

> [*Both forcing* Sir Oliver *out.*

*Enter* Sir Peter *and* Lady Teazle, Maria, *and* Rowley

Sir Pet. My old friend, Sir Oliver—hey! What in the name of wonder—here are dutiful nephews—assault their uncle at a first visit!

Lady Teaz. Indeed, Sir Oliver, 'twas well we came in to rescue you.

Row. Truly it was; for I perceive, Sir Oliver, the character of old Stanley was no protection to you.

Sir Oliv. Nor of Premium either: the necessities of the former could not extort a shilling from that benevolent gentleman; and with the other I stood a chance of faring worse than my ancestors, and being knocked down without being bid for.

Jos. Surf. Charles!

Chas. Surf. Joseph!

Jos. Surf. 'Tis now complete!

Chas. Surf. Very.

Sir Oliv. Sir Peter, my friend, and Rowley too—look on that elder nephew of mine. You know what he has already received from my bounty; and you also know how gladly I would have regarded half my fortune as held in trust for him: judge then my disappointment in discovering him to be destitute of truth, charity, and gratitude!

Sir Pet. Sir Oliver, I should be more surprised at this declaration, if I had not myself found him to be mean, treacherous, and hypocritical.

Lady Teaz. And if the gentleman pleads not guilty to these, pray let him call me to his character.

SIR PET. Then, I believe, we need add no more: if he knows himself, he will consider it as the most perfect punishment, that he is known to the world.

CHAS. SURF. If they talk this way to Honesty, what will they say to me, by and by?                    [*Aside.*

[SIR PETER, LADY TEAZLE, *and* MARIA *retire.*

SIR OLIV. As for that prodigal, his brother, there—

CHAS. SURF. Ay, now comes my turn: the damned family pictures will ruin me!                    [*Aside.*

JOS. SURF. Sir Oliver—uncle, will you honour me with a hearing?

CHAS. SURF. Now, if Joseph would make one of his long speeches, I might recollect myself a little.          [*Aside.*

SIR OLIV. [*To* JOSEPH SURFACE.] I suppose you would undertake to justify yourself?

JOS. SURF. I trust I could.

SIR OLIV. [*To* CHARLES SURFACE.] Well, sir!—and you could justify yourself too, I suppose?

CHAS. SURF. Not that I know of, Sir Oliver.

SIR OLIV. What!—Little Premium has been let too much into the secret, I suppose?

CHAS. SURF. True, sir; but they were family secrets, and should not be mentioned again, you know.

Row. Come, Sir Oliver, I know you cannot speak of Charles's follies with anger.

SIR OLIV. Odd's heart, no more I can; nor with gravity either. Sir Peter, do you know the rogue bargained with me for all his ancestors; sold me judges and generals by the foot, and maiden aunts as cheap as broken china.

CHAS. SURF. To be sure, Sir Oliver, I did make a little free with the family canvas, that's the truth on't. My ancestors may rise in judgment against me, there's no denying it; but believe me sincere when I tell you—and upon my soul I would not say so if I was not—that if I do not appear mortified at the exposure of my follies, it is because I feel at this moment the warmest satisfaction in seeing you, my liberal benefactor.

SIR OLIV. Charles, I believe you. Give me your hand again: the ill-looking little fellow over the settee has made your peace.

CHAS. SURF. Then, sir, my gratitude to the original is still increased.

LADY TEAZ. [*Advancing.*] Yet, I believe, Sir Oliver, here is one Charles is still more anxious to be reconciled to.

[*Pointing to* MARIA.

SIR OLIV. Oh, I have heard of his attachment there; and, with the young lady's pardon, if I construe right—that blush—

SIR PET. Well, child, speak your sentiments!

MAR. Sir, I have little to say, but that I shall rejoice to hear that he is happy; for me, whatever claim I had to his attention, I willingly resign to one who has a better title.

CHAS. SURF. How, Maria!

SIR PET. Heyday! what's the mystery now? While he appeared an incorrigible rake, you would give your hand to no one else; and now that he is likely to reform I'll warrant you won't have him!

MAR. His own heart and Lady Sneerwell know the cause.

CHAS. SURF. Lady Sneerwell!

JOS. SURF. Brother, it is with great concern I am obliged to speak on this point, but my regard to justice compels me, and Lady Sneerwell's injuries can no longer be concealed.

[*Opens the door.*

*Enter* LADY SNEERWELL

SIR PET. So! another French milliner! Egad, he has one in every room in the house, I suppose!

LADY SNEER. Ungrateful Charles! Well may you be surprised, and feel for the indelicate situation your perfidy has forced me into.

CHAS. SURF. Pray, uncle, is this another plot of yours? For, as I have life, I don't understand it.

JOS. SURF. I believe, sir, there is but the evidence of one person more necessary to make it extremely clear.

SIR PET. And that person, I imagine, is Mr Snake.— Rowley, you were perfectly right to bring him with us, and pray let him appear.

ROW. Walk in, Mr Snake.

*Enter* SNAKE

I thought his testimony might be wanted: however, it happens unluckily, that he comes to confront Lady Sneerwell, not to support her.

LADY SNEER. A villain! Treacherous to me at last! Speak, fellow, have you too conspired against me?

SNAKE. I beg your ladyship ten thousand pardons: you paid me extremely liberally for the lie in question; but I unfortunately have been offered double to speak the truth.

SIR PET. Plot and counter-plot, egad! I wish your ladyship joy of your negociation.

LADY SNEER. The torments of shame and disappointment on you all!                                              [*Going.*

LADY TEAZ. Hold, Lady Sneerwell—before you go, let me thank you for the trouble you and that gentleman have taken, in writing letters from me to Charles, and answering them yourself; and let me also request you to make my respects to the scandalous college of which you are president, and inform them that Lady Teazle, licentiate, begs leave to return the diploma they granted her, as she leaves off practice, and kills characters no longer.

LADY SNEER. You too, madam!—provoking—insolent! May your husband live these fifty years!          [*Exit.*

SIR PET. Oons! what a fury!

LADY TEAZ. A malicious creature, indeed!

SIR PET. What! not for her last wish?

LADY TEAZ. Oh, no!

SIR OLIV. Well, sir, and what have you to say now?

JOS. SURF. Sir, I am so confounded, to find that Lady Sneerwell could be guilty of suborning Mr Snake in this manner, to impose on us all, that I know not what to say: however, lest her revengeful spirit should prompt her to injure my brother, I had certainly better follow her directly. For the man who attempts to—                         [*Exit.*

SIR PET. Moral to the last!

SIR OLIV. Ay, and marry her, Joseph, if you can. Oil and vinegar!—egad you'll do very well together.

ROW. I believe we have no more occasion for Mr Snake at present?

SNAKE. Before I go, I beg pardon once for all, for whatever uneasiness I have been the humble instrument of causing to the parties present.

SIR PET. Well, well, you have made atonement by a good deed at last.

SNAKE. But I must request of the company, that it shall never be known.

SIR PET. Hey! what the plague! are you ashamed of having done a right thing once in your life?

SNAKE. Ah, sir, consider—I live by the badness of my character; and, if it were once known that I had been betrayed into an honest action, I should lose every friend I have in the world.

SIR OLIV. Well, well—we'll not traduce you by saying any thing in your praise, never fear.          [*Exit* SNAKE.

SIR PET. There's a precious rogue!

LADY TEAZ. See, Sir Oliver, there needs no persuasion now to reconcile your nephew and Maria.

SIR OLIV. Ay, ay, that's as it should be, and, egad, we'll have the wedding to-morrow morning.

CHAS. SURF. Thank you, dear uncle.

SIR PET. What, you rogue! don't you ask the girl's consent first?

CHAS. SURF. Oh, I have done that a long time—a minute ago—and she has looked yes.

MAR. For shame, Charles!—I protest, Sir Peter, there has not been a word—

SIR OLIV. Well, then, the fewer the better; may your love for each other never know abatement.

SIR PET. And may you live as happily together as Lady Teazle and I intend to do!

CHAS. SURF. Rowley, my old friend, I am sure you congratulate me; and I suspect that I owe you much.

SIR OLIV. You do, indeed, Charles.

SIR PET. Ay, honest Rowley always said you would reform.

CHAS. SURF. Why, as to reforming, Sir Peter, I'll make no promises, and that I take to be a proof that I intend to set about it. But here shall be my monitor—my gentle guide.— Ah! can I leave the virtuous path those eyes illumine?

Though thou, dear maid, shouldst waive thy beauty's sway,
Thou still must rule, because I will obey:
An humble fugitive from Folly view,
No sanctuary near but Love and you:

[*To the* Audience.

You can, indeed, each anxious fear remove,
For even Scandal dies, if you approve.

[*Exeunt omnes.*

# EPILOGUE

## BY MR. COLMAN

### SPOKEN BY LADY TEAZLE

I, who was late so volatile and gay,
Like a trade-wind must now blow all one way,
Bend all my cares, my studies, and my vows,
To one dull rusty weathercock—my spouse!
So wills our virtuous bard—the motley Bayes
Of crying epilogues and laughing plays!
Old bachelors, who marry smart young wives,
Learn from our play to regulate your lives:
Each bring his dear to town, all faults upon her—
London will prove the very source of honour.
Plunged fairly in, like a cold bath it serves,
When principles relax, to brace the nerves:
Such is my case; and yet I must deplore
That the gay dream of dissipation 's o'er.
And say, ye fair! was ever lively wife,
Born with a genius for the highest life,
Like me untimely blasted in her bloom,
Like me condemn'd to such a dismal doom?
Save money—when I just knew how to waste it!
Leave London—just as I began to taste it!
    Must I then watch the early crowing cock,
The melancholy ticking of a clock;
In a lone rustic hall for ever pounded,
With dogs, cats, rats, and squalling brats surrounded.
With humble curate can I now retire,
(While good Sir Peter boozes with the squire)
And at backgammon mortify my soul,
That pants for loo, or flutters at a vole?
Seven's the main! Dear sound that must expire,
Lost at hot cockles round a Christmas fire;

The transient hour of fashion too soon spent,
Farewell the tranquil mind, farewell content!
Farewell the plumèd head, the cushioned tête,
That takes the cushion from its proper seat!
That spirit-stirring drum!—card drums I mean,
Spadille—odd trick—pam—basto—king and queen!
And you, ye knockers, that, with brazen throat,
The welcome visitors' approach denote;
Farewell all quality of high renown,
Pride, pomp, and circumstance of glorious town!
Farewell! your revels I partake no more,
And Lady Teazle's occupation 's o'er!
All this I told our bard; he smiled, and said 'twas clear,
I ought to play deep tragedy next year.
Meanwhile he drew wise morals from his play,
And in these solemn periods stalked away:—
" Blessed were the fair like you; her faults who stopped
And closed her follies when the curtain dropped!
No more in vice or error to engage,
Or play the fool at large on life's great stage."

# SHE STOOPS TO CONQUER

BY

OLIVER GOLDSMITH

# INTRODUCTORY NOTE

OLIVER GOLDSMITH, *like his contemporary dramatist Sheridan, was an Irishman. He was born at Pallas, near Ballymahon, Longford, November 10, 1728, the son of Charles Goldsmith, a clergyman with narrow means and a large family. Through the help of relatives Oliver was able to get through his course at Trinity College, Dublin, and after various futile experiments he went to Edinburgh to study medicine. Deciding to finish his studies abroad, he set out for Leyden, whence he went traveling through France, Switzerland, and Italy, usually on foot, and earning his meals by playing to the peasants on the flute. Returning to England in 1756 in a state of destitution, he set up as a physician in London, later tried teaching, and in 1757 began his work as a literary hack in the employment of Griffiths, proprietor of the "Monthly Review." The next year he failed in an attempt to reenter the practise of medicine, and for the rest of his life was dependent on his pen and the generosity of his friends for a precarious livelihood.*

*Goldsmith's literary work began with writing for periodicals, and in this form appeared his earliest notable production, "The Chinese Letters," later republished as "The Citizen of the World." His reputation was increased by the publication of "The Traveller" in 1764, and still farther by that of "The Vicar of Wakefield" in 1766, so that he obtained abundance of work from publishers and came as near being in easy circumstances as his improvident nature permitted. In 1768 appeared his first attempt at drama, "The Good-Natured Man," which met with fair success. "The Deserted Village," issued in 1770, was immediately popular; and in 1773 "She Stoops to Conquer" was presented at Covent Garden and scored a great triumph. But Goldsmith's money was usually spent or given away before it was earned; and he died on April 4, 1774, deeply in debt.*

*Goldsmith shares with Sheridan the honor of being the only dramatist of his century whose plays are both read and acted to-day. "She Stoops to Conquer," while less brilliant in both dialogue and characterization than "The School for Scandal" is rich in amusing situations and still holds its audiences delighted with its genial and rollicking fun.*

### *To* SAMUEL JOHNSON, LL.D.

DEAR SIR,—By inscribing this slight performance to you, I do not mean so much to compliment you as myself. It may do me some honour to inform the public, that I have lived many years in intimacy with you. It may serve the interests of mankind also to inform them, that the greatest wit may be found in a character, without impairing the most unaffected piety.

I have, particularly, reason to thank you for your partiality to this performance. The undertaking a comedy not merely sentimental was very dangerous; and Mr. Colman, who saw this piece in its various stages, always thought it so. However, I ventured to trust it to the public; and, though it was necessarily delayed till late in the season, I have every reason to be grateful.

I am, dear Sir, your most sincere friend and admirer,

OLIVER GOLDSMITH.

# PROLOGUE

## BY DAVID GARRICK, ESQ.

*Enter* MR. WOODWARD, *dressed in black, and holding a handker-
chief to his eyes*

Excuse me, sirs, I pray—I can't yet speak—
I'm crying now—and have been all the week.
" 'Tis not alone this mourning suit," good masters:
" I've that within "—for which there are no plasters!
Pray, would you know the reason why I'm crying?
The Comic Muse, long sick, is now a-dying!
And if she goes, my tears will never stop;
For as a player, I can't squeeze out one drop:
I am undone, that's all—shall lose my bread—
I'd rather, but that's nothing—lose my head.
When the sweet maid is laid upon the bier,
Shuter and I shall be chief mourners here.
To her a mawkish drab of spurious breed,
Who deals in sentimentals, will succeed!
Poor Ned and I are dead to all intents;
We can as soon speak Greek as sentiments!
Both nervous grown, to keep our spirits up,
We now and then take down a hearty cup.
What shall we do? If Comedy forsake us,
They'll turn us out, and no one else will take us.
But why can't I be moral?—Let me try—
My heart thus pressing—fixed my face and eye—
With a sententious look, that nothing means,
(Faces are blocks in sentimental scenes)
Thus I begin: " All is not gold that glitters,
Pleasure seems sweet, but proves a glass of bitters.
When Ignorance enters, Folly is at hand:
Learning is better far than house and land.

Let not your virtue trip; who trips may stumble,
And virtue is not virtue, if she tumble."

I give it up—morals won't do for me;
To make you laugh, I must play tragedy.
One hope remains—hearing the maid was ill,
A Doctor comes this night to show his skill.
To cheer her heart, and give your muscles motion,
He, in Five Draughts prepar'd presents a potion:
A kind of magic charm—for be assur'd,
If you will swallow it, the maid is cur'd:
But desperate the Doctor, and her case is,
If you reject the dose, and make wry faces!
This truth he boasts, will boast it while he lives,
No poisonous drugs are mixed in what he gives.
Should he succeed, you'll give him his degree;
If not, within he will receive no fee!
The College *you,* must his pretensions back,
Pronounce him Regular, or dub him Quack.

# SHE STOOPS TO CONQUER

OR

# THE MISTAKES OF A NIGHT

### *A COMEDY*

## DRAMATIS PERSONÆ

#### MEN

| | |
|---|---|
| SIR CHARLES MARLOW . . . . | *Mr. Gardner* |
| YOUNG MARLOW (his son) . . . | *Mr. Lee Lewes* |
| HARDCASTLE . . . . . . | *Mr. Shuter* |
| HASTINGS . . . . . . | *Mr. Dubellamy* |
| TONY LUMPKIN . . . . . | *Mr. Quick* |
| DIGGORY . . . . . . | *Mr. Saunders* |

#### WOMEN

| | |
|---|---|
| MRS. HARDCASTLE . . . . | *Mrs. Green* |
| MISS HARDCASTLE . . . . | *Mrs. Bulkley* |
| MISS NEVILLE . . . . . | *Mrs. Kniveton* |
| Maid . . . . . . | *Miss Williams* |

Landlord, Servants, &c., &c.

## ACT THE FIRST

SCENE—*A Chamber in an old-fashioned House*

*Enter* MRS. HARDCASTLE *and* MR. HARDCASTLE

*Mrs. Hardcastle*

I VOW, Mr. Hardcastle, you're very particular. Is there a creature in the whole country but ourselves, that does not take a trip to town now and then, to rub off the rust a little? There's the two Miss Hoggs, and our neighbour Mrs. Grigsby, go to take a month's polishing every winter.

HARD. Ay, and bring back vanity and affectation to last them the whole year. I wonder why London cannot keep its own fools at home! In my time, the follies of the town crept slowly among us, but now they travel faster than a stage-coach. Its fopperies come down not only as inside passengers, but in the very basket.

MRS. HARD. Ay, your times were fine times indeed; you have been telling us of them for many a long year. Here we live in an old rumbling mansion, that looks for all the world like an inn, but that we never see company. Our best visitors are old Mrs. Oddfish, the curate's wife, and little Cripplegate, the lame dancing-master; and all our entertainment your old stories of Prince Eugene and the Duke of Marlborough. I hate such old-fashioned trumpery.

HARD. And I love it. I love everything that's old: old friends, old times, old manners, old books, old wine; and I believe, Dorothy (*taking her hand*), you'll own I have been pretty fond of an old wife.

MRS. HARD. Lord, Mr. Hardcastle, you're for ever at your Dorothys and your old wifes. You may be a Darby, but I'll be no Joan, I promise you. I'm not so old as you'd make me, by more than one good year. Add twenty to twenty, and make money of that.

HARD. Let me see; twenty added to twenty makes just fifty and seven.

MRS. HARD. It's false, Mr. Hardcastle; I was but twenty when I was brought to bed of Tony, that I had by Mr. Lumpkin, my first husband; and he's not come to years of discretion yet.

HARD. Nor ever will, I dare answer for him. Ay, you have taught him finely.

MRS. HARD. No matter. Tony Lumpkin has a good fortune. My son is not to live by his learning. I don't think a boy wants much learning to spend fifteen hundred a year.

HARD. Learning, quotha! a mere composition of tricks and mischief.

MRS. HARD. Humour, my dear; nothing but humour. Come, Mr. Hardcastle, you must allow the boy a little humour.

HARD. I'd sooner allow him a horse-pond. If burning the footmen's shoes, frightening the maids, and worrying the kittens be humour, he has it. It was but yesterday he fastened my wig to the back of my chair, and when I went to make a bow, I popt my bald head in Mrs. Frizzle's face.

MRS. HARD. And am I to blame? The poor boy was always too sickly to do any good. A school would be his death. When he comes to be a little stronger, who knows what a year or two's Latin may do for him?

HARD. Latin for him! A cat and fiddle. No, no; the alehouse and the stable are the only schools he'll ever go to.

MRS. HARD. Well, we must not snub the poor boy now, for I believe we sha'n't have him long among us. Anybody that looks in his face may see he's consumptive.

HARD. Ay, if growing too fat be one of the symptoms.

MRS. HARD. He coughs sometimes.

HARD. Yes, when his liquor goes the wrong way.

MRS. HARD. I'm actually afraid of his lungs.

HARD. And truly so am I; for he sometimes whoops like a speaking trumpet—(TONY *hallooing behind the scenes*)—O, there he goes—a very consumptive figure, truly.

#### Enter TONY, *crossing the stage*

MRS. HARD. Tony, where are you going, my charmer? Won't you give papa and I a little of your company, lovee?

TONY. I'm in haste, mother; I cannot stay.

MRS. HARD. You sha'n't venture out this raw evening, my dear; you look most shockingly.

TONY. I can't stay, I tell you. The Three Pigeons expects me down every moment. There's some fun going forward.

HARD. Ay; the alehouse, the old place; I thought so.

MRS. HARD. A low, paltry set of fellows.

TONY. Not so low, neither. There's Dick Muggins the exciseman, Jack Slang the horse doctor, little Aminadab that grinds the music box, and Tom Twist that spins the pewter platter.

MRS. HARD. Pray, my dear, disappoint them for one night at least.

TONY. As for disappointing them, I should not so much mind; but I can't abide to disappoint myself.

MRS. HARD. (*detaining him*). You sha'n't go.

TONY. I will, I tell you.

Mrs. Hard. I say you sha'n't.

Tony. We'll see which is strongest, you or I.

[*Exit, hauling her out.*

Hard. (*solus*). Ay, there goes a pair that only spoil each other. But is not the whole age in a combination to drive sense and discretion out of doors? There's my pretty darling Kate! the fashions of the times have almost infected her too. By living a year or two in town, she is as fond of gauze and French frippery as the best of them.

### *Enter* Miss Hardcastle

Hard. Blessings on my pretty innocence! drest out as usual, my Kate. Goodness! What a quantity of superfluous silk hast thou got about thee, girl! I could never teach the fools of this age, that the indigent world could be clothed out of the trimmings of the vain.

Miss Hard. You know our agreement, sir. You allow me the morning to receive and pay visits, and to dress in my own manner; and in the evening I put on my housewife's dress to please you.

Hard. Well, remember, I insist on the terms of our agreement; and, by the by, I believe I shall have occasion to try your obedience this very evening.

Miss Hard. I protest, sir, I don't comprehend your meaning.

Hard. Then to be plain with you, Kate, I expect the young gentleman I have chosen to be your husband from town this very day. I have his father's letter, in which he informs me his son is set out, and that he intends to follow himself shortly after.

Miss Hard. Indeed! I wish I had known something of this before. Bless me, how shall I behave? It's a thousand to one I sha'n't like him; our meeting will be so formal, and so like a thing of business, that I shall find no room for friendship or esteem.

Hard. Depend upon it, child, I'll never control your choice; but Mr. Marlow whom I have pitched upon, is the son of my old friend, Sir Charles Marlow, of whom you have heard me talk so often. The young gentleman has been bred a scholar, and is designed for an employment in the service of his country. I am told he's a man of an excellent understanding.

MISS HARD. Is he?

HARD. Very generous.

MISS HARD. I believe I shall like him.

HARD. Young and brave.

MISS HARD. I'm sure I shall like him.

HARD. And very handsome.

MISS HARD. My dear papa, say no more (*kissing his hand*), he's mine; I'll have him.

HARD. And, to crown all, Kate, he's one of the most bashful and reserved young fellows in all the world.

MISS HARD. Eh! you have frozen me to death again. That word *reserved* has undone all the rest of his accomplishments. A reserved lover, it is said, always makes a suspicious husband.

HARD. On the contrary, modesty seldom resides in a breast that is not enriched with nobler virtues. It was the very feature in his character that first struck me.

MISS HARD. He must have more striking features to catch me, I promise you. However, if he be so young, so handsome, and so everything as you mention, I believe he'll do still. I think I'll have him.

HARD. Ay, Kate, but there is still an obstacle. It's more than an even wager he may not have you.

MISS HARD. My dear papa, why will you mortify one so? Well, if he refuses, instead of breaking my heart at his indifference, I'll only break my glass for its flattery, set my cap to some newer fashion, and look out for some less difficult admirer.

HARD. Bravely resolved! In the meantime I'll go prepare the servants for his reception: as we seldom see company, they want as much training as a company of recruits the first day's muster. [*Exit.*

MISS HARD. (*Alone.*) Lud, this news of papa's puts me all in a flutter. Young, handsome: these he put last; but I put them foremost. Sensible, good-natured; I like all that. But then reserved and sheepish; that's much against him. Yet can't he be cured of his timidity, by being taught to be proud of his wife? Yes, and can't I—But I vow I'm disposing of the husband before I have secured the lover.

*Enter* MISS NEVILLE

MISS HARD. I'm glad you're come, Neville, my dear. Tell me, Constance, how do I look this evening? Is there anything whimsical about me? Is it one of my well-looking days, child? Am I in face to-day?

MISS NEV. Perfectly, my dear. Yet now I look again— bless me!—sure no accident has happened among the canary birds or the gold fishes. Has your brother or the cat been meddling? or has the last novel been too moving?

MISS HARD. No; nothing of all this. I have been threatened—I can scarce get it out—I have been threatened with a lover.

MISS NEV. And his name—

MISS HARD. Is Marlow.

MISS NEV. Indeed!

MISS HARD. The son of Sir Charles Marlow.

MISS NEV. As I live, the most intimate friend of Mr. Hastings, my admirer. They are never asunder. I believe you must have seen him when we lived in town.

MISS HARD. Never.

MISS NEV. He's a very singular character, I assure you. Among women of reputation and virtue he is the modestest man alive; but his acquaintance give him a very different character among creatures of another stamp: you understand me.

MISS HARD. An odd character indeed. I shall never be able to manage him. What shall I do? Pshaw, think no more of him, but trust to occurrences for success. But how goes on your own affair, my dear? has my mother been courting you for my brother Tony as usual?

MISS NEV. I have just come from one of our agreeable *tête-à-têtes*. She has been saying a hundred tender things, and setting off her pretty monster as the very pink of perfection.

MISS HARD. And her partiality is such, that she actually thinks him so. A fortune like yours is no small temptation.

Besides, as she has the sole management of it, I'm not surprised to see her unwilling to let it go out of the family.

Miss Nev. A fortune like mine, which chiefly consists in jewels, is no such mighty temptation. But at any rate, if my dear Hastings be but constant, I make no doubt to be too hard for her at last. However, I let her suppose that I am in love with her son; and she never once dreams that my affections are fixed upon another.

Miss Hard. My good brother holds out stoutly. I could almost love him for hating you so.

Miss Nev. It is a good-natured creature at bottom, and I'm sure would wish to see me married to anybody but himself. But my aunt's bell rings for our afternoon's walk round the improvements. *Allons!* Courage is necessary, as our affairs are critical.

Miss Hard. "Would it were bed-time, and all were well."

[*Exeunt.*

Scene—*An Alehouse Room. Several shabby Fellows with punch and tobacco.* Tony *at the head of the table, a little higher than the rest, a mallet in his hand*

Omnes. Hurrea! hurrea! hurrea! bravo!

First Fel. Now, gentlemen, silence for a song. The 'squire is going to knock himself down for a song.

Omnes. Ay, a song, a song!

Tony. Then I'll sing you, gentlemen, a song I made upon this alehouse, the Three Pigeons.

### SONG

Let schoolmasters puzzle their brain
   With grammar, and nonsense, and learning,
Good liquor, I stoutly maintain,
   Gives *genus* a better discerning.
Let them brag of their heathenish gods,
   Their Lethes, their Styxes, and Stygians,
Their Quis, and their Quæs, and their Quods,
   They're all but a parcel of Pigeons.
          Toroddle, toroddle, toroll.

When methodist preachers come down,
   A-preaching that drinking is sinful,

I'll wager the rascals a crown,
   They always preach best with a skinful.
But when you come down with your pence,
   For a slice of their scurvy religion,
I'll leave it to all men of sense,
   But you, my good friend, are the Pigeon.
               Toroddle, toroddle, toroll.

Then come, put the jorum about,
   And let us be merry and clever,
Our hearts and our liquors are stout,
   Here's the Three Jolly Pigeons for ever.
Let some cry up woodcock or hare,
   Your bustards, your ducks, and your widgeons;
But of all the *gay* birds in the air,
   Here's a health to the Three Jolly Pigeons.
               Toroddle, toroddle, toroll.

OMNES. Bravo, bravo!

FIRST FEL. The 'squire has got spunk in him.

SECOND FEL. I loves to hear him sing, bekeays he never gives us nothing that's low.

THIRD FEL. O damn anything that's low, I cannot bear it.

FOURTH FEL. The genteel thing is the genteel thing any time: if so be that a gentleman bees in a concatenation accordingly.

THIRD FEL. I likes the maxum of it, Master Muggins. What, though I am obligated to dance a bear, a man may be a gentleman for all that. May this be my poison, if my bear ever dances but to the very genteelest of tunes; "Water Parted," or "The Minuet in Ariadne."

SECOND FEL. What a pity it is the 'squire is not come to his own. It would be well for all the publicans within ten miles round of him.

TONY. Ecod, and so it would, Master Slang. I'd then show what it was to keep choice of company.

SECOND FEL. O he takes after his own father for that. To be sure old 'Squire Lumpkin was the finest gentleman I ever set my eyes on. For winding the straight horn, or beating a thicket for a hare, or a wench, he never had his fellow. It was a saying in the place, that he kept the best horses, dogs, and girls, in the whole county.

Tony. Ecod, and when I'm of age, I'll be no bastard, I promise you. I have been thinking of Bet Bouncer and the miller's grey mare to begin with. But come, my boys, drink about and be merry, for you pay no reckoning. Well, Stingo, what's the matter?

*Enter* Landlord

Land. There be two gentlemen in a post-chaise at the door. They have lost their way upo' the forest; and they are talking something about Mr. Hardcastle.

Tony. As sure as can be, one of them must be the gentleman that's coming down to court my sister. Do they seem to be Londoners?

Land. I believe they may. They look woundily like Frenchmen.

Tony. Then desire them to step this way, and I'll set them right in a twinkling. (*Exit* Landlord.) Gentlemen, as they mayn't be good enough company for you, step down for a moment, and I'll be with you in the squeezing of a lemon.

[*Exeunt mob.*

Tony (*solus*). Father-in-law has been calling me whelp and hound this half year. Now, if I pleased, I could be so revenged upon the old grumbletonian. But then I'm afraid— afraid of what? I shall soon be worth fifteen hundred a year, and let him frighten me out of *that* if he can.

*Enter* Landlord, *conducting* Marlow *and* Hastings

Mar. What a tedious uncomfortable day have we had of it! We were told it was but forty miles across the country, and we have come above threescore.

Hast. And all, Marlow, from that unaccountable reserve of yours, that would not let us inquire more frequently on the way.

Mar. I own, Hastings, I am unwilling to lay myself under an obligation to every one I meet, and often stand the chance of an unmannerly answer.

Hast. At present, however, we are not likely to receive any answer.

Tony. No offence, gentlemen. But I'm told you have been

inquiring for one Mr. Hardcastle in these parts. Do you know what part of the country you are in?

Hast. Not in the least, sir, but should thank you for information.

Tony. Nor the way you came?

Hast. No, sir; but if you can inform us—

Tony. Why, gentlemen, if you know neither the road you are going, nor where you are, nor the road you came, the first thing I have to inform you is, that—you have lost your way.

Mar. We wanted no ghost to tell us that.

Tony. Pray, gentlemen, may I be so bold so as to ask the place from whence you came?

Mar. That's not necessary towards directing us where we are to go.

Tony. No offence; but question for question is all fair, you know. Pray, gentlemen, is not this same Hardcastle a cross-grained, old-fashioned, whimsical fellow, with an ugly face, a daughter, and a pretty son?

Hast. We have not seen the gentleman; but he has the family you mention.

Tony. The daughter, a tall, trapesing, trolloping, talkative maypole; the son, a pretty, well-bred, agreeable youth, that everybody is fond of.

Mar. Our information differs in this. The daughter is said to be well-bred and beautiful; the son an awkward booby, reared up and spoiled at his mother's apron-string.

Tony. He-he-hem!—Then, gentlemen, all I have to tell you is, that you won't reach Mr. Hardcastle's house this night, I believe.

Hast. Unfortunate!

Tony. It's a damn'd long, dark, boggy, dirty, dangerous way. Stingo, tell the gentlemen the way to Mr. Hardcastle's! (*Winking upon the* Landlord.) Mr. Hardcastle's, of Quagmire Marsh, you understand me.

Land. Master Hardcastle's! Lock-a-daisy, my masters, you're come a deadly deal wrong! When you came to the bottom of the hill, you should have crossed down Squash Lane.

Mar. Cross down Squash Lane!

LAND. Then you were to keep straight forward, till you came to four roads.

MAR. Come to where four roads meet?

TONY. Ay; but you must be sure to take only one of them.

MAR. O, sir, you're facetious.

TONY. Then keeping to the right, you are to go sideways till you come upon Crackskull Common: there you must look sharp for the track of the wheel, and go forward till you come to farmer Murrain's barn. Coming to the farmer's barn, you are to turn to the right, and then to the left, and then to the right about again, till you find out the old mill—

MAR. Zounds, man! we could as soon find out the longitûde!

HAST. What's to be done, Marlow?

MAR. This house promises but a poor reception; though perhaps the landlord can accommodate us.

LAND. Alack, master, we have but one spare bed in the whole house.

TONY. And to my knowledge, that's taken up by three lodgers already. (*After a pause, in which the rest seem disconcerted.*) I have hit it. Don't you think, Stingo, our landlady could accommodate the gentlemen by the fire-side, with —three chairs and a bolster?

HAST. I hate sleeping by the fire-side.

MAR. And I detest your three chairs and a bolster.

TONY. You do, do you? then, let me see—what if you go on a mile further, to the Buck's Head; the old Buck's Head on the hill, one of the best inns in the whole county?

HAST. O ho! so we have escaped an adventure for this night, however.

LAND. (*apart to* TONY). Sure, you ben't sending them to your father's as an inn, be you?

TONY. Mum, you fool you. Let *them* find that out. (*To them.*) You have only to keep on straight forward, till you come to a large old house by the road side. You'll see a pair of large horns over the door. That's the sign. Drive up the yard, and call stoutly about you.

HAST. Sir, we are obliged to you. The servants can't miss the way?

TONY. No, no: but I tell you, though, the landlord is rich, and going to leave off business; so he wants to be thought a gentleman, saving your presence, he! he! he! He'll be for giving you his company; and, ecod, if you mind him, he'll persuade you that his mother was an alderman, and his aunt a justice of peace.

LAND. A troublesome old blade, to be sure; but a keeps as good wines and beds as any in the whole country.

MAR. Well, if he supplies us with these, we shall want no farther connection. We are to turn to the right, did you say?

TONY. No, no; straight forward. I'll just step myself, and show you a piece of the way. (*To the* Landlord.) Mum!

LAND. Ah, bless your heart, for a sweet, pleasant— damn'd mischievous son of a whore.　　　　　[*Exeunt.*

## ACT THE SECOND

SCENE—*An old-fashioned House*

*Enter* HARDCASTLE, *followed by three or four awkward* Servants

HARD. Well, I hope you are perfect in the table exercise I have been teaching you these three days. You all know your posts and your places, and can show that you have been used to good company, without ever stirring from home.

OMNES. Ay, ay.

HARD. When company comes you are not to pop out and stare, and then run in again, like frighted rabbits in a warren.

OMNES. No, no.

HARD. You, Diggory, whom I have taken from the barn, are to make a show at the side-table; and you, Roger, whom I have advanced from the plough, are to place yourself behind my chair. But you're not to stand so, with your hands in your pockets. Take your hands from your pockets, Roger; and from your head, you blockhead you. See how Diggory carries his hands. They're a little too stiff, indeed, but that's no great matter.

DIG. Ay, mind how I hold them. I learned to hold my hands this way when I was upon drill for the militia. And so being upon drill—

HARD. You must not be so talkative, Diggory. You must

be all attention to the guests. You must hear us talk, and not think of talking; you must see us drink, and not think of drinking; you must see us eat, and not think of eating.

Dig. By the laws, your worship, that's perfectly unpossible. Whenever Diggory sees yeating going forward, ecod, he's always wishing for a mouthful himself.

Hard. Blockhead! Is not a belly-full in the kitchen as good as a belly-full in the parlour? Stay your stomach with that reflection.

Dig. Ecod, I thank your worship, I'll make a shift to stay my stomach with a slice of cold beef in the pantry.

Hard. Diggory, you are too talkative.—Then, if I happen to say a good thing, or tell a good story at table, you must not all burst out a-laughing, as if you made part of the company.

Dig. Then ecod your worship must not tell the story of Ould Grouse in the gun-room: I can't help laughing at that— he! he! he!—for the soul of me. We have laughed at that these twenty years—ha! ha! ha!

Hard. Ha! ha! ha! The story is a good one. Well, honest Diggory, you may laugh at that—but still remember to be attentive. Suppose one of the company should call for a glass of wine, how will you behave? A glass of wine, sir, if you please (*to* Diggory).—Eh, why don't you move?

Dig. Ecod, your worship, I never have courage till I see the eatables and drinkables brought upo' the table, and then I'm as bauld as a lion.

Hard. What, will nobody move?

First Serv. I'm not to leave this pleace.

Second Serv. I'm sure it's no pleace of mine.

Third Serv. Nor mine, for sartain.

Dig. Wauns, and I'm sure it canna be mine.

Hard. You numskulls! and so while, like your betters, you are quarrelling for places, the guests must be starved. O you dunces! I find I must begin all over again—But don't I hear a coach drive into the yard? To your posts, you blockheads. I'll go in the mean time and give my old friend's son a hearty reception at the gate.          [*Exit* Hardcastle.

Dig. By the elevens, my pleace is gone quite out of my head.

Rog. I know that my pleace is to be everywhere.

First Serv. Where the devil is mine?

SECOND SERV. My pleace is to be nowhere at all; and so I'ze go about my business.

[*Exeunt* Servants, *running about as if frighted, different ways.*

*Enter* Servant *with candles, showing in*
MARLOW *and* HASTINGS

SERV. Welcome, gentlemen, very welcome! This way.

HAST. After the disappointments of the day, welcome once more, Charles, to the comforts of a clean room and a good fire. Upon my word, a very well-looking house; antique but creditable.

MAR. The usual fate of a large mansion. Having first ruined the master by good housekeeping, it at last comes to levy contributions as an inn.

HAST. As you say, we passengers are to be taxed to pay all these fineries. I have often seen a good sideboard, or a marble chimney-piece, though not actually put in the bill, inflame a reckoning confoundedly.

MAR. Travellers, George, must pay in all places: the only difference is, that in good inns you pay dearly for luxuries; in bad inns you are fleeced and starved.

HAST. You have lived very much among them. In truth, I have been often surprised, that you who have seen so much of the world, with your natural good sense, and your many opportunities, could never yet acquire a requisite share of assurance.

MAR. The Englishman's malady. But tell me, George, where could I have learned that assurance you talk of? My life has been chiefly spent in a college or an inn, in seclusion from that lovely part of the creation that chiefly teach men confidence. I don't know that I was ever familiarly acquainted with a single modest woman—except my mother— But among females of another class, you know—

HAST. Ay, among them you are impudent enough of all conscience.

MAR. They are of *us,* you know.

HAST. But in the company of women of reputation I never saw such an idiot, such a trembler; you look for all the world as if you wanted an opportunity of stealing out of the room.

MAR. Why, man, that's because I do want to steal out of the room. Faith, I have often formed a resolution to break the ice, and rattle away at any rate. But I don't know how, a single glance from a pair of fine eyes has totally overset my resolution. An impudent fellow may counterfeit modesty; but I'll be hanged if a modest man can ever counterfeit impudence.

HAST. If you could but say half the fine things to them that I have heard you lavish upon the bar-maid of an inn, or even a college bed-maker—

MAR. Why, George, I can't say fine things to them; they freeze, they petrify me. They may talk of a comet, or a burning mountain, or some such bagatelle; but, to me, a modest woman, drest out in all her finery, is the most tremendous object of the whole creation.

HAST. Ha! ha! ha! At this rate, man, how can you ever expect to marry?

MAR. Never; unless, as among kings and princes, my bride were to be courted by proxy. If, indeed, like an Eastern bridegroom, one were to be introduced to a wife he never saw before, it might be endured. But to go through all the terrors of a formal courtship, together with the episode of aunts, grandmothers, and cousins, and at last to blurt out the broad staring question of, Madam, will you marry me? No, no, that's a strain much above me, I assure you.

HAST. I pity you. But how do you intend behaving to the lady you are come down to visit at the request of your father?

MAR. As I behave to all other ladies. Bow very low, answer yes or no to all her demands—But for the rest, I don't think I shall venture to look in her face till I see my father's again.

HAST. I'm surprised that one who is so warm a friend can be so cool a lover.

MAR. To be explicit, my dear Hastings, my chief inducement down was to be instrumental in forwarding your happiness, not my own. Miss Neville loves you, the family don't know you; as my friend you are sure of a reception, and let honour do the rest.

Hast. My dear Marlow! But I'll suppress the emotion. Were I a wretch, meanly seeking to carry off a fortune, you should be the last man in the world I would apply to for assistance. But Miss Neville's person is all I ask, and that is mine, both from her deceased father's consent, and her own inclination.

Mar. Happy man! You have talents and art to captivate any woman. I'm doom'd to adore the sex, and yet to converse with the only part of it I despise. This stammer in my address, and this awkward prepossessing visage of mine, can never permit me to soar above the reach of a milliner's 'prentice, or one of the duchesses of Drury-lane. Pshaw! this fellow here to interrupt us.

*Enter* HARDCASTLE

Hard. Gentlemen, once more you are heartily welcome. Which is Mr. Marlow? Sir, you are heartily welcome. It's not my way, you see, to receive my friends with my back to the fire. I like to give them a hearty reception in the old style at my gate. I like to see their horses and trunks taken care of.

Mar. (*Aside.*) He has got our names from the servants already. (*To him.*) We approve your caution and hospitality, sir. (*To* HASTINGS.) I have been thinking, George, of changing our travelling dresses in the morning. I am grown confoundedly ashamed of mine.

Hard. I beg, Mr. Marlow, you'll use no ceremony in this house.

Hast. I fancy, George, you're right: the first blow is half the battle. I intend opening the campaign with the white and gold.

Hard. Mr. Marlow—Mr. Hastings—gentlemen—pray be under no constraint in this house. This is Liberty-hall, gentlemen. You may do just as you please here.

Mar. Yet, George, if we open the campaign too fiercely at first, we may want ammunition before it is over. I think to reserve the embroidery to secure a retreat.

Hard. Your talking of a retreat, Mr. Marlow, puts me in mind of the Duke of Marlborough, when we went to besiege Denain. He first summoned the garrison—

MAR. Don't you think the *ventre d'or* waistcoat will do with the plain brown?

HARD. He first summoned the garrison, which might consist of about five thousand men—

HAST. I think not: brown and yellow mix but very poorly.

HARD. I say, gentlemen, as I was telling you, he summoned the garrison, which might consist of about five thousand men—

MAR. The girls like finery.

HARD. Which might consist of about five thousand men, well appointed with stores, ammunition, and other implements of war. Now, says the Duke of Marlborough to George Brooks, that stood next to him—you must have heard of George Brooks—I'll pawn my dukedom, says he, but I take that garrison without spilling a drop of blood. So—

MAR. What, my good friend, if you gave us a glass of punch in the mean time; it would help us to carry on the siege with vigour.

HARD. Punch, sir! (*Aside.*) This is the most unaccountable kind of modesty I ever met with.

MAR. Yes, sir, punch. A glass of warm punch, after our journey, will be comfortable. This is Liberty-hall, you know.

HARD. Here's a cup, sir.

MAR. (*Aside.*) So this fellow, in his Liberty-hall, will only let us have just what he pleases.

HARD. (*Taking the cup.*) I hope you'll find it to your mind. I have prepared it with my own hands, and I believe you'll own the ingredients are tolerable. Will you be so good as to pledge me, sir? Here, Mr. Marlow, here is to our better acquaintance.                                        [*Drinks.*

MAR. (*Aside.*) A very impudent fellow this! but he's a character, and I'll humour him a little. Sir, my service to you.                                                            [*Drinks.*

HAST. (*Aside.*) I see this fellow wants to give us his company, and forgets that he's an innkeeper, before he has learned to be a gentleman.

MAR. From the excellence of your cup, my old friend, I suppose you have a good deal of business in this part of the country. Warm work, now and then, at elections, I suppose.

HARD. No, sir, I have long given that work over. Since

our betters have hit upon the expedient of electing each other, there is no business " for us that sell ale."

Hast. So, then, you have no turn for politics, I find.

Hard. Not in the least. There was a time, indeed, I fretted myself about the mistakes of government, like other people; but finding myself every day grow more angry, and the government growing no better, I left it to mend itself. Since that, I no more trouble my head about Hyder Ally, or Ally Cawn, than about Ally Croker. Sir, my service to you.

Hast. So that with eating above stairs, and drinking below, with receiving your friends within, and amusing them without, you lead a good pleasant bustling life of it.

Hard. I do stir about a great deal, that's certain. Half the differences of the parish are adjusted in this very parlour.

Mar. (*After drinking.*) And you have an argument in your cup, old gentleman, better than any in Westminster-hall.

Hard. Ay, young gentleman, that, and a little philosophy.

Mar. (*Aside.*) Well, this is the first time I ever heard of an innkeeper's philosophy.

Hast. So then, like an experienced general, you attack them on every quarter. If you find their reason manageable, you attack it with your philosophy; if you find they have no reason, you attack them with this. Here's your health, my philosopher.                                              [*Drinks.*

Hard. Good, very good, thank you; ha! ha! Your generalship puts me in mind of Prince Eugene, when he fought the Turks at the battle of Belgrade. You shall hear.

Mar. Instead of the battle of Belgrade, I believe it's almost time to talk about supper. What has your philosophy got in the house for supper?

Hard. For supper, sir! (*Aside.*) Was ever such a request to a man in his own house?

Mar. Yes, sir, supper, sir; I begin to feel an appetite. I shall make devilish work to-night in the larder, I promise you.

Hard. (*Aside.*) Such a brazen dog sure never my eyes beheld. (*To him.*) Why, really, sir, as for supper I can't well tell. My Dorothy and the cook-maid settle these things between them. I leave these kind of things entirely to them.

Mar. You do, do you?

Hard. Entirely. By the bye, I believe they are in actual

consultation upon what's for supper this moment in the kitchen.

MAR. Then I beg they'll admit me as one of their privy council. It's a way I have got. When I travel, I always choose to regulate my own supper. Let the cook be called. No offence I hope, sir.

HARD. O no, sir, none in the least; yet I don't know how; our Bridget, the cookmaid, is not very communicative upon these occasions. Should we send for her, she might scold us all out of the house.

HAST. Let's see your list of the larder then. I ask it as a favour. I always match my appetite to my bill of fare.

MAR. (*To* HARDCASTLE, *who looks at them with surprise.*) Sir, he's very right, and it's my way too.

HARD. Sir, you have a right to command here. Here, Roger, bring us the bill of fare for to-night's supper: I believe it's drawn out—Your manner, Mr. Hastings, puts me in mind of my uncle, Colonel Wallop. It was a saying of his, that no man was sure of his supper till he had eaten it.

HAST. (*Aside.*) All upon the high rope! His uncle a colonel! we shall soon hear of his mother being a justice of the peace. But let's hear the bill of fare.

MAR. (*Perusing.*) What's here? For the first course; for the second course; for the desert. The devil, sir, do you think we have brought down a whole Joiners' Company, or the corporation of Bedford, to eat up such a supper? Two or three little things, clean and comfortable, will do.

HAST. But let's hear it.

MAR. (*Reading.*) For the first course, at the top, a pig and prune sauce.

HAST. Damn your pig, I say.

MAR. And damn your prune sauce, say I.

HARD. And yet, gentlemen, to men that are hungry, pig with prune sauce is very good eating.

MAR. At the bottom, a calf's tongue and brains.

HAST. Let your brains be knocked out, my good sir, I don't like them.

MAR. Or you may clap them on a plate by themselves. I do.

HARD. (*Aside.*) Their impudence confounds me. (*To them.*) Gentlemen, you are my guests, make what altera-

tions you please. Is there anything else you wish to retrench
or alter, gentlemen?

MAR. Item, a pork pie, a boiled rabbit and sausages, a Flor-
entine, a shaking pudding, and a dish of tiff—taff—taffety
cream.

HAST. Confound your made dishes; I shall be as much at a
loss in this house as at a green and yellow dinner at the
French ambassador's table. I'm for plain eating.

HARD. I'm sorry, gentlemen, that I have nothing you like,
but if there be anything you have a particular fancy to—

MAR. Why, really, sir, your bill of fare is so exquisite, that
any one part of it is full as good as another. Send us what
you please. So much for supper. And now to see that our
beds are aired, and properly taken care of.

HARD. I entreat you'll leave that to me. You shall not stir
a step.

MAR. Leave that to you! I protest, sir, you must excuse
me, I always look to these things myself.

HARD. I must insist, sir, you'll make yourself easy on that
head.

MAR. You see I'm resolved on it. (*Aside.*) A very
troublesome fellow this, as I ever met with.

HARD. Well, sir, I'm resolved at least to attend you.
(*Aside.*) This may be modern modesty, but I never saw anything look so like old-fashioned impudence. [*Exeunt* Marlow
and Hardcastle.

HAST. (*Alone.*) So I find this fellow's civilities begin to
grow troublesome. But who can be angry at those assiduities
which are meant to please him? Ha! what do I see? Miss
Neville, by all that's happy!


*Enter* MISS NEVILLE

MISS NEV. My dear Hastings! To what unexpected good
fortune, to what accident, am I to ascribe this happy meeting?

HAST. Rather let me ask the same question, as I could
never have hoped to meet my dearest Constance at an inn.

MISS NEV. An inn! sure you mistake: my aunt, my guardian, lives here. What could induce you to think this house
an inn?

HAST. My friend, Mr. Marlow, with whom I came down, and I, have been sent here as to an inn, I assure you. A young fellow, whom we accidentally met at a house hard by, directed us hither.

MISS NEV. Certainly it must be one of my hopeful cousin's tricks, of whom you have heard me talk so often; ha! ha! ha!

HAST. He whom your aunt intends for you? he of whom I have such just apprehensions?

MISS NEV. You have nothing to fear from him, I assure you. You'd adore him, if you knew how heartily he despises me. My aunt knows it too, and has undertaken to court me for him, and actually begins to think she has made a conquest.

HAST. Thou dear dissembler! You must know, my Constance, I have just seized this happy opportunity of my friend's visit here to get admittance into the family. The horses that carried us down are now fatigued with their journey, but they'll soon be refreshed; and then, if my dearest girl will trust in her faithful Hastings, we shall soon be landed in France, where even among slaves the laws of marriage are respected.

MISS NEV. I have often told you, that though ready to obey you, I yet should leave my little fortune behind with reluctance. The greatest part of it was left me by my uncle, the India director, and chiefly consists in jewels. I have been for some time persuading my aunt to let me wear them. I fancy I'm very near succeeding. The instant they are put into my possession, you shall find me ready to make them and myself yours.

HAST. Perish the baubles! Your person is all I desire. In the mean time, my friend Marlow must not be let into his mistake. I know the strange reserve of his temper is such, that if abruptly informed of it, he would instantly quit the house before our plan was ripe for execution.

MISS NEV. But how shall we keep him in the deception? Miss Hardcastle is just returned from walking; what if we still continue to deceive him?—This, this way—

*[They confer.*

*Enter* MARLOW

MAR. The assiduities of these good people tease me beyond bearing. My host seems to think it ill manners to leave me alone, and so he claps not only himself, but his old-fashioned wife, on my back. They talk of coming to sup with us too; and then, I suppose, we are to run the gauntlet through all the rest of the family.—What have we got here?

HAST. My dear Charles! Let me congratulate you!—The most fortunate accident!—Who do you think is just alighted?

MAR. Cannot guess.

HAST. Our mistresses, boy, Miss Hardcastle and Miss Neville. Give me leave to introduce Miss Constance Neville to your acquaintance. Happening to dine in the neighbourhood, they called on their return to take fresh horses here. Miss Hardcastle has just stept into the next room, and will be back in an instant. Wasn't it lucky, eh!

MAR. (*Aside.*) I have been mortified enough of all conscience, and here comes something to complete my embarrassment.

HAST. Well, but wasn't it the most fortunate thing in the world?

MAR. Oh! yes. Very fortunate—a most joyful encounter —But our dresses, George, you know, are in disorder—What if we should postpone the happiness till to-morrow?—To-morrow at her own house—It will be every bit as convenient —and rather more respectful—To-morrow let it be.

[*Offering to go.*

MISS NEV. By no means, sir. Your ceremony will displease her. The disorder of your dress will show the ardour of your impatience. Besides, she knows you are in the house, and will permit you to see her.

MAR. O! the devil! how shall I support it? Hem! hem! Hastings, you must not go. You are to assist me, you know. I shall be confoundedly ridiculous. Yet, hang it! I'll take courage. Hem!

HAST. Pshaw, man! it's but the first plunge, and all's over. She's but a woman, you know.

MAR. And, of all women, she that I dread most to encounter.

*Enter* Miss Hardcastle, *as returned from
walking, a bonnet, &c.*

Hast. (*Introducing them.*)  Miss Hardcastle, Mr. Marlow.  I'm proud of bringing two persons of such merit together, that only want to know, to esteem each other.

Miss Hard. (*Aside.*)  Now for meeting my modest gentleman with a demure face, and quite in his own manner. (*After a pause, in which he appears very uneasy and disconcerted.*)  I'm glad of your safe arrival, sir.  I'm told you had some accidents by the way.

Mar. Only a few, madam.  Yes, we had some.  Yes, madam, a good many accidents, but should be sorry—madam —or rather glad of any accidents—that are so agreeably concluded.  Hem!

Hast. (*To him.*)  You never spoke better in your whole life.  Keep it up, and I'll insure you the victory.

Miss Hard. I'm afraid you flatter, sir.  You that have seen so much of the finest company, can find little entertainment in an obscure corner of the country.

Mar. (*Gathering courage.*)  I have lived, indeed, in the world, madam; but I have kept very little company.  I have been but an observer upon life, madam, while others were enjoying it.

Miss Nev. But that, I am told, is the way to enjoy it at last.

Hast. (*To him.*)  Cicero never spoke better.  Once more, and you are confirmed in assurance for ever.

Mar. (*To him.*)  Hem!  Stand by me, then, and when I'm down, throw in a word or two, to set me up again.

Miss Hard. An observer, like you, upon life were, I fear, disagreeably employed, since you must have had much more to censure than to approve.

Mar. Pardon me, madam.  I was always willing to be amused.  The folly of most people is rather an object of mirth than uneasiness.

Hast. (*To him.*)  Bravo, bravo.  Never spoke so well in your whole life.  Well, Miss Hardcastle, I see that you and Mr. Marlow are going to be very good company.  I believe our being here will but embarrass the interview.

Mar. Not in the least, Mr. Hastings.  We like your company of all things. (*To him.*) Zounds! George, sure you won't go, how can you leave us?

HAST. Our presence will but spoil conversation, so we'll retire to the next room. (*To him.*) You don't consider, man, that we are to manage a little *tête-à-tête* of our own.

[*Exeunt.*

MISS HARD. (*after a pause*). But you have not been wholly an observer, I presume, sir: the ladies, I should hope, have employed some part of your addresses.

MAR. (*Relapsing into timidity.*) Pardon me, madam, I—I—I—as yet have studied—only—to—deserve them.

MISS HARD. And that, some say, is the very worst way to obtain them.

MAR. Perhaps so, madam. But I love to converse only with the more grave and sensible part of the sex. But I'm afraid I grow tiresome.

MISS HARD. Not at all, sir; there is nothing I like so much as grave conversation myself; I could hear it for ever. Indeed, I have often been surprised how a man of sentiment could ever admire those light airy pleasures, where nothing reaches the heart.

MAR. It's—a disease—of the mind, madam. In the variety of tastes there must be some who, wanting a relish—for—um—a—um.

MISS HARD. I understand you, sir. There must be some, who, wanting a relish for refined pleasures, pretend to despise what they are incapable of tasting.

MAR. My meaning, madam, but infinitely better expressed. And I can't help observing—a—

MISS HARD. (*Aside.*) Who could ever suppose this fellow impudent upon some occasions? (*To him.*) You were going to observe, sir—

MAR. I was observing, madam—I protest, madam, I forget what I was going to observe.

MISS HARD. (*Aside.*) I vow and so do I. (*To him.*) You were observing, sir, that in this age of hypocrisy—something about hypocrisy, sir.

MAR. Yes, madam. In this age of hypocrisy there are few who upon strict inquiry do not—a—a—a—

MISS HARD. I understand you perfectly, sir.

MAR. (*Aside.*) Egad! and that's more than I do myself.

MISS HARD. You mean that in this hypocritical age there are few that do not condemn in public what they practise in private, and think they pay every debt to virtue when they praise it.

MAR. True, madam; those who have most virtue in their mouths, have least of it in their bosoms. But I'm sure I tire you, madam.

MISS HARD. Not in the least, sir; there's something so agreeable and spirited in your manner, such life and force—pray, sir, go on.

MAR. Yes, madam. I was saying—that there are some occasions, when a total want of courage, madam, destroys all the—and puts us—upon a—a—a—

MISS HARD. I agree with you entirely; a want of courage upon some occasions assumes the appearance of ignorance, and betrays us when we most want to excel. I beg you'll proceed.

MAR. Yes, madam. Morally speaking, madam—But I see Miss Neville expecting us in the next room. I would not intrude for the world.

MISS HARD. I protest, sir, I never was more agreeably entertained in all my life. Pray go on.

MAR. Yes, madam, I was—But she beckons us to join her. Madam, shall I do myself the honour to attend you?

MISS HARD. Well, then, I'll follow.

MAR. (*Aside.*) This pretty smooth dialogue has done for me.                                                    [*Exit.*

MISS HARD. (*Alone.*) Ha! ha! ha! Was there ever such a sober, sentimental interview? I'm certain he scarce looked in my face the whole time. Yet the fellow, but for his unaccountable bashfulness, is pretty well too. He has good sense, but then so buried in his fears, that it fatigues one more than ignorance. If I could teach him a little confidence, it would be doing somebody that I know of a piece of service. But who is that somebody?—That, faith, is a question I can scarce answer.                                    [*Exit.*

*Enter* Tony *and* Miss Neville, *followed by*
Mrs. Hardcastle *and* Hastings

Tony. What do you follow me for, cousin Con? I wonder you're not ashamed to be so very engaging.

Miss Nev. I hope, cousin, one may speak to one's own relations, and not be to blame.

Tony. Ay, but I know what sort of a relation you want to make me, though; but it won't do. I tell you, cousin Con, it won't do; so I beg you'll keep your distance, I want no nearer relationship.

[*She follows, coquetting him to the back scene.*

Mrs. Hard. Well! I vow, Mr. Hastings, you are very entertaining. There's nothing in the world I love to talk of so much as London, and the fashions, though I was never there myself.

Hast. Never there! You amaze me! From your air and manner, I concluded you had been bred all your life either at Ranelagh, St. James's, or Tower Wharf.

Mrs. Hard. O! sir, you're only pleased to say so. We country persons can have no manner at all. I'm in love with the town, and that serves to raise me above some of our neighbouring rustics; but who can have a manner, that has never seen the Pantheon, the Grotto Gardens, the Borough, and such places where the nobility chiefly resort? All I can do is to enjoy London at second-hand. I take care to know every *tête-à-tête* from the Scandalous Magazine, and have all the fashions, as they come out, in a letter from the two Miss Rickets of Crooked Lane. Pray how do you like this head, Mr. Hastings?

Hast. Extremely elegant and *dégagée,* upon my word, madam. Your friseur is a Frenchman, I suppose?

Mrs. Hard. I protest, I dressed it myself from a print in the Ladies' Memorandum-book for the last year.

Hast. Indeed! Such a head in a side box at the play-house would draw as many gazers as my Lady Mayoress at a City Ball.

Mrs. Hard. I vow, since inoculation began, there is no such thing to be seen as a plain woman; so one must dress a little particular, or one may escape in the crowd.

HAST. But that can never be your case, madam, in any dress. (*Bowing.*)

MRS. HARD. Yet, what signifies my dressing when I have such a piece of antiquity by my side as Mr. Hardcastle: all I can say will never argue down a single button from his clothes. I have often wanted him to throw off his great flaxen wig, and where he was bald, to plaster it over, like my Lord Pately, with powder.

HAST. You are right, madam; for, as among the ladies there are none ugly, so among the men there are none old.

MRS. HARD. But what do you think his answer was? Why, with his usual Gothic vivacity, he said I only wanted him to throw off his wig, to convert it into a *tête* for my own wearing.

HAST. Intolerable! At your age you may wear what you please, and it must become you.

MRS. HARD. Pray, Mr. Hastings, what do you take to be the most fashionable age about town?

HAST. Some time ago, forty was all the mode; but I'm told the ladies intend to bring up fifty for the ensuing winter.

MRS. HARD. Seriously. Then I shall be too young for the fashion.

HAST. No lady begins now to put on jewels till she's past forty. For instance, Miss there, in a polite circle, would be considered as a child, as a mere maker of samplers.

MRS. HARD. And yet Mrs. Niece thinks herself as much a woman, and is as fond of jewels, as the oldest of us all.

HAST. Your niece, is she? And that young gentleman, a brother of yours, I should presume?

MRS. HARD. My son, sir. They are contracted to each other. Observe their little sports. They fall in and out ten times a day, as if they were man and wife already. (*To them.*) Well, Tony, child, what soft things are you saying to your cousin Constance this evening?

TONY. I have been saying no soft things; but that it's very hard to be followed about so. Ecod! I've not a place in the house now that's left to myself, but the stable.

MRS. HARD. Never mind him, Con, my dear. He's in another story behind your back.

MISS NEV. There's something generous in my cousin's

manner. He falls out before faces to be forgiven in private.

TONY. That's a damned confounded—crack.

MRS. HARD. Ah! he's a sly one. Don't you think they are like each other about the mouth, Mr. Hastings? The Blenkinsop mouth to a T. They're of a size too. Back to back, my pretties, that Mr. Hastings may see you. Come, Tony.

TONY. You had as good not make me, I tell you. (*Measuring.*)

MISS NEV. O lud! he has almost cracked my head.

MRS. HARD. O, the monster! For shame, Tony. You a man, and behave so!

TONY. If I'm a man, let me have my fortin. Ecod! I'll not be made a fool of no longer.

MRS. HARD. Is this, ungrateful boy, all that I'm to get for the pains I have taken in your education? I that have rocked you in your cradle, and fed that pretty mouth with a spoon! Did not I work that waistcoat to make you genteel? Did not I prescribe for you every day, and weep while the receipt was operating?

TONY. Ecod! you had reason to weep, for you have been dosing me ever since I was born. I have gone through every receipt in the Complete Huswife ten times over; and you have thoughts of coursing me through Quincy next spring. But, ecod! I tell you, I'll not be made a fool of no longer.

MRS. HARD. Wasn't it all for your good, viper? Wasn't it all for your good?

TONY. I wish you'd let me and my good alone, then. Snubbing this way when I'm in spirits. If I'm to have any good, let it come of itself; not to keep dinging it, dinging it into one so.

MRS. HARD. That's false; I never see you when you're in spirits. No, Tony, you then go to the alehouse or kennel. I'm never to be delighted with your agreeable wild notes, unfeeling monster!

TONY. Ecod! mamma, your own notes are the wildest of the two.

MRS. HARD. Was ever the like? But I see he wants to break my heart, I see he does.

HAST. Dear madam, permit me to lecture the young gentleman a little.  I'm certain I can persuade him to his duty.

MRS. HARD. Well, I must retire.  Come, Constance, my love.  You see, Mr. Hastings, the wretchedness of my situation: was ever poor woman so plagued with a dear sweet, pretty, provoking, undutiful boy?

[*Exeunt* MRS. HARDCASTLE *and* MISS NEVILLE.

TONY. (*Singing.*) " There was a young man riding by, and fain would have his will.  Rang do didlo dee."—Don't mind her.  Let her cry.  It's the comfort of her heart.  I have seen her and sister cry over a book for an hour together; and they said they liked the book the better the more it made them cry.

HAST. Then you're no friend to the ladies, I find, my pretty young gentleman?

TONY. That's as I find 'um.

HAST. Not to her of your mother's choosing, I dare answer?  And yet she appears to me a pretty well-tempered girl.

TONY. That's because you don't know her as well as I.  Ecod!  I know every inch about her; and there's not a more bitter cantankerous toad in all Christendom.

HAST. (*Aside.*) Pretty encouragement this for a lover!

TONY. I have seen her since the height of that.  She has as many tricks as a hare in a thicket, or a colt the first day's breaking.

HAST. To me she appears sensible and silent.

TONY. Ay, before company.  But when she's with her playmate, she's as loud as a hog in a gate.

HAST. But there is a meek modesty about her that charms me.

TONY. Yes, but curb her never so little, she kicks up, and you're flung in a ditch.

HAST. Well, but you must allow her a little beauty.—Yes, you must allow her some beauty.

TONY. Bandbox!  She's all a made-up thing, mun.  Ah!  could you but see Bet Bouncer of these parts, you might then talk of beauty.  Ecod, she has two eyes as black as sloes, and cheeks as broad and red as a pulpit cushion.  She'd make two of she.

HAST. Well, what say you to a friend that would take this bitter bargain off your hands?

TONY. Anon.

HAST. Would you thank him that would take Miss Neville, and leave you to happiness and your dear Betsy?

TONY. Ay; but where is there such a friend, for who would take her?

HAST. I am he. If you but assist me, I'll engage to whip her off to France, and you shall never hear more of her.

TONY. Assist you! Ecod I will, to the last drop of my blood. I'll clap a pair of horses to your chaise that shall trundle you off in a twinkling, and may be get you a part of her fortin beside, in jewels, that you little dream of.

HAST. My dear 'squire, this looks like a lad of spirit.

TONY. Come along, then, and you shall see more of my spirit before you have done with me. (*Singing.*)

> "We are the boys
> That fears no noise
> Where the thundering cannons roar." [*Exeunt.*

## ACT THE THIRD

SCENE.—*A Room in* HARDCASTLE'S *House*

*Enter* HARDCASTLE, *alone*

HARD. What could my old friend Sir Charles mean by recommending his son as the modestest young man in town? To me he appears the most impudent piece of brass that ever spoke with a tongue. He has taken possession of the easy chair by the fire-side already. He took off his boots in the parlour, and desired me to see them taken care of. I'm desirous to know how his impudence affects my daughter. She will certainly be shocked at it.

*Enter* MISS HARDCASTLE, *plainly dressed*

HARD. Well, my Kate, I see you have changed your dress, as I bade you; and yet, I believe there was no great occasion.

MISS HARD. I find such a pleasure, sir, in obeying your commands, that I take care to observe them without ever debating their propriety.

HARD. And yet, Kate, I sometimes give you some cause, particularly when I recommended my modest gentleman to you as a lover to-day.

MISS HARD. You taught me to expect something extraordinary, and I find the original exceeds the description.

HARD. I was never so surprised in my life! He has quite confounded all my faculties!

MISS HARD. I never saw anything like it: and a man of the world too!

HARD. Ay, he learned it all abroad—what a fool was I, to think a young man could learn modesty by travelling. He might as soon learn wit at a masquerade.

MISS HARD. It seems all natural to him.

HARD. A good deal assisted by bad company and a French dancing-master.

MISS HARD. Sure you mistake, papa! A French dancing-master could never have taught him that timid look—that awkward address—that bashful manner—

HARD. Whose look? whose manner, child?

MISS HARD. Mr. Marlow's: his *mauvaise honte,* his timidity, struck me at the first sight.

HARD. Then your first sight deceived you; for I think him one of the most brazen first sights that ever astonished my senses.

MISS HARD. Sure, sir, you rally! I never saw any one so modest.

HARD. And can you be serious? I never saw such a bouncing, swaggering puppy since I was born. Bully Dawson was but a fool to him.

MISS HARD. Surprising! He met me with a respectful bow, a stammering voice, and a look fixed on the ground.

HARD. He met me with a loud voice, a lordly air, and a familiarity that made my blood freeze again.

MISS HARD. He treated me with diffidence and respect; censured the manners of the age; admired the prudence of girls that never laughed; tired me with apologies for being tiresome; then left the room with a bow; and " Madam, I would not for the world detain you."

HARD. He spoke to me as if he knew me all his life before; asked twenty questions, and never waited for an answer; interrupted my best remarks with some silly pun; and when I was in my best story of the Duke of Marlborough and Prince Eugene, he asked if I had not a good hand at making punch. Yes, Kate, he asked your father if he was a maker of punch!

MISS HARD. One of us must certainly be mistaken.

HARD. If he be what he has shown himself, I'm determined he shall never have my consent.

MISS HARD. And if he be the sullen thing I take him, he shall never have mine.

HARD. In one thing then we are agreed—to reject him.

MISS HARD. Yes; but upon conditions. For if you should find him less impudent, and I more presuming—if you find him more respectful, and I more importunate—I don't know —the fellow is well enough for a man—Certainly we don't meet many such at a horse-race in the country.

HARD. If we should find him so—But that's impossible. The first appearance has done my business. I'm seldom deceived in that.

MISS HARD. And yet there may be many good qualities under that first appearance.

HARD. Ay, when a girl finds a fellow's outside to her taste, she then sets about guessing the rest of his furniture. With her, a smooth face stands for good sense, and a genteel figure for every virtue.

MISS HARD. I hope, sir, a conversation begun with a compliment to my good sense, won't end with a sneer at my understanding?

HARD. Pardon me, Kate. But if young Mr. Brazen can find the art of reconciling contradictions, he may please us both, perhaps.

MISS HARD. And as one of us must be mistaken, what if we go to make further discoveries?

HARD. Agreed. But depend on't I'm in the right.

MISS HARD. And depend on't I'm not much in the wrong.
[*Exeunt.*

*Enter* TONY, *running in with a casket*

TONY. Ecod! I have got them. Here they are. My cousin Con's necklaces; bobs and all. My mother sha'n't cheat the poor souls out of their fortin neither. O! my genus, is that you?

*Enter* HASTINGS

HAST. My dear friend, how have you managed with your mother? I hope you have amused her with pretending love for your cousin, and that you are willing to be reconciled at last? Our horses will be refreshed in a short time, and we shall soon be ready to set off.

TONY. And here's something to bear your charges by the way (*giving the casket*); your sweetheart's jewels. Keep them: and hang those, I say, that would rob you of one of them.

HAST. But how have you procured them from your mother?

TONY. Ask me no questions, and I'll tell you no fibs. I procured them by the rule of thumb. If I had not a key to every drawer in mother's bureau, how could I go to the alehouse so often as I do? An honest man may rob himself of his own at any time.

HAST. Thousands do it every day. But to be plain with you; Miss Neville is endeavouring to procure them from her aunt this very instant. If she succeeds, it will be the most delicate way at least of obtaining them.

TONY. Well, keep them till you know how it will be. But I know how it will be well enough; she'd as soon part with the only sound tooth in her head.

HAST. But I dread the effects of her resentment, when she finds she has lost them.

TONY. Never you mind her resentment, leave *me* to manage that. I don't value her resentment the bounce of a cracker. Zounds! here they are. Morrice! Prance!

[*Exit* HASTINGS.

*Enter* MRS. HARDCASTLE *and* MISS NEVILLE

MRS. HARD. Indeed, Constance, you amaze me. Such a girl as you want jewels! It will be time enough for jewels, my dear, twenty years hence, when your beauty begins to want repairs.

MISS NEV. But what will repair beauty at forty, will certainly improve it at twenty, madam.

MRS. HARD. Yours, my dear, can admit of none. That natural blush is beyond a thousand ornaments. Besides, child, jewels are quite out at present. Don't you see half the ladies of our acquaintance, my Lady Kill-daylight and Mrs. Crump, and the rest of them, carry their jewels to town, and bring nothing but paste and marcasites back.

MISS NEV. But who knows, madam, but somebody that shall be nameless would like me best with all my little finery about me?

MRS. HARD. Consult your glasses, my dear, and then see if, with such a pair of eyes, you want any better sparklers. What do you think, Tony, my dear? does your cousin Con. want any jewels in your eyes to set off her beauty?

TONY. That's as thereafter may be.

MISS NEV. My dear aunt, if you knew how it would oblige me.

MRS. HARD. A parcel of old-fashioned rose and table-cut things. They would make you look like the court of King Solomon at a puppet-show. Besides, I believe, I can't readily come at them. They may be missing, for aught I know to the contrary.

TONY. (*Apart to* MRS. HARDCASTLE.) Then why don't you tell her so at once, as she's so longing for them? Tell her they're lost. It's the only way to quiet her. Say they're lost, and call me to bear witness.

MRS. HARD. (*Apart to* TONY.) You know, my dear, I'm only keeping them for you. So if I say they're gone, you'll bear me witness, will you? He! he! he!

TONY. Never fear me. Ecod! I'll say I saw them taken out with my own eyes.

MISS NEV. I desire them but for a day, madam. Just to be permitted to show them as relics, and then they may be locked up again.

MRS. HARD. To be plain with you, my dear Constance, if I could find them you should have them. They're missing, I assure you. Lost, for aught I know; but we must have patience wherever they are.

MISS NEV. I'll not believe it! this is but a shallow pre-

tence to deny me. I know they are too valuable to be so
slightly kept, and as you are to answer for the loss—

Mrs. Hard. Don't be alarmed, Constance. If they be
lost, I must restore an equivalent. But my son knows they
are missing, and not to be found.

Tony. That I can bear witness to. They are missing,
and not to be found; I'll take my oath on't.

Mrs. Hard. You must learn resignation, my dear; for
though we lose our fortune, yet we should not lose our
patience. See me, how calm I am.

Miss Nev. Ay, people are generally calm at the misfortunes of others.

Mrs. Hard. Now I wonder a girl of your good sense
should waste a thought upon such trumpery. We shall soon
find them; and in the mean time you shall make use of my
garnets till your jewels be found.

Miss Nev. I detest garnets.

Mrs. Hard. The most becoming things in the world to
set off a clear complexion. You have often seen how well
they look upon me. You *shall* have them.        [*Exit.*

Miss Nev. I dislike them of all things. You sha'n't stir.—
Was ever anything so provoking, to mislay my own jewels
and force me to wear her trumpery?

Tony. Don't be a fool. If she gives you the garnets, take
what you can get. The jewels are your own already. I
have stolen them out of her bureau, and she does not
know it. Fly to your spark, he'll tell you more of the
matter. Leave me to manage her.

Miss Nev. My dear cousin!

Tony. Vanish. She's here, and has missed them already.
[*Exit* Miss Neville.] Zounds! how she fidgets and spits
about like a Catherine wheel.

### Enter Mrs. Hardcastle

Mrs. Hard. Confusion! thieves! robbers! we are cheated,
plundered, broke open, undone.

Tony. What's the matter, what's the matter, mamma? I
hope nothing has happened to any of the good family!

Mrs. Hard. We are robbed. My bureau has been broken
open, the jewels taken out, and I'm undone.

Tony. Oh! is that all? Ha! ha! ha! By the laws, I never saw it acted better in my life. Ecod, I thought you was ruined in earnest, ha! ha! ha!

Mrs. Hard. Why, boy, I *am* ruined in earnest. My bureau has been broken open, and all taken away.

Tony. Stick to that: ha! ha! ha! stick to that. I'll bear witness, you know; call me to bear witness.

Mrs. Hard. I tell you, Tony, by all that's precious, the jewels are gone, and I shall be ruined for ever.

Tony. Sure I know they are gone, and I'm to say so.

Mrs. Hard. My dearest Tony, but hear me. They're gone, I say.

Tony. By the laws, mamma, you make me for to laugh, ha! ha! I know who took them well enough, ha! ha! ha!

Mrs. Hard. Was there ever such a blockhead, that can't tell the difference between jest and earnest? I tell you I'm not in jest, booby.

Tony. That's right, that's right; you must be in a bitter passion, and then nobody will suspect either of us. I'll bear witness that they are gone.

Mrs. Hard. Was there ever such a cross-grained brute, that won't hear me? Can you bear witness that you're no better than a fool? Was ever poor woman so beset with fools on one hand, and thieves on the other?

Tony. I can bear witness to that.

Mrs. Hard. Bear witness again, you blockhead you, and I'll turn you out of the room directly. My poor niece, what will become of her? Do you laugh, you unfeeling brute, as if you enjoyed my distress?

Tony. I can bear witness to that.

Mrs. Hard. Do you insult me, monster? I'll teach you to vex your mother, I will.

Tony. I can bear witness to that.

[*He runs off, she follows him.*

### *Enter* Miss Hardcastle *and* Maid

Miss Hard. What an unaccountable creature is that brother of mine, to send them to the house as an inn! ha! ha! I don't wonder at his impudence.

MAID. But what is more, madam, the young gentleman, as you passed by in your present dress, asked me if you were the bar-maid. He mistook you for the bar-maid, madam.

MISS HARD. Did he? Then as I live, I'm resolved to keep up the delusion. Tell me, Pimple, how do you like my present dress? Don't you think I look something like Cherry in the Beaux Stratagem?

MAID. It's the dress, madam, that every lady wears in the country, but when she visits or receives company.

MISS HARD. And are you sure he does not remember my face or person?

MAID. Certain of it.

MISS HARD. I vow, I thought so; for, though we spoke for some time together, yet his fears were such, that he never once looked up during the interview. Indeed, if he had, my bonnet would have kept him from seeing me.

MAID. But what do you hope from keeping him in his mistake?

MISS HARD. In the first place, I shall be seen, and that is no small advantage to a girl who brings her face to market. Then I shall perhaps make an acquaintance, and that's no small victory gained over one who never addresses any but the wildest of her sex. But my chief aim is, to take my gentleman off his guard, and, like an invisible champion of romance, examine the giant's force before I offer to combat.

MAID. But are you sure you can act your part, and disguise your voice so that he may mistake that, as he has already mistaken your person?

MISS HARD. Never fear me. I think I have got the true bar cant—Did your honour call?—Attend the Lion there—Pipes and tobacco for the Angel.—The Lamb has been outrageous this half hour.

MAID. It will do, madam. But he's here.    [*Exit* Maid.

### Enter MARLOW

MAR. What a bawling in every part of the house! I have scarce a moment's repose. If I go to the best room, there I find my host and his story: if I fly to the gallery, there we have my hostess with her curtsey down to the ground. I have at last got a moment to myself, and now for recollection.                    [*Walks and muses.*

Miss Hard. Did you call, sir? Did your honour call?

Mar. (*Musing.*) As for Miss Hardcastle, she's too grave and sentimental for me.

Miss Hard. Did your honour call? (*She still places herself before him, he turning away.*)

Mar. No, child. (*Musing.*) Besides, from the glimpse I had of her, I think she squints.

Miss Hard. I'm sure, sir, I heard the bell ring.

Mar. No, no. (*Musing.*) I have pleased my father, however, by coming down, and I'll to-morrow please myself by returning.                [*Taking out his tablets, and perusing.*

Miss Hard. Perhaps the other gentleman called, sir?

Mar. I tell you, no.

Miss Hard. I should be glad to know, sir. We have such a parcel of servants.

Mar. No, no, I tell you. (*Looks full in her face.*) Yes, child, I think I did call. I wanted—I wanted—I vow, child, you are vastly handsome.

Miss Hard. O la, sir, you'll make one ashamed.

Mar. Never saw a more sprightly malicious eye. Yes, yes, my dear, I did call. Have you got any of your—a— what d'ye call it in the house?

Miss Hard. No, sir, we have been out of that these ten days.

Mar. One may call in this house, I find, to very little purpose. Suppose I should call for a taste, just by way of a trial, of the nectar of your lips; perhaps I might be disappointed in that too.

Miss Hard. Nectar! nectar! That's a liquor there's no call for in these parts. French, I suppose. We sell no French wines here, sir.

Mar. Of true English growth, I assure you.

Miss Hard. Then it's odd I should not know it. We brew all sorts of wines in this house, and I have lived here these eighteen years.

Mar. Eighteen years! Why, one would think, child, you kept the bar before you were born. How old are you?

Miss Hard. O! sir, I must not tell my age. They say women and music should never be dated.

Mar. To guess at this distance, you can't be much above forty (*approaching*). Yet, nearer, I don't think so much (*approaching*). By coming close to some women they look younger still; but when we come very close indeed—(*attempting to kiss her*).

Miss Hard. Pray, sir, keep your distance. One would think you wanted to know one's age, as they do horses, by mark of mouth.

Mar. I protest, child, you use me extremely ill. If you keep me at this distance, how is it possible you and I can ever be acquainted?

Miss Hard. And who wants to be acquainted with you? I want no such acquaintance, not I. I'm sure you did not treat Miss Hardcastle, that was here awhile ago, in this obstropalous manner. I'll warrant me, before her you looked dashed, and kept bowing to the ground, and talked, for all the world, as if you was before a justice of peace.

Mar. (*Aside.*) Egad, she has hit it, sure enough! (*To her.*) In awe of her, child? Ha! ha! ha! A mere awkward squinting thing; no, no. I find you don't know me. I laughed and rallied her a little; but I was unwilling to be too severe. No, I could not be too severe, curse me!

Miss Hard. O! then, sir, you are a favourite, I find, among the ladies?

Mar. Yes, my dear, a great favourite. And yet hang me, I don't see what they find in me to follow. At the Ladies' Club in town I'm called their agreeable Rattle. Rattle, child, is not my real name, but one I'm known by. My name is Solomons; Mr. Solomons, my dear, at your service. (*Offering to salute her.*)

Miss Hard. Hold, sir; you are introducing me to your club, not to yourself. And you're so great a favourite there, you say?

Mar. Yes, my dear. There's Mrs. Mantrap, Lady Betty Blackleg, the countess of Sligo, Mrs. Langhorns, old Miss Biddy Buckskin, and your humble servant, keep up the spirit of the place.

Miss Hard. Then it's a very merry place, I suppose?

MAR. Yes, as merry as cards, supper, wine, and old women can make us.

MISS HARD. And their agreeable Rattle, ha! ha! ha!

MAR. (*Aside.*) Egad! I don't quite like this chit. She looks knowing, methinks. You laugh, child?

MISS HARD. I can't but laugh, to think what time they all have for minding their work or their family.

MAR. (*Aside.*) All's well; she don't laugh at me. (*To her.*) Do you ever work, child?

MISS HARD. Ay, sure. There's not a screen or quilt in the whole house but what can bear witness to that.

MAR. Odso! then you must show me your embroidery. I embroider and draw patterns myself a little. If you want a judge of your work, you must apply to me. (*Seizing her hand.*)

MISS HARD. Ay, but the colours do not look well by candlelight. You shall see all in the morning. (*Struggling.*)

MAR. And why not now, my angel? Such beauty fires beyond the power of resistance.—Pshaw! the father here! My old luck: I never nicked seven that I did not throw ames ace three times following.        [*Exit* MARLOW.

### *Enter* HARDCASTLE, *who stands in surprise*

HARD. So, madam. So, I find *this* is your *modest* lover. This is your humble admirer, that kept his eyes fixed on the ground, and only adored at humble distance. Kate, Kate, art thou not ashamed to deceive your father so?

MISS HARD. Never trust me, dear papa, but he's still the modest man I first took him for: you'll be convinced of it as well as I.

HARD. By the hand of my body, I believe his impudence is infectious! Didn't I see him seize your hand? Didn't I see him haul you about like a milkmaid? And now you talk of his respect and his modesty, forsooth!

MISS HARD. But if I shortly convince you of his modesty, that he has only the faults that will pass off with time, and the virtues that will improve with age, I hope you'll forgive him.

HARD. The girl would actually make one run mad! I tell you, I'll not be convinced. I am convinced. He has scarce been three hours in the house, and he has already encroached on all my prerogatives. You may like his impudence, and call it modesty, but my son-in-law, madam, must have very different qualifications.

MISS HARD. Sir, I ask but this night to convince you.

HARD. You shall not have half the time, for I have thoughts of turning him out this very hour.

MISS HARD. Give me that hour then, and I hope to satisfy you.

HARD. Well, an hour let it be then. But I'll have no trifling with your father. All fair and open, do you mind me?

MISS HARD. I hope, sir, you have ever found that I considered your commands as my pride; for your kindness is such, that my duty as yet has been inclination.  [*Exeunt.*

## ACT THE FOURTH

### SCENE.—*A Room in* HARDCASTLE'S *House*

#### *Enter* HASTINGS *and* MISS NEVILLE

HAST. You surprise me; Sir Charles Marlow expected here this night! Where have you had your information?

MISS NEV. You may depend upon it. I just saw his letter to Mr. Hardcastle, in which he tells him he intends setting out a few hours after his son.

HAST. Then, my Constance, all must be completed before he arrives. He knows me; and should he find me here, would discover my name, and perhaps my designs, to the rest of the family.

MISS NEV. The jewels, I hope, are safe?

HAST. Yes, yes, I have sent them to Marlow, who keeps the keys of our baggage. In the mean time, I'll go to prepare matters for our elopement. I have had the 'squire's promise of a fresh pair of horses; and if I should not see him again, will write him further directions.  [*Exit.*

MISS NEV. Well! success attend you. In the mean time I'll go and amuse my aunt with the old pretence of a violent passion for my cousin.  [*Exit.*

*Enter* MARLOW, *followed by a* Servant

MAR. I wonder what Hastings could mean by sending me so valuable a thing as a casket to keep for him, when he knows the only place I have is the seat of a post-coach at an inn-door. Have you deposited the casket with the landlady, as I ordered you? Have you put it into her own hands?

SER. Yes, your honour.

MAR. She said she'd keep it safe, did she?

SER. Yes, she said she'd keep it safe enough; she asked me how I came by it: and she said she had a great mind to make me give an account of myself.          [*Exit* Servant.

MAR. Ha! ha! ha! They're safe, however. What an unaccountable set of beings have we got amongst! This little bar-maid though runs in my head most strangely, and drives out the absurdities of all the rest of the family. She's mine, she must be mine, or I'm greatly mistaken.


*Enter* HASTINGS

HAST. Bless me! I quite forgot to tell her that I intended to prepare at the bottom of the garden. Marlow here, and in spirits too!

MAR. Give me joy, George. Crown me, shadow me with laurels! Well, George, after all, we modest fellows don't want for success among the women.

HAST. Some women, you mean. But what success has your honour's modesty been crowned with now, that it grows so insolent upon us?

MAR. Didn't you see the tempting, brisk, lovely little thing, that runs about the house with a bunch of keys to its girdle?

HAST. Well, and what then?

MAR. She's mine, you rogue you. Such fire, such motion, such eyes, such lips, but, egad! she would not let me kiss them though.

HAST. But are you so sure, so very sure of her?

MAR. Why, man, she talked of showing me her work above stairs, and I am to improve the pattern.

Hast. But how can you, Charles, go about to rob a woman of her honour?

Mar. Pshaw! pshaw! We all know the honour of the bar-maid of an inn. I don't intend to rob her, take my word for it; there's nothing in this house I shan't honestly pay for.

Hast. I believe the girl has virtue.

Mar. And if she has, I should be the last man in the world that would attempt to corrupt it.

Hast. You have taken care, I hope, of the casket I sent you to lock up? Is it in safety?

Mar. Yes, yes. It's safe enough. I have taken care of it. But how could you think the seat of a post-coach at an inn-door a place of safety? Ah! numskull! I have taken better precautions for you than you did for yourself— I have—

Hast. What?

Mar. I have sent it to the landlady to keep for you.

Hast. To the landlady!

Mar. The landlady.

Hast. You did?

Mar. I did. She's to be answerable for its forthcoming, you know.

Hast. Yes, she'll bring it forth with a witness.

Mar. Wasn't I right? I believe you'll allow that I acted prudently upon this occasion.

Hast. (*Aside.*) He must not see my uneasiness.

Mar. You seem a little disconcerted though, methinks. Sure nothing has happened?

Hast. No, nothing. Never was in better spirits in all my life. And so you left it with the landlady, who, no doubt, very readily undertook the charge.

Mar. Rather too readily. For she not only kept the casket, but, through her great precaution, was going to keep the messenger too. Ha! ha! ha!

Hast. He! he! he! They're safe, however.

Mar. As a guinea in a miser's purse.

Hast. (*Aside.*) So now all hopes of fortune are at an end, and we must set off without it. (*To him.*) Well, Charles, I'll leave you to your meditations on the pretty

bar-maid, and, he! he! he! may you be as successful for
yourself, as you have been for me!                    [*Exit.*

MAR. Thank ye, George: I ask no more.  Ha! ha! ha!


#### Enter HARDCASTLE

HARD. I no longer know my own house.  It's all topsy-
turvy.  His servants have got drunk already.  I'll bear it no
longer; and yet, from my respect for his father, I'll be
calm.  (*To him.*)  Mr. Marlow, your servant.  I'm your
very humble servant.  (*Bowing low.*)

MAR. Sir, your humble servant.  (*Aside.*)  What's to be
the wonder now?

HARD. I believe, sir, you must be sensible, sir, that no
man alive ought to be more welcome than your father's son,
sir.  I hope you think so?

MAR. I do from my soul, sir.  I don't want much en-
treaty.  I generally make my father's son welcome where-
ever he goes.

HARD. I believe you do, from my soul, sir.  But though
I say nothing to your own conduct, that of your servants
is insufferable.  Their manner of drinking is setting a
very bad example in this house, I assure you.

MAR. I protest, my very good sir, that is no fault of
mine.  If they don't drink as they ought, they are to
blame.  I ordered them not to spare the cellar.  I did, I
assure you.  (*To the side scene.*)  Here, let one of my
servants come up.  (*To him.*)  My positive directions were,
that as I did not drink myself, they should make up for
my deficiencies below.

HARD. Then they had your orders for what they do?
I'm satisfied!

MAR. They had, I assure you.  You shall hear from one
of themselves.


#### Enter Servant, *drunk*

MAR. You, Jeremy! Come forward, sirrah! What were
my orders?  Were you not told to drink freely, and call for
what you thought fit, for the good of the house?

HARD. (*Aside.*)  I begin to lose my patience.

JER. Please your honour, liberty and Fleet-street for ever! Though I'm but a servant, I'm as good as another man. I'll drink for no man before supper, sir, damme! Good liquor will sit upon a good supper, but a good supper will not sit upon—hiccup—on my conscience, sir.

MAR. You see, my old friend, the fellow is as drunk as he can possibly be. I don't know what you'd have more, unless you'd have the poor devil soused in a beer-barrel.

HARD. Zounds! he'll drive me distracted, if I contain myself any longer. Mr. Marlow—Sir; I have submitted to your insolence for more than four hours, and I see no likelihood of its coming to an end. I'm now resolved to be master here, sir; and I desire that you and your drunken pack may leave my house directly.

MAR. Leave your house!—Sure you jest, my good friend! What? when I'm doing what I can to please you.

HARD. I tell you, sir, you don't please me; so I desire you'll leave my house.

MAR. Sure you cannot be serious? At this time o' night, and such a night? You only mean to banter me.

HARD. I tell you, sir, I'm serious! and now that my passions are roused, I say this house is mine, sir; this house is mine, and I command you to leave it directly.

MAR. Ha! ha! ha! A puddle in a storm. I shan't stir a step, sir, I assure you. (*In a serious tone.*) This your house, fellow! It's my house. This is my house. Mine, while I choose to stay. What right have you to bid me leave this house, sir? I never met with such impudence, curse me; never in my whole life before.

HARD. Nor I, confound me if ever I did. To come to my house, to call for what he likes, to turn me out of my own chair, to insult the family, to order his servants to get drunk, and then to tell me, "This house is mine, sir." By all that's impudent, it makes me laugh. Ha! ha! ha! Pray, sir (*bantering*), as you take the house, what think you of taking the rest of the furniture? There's a pair of silver candlesticks, and there's a fire-screen, and here's a pair of brazen-nozed bellows; perhaps you may take a fancy to them?

MAR. Bring me your bill, sir; bring me your bill, and let's make no more words about it.

HARD. There are a set of prints, too. What think you of the Rake's Progress, for your own apartment?

MAR. Bring me your bill, I say; and I'll leave you and your infernal house directly.

HARD. Then there's a mahogany table that you may see your own face in.

MAR. My bill, I say.

HARD. I had forgot the great chair for your own particular slumbers, after a hearty meal.

MAR. Zounds! bring me my bill, I say, and let's hear no more on't.

HARD. Young man, young man, from your father's letter to me, I was taught to expect a well-bred modest man as a visitor here, but now I find him no better than a coxcomb and a bully; but he will be down here presently, and shall hear more of it.                                    [*Exit.*

MAR. How's this? Sure I have not mistaken the house. Everything looks like an inn. The servants cry, coming; the attendance is awkward; the bar-maid, too, to attend us. But she's here, and will further inform me. Whither so fast, child? A word with you.


*Enter* MISS HARDCASTLE

MISS HARD. Let it be short, then. I'm in a hurry. (*Aside.*) I believe he begins to find out his mistake. But it's too soon quite to undeceive him.

MAR. Pray, child, answer me one question. What are you, and what may your business in this house be?

MISS HARD. A relation of the family, sir.

MAR. What, a poor relation?

MISS HARD. Yes, sir. A poor relation, appointed to keep the keys, and to see that the guests want nothing in my power to give them.

MAR. That is, you act as the bar-maid of this inn.

MISS HARD. Inn! O law—what brought that in your head? One of the best families in the country keep an inn—Ha! ha! ha! old Mr. Hardcastle's house an inn!

Mar. Mr. Hardcastle's house! Is this Mr. Hardcastle's house, child?

Miss Hard. Ay, sure! Whose else should it be?

Mar. So then, all's out, and I have been damnably imposed on. O, confound my stupid head, I shall be laughed at over the whole town. I shall be stuck up in caricatura in all the print-shops. The *Dullissimo Maccaroni*. To mistake this house of all others for an inn, and my father's old friend for an innkeeper! What a swaggering puppy must he take me for! What a silly puppy do I find myself! There again, may I be hanged, my dear, but I mistook you for the bar-maid.

Miss Hard. Dear me! dear me! I'm sure there's nothing in my *behaviour* to put me on a level with one of that stamp.

Mar. Nothing, my dear, nothing. But I was in for a list of blunders, and could not help making you a subscriber. My stupidity saw everything the wrong way. I mistook your assiduity for assurance, and your simplicity for allurement. But it's over. This house I no more show *my* face in.

Miss Hard. I hope, sir, I have done nothing to disoblige you. I'm sure I should be sorry to affront any gentleman who has been so polite, and said so many civil things to me. I'm sure I should be sorry (*pretending to cry*) if he left the family upon my account. I'm sure I should be sorry if people said anything amiss, since I have no fortune but my character.

Mar. (*Aside.*) By Heaven! she weeps. This is the first mark of tenderness I ever had from a modest woman, and it touches me. (*To her.*) Excuse me, my lovely girl; you are the only part of the family I leave with reluctance. But to be plain with you, the difference of our birth, fortune, and education, makes an honourable connexion impossible; and I can never harbour a thought of seducing simplicity that trusted in my honour, of bringing ruin upon one whose only fault was being too lovely.

Miss Hard. (*Aside.*) Generous man! I now begin to admire him. (*To him.*) But I am sure my family is as good as Miss Hardcastle's; and though I'm poor, that's no great misfortune to a contented mind; and, until this moment, I never thought that it was bad to want a fortune.

Mar. And why now, my pretty simplicity?

Miss Hard. Because it puts me at a distance from one that, if I had a thousand pounds, I would give it all to.

Mar. (*Aside.*) This simplicity bewitches me so, that if I stay, I'm undone. I must make one bold effort, and leave her. (*To her.*) Your partiality in my favour, my dear, touches me most sensibly: and were I to live for myself alone, I could easily fix my choice. But I owe too much to the opinion of the world, too much to the authority of a father; so that—I can scarcely speak it—it affects me. Farewell. [*Exit.*

Miss Hard. I never knew half his merit till now. He shall not go, if I have power or art to detain him. I'll still preserve the character in which I *stooped to conquer;* but will undeceive my papa, who perhaps may laugh him out of his resolution. [*Exit.*

### Enter Tony *and* Miss Neville

Tony. Ay, you may steal for yourselves the next time. I have done my duty. She has got the jewels again, that's a sure thing; but she believes it was all a mistake of the servants.

Miss Nev. But, my dear cousin, sure you won't forsake us in this distress? If she in the least suspects that I'm going off, I shall certainly be locked up, or sent to my aunt Pedigree's, which is ten times worse.

Tony. To be sure, aunts of all kinds are damned bad things. But what can I do? I have got you a pair of horses that will fly like Whistle-jacket; and I'm sure you can't say but I have courted you nicely before her face. Here she comes, we must court a bit or two more, for fear she should suspect us. [*They retire, and seem to fondle.*

### Enter Mrs. Hardcastle

Mrs. Hard. Well, I was greatly fluttered, to be sure. But my son tells me it was all a mistake of the servants. I shan't be easy, however, till they are fairly married, and then let her keep her own fortune. But what do I see? fondling together, as I'm alive. I never saw Tony so sprightly before. Ah! have I caught you, my pretty doves? What, billing, exchanging stolen glances and broken murmurs? Ah!

TONY. As for murmurs, mother, we grumble a little now and then, to be sure. But there's no love lost between us.

MRS. HARD. A mere sprinkling, Tony, upon the flame, only to make it burn brighter.

MISS NEV. Cousin Tony promises to give us more of his company at home. Indeed, he shan't leave us any more. It won't leave us, cousin Tony, will it?

TONY. O! it's a pretty creature. No, I'd sooner leave my horse in a pound, than leave you when you smile upon one so. Your laugh makes you so becoming.

MISS NEV. Agreeable cousin! Who can help admiring that natural humour, that pleasant, broad, red, thoughtless (*patting his cheek*)—ah! it's a bold face.

MRS. HARD. Pretty innocence!

TONY. I'm sure I always loved cousin Con.'s hazel eyes, and her pretty long fingers, that she twists this way and that over the haspicholls, like a parcel of bobbins.

MRS. HARD. Ah! he would charm the bird from the tree. I was never so happy before. My boy takes after his father, poor Mr. Lumpkin, exactly. The jewels, my dear Con., shall be yours incontinently. You shall have them. Isn't he a sweet boy, my dear? You shall be married to-morrow, and we'll put off the rest of his education, like Dr. Drowsy's sermons, to a fitter opportunity.

*Enter* DIGGORY

DIG. Where's the 'squire? I have got a letter for your worship.

TONY. Give it to my mamma. She reads all my letters first.

DIG. I had orders to deliver it into your own hands.

TONY. Who does it come from?

DIG. Your worship mun ask that o' the letter itself.

TONY. I could wish to know though (*turning the letter, and gazing on it*).

MISS NEV. (*Aside.*) Undone! undone! A letter to him from Hastings. I know the hand. If my aunt sees it, we are ruined for ever. I'll keep her employed a little if I can. (*To* MRS. HARDCASTLE.) But I have not told you, madam, of my cousin's smart answer just now to Mr. Marlow. We so laughed.—You must know, madam.—This way a little, for he must not hear us.          [*They confer.*

TONY. (*Still gazing.*) A damned cramp piece of penmanship, as ever I saw in my life. I can read your print hand very well. But here are such handles, and shanks, and dashes, that one can scarce tell the head from the tail.— " To Anthony Lumpkin, Esquire." It's very odd, I can read the outside of my letters, where my own name is, well enough; but when I come to open it, it's all—buzz. That's hard, very hard; for the inside of the letter is always the cream of the correspondence.

MRS. HARD. Ha! ha! ha! Very well, very well. And so my son was too hard for the philosopher.

MISS NEV. Yes, madam; but you must hear the rest, madam. A little more this way, or he may hear us. You'll hear how he puzzled him again.

MRS. HARD. He seems strangely puzzled now himself, methinks.

TONY. (*Still gazing.*) A damned up and down hand, as if it was disguised in liquor.—(*Reading.*) Dear sir,—ay, that's that. Then there's an M, and a T, and an S, but whether the next be an izzard, or an R, confound me, I cannot tell.

MRS. HARD. What's that, my dear? Can I give you any assistance?

MISS NEV. Pray, aunt, let me read it. Nobody reads a cramp hand better than I. (*Twitching the letter from him.*) Do you know who it is from?

·TONY. Can't tell, except from Dick Ginger, the feeder.

MISS NEV. Ay, so it is. (*Pretending to read.*) Dear 'Squire, hoping that you're in health, as I am at this present. The gentlemen of the Shake-bag club has cut the gentlemen of Goose-green quite out of feather. The odds—um—odd battle—um—long fighting—um—here, here, it's all about cocks and fighting; it's of no consequence; here, put it up, put it up. (*Thrusting the crumpled letter upon him.*)

Tony. But I tell you, miss, it's of all the consequence in the world. I would not lose the rest of it for a guinea. Here, mother, do you make it out. Of no consequence! (*Giving* Mrs. Hardcastle *the letter.*)

Mrs. Hard. How's this?—(*Reads.*) "Dear 'Squire, I'm now waiting for Miss Neville, with a post-chaise and pair, at the bottom of the garden, but I find my horses yet unable to perform the journey. I expect you'll assist us with a pair of fresh horses, as you promised. Dispatch is necessary, as the *hag* (ay, the hag,) your mother, will otherwise suspect us! Yours, Hastings." Grant me patience. I shall run distracted! My rage chokes me.

Miss Nev. I hope, madam, you'll suspend your resentment for a few moments, and not impute to me any impertinence, or sinister design, that belongs to another.

Mrs. Hard. (*Curtseying very low.*) Fine spoken, madam, you are most miraculously polite and engaging, and quite the very pink of curtesy and circumspection, madam. (*Changing her tone.*) And you, you great ill-fashioned oaf, with scarce sense enough to keep your mouth shut: were you, too, joined against me? But I'll defeat all your plots in a moment. As for you, madam, since you have got a pair of fresh horses ready, it would be cruel to disappoint them. So, if you please, instead of running away with your spark, prepare, this moment, to run off with *me*. Your old aunt Pedigree will keep you secure, I'll warrant me. You too, sir, may mount your horse, and guard us upon the way. Here, Thomas, Roger, Diggory! I'll show you, that I wish you better than you do yourselves.          [*Exit.*

Miss Nev. So now I'm completely ruined.

Tony. Ay, that's a sure thing.

Miss Nev. What better could be expected from being connected with such a stupid fool,—and after all the nods and signs I made him?

Tony. By the laws, miss, it was your own cleverness, and not my stupidity, that did your business. You were so nice and so busy with your Shake-bags and Goose-greens, that I thought you could never be making believe.

### *Enter* HASTINGS

HAST. So, sir, I find by my servant, that you have shown my letter, and betrayed us. Was this well done, young gentleman?

TONY. Here's another. Ask miss there, who betrayed you. Ecod, it was her doing, not mine.

### *Enter* MARLOW

MAR. So I have been finely used here among you. Rendered contemptible, driven into ill manners, despised, insulted, laughed at.

TONY. Here's another. We shall have old Bedlam broke loose presently.

MISS NEV. And there, sir, is the gentleman to whom we all owe every obligation.

MAR. What can I say to him, a mere boy, an idiot, whose ignorance and age are a protection?

HAST. A poor contemptible booby, that would but disgrace correction.

MISS NEV. Yet with cunning and malice enough to make himself merry with all our embarrassments.

HAST. An insensible cub.

MAR. Replete with tricks and mischief.

TONY. Baw! damme, but I'll fight you both, one after the other—with baskets.

MAR. As for him, he's below resentment. But your conduct, Mr. Hastings, requires an explanation. You knew of my mistakes, yet would not undeceive me.

HAST. Tortured as I am with my own disappointments, is this a time for explanations? It is not friendly, Mr. Marlow.

MAR. But, sir—

MISS NEV. Mr. Marlow, we never kept on your mistake till it was too late to undeceive you.

*Enter* Servant

SER. My mistress desires you'll get ready immediately, madam. The horses are putting to. Your hat and things are in the next room. We are to go thirty miles before morning.                                    [*Exit* Servant.

MISS NEV. Well, well; I'll come presently.

MAR. (*To* HASTINGS.) Was it well done, sir, to assist in rendering me ridiculous? To hang me out for the scorn of all my acquaintance? Depend upon it, sir, I shall expect an explanation.

HAST. Was it well done, sir, if you're upon that subject to deliver what I entrusted to yourself, to the care of another, sir?

MISS NEV. Mr. Hastings! Mr. Marlow! Why will you increase my distress by this groundless dispute? I implore, I entreat you—

*Enter* Servant

SER. Your cloak, madam. My mistress is impatient.
                                    [*Exit* Servant.

MISS NEV. I come. Pray be pacified. If I leave you thus, I shall die with apprehension.

*Enter* Servant

SER. Your fan, muff, and gloves, madam. The horses are waiting.

MISS NEV. O, Mr. Marlow! if you knew what a scene of constraint and ill-nature lies before me, I'm sure it would convert your resentment into pity.

MAR. I'm so distracted with a variety of passions, that I don't know what I do. Forgive me, madam. George, forgive me. You know my hasty temper, and should not exasperate it.

HAST. The torture of my situation is my only excuse.

MISS NEV. Well, my dear Hastings, if you have that esteem for me that I think, that I am sure you have, your constancy for three years will but increase the happiness of our future connexion. If—

MRS. HARD.: (*Within.*) Miss Neville. Constance, why, Constance, I say.

MISS NEV. I'm coming. Well constancy, remember, constancy is the word.                                      [*Exit.*

HAST. My heart! how can I support this? To be so near happiness, and such happiness!

MAR. (*To* TONY.) You see now, young gentleman, the effects of your folly. What might be amusement to you, is here disappointment, and even distress.

TONY. (*From a reverie.*) Ecod, I have hit it. It's here. Your hands. Yours and yours, my poor Sulky!—My boots there, ho!—Meet me two hours hence at the bottom of the garden; and if you don't find Tony Lumpkin a more good-natured fellow than you thought for, I'll give you leave to take my best horse, and Bet Bouncer into the bargain. Come along. My boots, ho!                          [*Exeunt.*


## ACT THE FIFTH
### (SCENE *continued*)

### Enter HASTINGS *and* Servant.

HAST. You saw the old lady and Miss Neville drive off, you say?

SER. Yes, your honour. They went off in a post-coach, and the young 'squire went on horseback. They're thirty miles off by this time.

HAST. Then all my hopes are over.

SER. Yes, sir. Old Sir Charles has arrived. He and the old gentleman of the house have been laughing at Mr. Marlow's mistake this half hour. They are coming this way.

HAST. Then I must not be seen. So now to my fruitless appointment at the bottom of the garden. This is about the time.                                            [*Exit.*

### Enter SIR CHARLES *and* HARDCASTLE

HARD. Ha! ha! ha! The peremptory tone in which he sent forth his sublime commands!

Sir Cha. And the reserve with which I suppose he treated all your advances.

Hard. And yet he might have seen something in me above a common innkeeper, too.

Sir Cha. Yes, Dick, but he mistook you for an uncommon innkeeper, ha! ha! ha!

Hard. Well, I'm in too good spirits to think of anything but joy. Yes, my dear friend, this union of our families will make our personal friendships hereditary; and though my daughter's fortune is but small—

Sir Cha. Why, Dick, will you talk of fortune to *me?* My son is possessed of more than a competence already, and can want nothing but a good and virtuous girl to share his happiness and increase it. If they like each other, as you say they do—

Hard. *If,* man! I tell you they *do* like each other. My daughter as good as told me so.

Sir Cha. But girls are apt to flatter themselves, you know.

Hard. I saw him grasp her hand in the warmest manner myself; and here he comes to put you out of your *ifs,* I warrant him.

### *Enter* MARLOW

Mar. I come, sir, once more, to ask pardon for my strange conduct. I can scarce reflect on my insolence without confusion.

Hard. Tut, boy, a trifle! You take it too gravely. An hour or two's laughing with my daughter will set all to rights again. She'll never like you the worse for it.

Mar. Sir, I shall be always proud of her approbation.

Hard. Approbation is but a cold word, Mr. Marlow; if I am not deceived, you have something more than approbation thereabouts. You take me?

Mar. Really, sir, I have not that happiness.

Hard. Come, boy, I'm an old fellow and know what's what as well as you that are younger. I know what has passed between you; but mum.

Mar. Sure, sir, nothing has passed between us but the most profound respect on my side, and the most distant re-

HC XVIII—I

serve on hers. You don't think, sir, that my impudence has been passed upon all the rest of the family.

HARD. Impudence! No, I don't say that—not quite impudence—though girls like to be played with, and rumpled a little too, sometimes. But she has told no tales, I assure you.

MAR. I never gave her the slightest cause.

HARD. Well, well, I like modesty in its place well enough. But this is over-acting, young gentleman. You may be open. Your father and I will like you all the better for it.

MAR. May I die, sir, if I ever—

HARD. I tell you, she don't dislike you; and as I'm sure you like her—

MAR. Dear sir—I protest, sir—

HARD. I see no reason why you should not be joined as fast as the parson can tie you.

MAR. But hear me, sir—

HARD. Your father approves the match, I admire it; every moment's delay will be doing mischief. So—

MAR. But why won't you hear me? By all that's just and true, I never gave Miss Hardcastle the slightest mark of my attachment, or even the most distant hint to suspect me of affection. We had but one interview, and that was formal, modest, and uninteresting.

HARD. (*Aside.*) This fellow's formal modest impudence is beyond bearing.

SIR CHA. And you never grasped her hand, or made any protestations?

MAR. As Heaven is my witness, I came down in obedience to your commands. I saw the lady without emotion, and parted without reluctance. I hope you'll exact no farther proofs of my duty, nor prevent me from leaving a house in which I suffer so many mortifications.          [*Exit.*

SIR CHA. I'm astonished at the air of sincerity with which he parted.

HARD. And I'm astonished at the deliberate intrepidity of his assurance.

SIR CHA. I dare pledge my life and honour upon his truth.

HARD. Here comes my daughter, and I would stake my happiness upon her veracity.

*Enter* Miss Hardcastle

HARD. Kate, come hither, child. Answer us sincerely and without reserve: has Mr. Marlow made you any professions of love and affection?

MISS HARD. The question is very abrupt, sir. But since you require unreserved sincerity, I think he has.

HARD. (*To* SIR CHARLES.) You see.

SIR CHA. And pray, madam, have you and my son had more than one interview?

MISS HARD. Yes, sir, several.

HARD. (*To* SIR CHARLES.) You see.

SIR CHA. But did he profess any attachment?

MISS HARD. A lasting one.

SIR CHA. Did he talk of love?

MISS HARD. Much, sir.

SIR CHA. Amazing! And all this formally?

MISS HARD. Formally.

HARD. Now, my friend, I hope you are satisfied.

SIR CHA. And how did he behave, madam?

MISS HARD. As most profest admirers do: said some civil things of my face, talked much of his want of merit, and the greatness of mine; mentioned his heart, gave a short tragedy speech, and ended with pretended rapture.

SIR CHA. Now I'm perfectly convinced, indeed. I know his conversation among women to be modest and submissive: this forward canting ranting manner by no means describes him; and, I am confident, he never sat for the picture.

MISS HARD. Then, what, sir, if I should convince you to your face of my sincerity? If you and my papa in about half an hour, will place yourselves behind that screen, you shall hear him declare his passion to me in person.

SIR CHA. Agreed. And if I find him what you describe, all my happiness in him must have an end.          [*Exit.*

MISS HARD. And if you don't find him what I describe—I fear my happiness must never have a beginning. [*Exeunt.*

*SCENE changes to the back of the Garden*

*Enter* HASTINGS

HAST. What an idiot am I, to wait here for a fellow who probably takes a delight in mortifying me. He never intended to be punctual, and I'll wait no longer. What do I see? It is he! and perhaps with news of my Constance.


*Enter* TONY, *booted and spattered*

HAST. My honest 'squire! I now find you a man of your word. This looks like friendship.

TONY. Ay, I'm your friend, and the best friend you have in the world, if you knew but all. This riding by night, by the bye, is cursedly tiresome. It has shook me worse than the basket of a stage-coach.

HAST. But how? where did you leave your fellow-travellers? Are they in safety? Are they housed?

TONY. Five and twenty miles in two hours and a half is no such bad driving. The poor beasts have smoked for it: rabbit me, but I'd rather ride forty miles after a fox than ten with such varment.

HAST. Well, but where have you left the ladies? I die with impatience.

TONY. Left them! Why where should I leave them but where I found them?

HAST. This is a riddle.

TONY. Riddle me this, then. What's that goes round the house, and round the house, and never touches the house?

HAST. I'm still astray.

TONY. Why, that's it, mon. I have led them astray. By jingo, there's not a pond or a slough within five miles of the place but they can tell the taste of.

HAST. Ha! ha! ha! I understand: you took them in a round, while they supposed themselves going forward, and so you have at last brought them home again.

TONY. You shall hear. I first took them down Feather-bed Lane, where we stuck fast in the mud. I then rattled them **crack** over the stones of Up-and-down Hill. I then intro-

that forty miles in four hours was very good going. Hem.
As to be sure it was. Hem. I have got a sort of cold by
being out in the air. We'll go in, if you please. Hem.

HARD. But if you talked to yourself you did not answer
yourself. I'm certain I heard two voices, and am resolved
(*raising his voice*) to find the other out.

MRS. HARD. (*From behind.*) Oh! he's coming to find me
out. Oh!

TONY. What need you go, sir, if I tell you? Hem. I'll
lay down my life for the truth—hem—I'll tell you all, sir.

        [*Detaining him.*

HARD. I tell you I will not be detained. I insist on seeing.
It's in vain to expect I'll believe you.

MRS. HARD. (*Running forward from behind.*) O lud! he'll
murder my poor boy, my darling! Here, good gentleman,
whet your rage upon me. Take my money, my life, but
spare that young gentleman; spare my child, if you have
any mercy.

HARD. My wife, as I'm a Christian. From whence can
she come? or what does she mean?

MRS. HARD. (*Kneeling.*) Take compassion on us, good
Mr. Highwayman. Take our money, our watches, all we
have, but spare our lives. We will never bring you to
justice; indeed we won't, good Mr. Highwayman.

HARD. I believe the woman's out of her senses. What,
Dorothy, don't you know *me?*

MRS. HARD. Mr. Hardcastle, as I'm alive! My fears
blinded me. But who, my dear, could have expected to meet
you here, in this frightful place, so far from home? What
has brought you to follow us?

HARD. Sure, Dorothy, you have not lost your wits? So
far from home, when you are within forty yards of your own
door! (*To him.*) This is one of your old tricks, you
graceless rogue, you. (*To her.*) Don't you know the gate,
and the mulberry-tree; and don't you remember the horse-
pond, my dear?

MRS. HARD. Yes, I shall remember the horse-pond as long
as I live; I have caught my death in it. (*To* TONY.) And
is it to you, you graceless varlet, I owe all this? I'll teach you
to abuse your mother, I will.

TONY. Ecod, mother, all the parish says you have spoiled me, and so you may take the fruits on't.

MRS. HARD. I'll spoil you, I will.

[*Follows him off the stage.   Exit.*

HARD. There's morality, however, in his reply.       [*Exit.*


*Enter* HASTINGS *and* MISS NEVILLE

HAST. My dear Constance, why will you deliberate thus? If we delay a moment, all is lost for ever. Pluck up a little resolution, and we shall soon be out of the reach of her malignity.

MISS NEV. I find it impossible. My spirits are so sunk with the agitations I have suffered, that I am unable to face any new danger. Two or three years' patience will at last crown us with happiness.

HAST. Such a tedious delay is worse than inconstancy. Let us fly, my charmer. Let us date our happiness from this very moment. Perish fortune! Love and content will increase what we possess beyond a monarch's revenue. Let me prevail!

MISS NEV. No, Mr. Hastings, no. Prudence once more comes to my relief, and I will obey its dictates. In the moment of passion fortune may be despised, but it ever produces a lasting repentance. I'm resolved to apply to Mr. Hardcastle's compassion and justice for redress.

HAST. But though he had the will, he has not the power to relieve you.

MISS NEV. But he has influence, and upon that I am resolved to rely.

HAST. I have no hopes. But since you persist, I must reluctantly obey you.                          [*Exeunt.*


SCENE *changes*

*Enter* SIR CHARLES *and* MISS HARDCASTLE

SIR CHA. What a situation am I in! If what you say appears, I shall then find a guilty son. If what he says be true, I shall then lose one that, of all others, I most wished for a daughter.

Miss Hard. I am proud of your approbation, and to show I merit it, if you place yourselves as I directed, you shall hear his explicit declaration. But he comes.

Sir Cha. I'll to your father, and keep him to the appointment. [*Exit* Sir Charles.

*Enter* Marlow

Mar. Though prepared for setting out, I come once more to take leave; nor did I, till this moment, know the pain I feel in the separation.

Miss Hard. (*In her own natural manner.*) I believe these sufferings cannot be very great, sir, which you can so easily remove. A day or two longer, perhaps, might lessen your uneasiness, by showing the little value of what you now think proper to regret.

Mar. (*Aside.*) This girl every moment improves upon me. (*To her.*) It must not be, madam. I have already trifled too long with my heart. My very pride begins to submit to my passion. The disparity of education and fortune, the anger of a parent, and the contempt of my equals, begin to lose their weight; and nothing can restore me to myself but this painful effort of resolution.

Miss Hard. Then go, sir: I'll urge nothing more to detain you. Though my family be as good as hers you came down to visit, and my education, I hope, not inferior, what are these advantages without equal affluence? I must remain contented with the slight approbation of imputed merit; I must have only the mockery of your addresses, while all your serious aims are fixed on fortune.

*Enter* Hardcastle *and* Sir Charles *from behind*

Sir Cha. Here, behind this screen.

Hard. Ay, ay; make no noise. I'll engage my Kate covers him with confusion at last.

Mar. By heavens, madam! fortune was ever my smallest consideration. Your beauty at first caught my eye; for who could see that without emotion? But every moment that I converse with you steals in some new grace, heightens the picture, and gives it stronger expression. What at first

seemed rustic plainness, now appears refined simplicity.
What seemed forward assurance, now strikes me as the result
of courageous innocence and conscious virtue.

SIR CHA. What can it mean?  He amazes me!

HARD. I told you how it would be.  Hush!

MAR. I am now determined to stay, madam; and I have too
good an opinion of my father's discernment, when he sees
you, to doubt his approbation.

MISS HARD. No, Mr. Marlow, I will not, cannot detain
you.  Do you think I could suffer a connexion in which
there is the smallest room for repentance?  Do you
think I would take the mean advantage of a transient
passion, to load you with confusion?  Do you think I could
ever relish that happiness which was acquired by lessen-
ing yours?

MAR. By all that's good, I can have no happiness but what's
in your power to grant me!  Nor shall I ever feel repentance
but in not having seen your merits before.  I will stay even
contrary to your wishes; and though you should persist to
shun me, I will make my respectful assiduities atone for the
levity of my past conduct.

MISS HARD. Sir, I must entreat you'll desist.  As our acquaintance began, so let it end, in indifference.  I might have
given an hour or two to levity; but seriously, Mr. Marlow,
do you think I could ever submit to a connexion where
I must appear mercenary, and you imprudent?  Do you
think I could ever catch at the confident addresses of a
secure admirer?

MAR. (*Kneeling.*) Does this look like security?  Does this
look like confidence?  No, madam, every moment that shows
me your merit, only serves to increase my diffidence and confusion.  Here let me continue—

SIR CHA. I can hold it no longer.  Charles, Charles, how
hast thou deceived me!  Is this your indifference, your uninteresting conversation?

HARD. Your cold contempt; your formal interview!  What
have you to say now?

MAR. That I'm all amazement!  What can it mean?

HARD. It means that you can say and unsay things at
pleasure: that you can address a lady in private, and deny it

in public: that you have one story for us, and another for my daughter.

Mar. Daughter!—This lady your daughter?

Hard. Yes, sir, my only daughter; my Kate; whose else should she be?

Mar. Oh, the devil!

Miss Hard. Yes, sir, that very identical tall squinting lady you were pleased to take me for (*courtesying*); she that you addressed as the mild, modest, sentimental man of gravity, and the bold, forward, agreeable Rattle of the Ladies' Club. Ha! ha! ha!

Mar. Zounds! there's no bearing this; it's worse than death!

Miss Hard. In which of your characters, sir, will you give us leave to address you? As the faltering gentleman, with looks on the ground, that speaks just to be heard, and hates hypocrisy; or the loud confident creature, that keeps it up with Mrs. Mantrap, and old Miss Biddy Buckskin, till three in the morning? Ha! ha! ha!

Mar. O, curse on my noisy head. I never attempted to be impudent yet, that I was not taken down. I must be gone.

Hard. By the hand of my body, but you shall not. I see it was all a mistake, and I am rejoiced to find it. You shall not, sir, I tell you. I know she'll forgive you. Won't you forgive him, Kate? We'll all forgive you. Take courage, man. (*They retire, she tormenting him, to the back scene.*)

*Enter* Mrs. Hardcastle *and* Tony

Mrs. Hard. So, so, they're gone off. Let them go, I care not.

Hard. Who gone?

Mrs. Hard. My dutiful niece and her gentleman, Mr. Hastings, from town. He who came down with our modest visitor here.

Sir Cha. Who, my honest George Hastings? As worthy a fellow as lives, and the girl could not have made a more prudent choice.

Hard. Then, by the hand of my body, I'm proud of the connexion.

MRS. HARD. Well, if he has taken away the lady, he has not taken her fortune; that remains in this family to console us for her loss.

HARD. Sure, Dorothy, you would not be so mercenary?

MRS. HARD. Ay, that's my affair, not yours.

HARD. But you know if your son, when of age, refuses to marry his cousin, her whole fortune is then at her own disposal.

MRS. HARD. Ay, but he's not of age, and she has not thought proper to wait for his refusal.


*Enter* HASTINGS *and* MISS NEVILLE

MRS. HARD. (*Aside.*) What, returned so soon! I begin not to like it.

HAST. (*To* HARDCASTLE.) For my late attempt to fly off with your niece let my present confusion be my punishment. We are now come back, to appeal from your justice to your humanity. By her father's consent, I first paid her my addresses, and our passions were first founded in duty.

MISS NEV. Since his death, I have been obliged to stoop to dissimulation to avoid oppression. In an hour of levity, I was ready to give up my fortune to secure my choice. But I am now recovered from the delusion, and hope from your tenderness what is denied me from a nearer connexion.

MRS. HARD. Pshaw, pshaw! this is all but the whining end of a modern novel.

HARD. Be it what it will, I'm glad they're come back to reclaim their due. Come hither, Tony, boy. Do you refuse this lady's hand whom I now offer you?

TONY. What signifies my refusing? You know I can't refuse her till I'm of age, father.

HARD. While I thought concealing your age, boy, was likely to conduce to your improvement, I concurred with your mother's desire to keep it secret. But since I find she turns it to a wrong use, I must now declare you have been of age these three months.

TONY. Of age! Am I of age, father?

HARD. Above three months.

TONY. Then you'll see the first use I'll make of my liberty.

(*Taking* MISS NEVILLE'S *hand.*)   Witness all men by these presents, that I, Anthony Lumpkin, Esquire, of BLANK place, refuse you, Constantia Neville, spinster, of no place at all, for my true and lawful wife.   So Constance Neville may marry whom she pleases, and Tony Lumpkin is his own man again.

SIR CHA.  O brave 'squire!

HAST.  My worthy friend!

MRS. HARD.  My undutiful offspring!

MAR.  Joy, my dear George!  I give you joy sincerely.  And could I prevail upon my little tyrant here to be less arbitrary, I should be the happiest man alive, if you would return me the favour.

HAST.  (*To* MISS HARDCASTLE.)  Come, madam, you are now driven to the very last scene of all your contrivances.  I know you like him, I'm sure he loves you, and you must and shall have him.

HARD.  (*Joining their hands.*)  And I say so too.  And, Mr. Marlow, if she makes as good a wife as she has a daughter, I don't believe you'll ever repent your bargain.  So now to supper.  To-morrow we shall gather all the poor of the parish about us, and the mistakes of the night shall be crowned with a merry morning.  So, boy, take her; and as you have been mistaken in the mistress, my wish is, that you may never be mistaken in the wife.                    [*Exeunt Omnes.*

# THE CENCI

BY

**PERCY BYSSHE SHELLEY**

# INTRODUCTORY NOTE

PERCY BYSSHE SHELLEY *was born near Horsham, Sussex, England, on August 4, 1792, of a wealthy but undistinguished family. He was educated at Eton, where he was unpopular and persecuted, and at University College, Oxford, where he was interested in science, and from which he was expelled for the publication of a pamphlet on "The Necessity of Atheism." Going up to London, he met at the school attended by his sisters a girl of sixteen called Harriet Westbrook, whose accounts of the persecution she suffered won Shelley's sympathy and led him into a foolish marriage, he being nineteen and she sixteen. Within three years they had become estranged; she left him to return with her child to her father's house; and a month later he set out for the Continent with Mary, daughter of William Godwin, the political philosopher, under whose influence Shelley had been for a time. In 1816 Harriet was found drowned; Shelley formally married Mary Godwin; and the courts refused him the custody of his children. Meantime he was taking active part in political agitation on the side of liberty, and was producing a good deal of poetry. "Alastor" had been written in 1815, and "The Revolt of Islam" appeared in 1818. In that year he returned to Italy, where he remained till his death by drowning on July 8, 1822. His ashes were buried in Rome.*

*These last years were crowded with poetical production, "Prometheus Unbound," "The Cenci," the "Ode to the West Wind," "The Sensitive Plant," "Epipsychidion," "Adonais," and many of his finest lyrics belonging to this period. Of his dramatic work, the "Prometheus Unbound," a mythological drama on the redemption of mankind, in gorgeous lyrical verse, and "The Cenci" are the most important. In the latter he handled a terrible story of old Roman life with great delicacy and tremendous impressiveness. Partly under the influence of Shakespeare, partly from the nature of the subject, this play is more concrete and palpable than Shelley's work in general, and displays sides of his genius which might not otherwise have been suspected. Though impossible on the public stage, "The Cenci" has claims to be regarded, by virtue of its strength of characterization, its poetry, and its emotional intensity, as the greatest drama of the century.*

272

# DEDICATION

TO

## LEIGH HUNT, Esq.

My Dear Friend—I inscribe with your name, from a distant country, and after an absence whose months have seemed years, this the latest of my literary efforts.

Those writings which I have hitherto published, have been little else than visions which impersonate my own apprehensions of the beautiful and the just. I can also perceive in them the literary defects incidental to youth and impatience; they are dreams of what ought to be, or may be. The drama which I now present to you is a sad reality. I lay aside the presumptuous attitude of an instructor, and am content to paint, with such colours as my own heart furnishes, that which has been.

Had I known a person more highly endowed than yourself with all that it becomes a man to possess, I had solicited for this work the ornament of his name. One more gentle, honourable, innocent and brave; one of more exalted toleration for all who do and think evil, and yet himself more free from evil; one who knows better how to receive, and how to confer a benefit though he must ever confer far more than he can receive; one of simpler, and, in the highest sense of the word, of purer life and manners I never knew: and I had already been fortunate in friendships when your name was added to the list.

In that patient and irreconcilable enmity with domestic and political tyranny and imposture which the tenor of your life has illustrated, and which, had I health and talents, should illustrate mine, let us, comforting each other in our task, live and die.

All happiness attend you! Your affectionate friend,

Percy B. Shelley.

Rome, *May 29, 1819.*

# PREFACE

A MANUSCRIPT was communicated to me during my travels in Italy, which was copied from the archives of the Cenci Palace at Rome, and contains a detailed account of the horrors which ended in the extinction of one of the noblest and richest families of that city during the Pontificate of Clement VIII, in the year 1599. The story is, that an old man having spent his life in debauchery and wickedness, conceived at length an implacable hatred towards his children; which showed itself towards one daughter under the form of an incestuous passion, aggravated by every circumstance of cruelty and violence. This daughter, after long and vain attempts to escape from what she considered a perpetual contamination both of body and mind, at length plotted with her mother-in-law and brother to murder their common tyrant. The young maiden, who was uged to this tremendous deed by an impulse which overpowered its horror, was evidently a most gentle and amiable being, a creature formed to adorn and be admired, and thus violently thwarted from her nature by the necessity of circumstance and opinion. The deed was quickly discovered, and, in spite of the most earnest prayers made to the Pope by the highest persons in Rome, the criminals were put to death. The old man had during his life repeatedly bought his pardon from the Pope for capital crimes of the most enormous and unspeakable kind, at the price of a hundred thousand crowns; the death therefore of his victims can scarcely be accounted for by the love of justice. The Pope, among other motives for severity, probably felt that whoever killed the Count Cenci deprived his treasury of a certain and copious source of revenue.[1] Such a story, if told so as to present to the reader all the feelings of those who once acted it, their hopes and fears, their confidences and misgivings, their various interests, passions,

[1] The Papal Government formerly took the most extraordinary precautions against the publicity of facts which offer so tragical a demonstration of its own wickedness and weakness; so that the communication of the MS. had become, until very lately, a matter of some difficulty.

and opinions, acting upon and with each other, yet all conspiring to one tremendous end, would be as a light to make apparent some of the most dark and secret caverns of the human heart.

On my arrival at Rome I found that the story of the Cenci was a subject not to be mentioned in Italian society without awakening a deep and breathless interest; and that the feelings of the company never failed to incline to a romantic pity for the wrongs, and a passionate exculpation of the horrible deed to which they urged her, who has been mingled two centuries with the common dust. All ranks of people knew the outlines of this history, and participated in the overwhelming interest which it seems to have the magic of exciting in the human heart. I had a copy of Guido's picture of Beatrice which is preserved in the Colonna Palace, and my servant instantly recognized it as the portrait of *La Cenci*.

This national and universal interest which the story produces and has produced for two centuries and among all ranks of people in a great City, where the imagination is kept for ever active and awake, first suggested to me the conception of its fitness for a dramatic purpose. In fact it is a tragedy which has already received, from its capacity of awakening and sustaining the sympathy of men, approbation and success. Nothing remained as I imagined, but to clothe it to the apprehensions of my countrymen in such language and action as would bring it home to their hearts. The deepest and the sublimest tragic compositions, King Lear and the two plays in which the tale of Œdipus is told, were stories which already existed in tradition, as matters of popular belief and interest, before Shakspeare and Sophocles made them familiar to the sympathy of all succeeding generations of mankind.

This story of the Cenci is indeed eminently fearful and monstrous: any thing like a dry exhibition of it on the stage would be insupportable. The person who would treat such a subject must increase the ideal, and diminish the actual horror of the events, so that the pleasure which arises from the poetry which exists in these tempestuous sufferings and crimes may mitigate the pain of the contemplation of the moral deformity from which they spring. There must also be nothing attempted to make the exhibition subservient to what is vulgarly termed a moral purpose. The highest moral purpose aimed at in the highest species of the drama, is the teaching the human heart, through its sympathies and antipathies, the knowledge of itself; in proportion to the possession of which knowledge, every human being is wise, just, sincere, tolerant and kind. If dogmas can do more, it is well: but a drama is no fit place for the enforcement of them. Undoubtedly, no person can be truly dishonoured by the act of another; and the fit return to make to the most enormous injuries is kindness and forbearance, and a resolution to convert the injurer from his dark passions by peace and love. Revenge, retaliation, atonement, are pernicious mistakes. If Beatrice had thought in this manner she would have been wiser and better; but she would never have been a tragic character: the few whom such an exhibition would have interested, could never have been sufficiently interested for a dramatic purpose, from the want of finding sympathy in their interest among the mass who surround them. It is in the restless and anatomising casuistry with which men seek the justification of Beatrice, yet feel that she has done what needs justification; it is in the superstitious horror with which they contemplate alike her wrongs, and their revenge, that the dramatic character of what she did and suffered, consists.

I have endeavoured as nearly as possible to represent the characters as they probably were, and have sought to avoid the error of making them actuated by my own conceptions of right or wrong, false or true: thus under a thin veil converting names and actions of the sixteenth century into cold impersonations of my own mind. They are represented as Catholics, and as Catholics deeply tinged with religion. To a Protestant apprehension there will appear something unnatural in the earnest and perpetual sentiment of the relations between God and men which pervade the tragedy of the Cenci. It will especially be startled at the combination of an undoubting persuasion of the truth of the popular religion with a cool and determined perseverance in enormous guilt. But religion in Italy is not, as in Protestant countries, a cloak to be worn on particular days; or a passport which those who do not wish to be railed at carry with them to exhibit; or a gloomy passion for penetrating the impenetrable mysteries of our being, which terrifies its possessor at the darkness of the abyss to the brink of which it has conducted him. Religion coexists, as it were, in the mind of an Italian Catholic, with a faith in that of which all men have the most certain knowledge. It is interwoven with the whole fabric of life. It is adoration, faith, submission, penitence, blind admiration; not a rule for moral conduct. It has no necessary connection with any one virtue. The most atrocious villain may be rigidly devout, and without any shock to established faith, confess himself to be so. Religion pervades intensely the whole frame of society, and is according to the temper of the mind which it inhabits, a passion, a persuasion, an excuse, a refuge; never a check. Cenci himself built a chapel in the court of his Palace, and dedicated it to St. Thomas the Apostle, and established masses for the peace of his soul. Thus in the first scene of the fourth act Lucretia's design in exposing herself to the consequences of an expostulation with Cenci after having administered the opiate, was to induce him by a feigned tale to confess himself before death; this being esteemed by Catholics as essential to salvation; and she only relinquishes her purpose when she perceives that her perseverance would expose Beatrice to new outrages.

I have avoided with great care in writing this play the introduction of what is commonly called mere poetry, and I imagine there will scarcely be found a detached simile or a single isolated description, unless Beatrice's description of the chasm appointed for her father's murder should be judged to be of that nature.[2]

In a dramatic composition the imagery and the passion should interpenetrate one another, the former being reserved simply for the full development and illustration of the latter. Imagination is as the immortal God which should assume flesh for the redemption of mortal passion. It is thus that the most remote and the most familiar imagery may alike be fit for dramatic purposes when employed in the illustration of strong feeling, which raises what is low, and levels to the apprehension that which is lofty, casting over all the shadow of its own greatness. In other respects, I have written more carelessly; that is, without an over-fastidious and learned choice of words. In this respect I entirely agree with those modern critics who assert that in order to move men to true sympathy we must use the familiar language of men, and that our great ancestors the

[2] An idea in this speech was suggested by a most sublime passage in "El Purgatorio de San Patricio" of Calderon; the only plagiarism which I have intentionally committed in the whole piece.

ancient English poets are the writers, a study of whom might incite us to do that for our own age which they have done for theirs. But it must be the real language of men in general and not that of any particular class to whose society the writer happens to belong. So much for what I have attempted; I need not be assured that success is a very different matter; particularly for one whose attention has but newly been awakened to the study of dramatic literature.

I endeavoured whilst at Rome to observe such monuments of this story as might be accessible to a stranger. The portrait of Beatrice at the Colonna Palace is admirable as a work if art; it was taken by Guido during her confinement in prison. But it is most interesting as a just representation of one of the loveliest specimens of the workmanship of Nature. There is a fixed and pale composure upon the features: she seems sad and stricken down in spirit, yet the despair thus expressed is lightened by the patience of gentleness. Her head is bound with folds of white drapery from which the yellow strings of her golden hair escape, and fall about her neck. The moulding of her face is exquisitely delicate; the eyebrows are distinct and arched: the lips have that permanent meaning of imagination and sensibility which suffering has not repressed and which it seems as if death scarcely could extinguish. Her forehead is large and clear; her eyes which we are told were remarkable for their vivacity, are swollen with weeping and lustreless, but beautifully tender and serene. In the whole mien there is a simplicity and dignity which united with her exquisite loveliness and deep sorrow are inexpressibly pathetic. Beatrice Cenci appears to have been one of those rare persons in whom energy and gentleness dwell together without destroying one another: her nature was simple and profound. The crimes and miseries in which she was an actor and a sufferer are as the mask and the mantle in which circumstances clothed her for her impersonation on the scene of the world.

The Cenci Palace is of great extent; and though in part modernized, there yet remains a vast and gloomy pile of feudal architecture in the same state as during the dreadful scenes which are the subject of this tragedy. The Palace is situated in an obscure corner of Rome, near the quarter of the Jews, and from the upper windows you see the immense ruins of Mount Palatine half hidden under their profuse overgrowth of trees. There is a court in one part of the Palace (perhaps that in which Cenci built the Chapel to St. Thomas), supported by granite columns and adorned with antique friezes of fine workmanship, and built up, according to the ancient Italian fashion, with balcony over balcony of open-work. One of the gates of the Palace formed of immense stones and leading through a passage, dark and lofty and opening into gloomy subterranean chambers, struck me particularly.

Of the Castle of Petrella, I could obtain no further information than that which is to be found in the manuscript.

# THE CENCI

DRAMATIS PERSONÆ

COUNT FRANCESCO CENCI.
GIACOMO, } his Sons.
BERNARDO, }
CARDINAL CAMILLO.
ORSINO, a Prelate.
SAVELLA, the Pope's Legate.
OLIMPIO, } Assassins.
MARZIO, }
ANDREA, Servant to Cenci.
Nobles—Judges—Guards—Servants.
LUCRETIA, Wife of Cenci, and Step-mother of his children.
BEATRICE, his Daughter.

The SCENE lies principally in Rome, but changes during the fourth Act to Petrella, a castle among the Apulian Apennines.

*Time.* During the Pontificate of Clement VIII.

## ACT I

SCENE I.—*An Apartment in the Cenci Palace*

*Enter* COUNT CENCI, *and* CARDINAL CAMILLO
*Camillo*

THAT matter of the murder is hushed up
      If you consent to yield his Holiness
      Your fief that lies beyond the Pincian gate.—
It needed all my interest in the conclave
To bend him to this point: he said that you
Bought perilous impunity with your gold;
That crimes like yours if once or twice compounded
Enriched the Church, and respited from hell
An erring soul which might repent and live:—
But that the glory and the interest
Of the high throne he fills, little consist

With making it a daily mart of guilt
As manifold and hideous as the deeds
Which you scarce hide from men's revolted eyes.

CENCI. The third of my possessions—let it go!
Ay, I once heard the nephew of the Pope
Had sent his architect to view the ground,
Meaning to build a villa on my vines
The next time I compounded with his uncle:
I little thought he should outwit me so!
Henceforth no witness—not the lamp—shall see
That which the vassal threatened to divulge
Whose throat is choked with dust for his reward.
The deed he saw could not have rated higher
Than his most worthless life:—it angers me!
Respited me from Hell!—So may the Devil
Respite their souls from Heaven. No doubt Pope Clement,
And his most charitable nephews, pray
That the Apostle Peter and the saints
Will grant for their sake that I long enjoy
Strength, wealth, and pride, and lust, and length of days
Wherein to act the deeds which are the stewards
Of their revenue.—But much yet remains
To which they show no title.

CAMILLO.                    Oh, Count Cenci!
So much that thou mightst honourably live
And reconcile thyself with thine own heart
And with thy God, and with the offended world.
How hideously look deeds of lust and blood
Thro' those snow white and venerable hairs!—
Your children should be sitting round you now,
But that you fear to read upon their looks
The shame and misery you have written there.
Where is your wife? Where is your gentle daughter?
Methinks her sweet looks, which make all things else
Beauteous and glad, might kill the fiend within you.
Why is she barred from all society
But her own strange and uncomplaining wrongs?
Talk with me, Count,—you know I mean you well.
I stood beside your dark and fiery youth
Watching its bold and bad career, as men

Watch meteors, but it vanished not—I marked
Your desperate and remorseless manhood; now
Do I behold you in dishonoured age
Charged with a thousand unrepented crimes.
Yet I have ever hoped you would amend,
And in that hope have saved your life three times.

    CENCI. For which Aldobrandino owes you now
My fief beyond the Pincian—Cardinal,
One thing, I pray you, recollect henceforth,
And so we shall converse with less restraint.
A man you knew spoke of my wife and daughter—
He was accustomed to frequent my house;
So the next day *his* wife and daughter came
And asked if I had seen him; and I smiled:
I think they never saw him any more.

    CAMILLO. Thou execrable man, beware!—
    CENCI.                                            Of thee?
Nay this is idle:—We should know each other.
As to my character for what men call crime
Seeing I please my senses as I list,
And vindicate that right with force or guile
It is a public matter, and I care not
If I discuss it with you. I may speak
Alike to you and my own conscious heart—
For you give out that you have half reformed me,
Therefore strong vanity will keep you silent
If fear should not; both will, I do not doubt.
All men delight in sensual luxury,
All men enjoy revenge; and most exult
Over the tortures they can never feel—
Flattering their secret peace with others' pain.
But I delight in nothing else. I love
The sight of agony, and the sense of joy,
When this shall be another's, and that mine.
And I have no remorse and little fear,
Which are, I think, the checks of other men.
This mood has grown upon me, until now
Any design my captious fancy makes
The picture of its wish, and it forms none
But such as men like you would start to know,

Is as my natural food and rest debarred
Until it be accomplished.

CAMILLO. Art thou not
Most miserable?

CENCI. Why, miserable?—
No.—I am what your theologians call
Hardened;—which they must be in impudence,
So to revile a man's peculiar taste.
True, I was happier than I am, while yet
Manhood remained to act the thing I thought;
While lust was sweeter than revenge; and now
Invention palls:—Ay, we must all grow old—
And but that there yet remains a deed to act
Whose horror might make sharp an appetite
Duller than mine—I'd do—I know not what.
When I was young I thought of nothing else
But pleasure; and I fed on honey sweets:
Men, by St. Thomas! cannot live like bees,
And I grew tired:—yet, till I killed a foe,
And heard his groans, and heard his children's groans,
Knew I not what delight was else on earth,
Which now delights me little. I the rather
Look on such pangs as terror ill conceals,
The dry fixed eyeball; the pale quivering lip,
Which tell me that the spirit weeps within
Tears bitterer than the bloody sweat of Christ.
I rarely kill the body, which preserves,
Like a strong prison, the soul within my power,
Wherein I feed it with the breath of fear
For hourly pain.

CAMILLO. Hell's most abandoned fiend
Did never, in the drunkenness of guilt,
Speak to his heart as now you speak to me;
I thank my God that I believe you not.


*Enter* ANDREA

ANDREA. My Lord, a gentleman from Salamanca
Would speak with you.

CENCI. Bid him attend me in the grand saloon.
[*Exit* ANDREA.

CAMILLO. Farewell; and I will pray
Almighty God that thy false, impious words
Tempt not his spirit to abandon thee.    [*Exit* CAMILLO.
   CENCI. The third of my possessions! I must use
Close husbandry, or gold, the old man's sword,
Falls from my withered hand.  But yesterday
There came an order from the Pope to make
Fourfold provision for my cursèd sons;
Whom I had sent from Rome to Salamanca,
Hoping some accident might cut them off;
And meaning if I could to starve them there.
I pray thee, God, send some quick death upon them!
Bernardo and my wife could not be worse
If dead and damned:—then, as to Beatrice—
        (*Looking around him suspiciously.*)
I think they cannot hear me at that door;
What if they should?  And yet I need not speak
Though the heart triumphs with itself in words.
O, thou most silent air, that shalt not hear
What now I think!  Thou, pavement, which I tread
Towards her chamber,—let your echoes talk
Of my imperious step scorning surprise,
But not of my intent!—Andrea!


                    *Enter* ANDREA

ANDREA.                              My lord?
   CENCI. Bid Beatrice attend me in her chamber
This evening:—no, at midnight and alone    [*Exeunt.*


        SCENE II.—*A Garden in the Cenci Palace*

*Enter* BEATRICE *and* ORSINO, *as in conversation*
   BEATRICE. Pervert not truth,
Orsino.  You remember where we held
That conversation;—nay, we see the spot
Even from this cypress;—two long years are past
Since, on an April midnight, underneath
The moonlight ruins of mount Palatine,
I did confess to you my secret mind.

ORSINO. You said you loved me then.

BEATRICE. You are a Priest,
Speak to me not of love.

ORSINO. I may obtain
The dispensation of the Pope to marry.
Because I am a Priest do you believe
Your image, as the hunter some struck deer,
Follows me not whether I wake or sleep?

BEATRICE. As I have said, speak to me not of love;
Had you a dispensation I have not;
Nor will I leave this home of misery
Whilst my poor Bernard, and that gentle lady
To whom I owe life, and these virtuous thoughts,
Must suffer what I still have strength to share.
Alas, Orsino! All the love that once
I felt for you, is turned to bitter pain.
Ours was a youthful contract, which you first
Broke, by assuming vows no Pope will loose.
And thus I love you still, but holily,
Even as a sister or a spirit might;
And so I swear a cold fidelity.
And it is well perhaps we shall not marry.
You have a sly, equivocating vein
That suits me not.—Ah, wretched that I am!
Where shall I turn? Even now you look on me
As you were not my friend, and as if you
Discovered that I thought so, with false smiles
Making my true suspicion seem your wrong.
Ah no! forgive me; sorrow makes me seem
Sterner than else my nature might have been;
I have a weight of melancholy thoughts,
And they forbode,—but what can they forbode
Worse than I now endure?

ORSINO. All will be well.
Is the petition yet prepared? You know
My zeal for all you wish, sweet Beatrice;
Doubt not but I will use my utmost skill
So that the Pope attend to your complaint.

BEATRICE. Your zeal for all I wish;—Ah me, you are cold!
Your utmost skill . . . speak but one word . . . (aside) Alas!

Weak and deserted creature that I am,
Here I stand bickering with my only friend! [*To* ORSINO.
This night my father gives a sumptuous feast,
Orsino; he has heard some happy news
From Salamanca, from my brothers there,
And with this outward show of love he mocks
His inward hate. 'Tis bold hypocrisy,
For he would gladlier celebrate their deaths,
Which I have heard him pray for on his knees:
Great God! that such a father should be mine!
But there is mighty preparation made,
And all our kin, the Cenci, will be there,
And all the chief nobility of Rome.
And he has bidden me and my pale Mother
Attire ourselves in festival array.
Poor lady! She expects some happy change
In his dark spirit from this act; I none.
At supper I will give you the petition:
Till when—farewell.

    ORSINO. Farewell. (*Exit* BEATRICE.) I know the Pope
Will ne'er absolve me from my priestly vow
But by absolving me from the revenue
Of many a wealthy see; and, Beatrice,
I think to win thee at an easier rate.
Nor shall he read her eloquent petition:
He might bestow her on some poor relation
Of his sixth cousin, as he did her sister,
And I should be debarred from all access.
Then as to what she suffers from her father,
In all this there is much exaggeration:—
Old men are testy and will have their way;
A man may stab his enemy, or his vassal,
And live a free life as to wine and women,
And with a peevish temper may return
To a dull home, and rate his wife and children;
Daughters and wives call this foul tyranny.
I shall be well content if on my conscience
There rest no heavier sin than what they suffer
From the devices of my love—A net
From which she shall escape not. Yet I fear

Her subtle mind, her awe-inspiring gaze,
Whose beams anatomise me nerve by nerve
And lay me bare, and make me blush to see
My hidden thoughts.—Ah, no! A friendless girl
Who clings to me, as to her only hope:—
I were a fool, not less than if a panther
Were panic-stricken by the antelope's eye,
If she escape me.                                   [*Exit.*

SCENE III.—*A Magnificent Hall in the Cenci Palace.  A Banquet*

*Enter* CENCI, LUCRETIA, BEATRICE, ORSINO, CAMILLO, NOBLES

CENCI. Welcome, my friends and kinsmen; welcome ye,
Princes and Cardinals, pillars of the church,
Whose presence honours our festivity.
I have too long lived like an anchorite,
And in my absence from your merry meetings
An evil word is gone abroad of me;
But I do hope that you, my noble friends,
When you have shared the entertainment here,
And heard the pious cause for which 'tis given,
And we have pledged a health or two together,
Will think me flesh and blood as well as you;
Sinful indeed, for Adam made all so,
But tender-hearted, meek and pitiful.
     FIRST GUEST. In truth, My Lord, you seem too light of
          heart,
Too sprightly and companionable a man,
To act the deeds that rumour pins on you.
(*To his companion.*) I never saw such blithe and open cheer
In any eye!
     SECOND GUEST. Some most desired event,
In which we all demand a common joy,
Has brought us hither; let us hear it, Count.
     CENCI. It is indeed a most desired event.
If, when a parent from a parent's heart
Lifts from this earth to the great father of all
A prayer, both when he lays him down to sleep,
And when he rises up from dreaming it;

One supplication, one desire, one hope,
That he would grant a wish for his two sons,
Even all that he demands in their regard—
And suddenly beyond his dearest hope,
It is accomplished, he should then rejoice,
And call his friends and kinsmen to a feast,
And task their love to grace his merriment,
Then honour me thus far—for I am he.

BEATRICE (to *Lucretia*). Great God! How horrible!
    Some dreadful ill
Must have befallen my brothers.

LUCRETIA.                         Fear not, Child,
He speaks too frankly.

BEATRICE.                 Ah! My blood runs cold.
I fear that wicked laughter round his eye,
Which wrinkles up the skin even to the hair.

CENCI. Here are the letters brought from Salamanca;
Beatrice, read them to your mother. God!
I thank thee! In one night didst thou perform,
By ways inscrutable, the thing I sought.
My disobedient and rebellious sons
Are dead!—Why dead!—What means this change of cheer?
You hear me not, I tell you they are dead;
And they will need no food or raiment more:
The tapers that did light them the dark way
Are their last cost. The Pope, I think, will not
Expect I should maintain them in their coffins.
Rejoice with me—my heart is wondrous glad.

    [LUCRETIA *sinks, half-fainting;* BEATRICE *supports her.*

BEATRICE. It is not true!—Dear lady, pray look up.
Had it been true, there is a God in Heaven,
He would not live to boast of such a boon.
Unnatural man, thou knowest that it is false.

CENCI. Ay, as the word of God; whom here I call
To witness that I speak the sober truth;—
And whose most favouring Providence was shown
Even in the manner of their deaths. For Rocco
Was kneeling at the mass, with sixteen others,
When the church fell and crushed him to a mummy,
The rest escaped unhurt. Cristofano

Was stabbed in error by a jealous man,
Whilst she he loved was sleeping with his rival;
All in the self-same hour of the same night;
Which shows that Heaven has special care of me.
I beg those friends who love me, that they mark
The day a feast upon their calendars.
It was the twenty-seventh of December:
Ay, read the letters if you doubt my oath.

*[The Assembly appears confused; several of*
*the guests rise.*

FIRST GUEST. Oh, horrible! I will depart—
SECOND GUEST. And I.—
THIRD GUEST. No, stay!

I do believe it is some jest; tho' faith!
'Tis mocking us somewhat too solemnly.
I think his son has married the Infanta,
Or found a mine of gold in El dorado;
'Tis but to season some such news; stay, stay!
I see 'tis only raillery by his smile.

CENCI (*filling a bowl of wine, and lifting it up*). Oh,
thou bright wine whose purple splendour leaps
And bubbles gaily in this golden bowl
Under the lamp-light, as my spirits do,
To hear the death of my accursèd sons!
Could I believe thou wert their mingled blood,
Then would I taste thee like a sacrament,
And pledge with thee the mighty Devil in Hell,
Who, if a father's curses, as men say,
Climb with swift wings after their children's souls,
And drag them from the very throne of Heaven,
Now triumphs in my triumph!—But thou art
Superfluous; I have drunken deep of joy,
And I will taste no other wine to-night.
Here, Andrea! Bear the bowl around.

A GUEST (*rising*). Thou wretch!
Will none among this noble company
Check the abandoned villain?

CAMILLO. For God's sake
Let me dismiss the guests! You are insane,
Some ill will come of this.

SECOND GUEST.                    Seize, silence him!
FIRST GUEST.  I will!
THIRD GUEST.              And I?
CENCI (*addressing those who rise with a threatening
                    gesture*).  Who moves?  Who speaks?
                         (*turning to the Company*)
                              'tis nothing,
Enjoy yourselves.—Beware!  For my revenge
Is as the sealed commission of a king
That kills, and none dare name the murderer.
    [*The Banquet is broken up; several of the Guests are
    departing.*

BEATRICE.  I do entreat you, go not, noble guests;
What, although tyranny and impious hate
Stand sheltered by a father's hoary hair,
What, if 'tis he who clothed us in these limbs
Who tortures them, and triumphs?  What, if we,
The desolate and the dead, were his own flesh,
His children and his wife, whom he is bound
To love and shelter?  Shall we therefore find
No refuge in this merciless wide world?
O think what deep wrongs must have blotted out
First love, then reverence in a child's prone mind,
Till it thus vanquish shame and fear!  O think!
I have borne much, and kissed the sacred hand
Which crushed us to the earth, and thought its stroke
Was perhaps some paternal chastisement!
Have excused much, doubted; and when no doubt
Remained, have sought by patience, love, and tears
To soften him, and when this could not be
I have knelt down through the long sleepless nights
And lifted up to God, the father of all,
Passionate prayers: and when these were not heard
I have still borne,—until I meet you here,
Princes and kinsmen, at this hideous feast
Given at my brothers' deaths.  Two yet remain,
His wife remains and I, whom if ye save not,
Ye may soon share such merriment again
As fathers make over their children's graves.
O Prince Colonna, thou art our near kinsman,

Cardinal, thou art the Pope's chamberlain,
Camillo, thou art chief justiciary,
Take us away!

    CENCI. (*He has been conversing with* CAMILLO *during the
        first part of* BEATRICE'S *speech; he hears the conclusion,
        and now advances*). I hope my good friends here
Will think of their own daughters—or perhaps
Of their own throats—before they lend an ear
To this wild girl.

    BEATRICE (*not noticing the words of Cenci*). Dare no one
        look on me?
None answer? Can one tyrant overbear
The sense of many best and wisest men?
Or is it that I sue not in some form
Of scrupulous law, that ye deny my suit?
O God! That I were buried with my brothers!
And that the flowers of this departed spring
Were fading on my grave! And that my father
Were celebrating now one feast for all!

    CAMILLO. A bitter wish for one so young and gentle;
Can we do nothing?

    COLONNA.          Nothing that I see.
Count Cenci were a dangerous enemy:
Yet I would second any one.

    A CARDINAL.         And I.

    CENCI. Retire to your chamber, insolent girl!

    BEATRICE. Retire thou impious man! Ay hide thyself
Where never eye can look upon thee more!
Wouldst thou have honour and obedience
Who art a torturer? Father, never dream
Though thou mayst overbear this company,
But ill must come of ill.—Frown not on me!
Haste, hide thyself, lest with avenging looks
My brothers' ghosts should hunt thee from thy seat!
Cover thy face from every living eye,
And start if thou but hear a human step.
Seek out some dark and silent corner, there
Bow thy white head before offended God,
And we will kneel around, and fervently
Pray that he pity both ourselves, and thee.

CENCI. My friends, I do lament this insane girl
Has spoilt the mirth of our festivity.
Good night, farewell; I will not make you longer
Spectators of our dull domestic quarrels.
Another time.—

*[Exeunt all but* CENCI *and* BEATRICE.
My brain is swimming round;
Give me a bowl of wine! *[To* BEATRICE.
Thou painted viper!
Beast that thou art! Fair and yet terrible!
I know a charm shall make thee meek and tame,
Now get thee from my sight! *[Exit* BEATRICE.
Here, Andrea,
Fill up this goblet with Greek wine. I said
I would not drink this evening; but I must;
For, strange to say, I feel my spirits fail
With thinking what I have decreed to do.—

*[Drinking the wine.*
Be thou the resolution of quick youth
Within my veins, and manhood's purpose stern,
And age's firm, cold, subtle villainy;
As if thou wert indeed my children's blood
Which I did thirst to drink! The charm works well,
It must be done; it shall be done, I swear! *[Exit.*

## ACT II

### SCENE I.—*An Apartment in the Cenci Palace*

*Enter* LUCRETIA *and* BERNARDO

LUCRETIA. Weep not, my gentle boy; he struck but me
Who have borne deeper wrongs. In truth, if he
Had killed me, he had done a kinder deed.
O, God Almighty, do thou look upon us,
We have no other friend but only thee!
Yet weep not; though I love you as my own,
I am not your true mother.
BERNARDO. O more, more,
Than ever mother was to any child,
That have you been to me! Had he not been

My father, do you think that I should weep!
   LUCRETIA. Alas! Poor boy, what else couldst thou have
     done?

*Enter* BEATRICE

   BEATRICE. *(in a hurried voice)*. Did he pass this way?
     Have you seen him, brother?
Ah! No, that is his step upon the stairs;
'Tis nearer now; his hand is on the door;
Mother, if I to thee have ever been
A duteous child, now save me! Thou, great God,
Whose image upon earth a father is,
Dost thou indeed abandon me? He comes:
The door is opening now; I see his face;
He frowns on others, but he smiles on me,
Even as he did after the feast last night.


*Enter a servant*

Almighty God, how merciful thou art!
'Tis but Orsino's servant.—Well, what news?
   SERVANT. My master bids me say, the Holy Father
Has sent back your petition thus unopened. [*Giving a paper.*
And he demands at what hour 'twere secure
To visit you again?
   LUCRETIA.        At the Ave Mary.
                             [*Exit servant.*
So daughter, our last hope has failed; Ah me!
How pale you look; you tremble, and you stand
Wrapped in some fixed and fearful meditation,
As if one thought were over strong for you:
Your eyes have a chill glare; O, dearest child!
Are you gone mad? If not, pray speak to me.
   BEATRICE. You see I am not mad: I speak to you.
   LUCRETIA. You talked of something that your father did
After that dreadful feast? Could it be worse
Than when he smiled, and cried, My sons are dead!
And every one looked in his neighbour's face
To see if others were as white as he?
At the first word he spoke I felt the blood
Rush to my heart, and fell into a trance;

And when it past I sat all weak and wild;
Whilst you alone stood up, and with strong words
Checked his unnatural pride; and I could see
The devil was rebuked that lives in him.
Until this hour thus have you ever stood
Between us and your father's moody wrath
Like a protecting presence: your firm mind
Has been our only refuge and defence.
What can have thus subdued it? What can now
Have given you that cold melancholy look,
Succeeding to your unaccustomed fear?

BEATRICE. What is it that you say? I was just thinking
'Twere better not to struggle any more.
Men, like my father, have been dark and bloody,
Yet never—Oh! Before worse comes of it
'Twere wise to die: it ends in that at last.

LUCRETIA. O talk not so, dear child! Tell me at once
What did your father do or say to you?
He stayed not after that accursèd feast
One moment in your chamber.—Speak to me.

BERNARDO. O sister, sister, prithee, speak to us!

BEATRICE (*speaking very slowly with a forced calmness*).
        It was one word, Mother, one little word;
One look, one smile. (*Wildly.*) Oh! He has trampled me
Under his feet, and made the blood stream down
My pallid cheeks. And he has given us all
Ditch water, and the fever-stricken flesh
Of buffaloes, and bade us eat or starve,
And we have eaten.—He has made me look
On my beloved Bernardo, when the rust
Of heavy chains has gangrened his sweet limbs,
And I have never yet despaired—but now!
What could I say?                  [*Recovering herself.*
        Ah! No, 'tis nothing new.
The sufferings we all share have made me wild:
He only struck and cursed me as he passed;
He said, he looked, he did;—nothing at all
Beyond his wont, yet it disordered me.
Alas! I am forgetful of my duty,
I should preserve my senses for your sake.

LUCRETIA. Nay, Beatrice! have courage, my sweet girl,
If any one despairs it should be I
Who loved him once, and now must live with him
Till God in pity call for him or me.
For you may, like your sister, find some husband,
And smile, years hence, with children round your knees;
Whilst I, then dead, and all this hideous coil
Shall be remembered only as a dream.
    BEATRICE. Talk not to me, dear lady, of a husband.
Did you not nurse me when my mother died?
Did you not shield me and that dearest boy?
And had we any other friend but you
In infancy, with gentle words and looks,
To win our father not to murder us?
And shall I now desert you? May the ghost
Of my dead Mother plead against my soul
If I abandon her who filled the place
She left, with more, even, than a mother's love!
    BERNARDO. And I am of my sister's mind. Indeed
I would not leave you in this wretchedness,
Even though the Pope should make me free to live
In some blithe place, like others of my age,
With sports, and delicate food, and the fresh air.
O never think that I will leave you, Mother!
    LUCRETIA. My dear, dear children!


*Enter* CENCI *suddenly*

CENCI.                                What, Beatrice here!
Come hither! [*She shrinks back, and covers her face.*
                Nay, hide not your face, 'tis fair;
Look up! Why, yesternight you dared to look
With disobedient insolence upon me,
Bending a stern and an inquiring brow
On what I meant; whilst I then sought to hide
That which I came to tell you—but in vain.
    BEATRICE (*wildly, staggering towards the door*). O that
            the earth would gape! Hide me, O God!
    CENCI. Then it was I whose inarticulate words
Fell from my lips, and who with tottering steps

Fled from your presence, as you now from mine.
Stay, I command you—from this day and hour
Never again, I think, with fearless eye,
And brow superior, and unaltered cheek,
And that lip made for tenderness or scorn,
Shalt thou strike dumb the meanest of mankind;
Me least of all. Now get thee to thy chamber!
Thou too, loathed image of thy cursèd mother,

                                  [*To* BERNARDO.

Thy milky, meek face makes me sick with hate!

                      [*Exeunt* BEATRICE *and* BERNARDO.

(*Aside.*) So much has past between us as must make
Me bold, her fearful.—'Tis an awful thing
To touch such mischief as I now conceive:
So men sit shivering on the dewy bank,
And try the chill stream with their feet; once in . . .
How the delighted spirit pants for joy!

    LUCRETIA (*advancing timidly towards him*). O husband!
        Pray forgive poor Beatrice.
She meant not any ill.

    CENCI.                 Nor you perhaps?
Nor that young imp, whom you have taught by rote
Parricide with his alphabet? Nor Giacomo?
Nor those two most unnatural sons, who stirred
Enmity up against me with the Pope?
Whom in one night merciful God cut off:
Innocent lambs! They thought not any ill.
You were not here conspiring? You said nothing
Of how I might be dungeoned as a madman;
Or be condemned to death for some offence,
And you would be the witnesses?—This failing,
How just it were to hire assassins, or
Put sudden poison in my evening drink?
Or smother me when overcome by wine?
Seeing we had no other judge but God,
And he had sentenced me, and there were none
But you to be the executioners
Of his decree enregistered in heaven?
Oh, no! You said not this?

    LUCRETIA.              So help me God,

I never thought the things you charge me with!

CENCI. If you dare speak that wicked lie again
I'll kill you. What! It was not by your counsel
That Beatrice disturbed the feast last night?
You did not hope to stir some enemies
Against me, and escape, and laugh to scorn
What every nerve of you now trembles at?
You judged that men were bolder than they are;
Few dare to stand between their grave and me.

LUCRETIA. Look not so dreadfully! By my salvation
I knew not aught that Beatrice designed;
Nor do I think she designed any thing
Until she heard you talk of her dead brothers.

CENCI. Blaspheming liar! You are damned for this!
But I will take you where you may persuade
The stones you tread on to deliver you:
For men shall there be none but those who dare
All things—not question that which I command.
On Wednesday next I shall set out: you know
That savage rock, the Castle of Petrella:
'Tis safely walled, and moated round about:
Its dungeons underground, and its thick towers
Never told tales; though they have heard and seen
What might make dumb things speak.—Why do you linger?
Make speediest preparation for the journey! [Exit LUCRETIA.
The all-beholding sun yet shines; I hear
A busy stir of men about the streets;
I see the bright sky through the window panes:
It is a garish, broad, and peering day;
Loud, light, suspicious, full of eyes and ears,
And every little corner, nook, and hole
Is penetrated with the insolent light.
Come darkness! Yet, what is the day to me?
And wherefore should I wish for night, who do
A deed which shall confound both night and day?
'Tis she shall grope through a bewildering mist
Of horror: if there be a sun in heaven
She shall not dare to look upon its beams;
Nor feel its warmth. Let her then wish for night;
The act I think shall soon extinguish all

For me: I bear a darker deadlier gloom
Than the earth's shade, or interlunar air,
Or constellations quenched in murkiest cloud,
In which I walk secure and unbeheld
Towards my purpose.—Would that it were done!    [*Exit*

SCENE II.—*A Chamber in the Vatican*

*Enter* CAMILLO *and* GIACOMO, *in conversation*

CAMILLO. There is an obsolete and doubtful law
By which you might obtain a bare provision
Of food and clothing—
      GIACOMO.                Nothing more? Alas!
Bare must be the provision which strict law
Awards, and agèd, sullen avarice pays.
Why did my father not apprentice me
To some mechanic trade? I should have then
Been trained in no highborn necessities
Which I could meet not by my daily toil.
The eldest son of a rich nobleman
Is heir to all his incapacities;
He has wide wants, and narrow powers. If you,
Cardinal Camillo, were reduced at once
From thrice-driven beds of down, and delicate food,
An hundred servants, and six palaces,
To that which nature doth indeed require?—
      CAMILLO. Nay, there is reason in your plea; 'twere hard.
      GIACOMO. 'Tis hard for a firm man to bear: but I
Have a dear wife, a lady of high birth,
Whose dowry in ill hour I lent my father
Without a bond or witness to the deed:
And children, who inherit her fine senses,
The fairest creatures in this breathing world;
And she and they reproach me not. Cardinal,
Do you not think the Pope would interpose
And stretch authority beyond the law?
      CAMILLO. Though your peculiar case is hard, I know
The Pope will not divert the course of law.
After that impious feast the other night

I spoke with him, and urged him then to check
Your father's cruel hand; he frowned and said,
"Children are disobedient, and they sting
Their fathers' hearts to madness and despair,
Requiting years of care with contumely.
I pity the Count Cenci from my heart;
His outraged love perhaps awakened hate,
And thus he is exasperated to ill.
In the great war between the old and young
I, who have white hairs and a tottering body,
Will keep at least blameless neutrality."

*Enter* ORSINO

You, my good Lord Orsino, heard those words.
 ORSINO. What words?
 GIACOMO. Alas, repeat them not again!
There then is no redress for me, at least
None but that which I may achieve myself,
Since I am driven to the brink.—But, say,
My innocent sister and my only brother
Are dying underneath my father's eye.
The memorable torturers of this land,
Galeaz Visconti, Borgia, Ezzelin,
Never inflicted on the meanest slave
What these endure; shall they have no protection?
 CAMILLO. Why, if they would petition to the Pope
I see not how he could refuse it—yet
He holds it of most dangerous example
In aught to weaken the paternal power,
Being, as 'twere, the shadow of his own.
I pray you now excuse me. I have business
That will not bear delay.   [*Exit* CAMILLO
 GIACOMO.   But you, Orsino,
Have the petition: wherefore not present it?
 ORSINO. I have presented it, and backed it with
My earnest prayers, and urgent interest;
It was returned unanswered. I doubt not
But that the strange and execrable deeds
Alleged in it—in truth they might well baffle

Any belief—have turned the Pope's displeasure
Upon the accusers from the criminal:
So I should guess from what Camillo said.

GIACOMO. My friend, that palace-walking devil Gold
Has whispered silence to his Holiness:
And we are left, as scorpions ringed with fire.
What should we do but strike ourselves to death?
For he who is our murderous persecutor
Is shielded by a father's holy name,
Or I would—                    (*Stops abruptly.*)

ORSINO.        What? Fear not to speak your thought.
Words are but holy as the deeds they cover:
A priest who has forsworn the God he serves;
A judge who makes Truth weep at his decree;
A friend who should weave counsel, as I now,
But as the mantle of some selfish guile;
A father who is all a tyrant seems,
Were the profaner for his sacred name.

GIACOMO. Ask me not what I think; the unwilling brain
Feigns often what it would not; and we trust
Imagination with such phantasies
As the tongue dares not fashion into words,
Which have no words, their horror makes them dim
To the mind's eye.—My heart denies itself
To think what you demand.

ORSINO.                    But a friend's bosom
Is as the inmost cave of our own mind
Where we sit shut from the wide gaze of day,
And from the all-communicating air.
You look what I suspected—

GIACOMO.                    Spare me now!
I am as one lost in a midnight wood,
Who dares not ask some harmless passenger
The path across the wilderness, lest he,
As my thoughts are, should be—a murderer.
I know you are my friend, and all I dare
Speak to my soul that will I trust with thee.
But now my heart is heavy, and would take
Lone counsel from a night of sleepless care.
Pardon me, that I say farewell—farewell!

I would that to my own suspected self
I could address a word so full of peace.
   ORSINO. Farewell!—Be your thoughts better or more
      bold.                        [*Exit* GIACOMO.
I had disposed the Cardinal Camillo
To feed his hope with cold encouragement:
It fortunately serves my close designs
That 'tis a trick of this same family
To analyse their own and other minds.
Such self-anatomy shall teach the will
Dangerous secrets: for it tempts our powers,
Knowing what must be thought, and may be done,
Into the depth of darkest purposes:
So Cenci fell into the pit; even I,
Since Beatrice unveiled me to myself,
And made me shrink from what I cannot shun,
Show a poor figure to my own esteem,
To which I grow half reconciled. I'll do
As little mischief as I can; that thought
Shall fee the accuser conscience.
   (*After a pause.*)           Now what harm
If Cenci should be murdered?—Yet, if murdered,
Wherefore by me? And what if I could take
The profit, yet omit the sin and peril
In such an action? Of all earthly things
I fear a man whose blows outspeed his words;
And such is Cenci: and while Cenci lives
His daughter's dowry were a secret grave
If a priest wins her.—Oh, fair Beatrice!
Would that I loved thee not, or loving thee
Could but despise danger and gold and all
That frowns between my wish and its effect,
Or smiles beyond it! There is no escape . . .
Her bright form kneels beside me at the altar,
And follows me to the resort of men,
And fills my slumber with tumultuous dreams,
So when I wake my blood seems liquid fire;
And if I strike my damp and dizzy head
My hot palm scorches it: her very name,
But spoken by a stranger, makes my heart

Sicken and pant; and thus unprofitably
I clasp the phantom of unfelt delights
Till weak imagination half possesses
The self-created shadow.   Yet much longer
Will I not nurse this life of feverous hours:
From the unravelled hopes of Giacomo
I must work out my own dear purposes.
I see, as from a tower, the end of all:
Her father dead; her brother bound to me
By a dark secret, surer than the grave;
Her mother scared and unexpostulating
From the dread manner of her wish achieved:
And she!—Once more take courage my faint heart;
What dares a friendless maiden matched with thee?
I have such foresight as assures success:
Some unbeheld divinity doth ever,
When dread events are near, stir up men's minds
To black suggestions; and he prospers best,
Not who becomes the instrument of ill,
But who can flatter the dark spirit, that makes
Its empire and its prey of other hearts
Till it become his slave  .  .  .  as I will do.        [*Exit.*

## ACT III

SCENE I.—*An Apartment in the Cenci Palace*

LUCRETIA, *to her enter* BEATRICE

BEATRICE. (*She enters staggering, and speaks wildly.*)
        Reach me that handkerchief!—My brain is hurt;
My eyes are full of blood; just wipe them for me  .  .  .
I see but indistinctly  .  .  .
        LUCRETIA.                        My sweet child,
You have no wound; 'tis only a cold dew
That starts from your dear brow  .  .  .  Alas! Alas!
What has befallen?
        BEATRICE.              How comes this hair undone?
Its wandering strings must be what blind me so,
And yet I tied it fast.—O, horrible!

The pavement sinks under my feet! The walls
Spin round! I see a woman weeping there,
And standing calm and motionless, whilst I
Slide giddily as the world reels. . . . My God!
The beautiful blue heaven is flecked with blood!
The sunshine on the floor is black! The air
Is changed to vapours such as the dead breathe
In charnel pits! Pah! I am choked! There creeps
A clinging, black, contaminating mist
About me . . . 'tis substantial, heavy, thick,
I cannot pluck it from me, for it glues
My fingers and my limbs to one another,
And eats into my sinews, and dissolves
My flesh to a pollution, poisoning
The subtle, pure, and inmost spirit of life!
My God! I never knew what the mad felt
Before; for I am mad beyond all doubt!
(*More wildly.*) No, I am dead! These putrefying limbs
Shut round and sepulchre the panting soul
Which would burst forth into the wandering air! (*A pause.*)
What hideous thought was that I had even now?
'Tis gone; and yet its burthen remains here
O'er these dull eyes . . . upon this weary heart!
O, world! O, life! O, day! O, misery!

    LUCRETIA. What ails thee, my poor child? She answers
      not:
Her spirit apprehends the sense of pain,
But not its cause; suffering has dried away
The source from which it sprung . . .

    BEATRICE (*frantically*).              Like Parricide . . .
Misery has killed its father: yet its father
Never like mine . . . O, God! What thing am I?

    LUCRETIA. My dearest child, what has your father done?

    BEATRICE (*doubtfully*). Who art thou, questioner? I have
      no father.
(*Aside.*) She is the madhouse nurse who tends on me,
It is a piteous office.
(*To* LUCRETIA, *in a slow, subdued voice.*) Do you know
I thought I was that wretched Beatrice
Men speak of, whom her father sometimes hales

From hall to hall by the entangled hair;
At others, pens up naked in damp cells
Where scaly reptiles crawl, and starves her there,
Till she will eat strange flesh. This woful story
So did I overact in my sick dreams,
That I imagined . . . no, it cannot be!
Horrible things have been in this wild world,
Prodigious mixtures, and confusions strange
Of good and ill; and worse have been conceived
Than ever there was found a heart to do.
But never fancy imaged such a deed
As . . . (*Pauses, suddenly recollecting herself.*)
              Who art thou? Swear to me, ere I die
With fearful expectation, that indeed
Thou art not what thou seemest . . . Mother!

Lucretia.                                                    Oh!
My sweet child, know you . . .

Beatrice.                              Yet speak it not:
For then if this be truth, that other too
Must be a truth, a firm enduring truth,
Linked with each lasting circumstance of life,
Never to change, never to pass away.
Why so it is. This is the Cenci Palace;
Thou art Lucretia; I am Beatrice.
I have talked some wild words, but will no more.
Mother, come near me: from this point of time,
I am . . . (*Her voice dies away faintly.*)

Lucretia. Alas! What has befallen thee, child?
What has thy father done?

Beatrice.                           What have I done?
Am I not innocent? Is it my crime
That one with white hair and imperious brow,
Who tortured me from my forgotten years
As parents only dare, should call himself
My father, yet should be!—Oh, what am I?
What name, what place, what memory shall be mine?
What retrospects, outliving even despair?

Lucretia. He is a violent tyrant, surely, child:
We know that death alone can make us free;
His death or ours. But what can he have done

Of deadlier outrage or worse injury?
Thou art unlike thyself; thine eyes shoot forth
A wandering and strange spirit. Speak to me,
Unlock those pallid hands whose fingers twine
With one another.

BEATRICE.          'Tis the restless life
Tortured within them. If I try to speak
I shall go mad. Ay, something must be done;
What, yet I know not . . . something which shall
    make
The thing that I have suffered but a shadow
In the dread lightning which avenges it;
Brief, rapid, irreversible, destroying
The consequence of what it cannot cure.
Some such thing is to be endured or done:
When I know what, I shall be still and calm,
And never any thing will move me more.
But now!—Oh blood, which art my father's blood,
Circling thro' these contaminated veins,
If thou, poured forth on the polluted earth,
Could wash away the crime, and punishment
By which I suffer . . . no, that cannot be!
Many might doubt there were a God above
Who sees and permits evil, and so die:
That faith no agony shall obscure in me.

LUCRETIA. It must indeed have been some bitter wrong;
Yet what, I dare not guess. Oh, my lost child,
Hide not in proud impenetrable grief
Thy sufferings from my fear.

BEATRICE.               I hide them not.
What are the words which you would have me speak?
I, who can feign no image in my mind
Of that which has transformed me: I, whose thought
Is like a ghost shrouded and folded up
In its own formless horror: of all words,
That minister to mortal intercourse,
Which wouldst thou hear? For there is none to tell
My misery: if another ever knew
Aught like to it, she died as I will die,
And left it, as I must, without a name.

Death! Death! Our law and our religion call thee
A punishment and a reward . . . Oh, which
Have I deserved?

LUCRETIA.          The peace of innocence;
Till in your season you be called to heaven.
Whate'er you may have suffered, you have done
No evil. Death must be the punishment
Of crime, or the reward of trampling down
The thorns which God has strewed upon the path
Which leads to immortality.

BEATRICE.                Ay, death . . .
The punishment of crime. I pray thee, God,
Let me not be bewildered while I judge.
If I must live day after day, and keep
These limbs, the unworthy temple of thy spirit,
As a foul den from which what thou abhorrest
May mock thee, unavenged . . . it shall not be!
Self-murder . . . no, that might be no escape,
For thy decree yawns like a Hell between
Our will and it:—O! In this mortal world
There is no vindication and no law
Which can adjudge and execute the doom
Of that through which I suffer.


*Enter* ORSINO.

(*She approaches him solemnly.*) Welcome, Friend!
I have to tell you that, since last we met,
I have endured a wrong so great and strange,
That neither life nor death can give me rest.
Ask me not what it is, for there are deeds
Which have no form, sufferings which have no tongue.

ORSINO. And what is he who has thus injured you?
BEATRICE. The man they call my father: a dread
    name.
ORSINO. It cannot be . . .
BEATRICE.                What it can be, or not,
Forbear to think. It is, and it has been;
Advise me how it shall not be again.
I thought to die; but a religious awe

Restrains me, and the dread lest death itself
Might be no refuge from the consciousness
Of what is yet unexpiated.   Oh, speak!

ORSINO.   Accuse him of the deed, and let the law
avenge thee.

BEATRICE. Oh, ice-hearted counsellor!
If I could find a word that might make known
The crime of my destroyer; and that done,
My tongue should like a knife tear out the secret
Which cankers my heart's core; ay, lay all bare
So that my unpolluted fame should be
With vilest gossips a stale mouthèd story;
A mock, a bye-word, an astonishment:—
If this were done, which never shall be done,
Think of the offender's gold, his dreaded hate,
And the strange horror of the accuser's tale,
Baffling belief, and overpowering speech;
Scarce whispered, unimaginable, wrapt
In hideous hints . . . Oh, most assured redress!

ORSINO. You will endure it then?

BEATRICE.                           Endure?—Orsino,
It seems your counsel is small profit.

(*Turns from him, and speaks half to herself.*)
                                          Ay,
All must be suddenly resolved and done.
What is this undistinguishable mist
Of thoughts, which rise, like shadow after shadow,
Darkening each other?

ORSINO.                 Should the offender live?
Triumph in his misdeed? and make, by use,
His crime, whate'er it is, dreadful no doubt,
Thine element; until thou mayest become
Utterly lost; subdued even to the hue
Of that which thou permittest?

BEATRICE (*to herself*).            Mighty death!
Thou double-visaged shadow? Only judge!
Rightfullest arbiter!

(*She retires absorbed in thought.*)

LUCRETIA.             If the lightning
Of God has e'er descended to avenge . . .

ORSINO. Blaspheme not! His high Providence
    commits
Its glory on this earth, and their own wrongs
Into the hands of men; if they neglect
To punish crime . . .
    LUCRETIA. But if one, like this wretch,
Should mock, with gold, opinion, law, and power?
If there be no appeal to that which makes
The guiltiest tremble? If because our wrongs,
For that they are unnatural, strange, and monstrous,
Exceed all measure of belief? O God!
If, for the very reasons which should make
Redress most swift and sure, our injurer triumphs?
And we, the victims, bear worse punishment
Than that appointed for their torturer?
    ORSINO.                  Think not
But that there is redress where there is wrong,
So we be bold enough to seize it.
    LUCRETIA.             How?
If there were any way to make all sure,
I know not . . . but I think it might be good
To . . .
    ORSINO. Why, his late outrage to Beatrice;
For it is such, as I but faintly guess,
As makes remorse dishonour, and leaves her
Only one duty, how she may avenge:
You, but one refuge from ills ill endured;
Me, but one counsel . . .
    LUCRETIA.          For we cannot hope
That aid, or retribution, or resource
Will arise thence, where every other one
Might find them with less need. (BEATRICE *advances*.)
    ORSINO.            Then . . .
    BEATRICE.              Peace, Orsino!
And, honoured Lady, while I speak, I pray
That you put off, as garments overworn,
Forbearance and respect, remorse and fear,
And all the fit restraints of daily life,
Which have been borne from childhood, but which now
Would be a mockery to my holier plea.

As I have said, I have endured a wrong,
Which, though it be expressionless, is such
As asks atonement; both for what is past,
And lest I be reserved, day after day,
To load with crimes an overburthened soul,
And be . . . what ye can dream not. I have prayed
To God, and I have talked with my own heart,
And have unravelled my entangled will,
And have at length determined what is right.
Art thou my friend, Orsino? False or true?
Pledge thy salvation ere I speak.

  ORSINO.        I swear
To dedicate my cunning, and my strength,
My silence, and whatever else is mine,
To thy commands.

  LUCRETIA.   You think we should devise
His death?

  BEATRICE. And execute what is devised,
And suddenly. We must be brief and bold.

  ORSINO. And yet most cautious.

  LUCRETIA.      For the jealous laws
Would punish us with death and infamy
For that which it became themselves to do.

  BEATRICE.  Be cautious as ye may, but prompt.
  Orsino,
What are the means?

  ORSINO.   I know two dull, fierce outlaws,
Who think man's spirit as a worm's, and they
Would trample out, for any slight caprice,
The meanest or the noblest life. This mood
Is marketable here in Rome. They sell
What we now want.

  LUCRETIA.   To-morrow before dawn,
Cenci will take us to that lonely rock,
Petrella, in the Apulian Apennines.
If he arrive there . . .

  BEATRICE   He must not arrive.

  ORSINO. Will it be dark before you reach the
   tower?

  LUCRETIA. The sun will scarce be set.

BEATRICE.                    But I remember
Two miles on this side of the fort, the road
Crosses a deep ravine; 'tis rough and narrow,
And winds with short turns down the precipice;
And in its depth there is a mighty rock,
Which has, from unimaginable years,
Sustained itself with terror and with toil
Over a gulph, and with the agony
With which it clings seems slowly coming down;
Even as a wretched soul hour after hour,
Clings to the mass of life; yet clinging, leans;
And leaning, makes more dark the dread abyss
In which it fears to fall: beneath this crag
Huge as despair, as if in weariness,
The melancholy mountain yawns . . . below,
You hear but see not an impetuous torrent
Raging among the caverns, and a bridge
Crosses the chasm; and high above there grow,
With intersecting trunks, from crag to crag,
Cedars, and yews, and pines; whose tangled hair
Is matted in one solid roof of shade
By the dark ivy's twine.  At noonday here
'Tis twilight, and at sunset blackest night.

  ORSINO. Before you reach that bridge make
        some excuse
For spurring on your mules, or loitering
Until . . .
    BEATRICE.                    What sound is that?
    LUCRETIA. Hark! No, it cannot be a servant's step;
It must be Cenci, unexpectedly
Returned . . . Make some excuse for being here.

    BEATRICE (*To* ORSINO, *as she goes out.*) That step
        we hear approach must never pass
The bridge of which we spoke.
                        [*Exeunt* LUCRETIA *and* BEATRICE
  ORSINO.                    What shall I do?
Cenci must find me here, and I must bear
The imperious inquisition of his looks
As to what brought me hither: let me mask
Mine own in some inane and vacant smile.

*Enter* GIACOMO, *in a hurried manner*

How! Have you ventured hither? Know you then
That Cenci is from home?
    GIACOMO.               I sought him here;
And now must wait till he returns.
    ORSINO.                  Great God!
Weigh you the danger of this rashness?
    GIACOMO.                    Ay!
Does my destroyer know his danger? We
Are now no more, as once, parent and child,
But man to man; the oppressor to the oppressed;
The slanderer to the slandered; foe to foe:
He has cast Nature off, which was his shield,
And Nature casts him off, who is her shame;
And I spurn both. Is it a father's throat
Which I will shake, and say, I ask not gold;
I ask not happy years; nor memories
Of tranquil childhood; nor home-sheltered love;
Though all these hast thou torn from me, and more;
But only my fair fame; only one hoard
Of peace, which I thought hidden from thy hate,
Under the penury heaped on me by thee,
Or I will . . . God can understand and pardon,
Why should I speak with man?
    ORSINO.               Be calm, dear friend.
    GIACOMO. Well, I will calmly tell you what he did.
This old Francesco Cenci, as you know,
Borrowed the dowry of my wife from me,
And then denied the loan; and left me so
In poverty, the which I sought to mend
By holding a poor office in the state.
It had been promised to me, and already
I bought new clothing for my ragged babes,
And my wife smiled; and my heart knew repose.
When Cenci's intercession, as I found,
Conferred this office on a wretch, whom thus
He paid for vilest service. I returned
With this ill news, and we sate sad together
Solacing our despondency with tears

Of such affection and unbroken faith
As temper life's worst bitterness; when he,
As he is wont, came to upbraid and curse,
Mocking our poverty, and telling us
Such was God's scourge for disobedient sons.
And then, that I might strike him dumb with shame,
I spoke of my wife's dowry; but he coined
A brief yet specious tale, how I had wasted
The sum in secret riot; and he saw
My wife was touched, and he went smiling forth.
And when I knew the impression he had made,
And felt my wife insult with silent scorn
My ardent truth, and look averse and cold,
I went forth too: but soon returned again;
Yet not so soon but that my wife had taught
My children her harsh thoughts, and they all cried,
"Give us clothes, father! Give us better food!
What you in one night squander were enough
For months!" I looked, and saw that home was hell.
And to that hell will I return no more
Until mine enemy has rendered up
Atonement, or, as he gave life to me
I will, reversing nature's law . . .

    ORSINO.                     Trust me,
The compensation which thou seekest here
Will be denied.

    GIACOMO.     Then . . . Are you not my friend?
Did you not hint at the alternative,
Upon the brink of which you see I stand,
The other day when we conversed together?
My wrongs were then less. That word parricide,
Although I am resolved, haunts me like fear.

    ORSINO. It must be fear itself, for the bare word
Is hollow mockery. Mark, how wisest God
Draws to one point the threads of a just doom,
So sanctifying it: what you devise
Is, as it were, accomplished.

    GIACOMO.              Is he dead?

    ORSINO. His grave is ready. Know that since
      we met

Cenci has done an outrage to his daughter.
  GIACOMO. What outrage?
  ORSINO. That she speaks not, but you may
Conceive such half conjectures as I do,
From her fixed paleness, and the lofty grief
Of her stern brow bent on the idle air,
And her severe unmodulated voice,
Drowning both tenderness and dread; and last
From this; that whilst her step-mother and I,
Bewildered in our horror, talked together
With obscure hints; both self-misunderstood
And darkly guessing, stumbling, in our talk,
Over the truth, and yet to its revenge,
She interrupted us, and with a look
Which told before she spoke it, he must die: . . .
  GIACOMO. It is enough. My doubts are well
      appeased;
There is a higher reason for the act
Than mine; there is a holier judge than me,
A more unblamed avenger. Beatrice,
Who in the gentleness of thy sweet youth
Hast never trodden on a worm, or bruised
A living flower, but thou hast pitied it
With needless tears! Fair sister, thou in whom
Men wondered how such loveliness and wisdom
Did not destroy each other! Is there made
Ravage of thee? O, heart, I ask no more
Justification! Shall I wait, Orsino,
Till he return, and stab him at the door?
  ORSINO. Not so; some accident might interpose
To rescue him from what is now most sure;
And you are unprovided where to fly,
How to excuse or to conceal. Nay, listen:
All is contrived; success is so assured
That . . .

### Enter BEATRICE

  BEATRICE. 'Tis my brother's voice! You know
    me not?
  GIACOMO. My sister, my lost sister!

BEATRICE.                        Lost indeed!
I see Orsino has talked with you, and
That you conjecture things too horrible
To speak, yet far less than the truth.
          Now, stay not,
He might return: yet kiss me; I shall know
That then thou hast consented to his death.
Farewell, farewell! Let piety to God,
Brotherly love, justice and clemency,
And all things that make tender hardest hearts
Make thine hard, brother. Answer not . . . fare-
          well.                        [*Exeunt severally.*

SCENE II.—*A mean Apartment in* GIACOMO'S *House*

GIACOMO *alone*

GIACOMO. 'Tis midnight, and Orsino comes not
          yet.      [*Thunder, and the sound of a storm.*
What! can the everlasting elements
Feel with a worm like man? If so the shaft
Of mercy-wingèd lightning would not fall
On stones and trees. My wife and children sleep:
They are now living in unmeaning dreams:
But I must wake, still doubting if that deed
Be just which was most necessary. O,
Thou unreplenished lamp! whose narrow fire
Is shaken by the wind, and on whose edge
Devouring darkness hovers! Thou small flame,
Which, as a dying pulse rises and falls,
Still flickerest up and down, how very soon,
Did I not feed thee, wouldst thou fail and be
As thou hadst never been! So wastes and sinks
Even now, perhaps, the life that kindled mine:
But that no power can fill with vital oil
That broken lamp of flesh. Ha! 'tis the blood
Which fed these veins that ebbs till all is cold:
It is the form that moulded mine that sinks
Into the white and yellow spasms of death:
It is the soul by which mine was arrayed

In God's immortal likeness which now stands
Naked before Heaven's judgment seat!
   (*A bell strikes.*)                  One! Two!
The hours crawl on; and when my hairs are white,
My son will then perhaps be waiting thus,
Tortured between just hate and vain remorse;
Chiding the tardy messenger of news
Like those which I expect.  I almost wish
He be not dead, although my wrongs are great;
Yet . . . 'tis Orsino's step . . .


*Enter* ORSINO

                              Speak!
  ORSINO.                    I am come
To say he has escaped.
    GIACOMO.          Escaped!
    ORSINO.               And safe
Within Petrella.  He past by the spot
Appointed for the deed an hour too soon.
  GIACOMO. Are we the fools of such contingencies?
And do we waste in blind misgivings thus
The hours when we should act?  Then wind and
    thunder,
Which seemed to howl his knell, is the loud laughter
With which Heaven mocks our weakness!  I
    henceforth
Will ne'er repent of aught designed or done
But my repentance.
    ORSINO.       See, the lamp is out.
  GIACOMO. If no remorse is ours when the dim
    air
Has drank this innocent flame, why should we quail
When Cenci's life, that light by which ill spirits
See the worst deeds they prompt, shall sink for
    ever?
No, I am hardened.
    ORSINO. Why, what need of this?
Who feared the pale intrusion of remorse
In a just deed?  Altho' our first plan failed,

Doubt not but he will soon be laid to rest.
But light the lamp; let us not talk i' the dark.
    GIACOMO (*lighting the lamp*). And yet once
        quenched I cannot thus relume
My father's life: do you not think his ghost
Might plead that argument with God?
    ORSINO.                    Once gone
You cannot now recall your sister's peace;
Your own extinguished years of youth and hope;
Nor your wife's bitter words; nor all the taunts
Which, from the prosperous, weak misfortune takes;
Nor your dead mother; nor . . .
    GIACOMO.              O, speak no more!
I am resolved, although this very hand
Must quench the life that animated it.
    ORSINO. There is no need of that.  Listen: you
        know
Olimpio, the castellan of Petrella
In old Colonna's time; him whom your father
Degraded from his post?  And Marzio,
That desperate wretch, whom he deprived last year
Of a reward of blood, well earned and due?
    GIACOMO. I knew Olimpio; and they say he
        hated
Old Cenci so, that in his silent rage
His lips grew white only to see him pass.
Of Marzio I know nothing.
    ORSINO.             Marzio's hate
Matches Olimpio's.  I have sent these men,
But in your name and as at your request,
To talk with Beatrice and Lucretia.
    GIACOMO. Only to talk?
    ORSINO. The moments which even now
Pass onward to to-morrow's midnight hour
May memorise their flight with death: ere then
They must have talked, and may perhaps have done
And made an end . . .
    GIACOMO. Listen! What sound is that?
    ORSINO. The house-dog moans, and the beams
        crack: nought else.

GIACOMO. It is my wife complaining in her sleep:
I doubt not she is saying bitter things
Of me; and all my children round her dreaming
That I deny them sustenance.
    ORSINO.                      Whilst he
Who truly took it from them, and who fills
Their hungry rest with bitterness, now sleeps
Lapped in bad pleasures, and triumphantly
Mocks thee in visions of successful hate
Too like the truth of day.
    GIACOMO.               If e'er he wakes
Again, I will not trust to hireling hands . . .
    ORSINO. Why, that were well.  I must be gone;
        good-night:
When next we meet—may all be done!
    GIACOMO. .                And all
Forgotten: Oh, that I had never been!
                                   *[Exeunt.*

## ACT IV

SCENE I.—*An Apartment in the Castle of Petrella*

*Enter* CENCI

CENCI. She comes not; yet I left her even now
Vanquished and faint.  She knows the penalty
Of her delay: yet what if threats are vain?
Am I not now within Petrella's moat?
Or fear I still the eyes and ears of Rome?
Might I not drag her by the golden hair?
Stamp on her?  Keep her sleepless till her brain
Be overworn?  Tame her with chains and famine?
Less would suffice.  Yet so to leave undone
What I most seek!  No, 'tis her stubborn will
Which by its own consent shall stoop as low
As that which drags it down.

*Enter* LUCRETIA

                        Thou loathèd wretch!
Hide thee from my abhorrence; fly, begone!

Yet stay! Bid Beatrice come hither.

LUCRETIA.                                          Oh,
Husband! I pray for thine own wretched sake
Heed what thou dost. A man who walks like thee
Thro' crimes, and thro' the danger of his crimes,
Each hour may stumble o'er a sudden grave.
And thou art old; thy hairs are hoary gray;
As thou wouldst save thyself from death and hell,
Pity thy daughter; give her to some friend
In marriage: so that she may tempt thee not
To hatred, or worse thoughts, if worse there be.

CENCI. What! like her sister who has found a home
To mock my hate from with prosperity?
Strange ruin shall destroy both her and thee
And all that yet remain. My death may be
Rapid, her destiny outspeeds it. Go,
Bid her come hither, and before my mood
Be changed, lest I should drag her by the hair.

LUCRETIA. She sent me to thee, husband. At
      thy presence
She fell, as thou dost know, into a trance;
And in that trance she heard a voice which said,
"Cenci must die! Let him confess himself!
Even now the accusing Angel waits to hear
If God, to punish his enormous crimes,
Harden his dying heart!"

CENCI. Why—such things are . . .
No doubt divine revealings may be made.
'Tis plain I have been favoured from above,
For when I cursed my sons they died.—Ay . . . so . . .
As to the right or wrong that's talk . . . repent-
      ance . . .
Repentance is an easy moment's work
And more depends on God than me. Well . . .
      well . . .
I must give up the greater point, which was
To poison and corrupt her soul.

      [*A pause;* LUCRETIA *approaches anxiously, and then
      shrinks back as he speaks.*

                              One, two;

Ay . . . Rocco and Cristofano my curse
Strangled: and Giacomo, I think, will find
Life a worse Hell than that beyond the grave:
Beatrice shall, if there be skill in hate,
Die in despair, blaspheming: to Bernardo,
He is so innocent, I will bequeath
The memory of these deeds, and make his youth
The sepulchre of hope, where evil thoughts
Shall grow like weeds on a neglected tomb.
When all is done, out in the wide Campagna,
I will pile up my silver and my gold;
My costly robes, paintings and tapestries;
My parchments and all records of my wealth,
And make a bonfire in my joy, and leave
Of my possessions nothing but my name;
Which shall be an inheritance to strip
Its wearer bare as infamy. That done,
My soul, which is a scourge, will I resign
Into the hands of him who wielded it;
Be it for its own punishment or theirs,
He will not ask it of me till the lash
Be broken in its last and deepest wound;
Until its hate be all inflicted. Yet,
Lest death outspeed my purpose, let me make
Short work and sure . . .                    [*Going.*

   LUCRETIA. (*Stops him.*) Oh, stay! It was a feint:
She had no vision, and she heard no voice.
I said it but to awe thee.
   CENCI.                    That is well.
Vile palterer with the sacred truth of God,
Be thy soul choked with that blaspheming lie!
For Beatrice worse terrors are in store
To bend her to my will.
   LUCRETIA.            Oh! to what will?
What cruel sufferings more than she has known
Canst thou inflict?
   CENCI. Andrea! Go call my daughter,
And if she comes not tell her that I come.
What sufferings? I will drag her, step by step,
Thro' infamies unheard of among men:

She shall stand shelterless in the broad noon
Of public scorn, for acts blazoned abroad,
One among which shall be . . .   What? Canst
    thou guess?
She shall become (for what she most abhors
Shall have a fascination to entrap
Her loathing will) to her own conscious self
All she appears to others; and when dead,
As she shall die unshrived and unforgiven,
A rebel to her father and her God,
Her corpse shall be abandoned to the hounds;
Her name shall be the terror of the earth;
Her spirit shall approach the throne of God
Plague-spotted with my curses.  I will make
Body and soul a monstrous lump of ruin.


*Enter* ANDREA

ANDREA.  The Lady Beatrice . . .
CENCI.                              Speak, pale slave!  What
Said she?
ANDREA.  My Lord, 'twas what she looked; she
    said:
" Go tell my father that I see the gulf
Of Hell between us two, which he may pass,
I will not."                              [*Exit* ANDREA.
CENCI.    Go thou quick, Lucretia,
Tell her to come; yet let her understand
Her coming is consent: and say, moreover,
That if she come not I will curse her.
                    [*Exit* LUCRETIA.
                  Ha!
With what but with a father's curse doth God
Panic-strike armèd victory, and make pale
Cities in their prosperity?   The world's Father
Must grant a parent's prayer against his child
Be he who asks even what men call me.
Will not the deaths of her rebellious brothers
Awe her before I speak?  For I on them
Did imprecate quick ruin, and it came.

*Enter* LUCRETIA

Well; what?  Speak, wretch!

LUCRETIA.  She said, "I cannot come;
Go tell my father that I see a torrent
Of his own blood raging between us."

CENCI (*kneeling*).                              God!
Hear me!  If this most specious mass of flesh,
Which thou hast made my daughter; this my
        blood,
This particle of my divided being;
Or rather, this my bane and my disease,
Whose sight infects and poisons me; this devil
Which sprung from me as from a hell, was meant
To aught good use; if her bright loveliness
Was kindled to illumine this dark world;
If nursed by thy selectest dew of love
Such virtues blossom in her as should make
The peace of life, I pray thee for my sake,
As thou the common God and Father art
Of her, and me, and all; reverse that doom!
Earth, in the name of God, let her food be
Poison, until she be encrusted round
With leprous stains!  Heaven, rain upon her head
The blistering drops of the Maremma's dew,
Till she be speckled like a toad; parch up
Those love-enkindled lips, warp those fine limbs
To loathèd lameness!  All-beholding sun,
Strike in thine envy those life-darting eyes
With thine own blinding beams!

LUCRETIA.                              Peace! Peace!
For thine own sake unsay those dreadful words.
When high God grants he punishes such prayers.

CENCI (*leaping up, and throwing his right hand
        towards Heaven*). He does his will, I
        mine!  This in addition,
That if she have a child . . .

LUCRETIA.                              Horrible thought!

CENCI. That if she ever have a child; and thou,
Quick Nature! I adjure thee by thy God,

That thou be fruitful in her, and increase
And multiply, fulfilling his command,
And my deep imprecation! May it be
A hideous likeness of herself, that as
From a distorting mirror, she may see
Her image mixed with what she most abhors,
Smiling upon her from her nursing breast.
And that the child may from its infancy
Grow, day by day, more wicked and deformed,
Turning her mother's love to misery:
And that both she and it may live until
It shall repay her care and pain with hate,
Or what may else be more unnatural.
So he may hunt her through the clamorous scoffs
Of the loud world to a dishonoured grave.
Shall I revoke this curse? Go, bid her come,
Before my words are chronicled in Heaven.

[*Exit* LUCRETIA.

I do not feel as if I were a man,
But like a fiend appointed to chastise
The offences of some unremembered world.
My blood is running up and down my veins;
A fearful pleasure makes it prick and tingle:
I feel a giddy sickness of strange awe;
My heart is beating with an expectation
Of horrid joy.

*Enter* LUCRETIA
                    What? Speak!

LUCRETIA.                          She bids thee curse;
And if thy curses, as they cannot do,
Could kill her soul . . .

    CENCI. She would not come. 'Tis well,
I can do both: first take what I demand,
And then extort concession. To thy chamber!
Fly ere I spurn thee: and beware this night
That thou cross not my footsteps. It were safer
To come between the tiger and his prey.

[*Exit* LUCRETIA.

It must be late; mine eyes grow weary dim

With unaccustomed heaviness of sleep.
Conscience!   Oh, thou most insolent of lies!
They say that sleep, that healing dew of Heaven,
Steeps not in balm the foldings of the brain
Which thinks thee an impostor.   I will go
First to belie thee with an hour of rest,
Which will be deep and calm, I feel: and then . . .
O, multitudinous Hell, the fiends will shake
Thine arches with the laughter of their joy!
There shall be lamentation heard in Heaven
As o'er an angel fallen and upon Earth
All good shall droop and sicken, and ill things
Shall with a spirit of unnatural life
Stir and be quickened . . . even as I am now.  [*Exit.*

SCENE II.—*Before the Castle of Petrella*

*Enter* BEATRICE *and* LUCRETIA *above on the Ramparts*
   BEATRICE. They come not yet.
      LUCRETIA.               , 'Tis scarce midnight.
      BEATRICE.                   How slow
Behind the course of thought, even sick with speed,
Lags leaden footed time!
      LUCRETIA           The minutes pass . . .
If he should wake before the deed is done?
BEATRICE. O, mother!   He must never wake again.
What thou hast said persuades me that our act
Will but dislodge a spirit of deep hell
Out of a human form.
      LUCRETIA.            'Tis true he spoke
Of death and judgment with strange confidence
For one so wicked; as a man believing
In God, yet recking not of good or ill.
And yet to die without confession! . . .
      BEATRICE.                  Oh!
Believe that Heaven is merciful and just,
And will not add our dread necessity
To the amount of his offences.

*Enter* OLIMPIO *and* MARZIO, *below*

LUCRETIA.                                    See,
They come.

BEATRICE. All mortal things must hasten thus
To their dark end. Let us go down.

[*Exeunt* LUCRETIA *and* BEATRICE *from above.*

OLIMPIO. How feel you to this work?

MARZIO.                          As one who thinks
A thousand crowns excellent market price
For an old murderer's life. Your cheeks are pale.

OLIMPIO. It is the white reflection of your own,
Which you call pale.

MARZIO.               Is that their natural hue?

OLIMPIO.  Or 'tis my hate and the deferred desire
To wreak it, which extinguishes their blood.

MARZIO. You are inclined then to this business?

OLIMPIO.                                        Ay.
If one should bribe me with a thousand crowns
To kill a serpent which had stung my child,
I could not be more willing.


*Enter* BEATRICE *and* LUCRETIA, *below*
                              Noble ladies!

BEATRICE. Are ye resolved?

OLIMPIO.                    Is he asleep?

MARZIO.                                 Is all
Quiet?

LUCRETIA.   I mixed an opiate with his drink:
He sleeps so soundly . . .

BEATRICE.               That his death will be
But as a change of sin-chastising dreams,
A dark continuance of the Hell within him,
Which God extinguish! But ye are resolved?
Ye know it is a high and holy deed?

OLIMPIO. We are resolved.

MARZIO.                    As to the how this act
Be warranted, it rests with you.

BEATRICE.                      Well, follow!

OLIMPIO. Hush! Hark! What noise is that?

MARZIO. Ha! some one comes!

BEATRICE. Ye conscience-stricken cravens, rock to rest
Your baby hearts. It is the iron gate,
Which ye left open, swinging to the wind,
That enters whistling as in scorn. Come, follow!
And be your steps like mine, light, quick and bold.

[*Exeunt.*

SCENE III.—*An Apartment in the Castle*

*Enter* BEATRICE *and* LUCRETIA

LUCRETIA. They are about it now.

BEATRICE. Nay, it is done.

LUCRETIA. I have not heard him groan.

BEATRICE. He will not groan.

LUCRETIA. What sound is that?

BEATRICE. List! 'tis the tread of feet
About his bed.

LUCRETIA. My God!
If he be now a cold stiff corpse . . .

BEATRICE. O, fear not
What may be done, but what is left undone:
The act seals all.

*Enter* OLIMPIO *and* MARZIO
Is it accomplished?

MARZIO. What?

OLIMPIO. Did you not call?

BEATRICE. When?

OLIMPIO. Now.

BEATRICE. I ask if all is over?

OLIMPIO. We dare not kill an old and sleeping man;
His thin gray hair, his stern and reverent brow,
His veinèd hands crossed on his heaving breast,
And the calm innocent sleep in which he lay,
Quelled me. Indeed, indeed, I cannot do it.

MARZIO. But I was bolder; for I chid Olimpio,
And bade him bear his wrongs to his own grave

And leave me the reward.  And now my knife
Touched the loose wrinkled throat, when the old man
Stirred in his sleep, and said, " God ! hear, O, hear,
A father's curse ! What, art thou not our father ? "
And then he laughed.  I knew it was the ghost
Of my dead father speaking through his lips,
And could not kill him.

   BEATRICE.           Miserable slaves !
Where, if ye dare not kill a sleeping man,
Found ye the boldness to return to me
With such a deed undone ?  Base palterers !
Cowards and traitors !  Why, the very conscience
Which ye would sell for gold and for revenge
Is an equivocation : it sleeps over
A thousand daily acts disgracing men ;
And when a deed where mercy insults Heaven . . .
Why do I talk ?

   *[Snatching a dagger from one of them and raising it.*
                Hadst thou a tongue to say,
She murdered her own father, I must do it !
But never dream ye shall outlive him long !

   OLIMPIO. Stop, for God's sake !

   MARZIO.            I will go back and kill him.

   OLIMPIO. Give me the weapon, we must do thy will.

   BEATRICE. Take it ! Depart ! Return !

               *[Exeunt* OLIMPIO *and* MARZIO.
                    How pale thou art !
We do but that which 'twere a deadly crime
To leave undone.

   LUCRETIA.       Would it were done !

   BEATRICE.                Even whilst
That doubt is passing through your mind, the world
Is conscious of a change.  Darkness and Hell
Have swallowed up the vapour they sent forth
To blacken the sweet light of life.  My breath
Comes, methinks, lighter, and the jellied blood
Runs freely thro' my veins.  Hark !

*Enter* OLIMPIO *and* MARZIO

He is . . .

OLIMPIO.                                             Dead!

MARZIO. We strangled him that there might be no
　　blood;
And then we threw his heavy corpse i' the garden
Under the balcony; 'twill seem it fell.

BEATRICE (*giving them a bag of coin*). Here, take
　　this gold and hasten to your homes.
And, Marzio, because thou wast only awed
By that which made me tremble, wear thou this!
　　　　　　　　　　[*Clothes him in a rich mantle.*
It was the mantle which my grandfather
Wore in his high prosperity, and men
Envied his state: so may they envy thine.
Thou wert a weapon in the hand of God
To a just use. Live long and thrive! And, mark,
If thou hast crimes, repent: this deed is none.
　　　　　　　　　　　　[*A horn is sounded.*

LUCRETIA. Hark, 'tis the castle horn; my God! it
　　sounds
Like the last trump.

BEATRICE.                     Some tedious guest is coming.

LUCRETIA. The drawbridge is let down; there is a
　　tramp
Of horses in the court; fly, hide yourselves!
　　　　　　　　　　[*Exeunt* OLIMPIO *and* MARZIO.

BEATRICE. Let us retire to counterfeit deep rest;
I scarcely need to counterfeit it now:
The spirit which doth reign within these limbs
Seems strangely undisturbed. I could even sleep
Fearless and calm: all ill is surely past.　　[*Exeunt.*


SCENE IV.—*Another Apartment in the Castle*

*Enter on one side the Legate* SAVELLA, *introduced by a
Servant, and on the other* LUCRETIA *and* BERNARDO

SAVELLA. Lady, my duty to his Holiness
Be my excuse that thus unseasonably

I break upon your rest. I must speak with
Count Cenci; doth he sleep?

    LUCRETIA (*in a hurried and confused manner*). I
        think he sleeps;
Yet wake him not, I pray, spare me awhile,
He is a wicked and a wrathful man;
Should he be roused out of his sleep to-night,
Which is, I know, a hell of angry dreams,
It were not well; indeed it were not well.
Wait till day break . . . (*aside*) O, I am deadly sick!

    SAVELLA. I grieve thus to distress you, but the Count
Must answer charges of the gravest import,
And suddenly; such my commission is.

    LUCRETIA. (*with increased agitation*). I dare not
        rouse him: I know none who dare . . .
'Twere perilous; . . . you might as safely waken
A serpent; or a corpse in which some fiend
Were laid to sleep.

    SAVELLA.          Lady, my moments here
Are counted. I must rouse him from his sleep,
Since none else dare.

    LUCRETIA (*aside*). O, terror! O, despair!
(*To* BERNARDO.) Bernardo, conduct you the Lord
        Legate to
Your father's chamber.

                [*Exeunt* SAVELLA *and* BERNARDO.

*Enter* BEATRICE

    BEATRICE.          'Tis a messenger
Come to arrest the culprit who now stands
Before the throne of unappealable God.
Both Earth and Heaven, consenting arbiters,
Acquit our deed.

    LUCRETIA.     Oh, agony of fear!
Would that he yet might live! Even now I heard
The Legate's followers whisper as they passed
They had a warrant for his instant death.
All was prepared by unforbidden means
Which we must pay so dearly, having done.
Even now they search the tower, and find the body;

Now they suspect the truth; now they consult
Before they come to tax us with the fact;
O, horrible, 'tis all discovered!

BEATRICE.                              Mother,
What is done wisely, is done well.  Be bold
As thou art just.  'Tis like a truant child
To fear that others know what thou hast done,
Even from thine own strong consciousness, and thus
Write on unsteady eyes and altered cheeks
All thou wouldst hide.  Be faithful to thyself,
And fear no other witness but thy fear.
For if, as cannot be, some circumstance
Should rise in accusation, we can blind
Suspicion with such cheap astonishment,
Or overbear it with such guiltless pride,
As murderers cannot feign.  The deed is done,
And what may follow now regards not me.
I am as universal as the light;
Free as the earth-surrounding air; as firm
As the world's centre.  Consequence, to me,
Is as the wind which strikes the solid rock
But shakes it not.

                    [*A cry within and tumult*
VOICES.                    Murder! Murder! Murder!


                    *Enter* BERNARDO *and* SAVELLA

SAVELLA (*to his followers*).  Go search the castle
          round; sound the alarm;
Look to the gates that none escape!

BEATRICE.                              What now?

BERNARDO.  I know not what to say . . . my father's
          dead.

BEATRICE.  How; dead! he only sleeps; you mistake,
          brother.
His sleep is very calm, very like death;
'Tis wonderful how well a tyrant sleeps.
He is not dead?

BERNARDO.          Dead; murdered.

LUCRETIA (*with extreme agitation*).  Oh no, no,

He is not murdered though he may be dead;
I have alone the keys of those apartments.
    SAVELLA. Ha! Is it so?
    BEATRICE.             My Lord, I pray excuse us;
We will retire; my mother is not well:
She seems quite overcome with this strange horror.
                  [*Exeunt* LUCRETIA *and* BEATRICE.
    SAVELLA. Can you suspect who may have murdered
      him?
    BERNARDO. I know not what to think.
    SAVELLA.             Can you name any
Who had an interest in his death?
    BERNARDO.           Alas!
I can name none who had not, and those most
Who most lament that such a deed is done;
My mother, and my sister, and myself.
    SAVELLA. 'Tis strange! There were clear marks of
      violence.
I found the old man's body in the moonlight
Hanging beneath the window of his chamber,
Among the branches of a pine: he could not
Have fallen there, for all his limbs lay heaped
And effortless; 'tis true there was no blood . . .
Favour me, Sir; it much imports your house ·
That all should be made clear; to tell the ladies
That I request their presence.     [*Exit* BERNARDO.


        *Enter* GUARDS *bringing in* MARZIO
    GUARD.              We have one.
    OFFICER. My Lord, we found this ruffian and
      another
Lurking among the rocks; there is no doubt
But that they are the murderers of Count Cenci;
Each had a bag of coin; this fellow wore
A gold-inwoven robe, which shining bright
Under the dark rocks to the glimmering moon
Betrayed them to our notice: the other fell
Desperately fighting.
    SAVELLA.        What does he confess?

OFFICER. He keeps firm silence; but these lines found
     on him
May speak.

SAVELLA. Their language is at least sincere. [*Reads.*

"To THE LADY BEATRICE.—That the atonement
of what my nature sickens to conjecture may soon
arrive, I send thee, at thy brother's desire, those
who will speak and do more than I dare write.
. . . Thy devoted servant,          ORSINO."

*Enter* LUCRETIA, BEATRICE, *and* BERNARDO
Knowest thou this writing, Lady?

BEATRICE.                           No.

SAVELLA.                                  Nor thou?

LUCRETIA. (*Her conduct throughout the scene is
     marked by extreme agitation.*) Where was it
     found? What is it? It should be
Orsino's hand! It speaks of that strange horror
Which never yet found utterance, but which made
Between that hapless child and her dead father
A gulf of obscure hatred.

SAVELLA.                Is it so?
Is it true, Lady, that thy father did
Such outrages as to awaken in thee
Unfilial hate?

BEATRICE.    Not hate, 'twas more than hate:
This is most true, yet wherefore question me?

SAVELLA. There is a deed demanding question done;
Thou hast a secret which will answer not.

BEATRICE. What sayest? My Lord, your words are
     bold and rash.

SAVELLA. I do arrest all present in the name
Of the Pope's Holiness. You must to Rome.

LUCRETIA. O, not to Rome. Indeed we are not guilty.

BEATRICE. Guilty! Who dares talk of guilt? My
     Lord,
I am more innocent of parricide
Than is a child born fatherless. . . . Dear mother,
Your gentleness and patience are no shield

For this keen-judging world, this two-edged lie,
Which seems, but is not. What! will human laws,
Rather will ye who are their ministers,
Bar all access to retribution first,
And then, when Heaven doth interpose to do
What ye neglect, arming familiar things
To the redress of an unwonted crime,
Make ye the victims who demanded it
Culprits? 'Tis ye are culprits! That poor wretch
Who stands so pale, and trembling, and amazed,
If it be true he murdered Cenci, was
A sword in the right hand of justest God.
Wherefore should I have wielded it? Unless
The crimes which mortal tongue dare never name
God therefore scruples to avenge.

    SAVELLA.            You own
That you desired his death?

    BEATRICE.            It would have been
A crime no less than his, if for one moment
That fierce desire had faded in my heart.
'Tis true I did believe, and hope, and pray,
Ay, I even knew . . . for God is wise and just,
That some strange sudden death hung over him.
'Tis true that this did happen, and most true
There was no other rest for me on earth,
No other hope in Heaven . . . now what of this?

    SAVELLA. Strange thoughts beget strange deeds; and
      here are both:
I judge thee not.

    BEATRICE.      And yet, if you arrest me,
You are the judge and executioner
Of that which is the life of life: the breath
Of accusation kills an innocent name,
And leaves for lame acquittal the poor life
Which is a mask without it. 'Tis most false
That I am guilty of foul parricide;
Although I must rejoice, for justest cause,
That other hands have sent my father's soul
To ask the mercy he denied to me.
Now leaves us free; stain not a noble house

With vague surmises of rejected crime;
Add to our sufferings and your own neglect
No heavier sum: let them have been enough:
Leave us the wreck we have.

    SAVELLA.                    I dare not, Lady.
I pray that you prepare yourselves for Rome:
There the Pope's further pleasure will be known.

    LUCRETIA. O, not to Rome! O, take us not to Rome!

    BEATRICE. Why not to Rome, dear mother? There
        as here
Our innocence is as an armèd heel
To trample accusation. God is there
As here, and with his shadow ever clothes
The innocent, the injured and the weak;
And such are we. Cheer up, dear Lady, lean
On me; collect your wandering thoughts. My Lord,
As soon as you have taken some refreshment,
And had all such examinations made
Upon the spot, as may be necessary
To the full understanding of this matter,
We shall be ready. Mother; will you come?

    LUCRETIA. Ha! they will bind us to the rack, and
        wrest
Self-accusation from our agony!
Will Giacomo be there? Orsino? Marzio?
All present; all confronted; all demanding
Each from the other's countenance the thing
Which is in every heart! O, misery!

                *[She faints, and is borne out.*

    SAVELLA. She faints: an ill appearance, this.

    BEATRICE.                            My Lord,
She knows not yet the uses of the world.
She fears that power is as a beast which grasps
And loosens not: a snake whose look transmutes
All things to guilt which is its nutriment.
She cannot know how well the supine slaves
Of blind authority read the truth of things
When written on a brow of guilelessness:
She sees not yet triumphant Innocence
Stand at the judgment-seat of mortal man,

A judge and an accuser of the wrong
Which drags it there. Prepare yourself, my Lord;
Our suite will join yours in the court below. [*Exeunt.*

## ACT V

### Scene I.—*An Apartment in* Orsino's *Palace*

#### *Enter* Orsino *and* Giacomo

Giacomo. Do evil deeds thus quickly come to end?
O, that the vain remorse which must chastise
Crimes done, had but as loud a voice to warn
As its keen sting is mortal to avenge!
O, that the hour when present had cast off
The mantle of its mystery, and shown
The ghastly form with which it now returns
When its scared game is roused, cheering the hounds
Of conscience to their prey! Alas! Alas!
It was a wicked thought, a piteous deed,
To kill an old and hoary-headed father.
  Orsino. It has turned out unluckily, in truth.
  Giacomo. To violate the sacred doors of sleep;
To cheat kind nature of the placid death
Which she prepares for overwearied age;
To drag from Heaven an unrepentant soul
Which might have quenched in reconciling prayers
A life of burning crimes . . .
  Orsino.                     You cannot say
I urged you to the deed.
  Giacomo.               O, had I never
Found in thy smooth and ready countenance
The mirror of my darkest thoughts; hadst thou
Never with hints and questions made me look
Upon the monster of my thought, until
It grew familiar to desire . . .
  Orsino.                       'Tis thus
Men cast the blame of their unprosperous acts
Upon the abettors of their own resolve;
Or anything but their weak, guilty selves.
And yet, confess the truth, it is the peril

In which you stand that gives you this pale sickness
Of penitence; confess 'tis fear disguised
From its own shame that takes the mantle now
Of thin remorse.  What if we yet were safe?

GIACOMO. How can that be?  Already Beatrice,
Lucretia and the murderer are in prison.
I doubt not officers are, whilst we speak,
Sent to arrest us.

ORSINO.            I have all prepared
For instant flight.  We can escape even now,
So we take fleet occasion by the hair.

GIACOMO. Rather expire in tortures, as I may.
What! will you cast by self-accusing flight
Assured conviction upon Beatrice?
She, who alone in this unnatural work,
Stands like God's angel ministered upon
By fiends; avenging such a nameless wrong
As turns black parricide to piety;
Whilst we for basest ends . . . I fear, Orsino,
While I consider all your words and looks,
Comparing them with your proposal now,
That you must be a villain.  For what end
Could you engage in such a perilous crime,
Training me on with hints, and signs, and smiles,
Even to this gulf?  Thou art no liar?  No,
Thou art a lie!  Traitor and murderer!
Coward and slave!  But, no, defend thyself; [*Drawing.*
Let the sword speak what the indignant tongue
Disdains to brand thee with.

ORSINO.                  Put up your weapon.
Is it the desperation of your fear
Makes you thus rash and sudden with a friend,
Now ruined for your sake?  If honest anger
Have moved you, know, that what I just proposed
Was but to try you.  As for me, I think,
Thankless affection led me to this point,
From which, if my firm temper could repent,
I cannot now recede.  Even whilst we speak
The ministers of justice wait below:
They grant me these brief moments.  Now if you

Have any word of melancholy comfort
To speak to your pale wife, 'twere best to pass
Out at the postern, and avoid them so.

GIACOMO. O, generous friend! How canst thou pardon me?
Would that my life could purchase thine!

ORSINO.                                    That wish
Now comes a day too late. Haste; fare thee well!
Hear'st thou not steps along the corridor?

[*Exit* GIACOMO.

I'm sorry for it; but the guards are waiting
At his own gate, and such was my contrivance
That I might rid me both of him and them.
I thought to act a solemn comedy
Upon the painted scene of this new world,
And to attain my own peculiar ends
By some such plot of mingled good and ill
As others weave; but there arose a Power
Which graspt and snapped the threads of my device
And turned it to a net of ruin . . . Ha!

[*A shout is heard.*

Is that my name I hear proclaimed abroad?
But I will pass, wrapt in a vile disguise;
Rags on my back, and a false innocence
Upon my face, thro' the misdeeming crowd
Which judges by what seems. 'Tis easy then
For a new name and for a country new,
And a new life, fashioned on old desires,
To change the honours of abandoned Rome.
And these must be the masks of that within,
Which must remain unaltered . . . Oh, I fear
That what is past will never let me rest!
Why, when none else is conscious, but myself,
Of my misdeeds, should my own heart's contempt
Trouble me? Have I not the power to fly
My own reproaches? Shall I be the slave
Of . . . what? A word? which those of this false
world
Employ against each other, not themselves;
As men wear daggers not for self-offence.

But if I am mistaken, where shall I
Find the disguise to hide me from myself,
As now I skulk from every other eye?

[*Exit.*

SCENE II.—*A Hall of Justice*

CAMILLO, JUDGES, etc., *are discovered seated;* MARZIO
*is led in*

FIRST JUDGE. Accused, do you persist in your denial?
I ask you, are you innocent, or guilty?
I demand who were the participators
In your offence?  Speak truth and the whole truth.
MARZIO. My God! I did not kill him; I know nothing;
Olimpio sold the robe to me from which
You would infer my guilt.
SECOND JUDGE.          Away with him!
FIRST JUDGE. Dare you, with lips yet white from the
     rack's kiss
Speak false?  Is it so soft a questioner,
That you would bandy lover's talk with it
Till it wind out your life and soul?  Away!
MARZIO. Spare me! O, spare! I will confess.
FIRST JUDGE.                    Then speak.
MARZIO. I strangled him in his sleep.
FIRST JUDGE.                Who urged you to it?
MARZIO. His own son Giacomo, and the young prelate
Orsino sent me to Petrella; there
The ladies Beatrice and Lucretia
Tempted me with a thousand crowns, and I
And my companion forthwith murdered him.
Now let me die.
FIRST JUDGE. This sounds as bad as truth.  Guards,
     there,
Lead forth the prisoner!

*Enter* LUCRETIA, BEATRICE, *and* GIACOMO, *guarded*

                    Look upon this man;
When did you see him last?
BEATRICE.                We never saw him.

MARZIO. You know me too well, Lady Beatrice.
BEATRICE. I know thee! How? where? when?
MARZIO.                              You know 'twas I
Whom you did urge with menaces and bribes
To kill your father. When the thing was done
You clothed me in a robe of woven gold
And bade me thrive: how I have thriven, you see.
You, my Lord Giacomo, Lady Lucretia,
You know that what I speak is true.

[BEATRICE *advances towards him; he covers his face,
and shrinks back.*

                                   O, dart
The terrible resentment of those eyes
On the dead earth! Turn them away from me!
They wound: 'twas torture forced the truth. My
    Lords,
Having said this let me be led to death.

  BEATRICE. Poor wretch, I pity thee: yet stay awhile.
  CAMILLO. Guards, lead him not away.
  BEATRICE.                        Cardinal Camillo,
You have a good repute for gentleness
And wisdom: can it be that you sit here
To countenance a wicked farce like this?
When some obscure and trembling slave is dragged
From sufferings which might shake the sternest heart
And bade to answer, not as he believes,
But as those may suspect or do desire
Whose questions thence suggest their own reply:
And that in peril of such hideous torments
As merciful God spares even the damned. Speak
    now
The thing you surely know, which is that you,
If your fine frame were stretched upon that wheel,
And you were told: "Confess that you did poison
Your little nephew; that fair blue-eyed child
Who was the loadstar of your life:"—and though
All see, since his most swift and piteous death,
That day and night, and heaven and earth, and time,
And all the things hoped for or done therein
Are changed to you, through your exceeding grief,

Yet you would say, " I confess anything:"
And beg from your tormentors, like that slave,
The refuge of dishonourable death.
I pray thee, Cardinal, that thou assert
My innocence.

    CAMILLO (*much moved*).   What shall we think, my
        Lords?
Shame on these tears! I thought the heart was frozen
Which is their fountain.   I would pledge my soul
That she is guiltless.

    JUDGE.                    Yet she must be tortured.
    CAMILLO. I would as soon have tortured mine own
        nephew
(If he now lived he would be just her age;
His hair, too, was her colour, and his eyes
Like hers in shape, but blue and not so deep)
As that most perfect image of God's love
That ever came sorrowing upon the earth.
She is as pure as speechless infancy!

    JUDGE. Well, be her purity on your head, my Lord,
If you forbid the rack.   His Holiness
Enjoined us to pursue this monstrous crime
By the severest forms of law; nay even
To stretch a point against the criminals.
The prisoners stand accused of parricide
Upon such evidence as justifies
Torture.

    BEATRICE. What evidence?   This man's?
    JUDGE.                                          Even so.
    BEATRICE. (*To Marzio*.) Come near.   And who art
        thou thus chosen forth
Out of the multitude of living men
To kill the innocent?

    MARZIO.                    I am Marzio,
Thy father's vassal.

    BEATRICE.                    Fix thine eyes on mine;
Answer to what I ask.

                (*Turning to the Judges*.)
                      I prithee mark
His countenance: unlike bold calumny

Which sometimes dares not speak the thing it looks,
He dares not look the thing he speaks, but bends
His gaze on the blind earth.
    (*To* MARZIO.)                    What! wilt thou say
That I did murder my own father?
    MARZIO.                              Oh!
Spare me!  My brain swims round . . . I cannot
        speak . . .
It was that horrid torture forced the truth.
Take me away!  Let her not look on me!
I am a guilty miserable wretch,
I have said all I know; now, let me die!
    BEATRICE. My Lords, if by my nature I had been
So stern, as to have planned the crime alleged,
Which your suspicions dictate to this slave,
And the rack makes him utter, do you think
I should have left this two-edged instrument
Of my misdeed; this man, this bloody knife
With my own name engraven on the heft,
Lying unsheathed amid a world of foes,
For my own death?  That with such horrible need
For deepest silence, I should have neglected
So trivial a precaution, as the making
His tomb the keeper of a secret written
On a thief's memory?  What is his poor life?
What are a thousand lives?  A parricide
Had trampled them like dust; and, see, he lives!
    (*Turning to* MARZIO.)  And thou . . .
    MARZIO.                         Oh, spare me!
                            Speak to me no more!
That stern yet piteous look, those solemn tones,
Wound worse than torture.
    (*To the Judges.*)        I have told it all;
For pity's sake lead me away to death.
    CAMILLO. Guards, lead him nearer the Lady Beatrice,
He shrinks from her regard like autumn's leaf
From the keen breath of the serenest north.
    BEATRICE. O thou who tremblest on the giddy verge
Of life and death, pause ere thou answerest me;
So mayst thou answer God with less dismay:

What evil have we done thee? I, alas!
Have lived but on this earth a few sad years
And so my lot was ordered, that a father
First turned the moments of awakening life
To drops, each poisoning youth's sweet hope; and then
Stabbed with one blow my everlasting soul;
And my untainted fame; and even that peace
Which sleeps within the core of the heart's heart;
But the wound was not mortal; so my hate
Became the only worship I could lift
To our great father, who in pity and love,
Armed thee, as thou dost say, to cut him off;
And thus his wrong becomes my accusation;
And art thou the accuser? If thou hopest
Mercy in heaven, show justice upon earth:
Worse than a bloody hand is a hard heart.
If thou hast done murders, made thy life's path
Over the trampled laws of God and man,
Rush not before thy Judge, and say: " My maker,
I have done this and more; for there was one
Who was most pure and innocent on earth;
And because she endured what never any
Guilty or innocent endured before:
Because her wrongs could not be told, not thought;
Because thy hand at length did rescue her;
I with my words killed her and all her kin."
Think, I adjure you, what it is to slay
The reverence living in the minds of men
Towards our ancient house, and stainless fame!
Think what it is to strangle infant pity,
Cradled in the belief of guileless looks,
Till it become a crime to suffer. Think
What 'tis to blot with infamy and blood
All that which shows like innocence, and is,
Hear me, great God! I swear, most innocent,
So that the world lose all discrimination
Between the sly, fierce, wild regard of guilt,
And that which now compels thee to reply
To what I ask: Am I, or am I not
A parricide?

MARZIO.     Thou art not!

JUDGE.                    What is this?

MARZIO. I here declare those whom I did accuse
Are innocent. 'Tis I alone am guilty.

JUDGE. Drag him away to torments; let them be
Subtle and long drawn out, to tear the folds
Of the heart's inmost cell. Unbind him not
Till he confess.

MARZIO.          Torture me as ye will:
A keener pain has wrung a higher truth
From my last breath. She is most innocent!
Bloodhounds, not men, glut yourselves well with me;
I will not give you that fine piece of nature
To rend and ruin.

                         [*Exit* MARZIO, *guarded.*

CAMILLO.          What say ye now, my Lords?

JUDGE. Let tortures strain the truth till it be white
As snow thrice sifted by the frozen wind.

CAMILLO. Yet stained with blood.

JUDGE (*to* BEATRICE). Know you this paper, Lady?

BEATRICE. Entrap me not with questions. Who
          stands here
As my accuser? Ha! wilt thou be he,
Who art my judge? Accuser, witness, judge,
What, all in one? Here is Orsino's name;
Where is Orsino? Let his eye meet mine.
What means this scrawl? Alas! ye know not what,
And therefore on the chance that it may be
Some evil, will ye kill us?


*Enter an Officer*

OFFICER.                    Marzio's dead.

JUDGE. What did he say?

OFFICER.                    Nothing. As soon as we
Had bound him on the wheel, he smiled on us,
As one who baffles a deep adversary;
And holding his breath, died.

JUDGE.                    There remains nothing
But to apply the question to those prisoners,

Who yet remain stubborn.

    CAMILLO.                I overrule
Further proceedings, and in the behalf
Of these most innocent and noble persons
Will use my interest with the Holy Father.

    JUDGE. Let the Pope's pleasure then be done.  Meanwhile
Conduct these culprits each to separate cells;
And be the engines ready: for this night
If the Pope's resolution be as grave,
Pious, and just as once, I'll wring the truth
Out of those nerves and sinews, groan by groan.

                                      [*Exeunt.*


SCENE III.—*The Cell of a Prison*


BEATRICE *is discovered asleep on a couch.  Enter* BERNARDO

    BERNARDO.  How gently slumber rests upon her face,
Like the last thoughts of some day sweetly spent
Closing in night and dreams, and so prolonged.
After such torments as she bore last night,
How light and soft her breathing comes.  Ay, me!
Methinks that I shall never sleep again.
But I must shake the heavenly dew of rest
From this sweet folded flower, thus . . . wake! awake!
What, sister, canst thou sleep?

    BEATRICE (*awaking*).        I was just dreaming
That we were all in Paradise.  Thou knowest
This cell seems like a kind of Paradise
After our father's presence.

    BERNARDO.             Dear, dear sister,
Would that thy dream were not a dream!  O God!
How shall I tell?

    BEATRICE.        What wouldst thou tell, sweet
        brother?

    BERNARDO.  Look not so calm and happy, or even
        whilst
I stand considering what I have to say
My heart will break.

    BEATRICE.        See now, thou mak'st me weep:

How very friendless thou wouldst be, dear child,
If I were dead. Say what thou hast to say.

BERNARDO. They have confessed; they could endure
no more
The tortures . . .

BEATRICE. Ha! What was there to confess?
They must have told some weak and wicked lie
To flatter their tormentors. Have they said
That they were guilty? O white innocence,
That thou shouldst wear the mask of guilt to hide
Thine awful and serenest countenance
From those who know thee not!


*Enter* JUDGE *with* LUCRETIA *and*
GIACOMO, *guarded*

Ignoble hearts!
For some brief spasms of pain, which are at least
As mortal as the limbs through which they pass,
Are centuries of high splendour laid in dust?
And that eternal honour which should live
Sunlike, above the reek of mortal fame,
Changed to a mockery and a bye-word? What!
Will you give up these bodies to be dragged
At horses' heels, so that our hair should sweep
The footsteps of the vain and senseless crowd,
Who, that they may make our calamity
Their worship and their spectacle, will leave
The churches and the theatres as void
As their own hearts? Shall the light multitude
Fling, at their choice, curses or faded pity,
Sad funeral flowers to deck a living corpse,
Upon us as we pass to pass away,
And leave . . . what memory of our having been?
Infamy, blood, terror, despair? O thou,
Who wert a mother to the parentless,
Kill not thy child! Let not her wrongs kill thee!
Brother, lie down with me upon the rack,
And let us each be silent as a corpse;
It soon will be as soft as any grave.

'Tis but the falsehood it can wring from fear
Makes the rack cruel.
    GIACOMO.          They will tear the truth
Even from thee at last, those cruel pains:
For pity's sake say thou art guilty now.
    LUCRETIA. Oh, speak the truth! Let us all quickly
      die;
And after death, God is our judge, not they;
He will have mercy on us.
    BERNARDO.         If indeed
It can be true, say so, dear sister mine;
And then the Pope will surely pardon you,
And all be well.
    JUDGE.        Confess, or I will warp
Your limbs with such keen tortures . . .
    BEATRICE.             Tortures! Turn
The rack henceforth into a spinning wheel!
Torture your dog, that he may tell when last
He lapped the blood his master shed . . . not me!
My pangs are of the mind, and of the heart,
And of the soul; ay, of the inmost soul,
Which weeps within tears as of burning gall
To see, in this ill world where none are true,
My kindred false to their deserted selves.
And with considering all the wretched life
Which I have lived, and its now wretched end,
And the small justice shown by Heaven and Earth
To me or mine; and what a tyrant thou art,
And what slaves these; and what a world we make,
The oppressor and the oppressed . . . such pangs compel
My answer. What is it thou wouldst with me?
    JUDGE. Art thou not guilty of thy father's death?
    BEATRICE. Or wilt thou rather tax high judging God
That he permitted such an act as that
Which I have suffered, and which he beheld;
Made it unutterable, and took from it
All refuge, all revenge, all consequence,
But that which thou hast called my father's death?
Which is or is not what men call a crime,
Which either I have done, or have not done;

Say what ye will. I shall deny no more.
If ye desire it thus, thus let it be,
And so an end of all. Now do your will;
No other pains shall force another word.

JUDGE. She is convicted, but has not confessed.
Be it enough. Until their final sentence
Let none have converse with them. You, young Lord,
Linger not here!

BEATRICE.          Oh, tear him not away!

JUDGE. Guards do your duty.

BERNARDO (*embracing* BEATRICE).

                         Oh! would ye divide
Body from soul?

OFFICER.          That is the headsman's business.

[*Exeunt all but* LUCRETIA,
BEATRICE, *and* GIACOMO.

GIACOMO. Have I confessed? Is it all over now?
No hope! No refuge! O weak, wicked tongue
Which hast destroyed me, would that thou hadst been
Cut out and thrown to dogs first! To have killed
My father first, and then betrayed my sister;
Ay, thee! the one thing innocent and pure
In this black guilty world, to that which I
So well deserve! My wife! my little ones!
Destitute, helpless, and I . . . Father! God!
Canst thou forgive even the unforgiving,
When their full hearts break thus, thus! . . .

[*Covers his face and weeps.*

LUCRETIA.          O my child!
To what a dreadful end are we all come!
Why did I yield? Why did I not sustain
Those torments? Oh, that I were all dissolved
Into these fast and unavailing tears,
Which flow and feel not!

BEATRICE.          What 'twas weak to do,
'Tis weaker to lament, once being done;
Take cheer! The God who knew my wrong, and made
Our speedy act the angel of his wrath,
Seems, and but seems, to have abandoned us.
Let us not think that we shall die for this.

Brother, sit near me; give me your firm hand,
You had a manly heart. Bear up! Bear up!
O dearest Lady, put your gentle head
Upon my lap, and try to sleep awhile:
Your eyes look pale, hollow and overworn,
With heaviness of watching and slow grief.
Come, I will sing you some low, sleepy tune,
Not cheerful, nor yet sad; some dull old thing,
Some outworn and unused monotony,
Such as our country gossips sing and spin,
Till they almost forget they live: lie down!
So, that will do. Have I forgot the words?
Faith! They are sadder than I thought they were.

### Song

False friend, wilt thou smile or weep
When my life is laid asleep?
Little cares for a smile or a tear,
The clay-cold corpse upon the bier!
        Farewell! Heigho!
        What is this whispers low?
There is a snake in thy smile, my dear;
And bitter poison within thy tear.

Sweet sleep, were death like to thee,
Or if thou couldst mortal be,
I would close these eyes of pain;
When to wake? Never again.
        O World! Farewell!
        Listen to the passing bell!
It says, thou and I must part,
With a light and a heavy heart.

                              [*The scene closes.*

### Scene IV.—*A Hall of the Prison*

*Enter* Camillo *and* Bernardo

CAMILLO.   The Pope is stern; not to be moved or bent.
He looked as calm and keen as is the engine

Which tortures and which kills, exempt itself
From aught that it inflicts; a marble form,
A rite, a law, a custom: not a man.
He frowned, as if to frown had been the trick
Of his machinery, on the advocates
Presenting the defences, which he tore
And threw behind, muttering with hoarse, harsh voice:
" Which among ye defended their old father
Killed in his sleep? " Then to another: " Thou
Dost this in virtue of thy place; 'tis well."
He turned to me then, looking deprecation,
And said these three words, coldly: " They must die."

  BERNARDO. And yet you left him not?
  CAMILLO.       I urged him still;
Pleading, as I could guess, the devilish wrong
Which prompted your unnatural parent's death.
And he replied: " Paolo Santa Croce
Murdered his mother yester evening,
And he is fled. Parricide grows so rife
That soon, for some just cause no doubt, the young
Will strangle us all, dozing in our chairs.
Authority, and power, and hoary hair
Are grown crimes capital. You are my nephew,
You come to ask their pardon; stay a moment;
Here is their sentence; never see me more
Till, to the letter, it be all fulfilled."

  BERNARDO. O God, not so! I did believe indeed
That all you said was but sad preparation
For happy news. Oh, there are words and looks
To bend the sternest purpose! Once I knew them,
Now I forget them at my dearest need.
What think you if I seek him out, and bathe
His feet and robe with hot and bitter tears?
Importune him with prayers, vexing his brain
With my perpetual cries, until in rage
He strike me with his pastoral cross, and trample
Upon my prostrate head, so that my blood
May stain the senseless dust on which he treads,
And remorse waken mercy? I will do it!
Oh, wait till I return!     [*Rushes out.*

CAMILLO. Alas! poor boy!
A wreck-devoted seaman thus might pray
To the deaf sea.

*Enter* LUCRETIA, BEATRICE, *and*
GIACOMO, *guarded*

BEATRICE. I hardly dare to fear
That thou bring'st other news than a just pardon.
CAMILLO. May God in heaven be less inexorable
To the Pope's prayers, than he has been to mine.
Here is the sentence and the warrant.
BEATRICE (*wildly*). O
My God! Can it be possible I have
To die so suddenly? So young to go
Under the obscure, cold, rotting, wormy ground!
To be nailed down into a narrow place;
To see no more sweet sunshine; hear no more
Blithe voice of living thing; muse not again
Upon familiar thoughts, sad, yet thus lost—
How fearful! to be nothing! Or to be . . .
What? Oh, where am I? Let me not go mad!
Sweet Heaven, forgive weak thoughts! If there
     should be
No God, no Heaven, no Earth in the void world;
The wide, gray, lampless, deep, unpeopled world!
If all things then should be . . . my father's spirit,
His eye, his voice, his touch surrounding me;
The atmosphere and breath of my dead life!
If sometimes, as a shape more like himself,
Even the form which tortured me on earth,
Masked in gray hairs and wrinkles, he should come
And wind me in his hellish arms, and fix
His eyes on mine, and drag me down, down, down!
For was he not alone omnipotent
On Earth, and ever present? Even tho' dead,
Does not his spirit live in all that breathe,
And work for me and mine still the same ruin,
Scorn, pain, despair? Who ever yet returned
To teach the laws of death's untrodden realm?

Unjust perhaps as those which drive us now,
Oh, whither, whither?

LUCRETIA.                    Trust in God's sweet love,
The tender promises of Christ: ere night,
Think, we shall be in Paradise.

BEATRICE.                    'Tis past!
Whatever comes my heart shall sink no more.
And yet, I know not why, your words strike chill:
How tedious, false and cold seem all things. I
Have met with much injustice in this world;
No difference has been made by God or man,
Or any power moulding my wretched lot,
'Twixt good or evil, as regarded me.
I am cut off from the only world I know,
From light, and life, and love, in youth's sweet prime.
You do well telling me to trust in God,
I hope I do trust in him. In whom else
Can any trust? And yet my heart is cold.

> [*During the latter speeches* GIACOMO *has re-
> tired conversing with* CAMILLO, *who now
> goes out;* GIACOMO *advances.*

GIACOMO. Know you not, Mother . . . Sister, know
        you not?
Bernardo even now is gone to implore
The Pope to grant our pardon.

LUCRETIA.                    Child, perhaps
It will be granted. We may all then live
To make these woes a tale for distant years:
Oh, what a thought! It gushes to my heart
Like the warm blood.

BEATRICE.            Yet both will soon be cold.
Oh, trample out that thought! Worse than despair,
Worse than the bitterness of death, is hope:
It is the only ill which can find place
Upon the giddy, sharp and narrow hour
Tottering beneath us. Plead with the swift frost
That it should spare the eldest flower of spring:
Plead with awakening earthquake, o'er whose couch
Even now a city stands, strong, fair, and free;
Now stench and blackness yawn, like death. Oh, plead

With famine, or wind-walking Pestilence,
Blind lightning, or the deaf sea, not with man!
Cruel, cold, formal man; righteous in words,
In deeds a Cain.  No, Mother, we must die:
Since such is the reward of innocent lives;
Such the alleviation of worst wrongs.
And whilst our murderers live, and hard, cold men,
Smiling and slow, walk thro' a world of tears
To death as to life's sleep; 'twere just the grave
Were some strange joy for us.  Come, obscure Death,
And wind me in thine all-embracing arms!
Like a fond mother hide me in thy bosom,
And rock me to the sleep from which none wake.
Live ye, who live, subject to one another
As we were once, who now . . .

                                 [BERNARDO *rushes in.*

   BERNARDO.                    Oh, horrible,
That tears, that looks, that hope poured forth in prayer,
Even till the heart is vacant and despairs,
Should all be vain!  The ministers of death
Are waiting round the doors.  I thought I saw
Blood on the face of one . . . What if 'twere fancy?
Soon the heart's blood of all I love on earth
Will sprinkle him, and he will wipe it off
As if 'twere only rain.  O life! O world!
Cover me! let me be no more!  To see
That perfect mirror of pure innocence
Wherein I gazed, and grew happy and good,
Shivered to dust!  To see thee, Beatrice,
Who made all lovely thou didst look upon . . .
Thee, light of life . . . dead, dark! while I say, sister,
To hear I have no sister; and thou, Mother,
Whose love was as a bond to all our loves . . .
Dead!  The sweet bond broken!


              *Enter* CAMILLO *and Guards*

                    They come!  Let me
Kiss those warm lips before their crimson leaves
Are blighted . . . white . . . cold.  Say farewell, before

Death chokes that gentle voice! Oh, let me hear
You speak!

BEATRICE. Farewell, my tender brother. Think
Of our sad fate with gentleness, as now;
And let mild, pitying thoughts lighten for thee
Thy sorrow's load. Err not in harsh despair,
But tears and patience. One thing more, my child,
For thine own sake be constant to the love
Thou bearest us; and to the faith that I,
Tho' wrapt in a strange cloud of crime and shame,
Lived ever holy and unstained. And tho'
Ill tongues shall wound me, and our common name
Be as a mark stamped on thine innocent brow
For men to point at as they pass, do thou
Forbear, and never think a thought unkind
Of those, who perhaps love thee in their graves.
So mayest thou die as I do; fear and pain
Being subdued. Farewell! Farewell! Farewell!

BERNARDO. I cannot say, farewell!

CAMILLO.                O Lady Beatrice!

BEATRICE. Give yourself no unnecessary pain,
My dear Lord Cardinal. Here, Mother, tie
My girdle for me, and bind up this hair
In any simple knot; ay, that does well.
And yours I see is coming down. How often
Have we done this for one another, now
We shall not do it any more. My Lord,
We are quite ready. Well, 'tis very well.

# A BLOT IN THE 'SCUTCHEON

BY

ROBERT BROWNING

# INTRODUCTORY NOTE

ROBERT BROWNING *stands, in respect to his origin and his career, in marked contrast to the two aristocratic poets beside whose dramas his "Blot in the 'Scutcheon" is here printed. His father was a bank clerk and a dissenter at a time when dissent meant exclusion from Society; the poet went neither to one of the great public schools nor to Oxford or Cambridge; and no breath of scandal touched his name. Born in London in 1812, he was educated largely by private tutors, and spent two years at London University, but the influence of his father, a man of wide reading and cultivated tastes, was probably the most important element in his early training. He drew well, was something of a musician, and wrote verses from an early age, though it was the accidental reading of a volume of Shelley which first kindled his real inspiration. This indebtedness is beautifully acknowledged in his first published poem, "Pauline" (1833).*

*Apart from frequent visits to Italy, there is little of incident to chronicle in Browning's life, with the one great exception of his more than fortunate marriage in 1846 to Elizabeth Barrett, the greatest of English poetesses.*

*Browning's dramatic period extended from 1835 to the time of his marriage, and produced some nine plays, not all of which, however, were intended for the stage. "Paracelsus," the first of the series, has been fairly described as a "conversational drama," and "Pippa Passes," though it has been staged, is essentially a poem to read. The historical tragedy of "Strafford" has been impressively performed, but "King Victor and King Charles," "The Return of the Druses," "Colombe's Birthday," "A Soul's Tragedy," and "Luria," while interesting in many ways, can hardly be regarded as successful stage-plays. "A Blot in the 'Scutcheon" was performed at Drury Lane, but its chances of a successful run were spoiled by the jealousy of Macready, the manager.*

*The main cause of Browning's weakness as a playwright lay in the fact that he was so much more interested in psychology than in action. But in the present tragedy this defect is less prominent than usual, and in spite of flaws in construction, it reaches a high pitch of emotional intensity, the characters are drawn with vividness, and the lines are rich in poetry.*

# A BLOT IN THE 'SCUTCHEON

## A TRAGEDY

### (1843)

#### DRAMATIS PERSONÆ

MILDRED TRESHAM.    GUENDOLEN TRESHAM.
THOROLD, Earl Tresham.    AUSTIN TRESHAM.
HENRY, Earl Mertoun.
GERARD, *and other retainers of* Lord Tresham.

*Time, 17—*

## ACT I

SCENE I.—*The Interior of a Lodge in* Lord Tresham's *Park. Many* Retainers *crowded at the window, supposed to command a view of the entrance to his Mansion.*

GERARD, *the Warrener, his back to a table on which are flagons, etc.*

*First Retainer*

AY, do! push, friends, and then you'll push down me!
    —What for? Does any hear a runner's foot
    Or a steed's trample or a coach-wheel's cry?
Is the Earl come or his least poursuivant?
But there's no breeding in a man of you
Save Gerard yonder: here's a half-place yet,
Old Gerard!

GERARD. Save your courtesies, my friend. Here is my
        place.

SECOND RETAINER. Now, Gerard, out with it!
What makes you sullen, this of all the days
I' the year? To-day that young rich bountiful
Handsome Earl Mertoun, whom alone they match
With our Lord Tresham through the country-side,

357

Is coming here in utmost bravery
To ask our master's sister's hand?
   GERARD.                       What then?
   SECOND RETAINER. What then?   Why, you, she speaks
      to, if she meets
Your worship, smiles on as you hold apart
The boughs to let her through her forest walks,
You, always favourite for your no-deserts,
You've heard, these three days, how Earl Mertoun sues
To lay his heart and house and broad lands too
At Lady Mildred's feet: and while we squeeze
Ourselves into a mousehole lest we miss
One congee of the least page in his train,
You sit o' one side—"there's the Earl," say I—
"What then?" say you!
   THIRD RETAINER.         I'll wager he has let
Both swans he tamed for Lady Mildred swim
Over the falls and gain the river!
   GERARD.               Ralph,
Is not to-morrow my inspecting-day
For you and for your hawks?
   FOURTH RETAINER.        Let Gerard be!
He's coarse-grained, like his carved black cross-bow stock.
Ha, look now, while we squabble with him, look!
Well done, now—is not this beginning, now,
To purpose?
   FIRST RETAINER. Our retainers look as fine—
That's comfort. Lord, how Richard holds himself
With his white staff! Will not a knave behind
Prick him upright?
   FOURTH RETAINER. He's only bowing, fool!
The Earl's man bent us lower by this much.
   FIRST RETAINER.   That's comfort.  Here's a very
      cavalcade!
   THIRD RETAINER. I don't see wherefore Richard, and
      his troop
Of silk and silver varlets there, should find
Their perfumed selves so indispensable
On high days, holidays! Would it so disgrace
Our family, if I, for instance, stood—

In my right hand a cast of Swedish hawks,
A leash of greyhounds in my left?—
    GERARD.                            —With Hugh
The logman for supporter, in his right
The bill-hook, in his left the brushwood-shears!
    THIRD RETAINER. Out on you, crab! What next, what
        next? The Earl!
    FIRST RETAINER.   Oh Walter, groom, our horses, do
        they match
The Earl's? Alas, that first pair of the six—
They paw the ground—Ah Walter! and that brute
Just on his haunches by the wheel!
    SIXTH RETAINER.                Ay—ay!
You, Philip, are a special hand, I hear,
At soups and sauces: what's a horse to you?
D'ye mark that beast they've slid into the midst
So cunningly?—then, Philip, mark this further;
No leg has he to stand on!
    FIRST RETAINER.         No? that's comfort.
    SECOND RETAINER. Peace, Cook! The Earl descends.
        Well, Gerard, see
The Earl at least! Come, there's a proper man,
I hope! Why, Ralph, no falcon, Pole or Swede,
Has got a starrier eye.
    THIRD RETAINER.      His eyes are blue:
But leave my hawks alone!
    FOURTH RETAINER.       So young, and yet
So tall and shapely!
    FIFTH RETAINER. Here's Lord Tresham's self!
There now—there's what a nobleman should be!
He's older, graver, loftier, he's more like
A House's head.
    SECOND RETAINER. But you'd not have a boy
—And what's the Earl beside?—possess too soon
That stateliness?
    FIRST RETAINER. Our master takes his hand—
Richard and his white staff are on the move—
Back fall our people—(tsh!—there's Timothy
Sure to get tangled in his ribbon-ties,
And Peter's cursed rosette's a-coming off!)

—At last I see our lord's back and his friend's;
And the whole beautiful bright company
Close round them—in they go! [*Jumping down from
        the window-bench, and making for the table and its
        jugs.*] Good health, long life,
Great joy to our Lord Tresham and his House!
    SIXTH RETAINER. My father drove his father first to
        court,
After his marriage-day—ay, did he!
    SECOND RETAINER.                         God bless
Lord Tresham, Lady Mildred, and the Earl!
Here, Gerard, reach your beaker!
    GERARD.                         Drink, my boys!
Don't mind me—all's not right about me—drink!
    SECOND RETAINER [*aside*]. He's vexed, now, that he
        let the show escape!
    [*To* GERARD.] Remember that the Earl returns this way.
    GERARD. That way?
    SECOND RETAINER. Just so.
    GERARD.                         Then my way's here.
                                                [*Goes.*
    SECOND RETAINER.                         Old Gerard
Will die soon—mind, I said it! He was used
To care about the pitifullest thing
That touched the House's honour, not an eye
But his could see wherein: and on a cause
Of scarce a quarter this importance, Gerard
Fairly had fretted flesh and bone away
In cares that this was right, nor that was wrong,
Such point decorous, and such square by rule—
He knew such niceties, no herald more:
And now—you see his humour: die he will!
    SECOND RETAINER. God help him! Who's for the
        great servants' hall
To hear what's going on inside! They'd follow
Lord Tresham into the saloon.
    THIRD RETAINER.                         I!—
    FOURTH RETAINER.                         I!—
Leave Frank alone for catching, at the door,
Some hint of how the parley goes inside!

Prosperity to the great House once more!
Here's the last drop!

FIRST RETAINER. Have at you! Boys, hurrah!

SCENE II.—*A Saloon in the Mansion*

*Enter* LORD TRESHAM, LORD MERTOUN, AUSTIN, *and*
GUENDOLEN

TRESHAM. I welcome you, Lord Mertoun, yet once
more,
To this ancestral roof of mine. Your name
—Noble among the noblest in itself,
Yet taking in your person, fame avers,
New price and lustre,—(as that gem you wear,
Transmitted from a hundred knightly breasts,
Fresh chased and set and fixed by its last lord,
Seems to re-kindle at the core)—your name
Would win you welcome!—

MERTOUN. Thanks!

TRESHAM. —But add to that,
The worthiness and grace and dignity
Of your proposal for uniting both
Our Houses even closer than respect
Unites them now—add these, and you must grant
One favour more, nor that the least,—to think
The welcome I should give;—'tis given! My lord,
My only brother, Austin: he's the king's.
Our cousin, Lady Guendolen—betrothed
To Austin: all are yours.

MERTOUN. I thank you—less
For the expressed commendings which your seal,
And only that, authenticates—forbids
My putting from me . . . to my heart I take
Your praise . . . but praise less claims my gratitude
Than the indulgent insight it implies
Of what must needs be uppermost with one
Who comes, like me, with the bare leave to ask,
In weighed and measured unimpassioned words,
A gift, which, if as calmly 'tis denied,

He must withdraw, content upon his cheek,
Despair within his soul. That I dare ask
Firmly, near boldly, near with confidence
That gift, I have to thank you. Yes, Lord Tresham,
I love your sister—as you'd have one love
That lady . . . oh more, more I love her! Wealth,
Rank, all the world thinks me, they're yours, you know,
To hold or part with, at your choice—but grant
My true self, me without a rood of land,
A piece of gold, a name of yesterday,
Grant me that lady, and you . . . Death or life?
 GUENDOLEN. [*apart to* AUSTIN]. Why, this is loving,
  Austin!
 AUSTIN.  He's so young!
 GUENDOLEN. Young? Old enough, I think, to half
  surmise
He never had obtained an entrance here,
Were all this fear and trembling needed.
 AUSTIN.        Hush!
He reddens.
 GUENDOLEN. Mark him, Austin; that's true love!
Ours must begin again.
 TRESHAM.    We'll sit, my lord.
Ever with best desert goes diffidence.
I may speak plainly nor be misconceived
That I am wholly satisfied with you
On this occasion, when a falcon's eye
Were dull compared with mine to search out faults,
Is somewhat. Mildred's hand is hers to give
Or to refuse.
 MERTOUN.  But you, you grant my suit?
I have your word if hers?
 TRESHAM.    My best of words
If hers encourage you. I trust it will.
Have you seen Lady Mildred, by the way?
 MERTOUN. I . . . I . . . our two demesnes, remem-
  ber, touch,
I have been used to wander carelessly
After my stricken game: the heron roused
Deep in my woods, has trailed its broken wing

Thro' thicks and glades a mile in yours,—or else
Some eyass ill-reclaimed has taken flight
And lured me after her from tree to tree,
I marked not whither. I have come upon
The lady's wondrous beauty unaware,
And—and then . . . I have seen her.

GUENDOLEN [*aside to* AUSTIN]. Note that mode
Of faltering out that, when a lady passed,
He, having eyes, did see her! You had said—
"On such a day I scanned her, head to foot;
Observed a red, where red should not have been,
Outside her elbow; but was pleased enough
Upon the whole." Let such irreverent talk
Be lessoned for the future!

TRESHAM. What's to say
May be said briefly. She has never known
A mother's care; I stand for father too.
Her beauty is not strange to you, it seems—
You cannot know the good and tender heart,
Its girl's trust and its woman's constancy,
How pure yet passionate, how calm yet kind,
How grave yet joyous, how reserved yet free
As light where friends are—how imbued with lore
The world most prizes, yet the simplest, yet
The . . . one might know I talked of Mildred—thus
We brothers talk!

MERTOUN. I thank you.

TRESHAM. In a word,
Control's not for this lady; but her wish
To please me outstrips in its subtlety
My power of being pleased: herself creates
The want she means to satisfy. My heart
Prefers your suit to her as 'twere its own.
Can I say more?

MERTOUN. No more—thanks, thanks—no more!

TRESHAM. This matter then discussed . . .

MERTOUN. —We'll waste no breath
On aught less precious. I'm beneath the roof
Which holds her: while I thought of that, my speech
To you would wander—as it must not do,

Since as you favour me I stand or fall.
I pray you suffer that I take my leave!

TRESHAM. With less regret 'tis suffered, that again
We meet, I hope, so shortly.

MERTOUN.                         We? again?—
Ah yes, forgive me—when shall . . . you will crown
Your goodness by forthwith apprising me
When . . . if . . . the lady will appoint a day
For me to wait on you—and her.

TRESHAM.                         So soon
As I am made acquainted with her thoughts
On your proposal—howsoe'er they lean—
A messenger shall bring you the result.

MERTOUN. You cannot bind me more to you, my lord.
Farewell till we renew . . . I trust, renew
A converse ne'er to disunite again.

TRESHAM. So may it prove!

MERTOUN.                         You, lady, you, sir, take
My humble salutation!

GUENDOLEN *and* AUSTIN.    Thanks!

TRESHAM.                         Within there!

[Servants *enter*. TRESHAM *conducts* MERTOUN *to
the door. Meantime* AUSTIN *remarks,*

                                              Well,

Here I have an advantage of the Earl,
Confess now! I'd not think that all was safe
Because my lady's brother stood my friend!
Why, he makes sure of her—" do you say yes—
She'll not say, no,"—what comes it to beside?
I should have prayed the brother, " speak this speech,
For Heaven's sake urge this on her—put in this—
Forget not, as you'd save me, t'other thing,—
Then set down what she says, and how she looks,
And if she smiles, and " (in an under breath)
" Only let her accept me, and do you
And all the world refuse me, if you dare!"

GUENDOLEN. That way you'd take, friend Austin?
    What a shame
I was your cousin, tamely from the first
Your bride, and all this fervour's run to waste!

Do you know you speak sensibly to-day?
The Earl's a fool.

AUSTIN.          Here's Thorold. Tell him so!

TRESHAM [*returning*]. Now, voices, voices! 'St! the
    lady's first!

How seems he?—seems he not . . . come, faith give
    fraud
The mercy-stroke whenever they engage!
Down with fraud, up with faith! How seems the Earl?
A name! a blazon! if you knew their worth,
As you will never! come—the Earl?

GUENDOLEN.                              He's young.

TRESHAM. What's she? an infant save in heart and
    brain.
Young! Mildred is fourteen, remark! And you . . .
Austin, how old is she?

GUENDOLEN.          There's tact for you!
I meant that being young was good excuse
If one should tax him . . .

TRESHAM.                    Well?

GUENDOLEN.                              —With lacking wit.

TRESHAM. He lacked wit? Where might he lack wit, so
    please you?

GUENDOLEN. In standing straighter than the steward's
    rod
And making you the tiresomest harangue,
Instead of slipping over to my side
And softly whispering in my ear, " Sweet lady,
Your cousin there will do me detriment
He little dreams of: he's absorbed, I see,
In my old name and fame—be sure he'll leave
My Mildred, when his best account of me
Is ended, in full confidence I wear
My grandsire's periwig down either cheek.
I'm lost unless your gentleness vouchsafes " . . .

TRESHAM . . . " To give a best of best accounts, your-
    self,
Of me and my demerits." You are right!
He should have said what now I say for him.
Yon golden creature, will you help us all?

Here's Austin means to vouch for much, but you
—You are . . . what Austin only knows!  Come up,
All three of us: she's in the library
No doubt, for the day's wearing fast.  Precede!
    GUENDOLEN. Austin, how we must—!
    TRESHAM.             Must what?  Must speak truth,
Malignant tongue!  Detect one fault in him!
I challenge you!
    GUENDOLEN.     Witchcraft's a fault in him,
For you're bewitched.
    TRESHAM.        What's urgent we obtain
Is, that she soon receive him—say, to-morrow—,
Next day at furthest.
    GUENDOLEN.       Ne'er instruct me!
    TRESHAM.                  Come!
—He's out of your good graces, since forsooth,
He stood not as he'd carry us by storm
With his perfections!  You're for the composed
Manly assured becoming confidence!
—Get her to say, " to-morrow," and I'll give you . . .
I'll give you black Urganda, to be spoiled
With petting and snail-paces.  Will you?  Come!


SCENE  III.—MILDRED'S  *Chamber.  A  Painted  Window  overlooks
the  Park*


MILDRED *and* GUENDOLEN
    GUENDOLEN. Now, Mildred, spare those pains.  I have
      not left
Our talkers in the library, and climbed
The wearisome ascent to this your bower
In company with you,—I have not dared . . .
Nay, worked such prodigies as sparing you
Lord Mertoun's pedigree before the flood,
Which Thorold seemed in very act to tell
—Or bringing Austin to pluck up that most
Firm-rooted heresy—your suitor's eyes,
He would maintain, were grey instead of blue—
I think I brought him to contrition!—Well,
I have not done such things, (all to deserve

A minute's quiet cousin's talk with you,)
To be dismissed so coolly.

    MILDRED.                      Guendolen!
What have I done? what could suggest . . .

    GUENDOLEN.                  There, there!
Do I not comprehend you'd be alone
To throw those testimonies in a heap,
Thorold's enlargings, Austin's brevities,
With that poor silly heartless Guendolen's
Ill-time misplaced attempted smartnesses—
And sift their sense out? now, I come to spare you
Nearly a whole night's labour.  Ask and have!
Demand, be answered!  Lack I ears and eyes?
Am I perplexed which side of the rock-table
The Conqueror dined on when he landed first,
Lord Mertoun's ancestor was bidden take—
The bow-hand or the arrow-hand's great meed?
Mildred, the Earl has soft blue eyes!

    MILDRED.                    My brother—
Did he . . . you said that he received him well?

    GUENDOLEN. If I said only " well " I said not much.
Oh, stay—which brother?

    MILDRED.             Thorold! who—who else?

    GUENDOLEN. Thorold (a secret) is too proud by
        half,—
Nay, hear me out—with us he's even gentler
Than we are with our birds.  Of this great House
The least retainer that e'er caught his glance
Would die for him, real dying—no mere talk:
And in the world, the court, if men would cite
The perfect spirit of honour, Thorold's name
Rises of its clear nature to their lips.
But he should take men's homage, trust in it,
And care no more about what drew it down.
He has desert, and that, acknowledgment;
Is he content?

    MILDRED.     You wrong him, Guendolen.

    GUENDOLEN. He's proud, confess; so proud with
        brooding o'er
The light of his interminable line,

An ancestry with men all paladins,
And women all . . .
   MILDRED.          Dear Guendolen, 'tis late!
When yonder purple pane the climbing moon
Pierces, I know 'tis midnight.
   GUENDOLEN.         Well, that Thorold
Should rise up from such musings, and receive
One come audaciously to graft himself
Into this peerless stock, yet find no flaw,
No slightest spot in such an one . . .
   MILDRED.          Who finds
A spot in Mertoun?
   GUENDOLEN.     Not your brother; therefore,
Not the whole world.
   MILDRED.     I am weary, Guendolen.
Bear with me!
   GUENDOLEN.   I am foolish.
   MILDRED.        Oh no, kind!
But I would rest.
   GUENDOLEN.   Good night and rest to you!
I said how gracefully his mantle lay
Beneath the rings of his light hair?
   MILDRED.        Brown hair.
   GUENDOLEN. Brown? why, it *is* brown: how could you
    know that?
   MILDRED. How? did not you—Oh, Austin 'twas, de-
    clared
His hair was light, not brown—my head!—and look,
The moon-beam purpling the dark chamber! Sweet,
Good night!
   GUENDOLEN. Forgive me—sleep the soundlier for me!
               [*Going, she turns suddenly.*
                    Mildred!

Perdition! all's discovered! Thorold finds
—That the Earl's greatest of all grandmothers
Was grander daughter still—to that fair dame
Whose garter slipped down at the famous dance! [*Goes.*
   MILDRED. Is she—can she be really gone at last?
My heart! I shall not reach the window. Needs
Must I have sinned much, so to suffer.

*[She lifts the small lamp which is suspended before
the Virgin's image in the window, and places it by
the purple pane.*

There!

*[She returns to the seat in front.*

Mildred and Mertoun! Mildred, with consent
Of all the world and Thorold, Mertoun's bride!
Too late! 'Tis sweet to think of, sweeter still
To hope for, that this blessed end soothes up
The curse of the beginning; but I know
It comes too late: 'twill sweetest be of all
To dream my soul away and die upon.

*[A noise without.*

The voice! Oh why, why glided sin the snake
Into the paradise Heaven meant us both?

*[The window opens softly. A low voice sings.*


*There's a woman like a dew-drop, she's so purer than
      the purest;*
*And her noble heart's the noblest, yes, and her sure
      faith's the surest:*
*And her eyes are dark and humid, like the depth on
      depth of lustre*
*Hid i' the harebell, while her tresses, sunnier than the
      wild-grape cluster,*
*Gush in golden tinted plenty down her neck's rose-
      misted marble:*
*Then her voice's music . . . call it the well's bubbling,
      the bird's warble!*


*[A figure wrapped in a mantle appears at the window.*

*And this woman says, "My days were sunless and my
      nights were moonless,*
*Parched the pleasant April herbage, and the lark's
      heart's outbreak tuneless,*
*If you loved me not!" And I who—(ah, for words
      of flame!) adore her,*
*Who am mad to lay my spirit prostrate palpably before
      her—*

[*He enters, approaches her seat, and bends over her.*
*I may enter at her portal soon, as now her lattice takes*
*me,*
*And by noontide as by midnight make her mine, as*
*hers she makes me!*

[*The* EARL *throws off his slouched hat and long cloak.*

My very heart sings, so I sing, Beloved!
   MILDRED. Sit, Henry—do not take my hand!
   MERTOUN.                    'Tis mine.
The meeting that appalled us both so much
Is ended.
   MILDRED. What begins now?
   MERTOUN.                Happiness
Such as the world contains not.
   MILDRED.             That is it.
Our happiness would, as you say, exceed
The whole world's best of blisses: we—do we
Deserve that? Utter to your soul, what mine
Long since, Beloved, has grown used to hear,
Like a death-knell, so much regarded once,
And so familiar now; this will not be!
   MERTOUN. Oh, Mildred, have I met your brother's face?
Compelled myself—if not to speak untruth,
Yet to disguise, to shun, to put aside
The truth, as—what had e'er prevailed on me
Save you to venture? Have I gained at last
Your brother, the one scarer of your dreams,
And waking thoughts' sole apprehension too?
Does a new life, like a young sunrise, break
On the strange unrest of our night, confused
With rain and stormy flaw—and will you see
No dripping blossoms, no fire-tinted drops
On each live spray, no vapour steaming up,
And no expressless glory in the East?
When I am by you, to be ever by you,
When I have won you and may worship you,
Oh, Mildred, can you say "this will not be"?
   MILDRED. Sin has surprised us, so will punishment.

MERTOUN. No—me alone, who sinned alone!

MILDRED. The night
You likened our past life to—was it storm
Throughout to you then, Henry?

MERTOUN. Of your life
I spoke—what am I, what my life, to waste
A thought about when you are by me?—you
It was, I said my folly called the storm
And pulled the night upon. 'Twas day with me—
Perpetual dawn with me.

MILDRED. Come what, come will,
You have been happy: take my hand!

MERTOUN [after a pause]. How good
Your brother is! I figured him a cold—
Shall I say, haughty man?

MILDRED. They told me all.
I know all.

MERTOUN. It will soon be over.

MILDRED. Over?
Oh, what is over? what must I live through
And say, "'tis over"? Is our meeting over?
Have I received in presence of them all
The partner of my guilty love—with brow
Trying to seem a maiden's brow—with lips
Which make believe that when they strive to form
Replies to you and tremble as they strive,
It is the nearest ever they approached
A stranger's . . . Henry, yours that stranger's . . . lip—
With cheek that looks a virgin's, and that is . . .
Ah God, some prodigy of thine will stop
This planned piece of deliberate wickedness
In its birth even! some fierce leprous spot
Will mar the brow's dissimulating! I
Shall murmur no smooth speeches got by heart,
But, frenzied, pour forth all our woeful story,
The love, the shame, and the despair—with them
Round me aghast as round some cursed fount
That should spirt water, and spouts blood. I'll not
. . . Henry, you do not wish that I should draw
This vengeance down? I'll not affect a grace

That's gone from me—gone once, and gone for ever!

MERTOUN. Mildred, my honour is your own. I'll share
Disgrace I cannot suffer by myself.
A word informs your brother I retract
This morning's offer; time will yet bring forth
Some better way of saving both of us.

MILDRED. I'll meet their faces, Henry!

MERTOUN.                          When? to-morrow!
Get done with it!

MILDRED.          Oh, Henry, not to-morrow!
Next day! I never shall prepare my words
And looks and gestures sooner.—How you must
Despise me!

MERTOUN. Mildred, break it if you choose,
A heart the love of you uplifted—still
Uplifts, thro' this protracted agony,
To heaven! but Mildred, answer me,—first pace
The chamber with me—once again—now, say
Calmly the part, the  . . . what it is of me
You see contempt (for you did say contempt)
—Contempt for you in! I would pluck it off
And cast it from me!—but no—no, you'll not
Repeat that?—will you, Mildred, repeat that?

MILDRED. Dear Henry!

MERTOUN.          I was scarce a boy—e'en now
What am I more? And you were infantine
When first I met you; why, your hair fell loose
On either side! My fool's-cheek reddens now
Only in the recalling how it burned
That morn to see the shape of many a dream
—You know we boys are prodigal of charms
To her we dream of—I had heard of one,
Had dreamed of her, and I was close to her,
Might speak to her, might live and die her own,
Who knew? I spoke. Oh, Mildred, feel you not
That now, while I remember every glance
Of yours, each word of yours, with power to test
And weigh them in the diamond scales of pride,
Resolved the treasure of a first and last
Heart's love shall have been bartered at its worth,

—That now I think upon your purity
And utter ignorance of guilt—your own
Or other's guilt—the girlish undisguised
Delight at a strange novel prize—(I talk
A silly language, but interpret, you!)
If I, with fancy at its full, and reason
Scarce in its germ, enjoined you secrecy,
If you had pity on my passion, pity
On my protested sickness of the soul
To sit beside you, hear you breathe, and watch
Your eyelids and the eyes beneath—if you
Accorded gifts and knew not they were gifts—
If I grew mad at last with enterprise
And must behold my beauty in her bower
Or perish—(I was ignorant of even
My own desires—what then were you?) if sorrow—
Sin—if the end came—must I now renounce
My reason, blind myself to light, say truth
Is false and lie to God and my own soul?
Contempt were all of this!

    MILDRED.             Do you believe . . .
Or, Henry, I'll not wrong you—you believe
That I was ignorant. I scarce grieve o'er
The past. We'll love on; you will love me still.

    MERTOUN. Oh, to love less what one has injured!
       Dove,
Whose pinion I have rashly hurt, my breast—
Shall my heart's warmth not nurse thee into strength?
Flower I have crushed, shall I not care for thee?
Bloom o'er my crest, my fight-mark and device!
Mildred, I love you and you love me.

    MILDRED.           Go!
Be that your last word. I shall sleep to-night.

    MERTOUN. This is not our last meeting?

    MILDRED.           One night more.

    MERTOUN. And then—think, then!

    MILDRED.        Then, no sweet courtship-days,
No dawning consciousness of love for us,
No strange and palpitating births of sense
From words and looks, no innocent fears and hopes,

Reserves and confidences: morning's over!

MERTOUN. How else should love's perfected noontide
follow?

All the dawn promised shall the day perform.

MILDRED. So may it be! but—

You are cautious, Love?

Are sure that unobserved you scaled the walls?

MERTOUN. Oh, trust me! Then our final meeting's
fixed

To-morrow night?

MILDRED.         Farewell! stay, Henry . . . wherefore?

His foot is on the yew-tree bough; the turf

Receives him: now the moonlight as he runs

Embraces him—but he must go—is gone.

Ah, once again he turns—thanks, thanks, my Love!

He's gone. Oh, I'll believe him every word!

I was so young, I loved him so, I had

No mother, God forgot me, and I fell.

There may be pardon yet: all's doubt beyond!

Surely the bitterness of death is past.


## ACT II

SCENE.—*The Library*

*Enter* LORD TRESHAM, *hastily*

TRESHAM. This way! In, Gerard, quick!

[*As* GERARD *enters,* TRESHAM *secures the door.*

Now speak! or, wait—

I'll bid you speak directly.          [*Seats himself.*

Now repeat

Firmly and circumstantially the tale

You just now told me; it eludes me; either

I did not listen, or the half is gone

Away from me. How long have you lived here?

Here in my house, your father kept our woods

Before you?

GERARD.  —As his father did, my lord.

I have been eating, sixty years almost,

Your bread.

TRESHAM. Yes, yes.  You ever were of all
The servants in my father's house, I know,
The trusted one.  You'll speak the truth.
GERARD.                                   I'll speak
God's truth.  Night after night . . .
TRESHAM.                          Since when?
GERARD.                                   At least
A month—each midnight has some man access
To Lady Mildred's chamber.
TRESHAM.                          Tush, " access "—
No wide words like " access " to me!
GERARD.                          He runs
Along the woodside, crosses to the South,
Takes the left tree that ends the avenue . . .
TRESHAM. The last great yew-tree?
GERARD.                          You might stand upon
The main boughs like a platform.  Then he . . .
TRESHAM.                                   Quick!
GERARD. Climbs up, and, where they lessen at the top,
—I cannot see distinctly, but he throws,
I think—for this I do not vouch—a line
That reaches to the lady's casement—
TRESHAM.                          —Which
He enters not!  Gerard, some wretched fool
Dares pry into my sister's privacy!
When such are young, it seems a precious thing
To have approached,—to merely have approached,
Got sight of the abode of her they set
Their frantic thoughts upon.  He does not enter?
Gerard?
GERARD. There is a lamp that's full i' the midst.
Under a red square in the painted glass
Of Lady Mildred's  .  .  .
TRESHAM.                  Leave that name out!  Well?
That lamp?
GERARD.   Is moved at midnight higher up
To one pane—a small dark-blue pane; he waits
For that among the boughs: at sight of that,
I see him, plain as I see you, my lord,
Open the lady's casement, enter there . . .

TRESHAM.—And stay?

GERARD. An hour, two hours.

TRESHAM. And this you saw
Once?—twice?—quick!

GERARD. Twenty times.

TRESHAM. And what brings you
Under the yew-trees?

GERARD. The first night I left
My range so far, to track the stranger stag
That broke the pale, I saw the man.

TRESHAM. Yet sent
No cross-bow shaft through the marauder?

GERARD. But
He came, my lord, the first time he was seen,
In a great moonlight, light as any day,
*From* Lady Mildred's chamber.

TRESHAM [*after a pause*]. You have no cause
—Who could have cause to do my sister wrong?

GERARD. Oh, my lord, only once—let me this once
Speak what is on my mind! Since first I noted
All this, I've groaned as if a fiery net
Plucked me this way and that—fire if I turned
To her, fire if I turned to you, and fire
If down I flung myself and strove to die.
The lady could not have been seven years old
When I was trusted to conduct her safe
Through the deer-herd to stroke the snow-white
    fawn
I brought to eat bread from her tiny hand
Within a month. She ever had a smile
To greet me with—she . . . if it could undo
What's done, to lop each limb from off this trunk . . .
All that is foolish talk, not fit for you—
I mean, I could not speak and bring her hurt
For Heaven's compelling. But when I was fixed
To hold my peace, each morsel of your food
Eaten beneath your roof, my birth-place too,
Choked me. I wish I had grown mad in doubts
What it behoved me do. This morn it seemed
Either I must confess to you or die:

Now it is done, I seem the vilest worm
That crawls, to have betrayed my lady.

TRESHAM. No—
No, Gerard!

GERARD. Let me go!

TRESHAM. A man, you say:
What man? Young? Not a vulgar hind? What dress?

GERARD. A slouched hat and a large dark foreign cloak
Wraps his whole form; even his face is hid;
But I should judge him young: no hind, be sure!

TRESHAM. Why?

GERARD. He is ever armed: his sword projects
Beneath the cloak.

TRESHAM. Gerard,—I will not say
No word, no breath of this!

GERARD. Thank, thanks, my lord!
[*Goes.*

TRESHAM [*paces the room. After a pause*]. Oh,
thoughts absurd!—as with some monstrous fact
Which, when ill thoughts beset us, seems to give
Merciful God that made the sun and stars,
The waters and the green delights of earth,
The lie! I apprehend the monstrous fact—
Yet know the maker of all worlds is good,
And yield my reason up, inadequate
To reconcile what yet I do behold—
Blasting my sense! There's cheerful day outside:
This is my library, and this the chair
My father used to sit in carelessly
After his soldier-fashion, while I stood
Between his knees to question him: and here
Gerard our grey retainer,—as he says,
Fed with our food, from sire to son, an age,—
Has told a story—I am to believe!
That Mildred . . . oh, no, no! both tales are true,
Her pure cheek's story and the forester's!
Would she, or could she, err—much less, confound
All guilts of treachery, of craft, of . . . Heaven
Keep me within its hand!—I will sit here
Until thought settle and I see my course.

Avert, oh God, only this woe from me!

[*As he sinks his head between his arms on the table.*
*GUENDOLEN's voice is heard at the door.*

Lord Tresham! [*She knocks.*] Is Lord Tresham there?

[TRESHAM, *hastily turning, pulls down the first*
*book above him and opens it.*

TRESHAM.                              Come in! [*She enters.*
Ha, Guendolen!—good morning.
   GUENDOLEN.                          Nothing more?
   TRESHAM. What should I say more?
   GUENDOLEN. Pleasant question! more?
This more. Did I besiege poor Mildred's brain
Last night till close on morning with " the Earl,"
" The Earl "—whose worth did I asseverate
Till I am very fain to hope that . . . Thorold,
What is all this? You are not well!
   TRESHAM.                              Who, I?
You laugh at me.
   GUENDOLEN.        Has what I'm fain to hope,
Arrived then? Does that huge tome show some blot
In the Earl's 'scutcheon come no longer back
Than Arthur's time?
   TRESHAM.              When left you Mildred's chamber?
   GUENDOLEN. Oh, late enough, I told you! The main
     thing
To ask is, how I left her chamber,—sure,
Content yourself, she'll grant this paragon
Of Earls no such ungracious . . .
   TRESHAM.                          Send her here!
   GUENDOLEN. Thorold?
   TRESHAM.              I mean—acquaint her, Guendolen,
—But mildly!
   GUENDOLEN.    Mildly?
   TRESHAM.                  Ah, you guessed aright!
I am not well: there is no hiding it.
But tell her I would see her at her leisure—
That is, at once! here in the library!
The passage in that old Italian book

We hunted for so long is found, say, found—
And if I let it slip again . . . you see,
That she must come—and instantly!

GUENDOLEN.           I'll die
Piecemeal, record that, if there have not gloomed
Some blot i' the 'scutcheon!

TRESHAM.        Go! or, Guendolen,
Be you at call,—with Austin if you choose,—
In the adjoining gallery! There go!  [GUENDOLEN *goes*.
Another lesson to me! You might bid
A child disguise his heart's sore, and conduct
Some sly investigation point by point
With a smooth brow, as well as bid me catch
The inquisitorial cleverness some praise.
If you had told me yesterday, " There's one
You needs must circumvent and practise with,
Entrap by policies, if you would worm
The truth out: and that one is—Mildred! " There,
There—reasoning is thrown away on it!
Prove she's unchaste . . . why, you may after prove
That she's a poisoner, traitress, what you will!
Where I can comprehend nought, nought's to say,
Or do, or think. Force on me but the first
Abomination,—then outpour all plagues,
And I shall ne'er make count of them.


*Enter* MILDRED

MILDRED.               What book
Is it I wanted, Thorold? Guendolen
Thought you were pale; you are not pale. That book?
That's Latin surely.

TRESHAM.       Mildred, here's a line,
(Don't lean on me: I'll English it for you)
" Love conquers all things." What love conquers them?
What love should you esteem—best love?

MILDRED.              True love.

TRESHAM. I mean, and should have said, whose love
    is best
Of all that love or that profess to love?

MILDRED. The list's so long: there's father's,
    mother's, husband's . . .
TRESHAM. Mildred, I do believe a brother's love
For a sole sister must exceed them all.
For see now, only see! there's no alloy
Of earth that creeps into the perfect'st gold
Of other loves—no gratitude to claim;
You never gave her life, not even aught
That keeps life—never tended her, instructed,
Enriched her—so, your love can claim no right
O'er her save pure love's claim: that's what I call
Freedom from earthliness. You'll never hope
To be such friends, for instance, she and you,
As when you hunted cowslips in the woods,
Or played together in the meadow hay.
Oh yes—with age, respect comes, and your worth
Is felt, there's growing sympathy of tastes,
There's ripened friendship, there's confirmed esteem:
—Much head these make against the newcomer!
The startling apparition, the strange youth—
Whom one half-hour's conversing with, or, say,
Mere gazing at, shall change (beyond all change
This Ovid ever sang about) your soul
. . . Her soul, that is,—the sister's soul! With her
'Twas winter yesterday; now, all is warmth,
The green leaf's springing and the turtle's voice,
"Arise and come away!" Come whither?—far
Enough from the esteem, respect, and all
The brother's somewhat insignificant
Array of rights! All which he knows before,
Has calculated on so long ago!
I think such love, (apart from yours and mine,)
Contented with its little term of life,
Intending to retire betimes, aware
How soon the background must be placed for it,
—I think, am sure, a brother's love exceeds
All the world's love in its unworldliness.
    MILDRED. What is this for?
    TRESHAM.                This, Mildred, is it for!
Or, no, I cannot go to it so soon!

That's one of many points my haste left out—
Each day, each hour throws forth its silk-slight
    film
Between the being tied to you by birth,
And you, until those slender threads compose
A web that shrouds her daily life of hopes
And fears and fancies, all her life, from yours:
So close you live and yet so far apart!
And must I rend this web, tear up, break down
The sweet and palpitating mystery
That makes her sacred? You—for you I mean,
Shall I speak, shall I not speak?

  MILDRED.             Speak!

  TRESHAM.                 I will.

Is there a story men could—any man
Could tell of you, you would conceal from me?
I'll never think there's falsehood on that lip.
Say " There is no such story men could tell,"
And I'll believe you, though I disbelieve
The world—the world of better men than I,
And women such as I suppose you. Speak!
[*After a pause.*] Not speak? Explain then! Clear
    it up then! Move
Some of the miserable weight away
That presses lower than the grave. Not speak?
Some of the dead weight, Mildred! Ah, if I
Could bring myself to plainly make their charge
Against you! Must I, Mildred? Silent still?
[*After a pause.*] Is there a gallant that has night by
    night
Admittance to your chamber?
             [*After a pause.*] Then, his name!
Till now, I only had a thought for you:
But now,—his name!

  MILDRED. Thorold, do you devise
Fit expiation for my guilt, if fit
There be! 'Tis nought to say that I'll endure
And bless you,—that my spirit yearns to purge
Her stains off in the fierce renewing fire:
But do not plunge me into other guilt!

Oh, guilt enough! I cannot tell his name.

TRESHAM. Then judge yourself! How should I
    act? Pronounce!

MILDRED. Oh, Thorold, you must never tempt me
    thus!

To die here in this chamber by that sword
Would seem like punishment: so should I glide,
Like an arch-cheat, into extremest bliss!
'Twere easily arranged for me: but you—
What would become of you?

TRESHAM.              And what will now
Become of me? I'll hide your shame and mine
From every eye; the dead must heave their hearts
Under the marble of our chapel-floor;
They cannot rise and blast you. You may wed
Your paramour above our mother's tomb;
Our mother cannot move from 'neath your foot.
We too will somehow wear this one day out:
But with to-morrow hastens here—the Earl!
The youth without suspicion. Face can come
From Heaven and heart from . . . whence proceed
    such hearts?
I have dispatched last night at your command
A missive bidding him present himself
To-morrow—here—thus much is said; the rest
Is understood as if 'twere written down—
"His suit finds favor in your eyes." Now dictate
This morning's letter that shall countermand
Last night's—do dictate that!

MILDRED.            But, Thorold—if
I will receive him as I said?

TRESHAM.           The Earl?

MILDRED. I will receive him.

TRESHAM [*starting up*].     Ho there! Guendolen!


GUENDOLEN *and* AUSTIN *enter*

And, Austin, you are welcome, too! Look there!
The woman there!

AUSTIN *and* GUENDOLEN. How? Mildred?

TRESHAM. Mildred once!
Now the receiver night by night, when sleep
Blesses the inmates of her father's house,
—I say, the soft sly wanton that receives
Her guilt's accomplice 'neath this roof which holds
You, Guendolen, you, Austin, and has held
A thousand Treshams—never one like her!
No lighter of the signal-lamp her quick
Foul breath near quenches in hot eagerness
To mix with breath as foul! no loosener
O' the lattice, practised in the stealthy tread,
The low voice and the noiseless come-and-go!
Not one composer of the bacchant's mien
Into—what you thought Mildred's, in a word!
Know her!
    GUENDOLEN. Oh, Mildred, look to me, at least!
Thorold—she's dead, I'd say, but that she stands
Rigid as stone and whiter!
    TRESHAM. You have heard . . .
    GUENDOLEN. Too much! You must proceed no
        further.
    MILDRED. Yes—
Proceed! All's truth. Go from me!
    TRESHAM. All is truth,
She tells you! Well, you know, or ought to know,
All this I would forgive in her. I'd con
Each precept the harsh world enjoins, I'd take
Our ancestors' stern verdicts one by one,
I'd bind myself before them to exact
The prescribed vengeance—and one word of hers,
The sight of her, the bare least memory
Of Mildred, my one sister, my heart's pride
Above all prides, my all in all so long,
Would scatter every trace of my resolve.
What were it silently to waste away
And see her waste away from this day forth,
Two scathed things with leisure to repent,
And grow acquainted with the grave, and die
Tired out if not at peace, and be forgotten?
It were not so impossible to bear.

But this—that, fresh from last night's pledge renewed
Of love with the successful gallant there,
She calmly bids me help her to entice,
Inveigle an unconscious trusting youth
Who thinks her all that's chaste and good and pure,
—Invites me to betray him . . . who so fit
As honour's self to cover shame's arch-deed?
—That she'll receive Lord Mertoun—(her own
    phrase)—
This, who could bear? Why, you have heard of
    thieves,
Stabbers, the earth's disgrace, who yet have laughed,
" Talk not to me of torture—I'll betray
No comrade I've pledged faith to ! "—you have
    heard
Of wretched women—all but Mildreds—tied
By wild illicit ties to losels vile
You'd tempt them to forsake; and they'll reply
" Gold, friends, repute, I left for him, I find
In him, why should I leave him then, for gold,
Repute or friends? "—and you have felt your heart
Respond to such poor outcasts of the world
As to so many friends; bad as you please,
You've felt they were God's men and women still,
So, not to be disowned by you. But she
That stands there, calmly gives her lover up
As means to wed the Earl that she may hide
Their intercourse the surelier: and, for this,
I curse her to her face before you all.
Shame hunt her from the earth ! Then Heaven do
    right
To both ! It hears me now—shall judge her then !
    [*As* MILDRED *faints and falls,* TRESHAM *rushes out.*
    AUSTIN. Stay, Tresham, we'll accompany you !
    GUENDOLEN.                      We?
What, and leave Mildred? We? Why, where's my
    place
But by her side, and where yours but by mine?
Mildred—one word ! Only look at me, then !
    AUSTIN. No, Guendolen ! I echo Thorold's voice.

She is unworthy to behold . . .
  GUENDOLEN.                  Us two?
If you spoke on reflection, and if I
Approved your speech—if you (to put the thing
At lowest) you the soldier, bound to make
The king's cause yours and fight for it, and throw
Regard to others of its right or wrong,
—If with a death-white woman you can help,
Let alone sister, let alone a Mildred,
You left her—or if I, her cousin, friend
This morning, playfellow but yesterday,
Who said, or thought at least a thousand times,
"I'd serve you if I could," should now face round
And say, "Ah, that's to only signify
I'd serve you while you're fit to serve yourself:
So long as fifty eyes await the turn
Of yours to forestall its yet half-formed wish,
I'll proffer my assistance you'll not need—
When every tongue is praising you, I'll join
The praisers' chorus—when you're hemmed about
With lives between you and detraction—lives
To be laid down if a rude voice, rash eye,
Rough hand should violate the sacred ring
Their worship throws about you,—then indeed,
Who'll stand up for you stout as I?" If so
We said, and so we did,—not Mildred there
Would be unworthy to behold us both,
But we should be unworthy,. both of us.
To be beheld by—by—your meanest dog,
Which, if that sword were broken in your face
Before a crowd, that badge torn off your breast,
And you cast out with hooting and contempt,
—Would push his way thro' all the hooters, gain
Your side, go off with you and all your shame
To the next ditch you choose to die in! Austin,
Do you love me? Here's Austin, Mildred,—here's
Your brother says he does not believe half—
No, nor half that—of all he heard! He says,
Look up and take his hand!
  AUSTIN.               Look up and take

My hand, dear Mildred!
MILDRED.                    I—I was so young!
Beside, I loved him, Thorold—and I had
No mother; God forgot me: so, I fell.
GUENDOLEN. Mildred!
MILDRED.                    Require no further! Did I dream
That I could palliate what is done? All's true.
Now, punish me! A woman takes my hand?
Let go my hand! You do not know, I see.
I thought that Thorold told you.
GUENDOLEN.                    What is this?
Where start you to?
MILDRED.                    Oh, Austin, loosen me!
You heard the whole of it—your eyes were worse,
In their surprise, than Thorold's! Oh, unless
You stay to execute his sentence, loose
My hand! Has Thorold gone, and are you here?
GUENDOLEN. Here, Mildred, we two friends of yours
          will wait
Your bidding; be you silent, sleep or muse!
Only, when you shall want your bidding done,
How can we do it if we are not by?
Here's Austin waiting patiently your will!
One spirit to command, and one to love
And to believe in it and do its best,
Poor as that is, to help it—why, the world
Has been won many a time, its length and breadth,
By just such a beginning!
MILDRED.                         I believe
If once I threw my arms about your neck
And sunk my head upon your breast, that I
Should weep again.
GUENDOLEN.          Let go her hand now, Austin!
Wait for me. Pace the gallery and think
On the world's seemings and realities,
Until I call you.                    [AUSTIN *goes.*
MILDRED. No—I cannot weep.
No more tears from this brain—no sleep—no tears!
O Guendolen, I love you!
GUENDOLEN.               Yes: and "love"

Is a short word that says so very much!
It says that you confide in me.

MILDRED.                            Confide!

GUENDOLEN. Your lover's name, then! I've so much
    to learn,
Ere I can work in your behalf!

MILDRED.                        My friend,
You know I cannot tell his name.

GUENDOLEN.                        At least
He is your lover? and you love him too?

MILDRED. Ah, do you ask me that,—but I am fallen
So low!

GUENDOLEN. You love him still, then?

MILDRED.                            My sole prop
Against the guilt that crushes me! I say,
Each night ere I lie down, "I was so young—
I had no mother, and I loved him so!"
And then God seems indulgent, and I dare
Trust him my soul in sleep.

GUENDOLEN.                    How could you let us
E'en talk to you about Lord Mertoun then?

MILDRED. There is a cloud around me.

GUENDOLEN.                            But you said
You would receive his suit in spite of this?

MILDRED. I say there is a cloud . . .

GUENDOLEN.                            No cloud to me!
Lord Mertoun and your lover are the same!

MILDRED. What maddest fancy . . .

GUENDOLEN [*calling aloud.*] Austin! (spare your
    pains—
When I have got a truth, that truth I keep)—

MILDRED. By all you love, sweet Guendolen, forbear!
Have I confided in you . . .

GUENDOLEN.                    Just for this!
Austin!—Oh, not to guess it at the first!
But I did guess it—that is, I divined,
Felt by an instinct how it was: why else
Should I pronounce you free from all that heap
Of sins which had been irredeemable?
I felt they were not yours—what other way

Than this, not yours? The secret's wholly mine!

MILDRED. If you would see me die before his face . . .

GUENDOLEN. I'd hold my peace! And if the Earl
    returns

To-night?

MILDRED. Ah Heaven, he's lost!

GUENDOLEN.                     I thought so. Austin!

*Enter* AUSTIN

Oh, where have you been hiding?

AUSTIN.                   Thorold's gone,

I know not how, across the meadow-land.

I watched him till I lost him in the skirts

O' the beech-wood.

GUENDOLEN.        Gone? All thwarts us.

MILDRED.                      Thorold too?

GUENDOLEN. I have thought. First lead this Mildred
    to her room.

Go on the other side; and then we'll seek

Your brother: and I'll tell you, by the way,

The greatest comfort in the world. You said

There was a clue to all. Remember, Sweet,

He said there was a clue! I hold it. Come!

## ACT III

SCENE I.—*The end of the Yew-tree Avenue under* MILDRED'S *Window.
A light seen through a central red pane*

*Enter* TRESHAM *through the trees*

Again here! But I cannot lose myself.

The heath—the orchard—I have traversed glades

And dells and bosky paths which used to lead

Into green wild-wood depths, bewildering

My boy's adventurous step. And now they tend

Hither or soon or late; the blackest shade

Breaks up, the thronged trunks of the trees ope wide,

And the dim turret I have fled from, fronts

Again my step; the very river put

Its arm about me and conducted me
To this detested spot.  Why then, I'll shun
Their will no longer: do your will with me!
Oh, bitter!  To have reared a towering scheme
Of happiness, and to behold it razed,
Were nothing: all men hope, and see their hopes
Frustrate, and grieve awhile, and hope anew.
But I . . . to hope that from a line like ours
No horrid prodigy like this would spring,
Were just as though I hoped that from these old
Confederates against the sovereign day,
Children of older and yet older sires,
Whose living coral berries dropped, as now
On me, on many a baron's surcoat once,
On many a beauty's whimple—would proceed
No poison-tree, to thrust, from hell its root,
Hither and thither its strange snaky arms.
Why came I here?  What must I do?  [*A bell strikes.*]
        A bell?
Midnight! and 'tis at midnight . . . Ah, I catch
—Woods, river, plains, I catch your meaning now,
And I obey you!  Hist!  This tree will serve.
        [*He retires behind one of the trees.  After a pause,
                        enter* MERTOUN *cloaked as before.*
    MERTOUN.  Not time!  Beat out thy last voluptuous
        beat
Of hope and fear, my heart!  I thought the clock
I' the chapel struck as I was pushing through
The ferns.  And so I shall no more see rise
My love-star!  Oh, no matter for the past!
So much the more delicious task to watch
Mildred revive: to pluck out, thorn by thorn,
All traces of the rough forbidden path
My rash love lured her to!  Each day must see
Some fear of hers effaced, some hope renewed:
Then there will be surprises, unforeseen
Delights in store.  I'll not regret the past.
        [*The light is placed above in the purple pane.*
And see, my signal rises, Mildred's star!
I never saw it lovelier than now

It rises for the last time. If it sets,
'Tis that the re-assuring sun may dawn.

> [*As he prepares to ascend the last tree of the avenue,*
> TRESHAM *arrests his arm.*

Unhand me—peasant, by your grasp! Here's gold.
'Twas a mad freak of mine. I said I'd pluck
A branch from the white-blossomed shrub beneath
The casement there. Take this, and hold your peace.

TRESHAM. Into the moonlight yonder, come with me!
Out of the shadow!

MERTOUN.　　　　I am armed, fool!

TRESHAM.　　　　　　　　　　Yes,
Or no? You'll come into the light, or no?
My hand is on your throat—refuse!—

MERTOUN.　　　　　　　　That voice!
Where have I heard . . . no—that was mild and slow.
I'll come with you.　　　　　[*They advance.*

TRESHAM.　　　You're armed: that's well. Declare
Your name: who are you?

MERTOUN.　　　　　　(Tresham!—she is lost!)

TRESHAM. Oh, silent? Do you know, you bear your-
　　　self
Exactly as, in curious dreams I've had
How felons, this wild earth is full of, look
When they're detected, still your kind has looked!
The bravo holds an assured countenance,
The thief is voluble and plausible,
But silently the slave of lust has crouched
When I have fancied it before a man.
Your name!

MERTOUN.　　　　I do conjure Lord Tresham—ay,
Kissing his foot, if so I might prevail—
That he for his own sake forbear to ask
My name! As heaven's above, his future weal
Or woe depends upon my silence! Vain!
I read your white inexorable face.
Know me, Lord Tresham!

> [*He throws off his disguises.*

TRESHAM.　　　　　　Mertoun!

> [*After a pause.*] Draw now!

MERTOUN.                              Hear me
But speak first!

TRESHAM.          Not one least word on your life!
Be sure that I will strangle in your throat
The least word that informs me how you live
And yet seem what you seem! No doubt 'twas you
Taught Mildred still to keep that face and sin.
We should join hands in frantic sympathy
If you once taught me the unteachable,
Explained how you can live so and so lie.
With God's help I retain, despite my sense,
The old belief—a life like yours is still
Impossible. Now draw!

MERTOUN.                    Not for my sake,
Do I entreat a hearing—for your sake,
And most, for her sake!

TRESHAM.                  Ha, ha, what should I
Know of your ways? A miscreant like yourself,
How must one rouse his ire? A blow?—that's pride
No doubt, to him! One spurns him, does one not?
Or sets the foot upon his mouth, or spits
Into his face! Come! Which, or all of these?

    MERTOUN. 'Twixt him and me and Mildred, Heaven
        be judge!

Can I avoid this? Have your will, my lord!
        [*He draws and, after a few passes, falls.*

    TRESHAM. You are not hurt?

MERTOUN.                      You'll hear me now!

TRESHAM.                              But rise!

    MERTOUN. Ah, Tresham, say I not "you'll hear me
    now!"

And what procures a man the right to speak
In his defence before his fellow man,
But—I suppose—the thought that presently
He may have leave to speak before his God
His whole defence?

TRESHAM.                Not hurt? It cannot be!
You made no effort to resist me. Where
Did my sword reach you? Why not have returned
My thrusts? Hurt where?

MERTOUN. My lord—

TRESHAM. How young he is!

MERTOUN. Lord Tresham, I am very young, and yet
I have entangled other lives with mine.
Do let me speak, and do believe my speech!
That when I die before you presently,—

TRESHAM. Can you stay here till I return with help?

MERTOUN. Oh, stay by me! When I was less than
     boy
I did you grievous wrong and knew it not—
Upon my honour, knew it not! Once known,
I could not find what seemed a better way
To right you than I took: my life—you feel
How less than nothing were the giving you
The life you've taken! But I thought my way
The better—only for your sake and hers:
And as you have decided otherwise,
Would I had an infinity of lives
To offer you! Now say—instruct me—think!
Can you, from the brief minutes I have left,
Eke out my reparation? Oh think—think!
For I must wring a partial—dare I say,
Forgiveness from you, ere I die?

TRESHAM. I do
Forgive you.

MERTOUN. Wait and ponder that great word!
Because, if you forgive me, I shall hope
To speak to you of—Mildred!

TRESHAM. Mertoun, haste
And anger have undone us. 'Tis not you
Should tell me for a novelty you're young,
Thoughtless, unable to recall the past.
Be but your pardon ample as my own!

MERTOUN. Ah, Tresham, that a sword-stroke and a
     drop
Of blood or two, should bring all this about
Why, 'twas my very fear of you, my love
Of you—(what passion like a boy's for one
Like you?)—that ruined me! I dreamed of you—
You, all accomplished, courted everywhere,

The scholar and the gentleman.  I burned
To knit myself to you: but I was young,
And your surpassing reputation kept me
So far aloof!  Oh, wherefore all that love?
With less of love, my glorious yesterday
Of praise and gentlest words and kindest looks,
Had taken place perchance six months ago.
Even now, how happy we had been!  And yet
I know the thought of this escaped you, Tresham!
Let me look up into your face; I feel
'Tis changed above me: yet my eyes are glazed.
Where? where?

> [*As he endeavours to raise himself, his eye catches*
> *the lamp.*

                Ah, Mildred!  What will Mildred do?
Tresham, her life is bound up in the life
That's bleeding fast away!  I'll live—must live,
There, if you'll only turn me I shall live
And save her!  Tresham—oh, had you but heard!
Had you but heard!  What right was yours to set
The thoughtless foot upon her life and mine,
And then say, as we perish, "Had I thought,
All had gone otherwise"?  We've sinned and die:
Never you sin, Lord Tresham! for you'll die,
And God will judge you.

TRESHAM.             Yes, be satisfied!
That process is begun.

MERTOUN.         And she sits there
Waiting for me!  Now, say you this to her—
You, not another—say, I saw him die
As he breathed this, " I love her "—you don't know
What those three small words mean!  Say, loving her
Lowers me down the bloody slope to death
With memories . . . I speak to her, not you,
Who had no pity, will have no remorse,
Perchance intend her . . . Die along with me,
Dear Mildred! 'tis so easy, and you'll 'scape
So much unkindness!  Can I lie at rest,
With rude speech spoken to you, ruder deeds
Done to you?—heartless men shall have my heart,

And I tied down with grave-clothes and the worm,
Aware, perhaps, of every blow—oh God!—
Upon those lips—yet of no power to tear
The felon stripe by stripe! Die, Mildred! Leave
Their honourable world to them! For God
We're good enough, though the world casts us out.
                              [*A whistle is heard.*

TRESHAM.  Ho, Gerard!


*Enter* GERARD, AUSTIN *and* GUENDOLEN, *with lights*
                    No one speak! You see what's done.
I cannot bear another voice.
    MERTOUN.                    There's light—
Light all about me, and I move to it.
Tresham, did I not tell you—did you not
Just promise to deliver words of mine
To Mildred?
    TRESHAM. I will bear those words to her.
    MERTOUN. Now?
    TRESHAM.          Now. Lift you the body, and leave me
The head.
              [*As they have half raised* MERTOUN, *he turns
                                        suddenly.*

    MERTOUN. I knew they turned me: turn me not from
        her!
There! stay you! there!                        [*Dies.*
    GUENDOLEN [*after a pause*]. Austin, remain you here
With Thorold until Gerard comes with help:
Then lead him to his chamber. I must go
To Mildred.
    TRESHAM. Guendolen, I hear each word
You utter. Did you hear him bid me give
His message? Did you hear my promise? I,
And only I, see Mildred.
    GUENDOLEN.              She will die.
    TRESHAM. Oh no, she will not die! I dare not hope
She'll die. What ground have you to think she'll die?
Why, Austin's with you!
    AUSTIN.                    Had we but arrived

Before you fought!

TRESHAM. There was no fight at all.
He let me slaughter him—the boy! I'll trust
The body there to you and Gerard—thus!
Now bear him on before me.

AUSTIN. Whither bear him?

TRESHAM. Oh, to my chamber! When we meet there next,
We shall be friends.

[*They bear out the body of* MERTOUN.
Will she die, Guendolen?

GUENDOLEN. Where are you taking me?

TRESHAM. He fell just here.
Now answer me. Shall you in your whole life
—You who have nought to do with Mertoun's fate,
Now you have seen his breast upon the turf,
Shall you e'er walk this way if you can help?
When you and Austin wander arm-in-arm
Through our ancestral grounds, will not a shade
Be ever on the meadow and the waste—
Another kind of shade than when the night
Shuts the woodside with all its whispers up?
But will you ever so forget his breast
As carelessly to cross this bloody turf
Under the black yew avenue? That's well!
You turn your head: and I then?—

GUENDOLEN. What is done
Is done. My care is for the living. Thorold,
Bear up against this burden: more remains
To set the neck to!

TRESHAM. Dear and ancient trees
My fathers planted, and I loved so well!
What have I done that, like some fabled crime
Of yore, lets loose a Fury leading thus
Her miserable dance amidst you all?
Oh, never more for me shall winds intone
With all your tops a vast antiphony,
Demanding and responding in God's praise!
Hers ye are now, not mine! Farewell—farewell!

Scene II.—Mildred's *Chamber*

Mildred *alone*

He comes not! I have heard of those who seemed
Resourceless in prosperity,—you thought
Sorrow might slay them when she listed; yet
Did they so gather up their diffused strength
At her first menace, that they bade her strike,
And stood and laughed her subtlest skill to scorn.
Oh, 'tis not so with me! The first woe fell,
And the rest fall upon it, not on me:
Else should I bear that Henry comes not?—fails
Just this first night out of so many nights?
Loving is done with. Were he sitting now,
As so few hours since, on that seat, we'd love
No more—contrive no thousand happy ways
To hide love from the loveless, any more.
I think I might have urged some little point
In my defence, to Thorold; he was breathless
For the least hint of a defence: but no,
The first shame over, all that would might fall.
No Henry! Yet I merely sit and think
The morn's deed o'er and o'er. I must have crept
Out of myself. A Mildred that has lost
Her lover—oh, I dare not look upon
Such woe! I crouch away from it! 'Tis she,
Mildred, will break her heart, not I! The world
Forsakes me: only Henry's left me—left?
When I have lost him, for he does not come,
And I sit stupidly . . . Oh Heaven, break up
This worse than anguish, this mad apathy,
By any means or any messenger!

    Tresham [*without*]. Mildred!
    Mildred.            Come in! Heaven hears me!
    [*Enter* Tresham.]         You? alone?
Oh, no more cursing!
    Tresham.       Mildred, I must sit.
There—you sit!
    Mildred.     Say it, Thorold—do not look
The curse! deliver all you come to say!

What must become of me? Oh, speak that thought
Which makes your brow and cheeks so pale!

TRESHAM.                                         My thought?

MILDRED. All of it!

TRESHAM.                    How we waded years—ago—
After those water-lilies, till the plash,
I know not how, surprised us; and you dared
Neither advance nor turn back: so, we stood
Laughing and crying until Gerard came—
Once safe upon the turf, the loudest too,
For once more reaching the relinquished prize!
How idle thoughts are, some men's, dying men's!
Mildred,—

MILDRED. You call me kindlier by my name
Than even yesterday: what is in that?

TRESHAM. It weighs so much upon my mind that I
This morning took an office not my own!
I might . . . of course, I must be glad or grieved,
Content or not, at every little thing
That touches you. I may with a wrung heart
Even reprove you, Mildred; I did more:
Will you forgive me?

MILDRED.                    Thorold? do you mock?
Oh no . . . and yet you bid me . . . say that word!

TRESHAM. Forgive me, Mildred!—are you silent,
    Sweet?

MILDRED [*starting up*]. Why does not Henry Mertoun
    come to-night?
Are you, too, silent?

[*Dashing his mantle aside, and pointing to his scabbard,
                                    which is empty.*

                              Ah, this speaks for you!
You've murdered Henry Mertoun! Now proceed!
What is it I must pardon? This and all?
Well, I do pardon you—I think I do.
Thorold, how very wretched you must be!

TRESHAM. He bade me tell you . . .

MILDRED.                              What I do forbid
Your utterance of! So much that you may tell

And will not—how you murdered him . . . but, no!
You'll tell me that he loved me, never more
Than bleeding out his life there: must I say
"Indeed," to that? Enough! I pardon you.

    TRESHAM. You cannot, Mildred! for the harsh words,
        yes:
Of this last deed Another's judge: whose doom
I wait in doubt, despondency and fear.

    MILDRED. Oh, true! There's nought for me to pardon!
        True!
You loose my soul of all its cares at once.
Death makes me sure of him for ever! You
Tell me his last words? He shall tell me them,
And take my answer—not in words, but reading
Himself the heart I had to read him late,
Which death . . .

    TRESHAM.         Death? You are dying too? Well
        said
Of Guendolen! I dared not hope you'd die:
But she was sure of it.

    MILDRED.         Tell Guendolen
I loved her, and tell Austin . . .

    TRESHAM.             Him you loved:
And me?

    MILDRED. Ah, Thorold! Was't not rashly done
To quench that blood, on fire with youth and hope
And love of me—whom you loved too, and yet
Suffered to sit here waiting his approach
While you were slaying him? Oh, doubtlessly
You let him speak his poor confused boy's-speech
—Do his poor utmost to disarm your wrath
And respite me!—you let him try to give
The story of our love and ignorance,
And the brief madness and the long despair—
You let him plead all this, because your code
Of honour bids you hear before you strike:
But at the end, as he looked up for life
Into your eyes—you struck him down!

    TRESHAM.            No! No!
Had I but heard him—had I let him speak

Half the truth—less—had I looked long on him
I had desisted! Why, as he lay there,
The moon on his flushed cheek, I gathered all
The story ere he told it: I saw through
The troubled surface of his crime and yours
A depth of purity immovable,
Had I but glanced, where all seemed turbidest
Had gleamed some inlet to the calm beneath;
I would not glance: my punishment's at hand.
There, Mildred, is the truth! and you—say on—
You curse me?

MILDRED.        As I dare approach that Heaven
Which has not bade a living thing despair,
Which needs no code to keep its grace from stain,
But bids the vilest worm that turns on it
Desist and be forgiven,—I—forgive not,
But bless you, Thorold, from my soul of souls!

                                [*Falls on his neck.*

There! Do not think too much upon the past!
The cloud that's broke was all the same a cloud
While it stood up between my friend and you;
You hurt him 'neath its shadow: but is that
So past retrieve? I have his heart, you know;
I may dispose of it: I give it you!
It loves you as mine loves! Confirm me, Henry!

                                          [*Dies.*

   TRESHAM. I wish thee joy, Beloved! I am glad
In thy full gladness!

   GUENDOLEN [*without*]. Mildred! Tresham!

                   [*Entering with* AUSTIN.] Thorold,
I could desist no longer. Ah, she swoons!
That's well.

   TRESHAM. Oh, better far than that!
   GUENDOLEN.                    She's dead!
Let me unlock her arms!

   TRESHAM.              She threw them thus
About my neck, and blessed me, and then died:
You'll let them stay now, Guendolen!

   AUSTIN                              Leave her
And look to him! What ails you, Thorold?

GUENDOLEN.                                    White
As she, and whiter! Austin! quick—this side!

AUSTIN. A froth is oozing through his clenched
    teeth;
Both lips, where they're not bitten through, are black:
Speak, dearest Thorold!

TRESHAM. Something does weigh down
My neck beside her weight: thanks: I should fall
But for you, Austin, I believe!—there, there,
'Twill pass away soon!—ah,—I had forgotten:
I am dying.

GUENDOLEN. Thorold—Thorold—why was this?

TRESHAM. I said, just as I drank the poison off,
The earth would be no longer earth to me,
The life out of all life was gone from me.
There are blind ways provided, the fore-done
Heart-weary player in this pageant-world
Drops out by, letting the main masque defile
By the conspicuous portal: I am through—
Just through!

GUENDOLEN. Don't leave him, Austin! Death is
    close.

TRESHAM. Already Mildred's face is peacefuller,
I see you, Austin—feel you; here's my hand,
Put yours in it—you, Guendolen, yours too!
You're lord and lady now—you're Treshams; name
And fame are yours: you hold our 'scutcheon up.
Austin, no blot on it! You see how blood
Must wash one blot away: the first blot came
And the first blood came. To the vain world's eye
All's gules again: no care to the vain world,
From whence the red was drawn!

AUSTIN. No blot shall come!

TRESHAM. I said that: yet it did come. Should it
    come,
Vengeance is God's, not man's. Remember me! [*Dies.*

GUENDOLEN [*letting fall the pulseless arm*]. Ah,
    Thorold, we can but—remember you!

# MANFRED

BY
LORD BYRON

# INTRODUCTORY NOTE

GEORGE GORDON, *sixth Lord Byron, was the son of a profligate guardsman and an eccentric Scottish heiress. He was born in London on January 22, 1788, educated at Harrow and Trinity College, Cambridge, and came into prominence with the publication of "English Bards and Scotch Reviewers" (1809), a satire provoked by an adverse criticism of his youthful "Hours of Idleness" in the "Edinburgh Review." After two years of travel on the Continent, he published the first two cantos of "Childe Harold," and in 1815 married Miss Millbanke, a prospective heiress. She left him a year later, and in the scandal which accompanied the separation Byron became very unpopular. He left England never to return, and spent most of his remaining years in Italy.*

*It is unnecessary to follow in detail the history of his life abroad. In spite of great irregularities in conduct, Byron continued to write copiously, seldom with care or attention to finish, but often with brilliance. His Oriental tales, which made him the hero of the sentimental readers of the day, "The Giaour," "The Bride of Abydos," "The Corsair," had been written in the years preceding his marriage; "Manfred," his first and in many respects his most interesting drama, appeared in 1817; "Don Juan" came out at intervals from 1819 to 1824; and during the same period he produced with extraordinary rapidity a group of plays of which the so-called mystery, "Cain," is the most important. "The Vision of Judgment," a merciless satire on Southey's apotheosis of George III, followed in 1822.*

*Byron had been interested in revolutionary politics in Italy, and when the Greeks revolted against the Turks in 1823 he joined them as a volunteer; but before he saw fighting he died of fever at Missolonghi, April 19, 1824. His death at least was worthy of the noblest passion of his life, the passion for liberty.*

*For dramatic writing Byron was not favorably endowed. His egotism was too persistent to enable him to enter vitally and sympathetically into a variety of characters, and the hero of his plays, as of his poems, is usually himself more or less disguised. Yet some of his most eloquent lines are to be found in his dramas, and "Manfred" is an impressive and characteristic product of one of the most brilliantly gifted of English poets.*

# MANFRED

## A DRAMATIC POEM

' There are more things in heaven and earth, Horatio,
Than are dreamt of in your philosophy.'

### DRAMATIS PERSONÆ

| | |
|---|---|
| MANFRED | WITCH OF THE ALPS |
| CHAMOIS HUNTER | ARIMANES |
| ABBOT OF ST. MAURICE | NEMESIS |
| MANUEL | THE DESTINIES |
| HERMAN | SPIRITS, etc. |

*The scene of the Drama is amongst the Higher Alps—partly in the
Castle of Manfred, and partly in the Mountains.*

## ACT I

SCENE I.—MANFRED *alone.—Scene, a Gothic Gallery.*
*Time, Midnight.*

*Manfred*

THE lamp must be replenish'd, but even then
It will not burn so long as I must watch.
My slumbers—if I slumber—are not sleep,
But a continuance of enduring thought,
Which then I can resist not: in my heart
There is a vigil, and these eyes but close
To look within; and yet I live, and bear
The aspect and the form of breathing men.
But grief should be the instructor of the wise;
Sorrow is knowledge: they who know the most
Must mourn the deepest o'er the fatal truth, '
The Tree of Knowledge is not that of Life.
Philosophy and science, and the springs
Of wonder, and the wisdom of the world,

I have essay'd, and in my mind there is
A power to make these subject to itself—
But they avail not: I have done men good,
And I have met with good even among men—
But this avail'd not: I have had my foes,
And none have baffled, many fallen before me—
But this avail'd not:—Good, or evil, life,
Powers, passions, all I see in other beings,
Have been to me as rain unto the sands,
Since that all-nameless hour. I have no dread,
And feel the curse to have no natural fear,
Nor fluttering throb, that beats with hopes or wishes,
Or lurking love of something on the earth.
Now to my task.—
     Mysterious Agency!
Ye spirits of the unbounded Universe,
Whom I have sought in darkness and in light!
Ye, who do compass earth about, and dwell
In subtler essence! ye, to whom the tops
Of mountains inaccessible are haunts,
And earth's and ocean's caves familiar things—
I call upon ye by the written charm
Which gives me power upon you—Rise! appear!
         *[A pause.*

They come not yet.—Now by the voice of him
Who is the first among you; by this sign,
Which makes you tremble; by the claims of him
Who is undying,—Rise! appear!—Appear!
         *[A pause.*

If it be so.—Spirits of earth and air,
Ye shall not thus elude me: by a power,
Deeper than all yet urged, a tyrant-spell,
Which had its birthplace in a star condemn'd,
The burning wreck of a demolish'd world,
A wandering hell in the eternal space;
By the strong curse which is upon my soul,
The thought which is within me and around me,
I do compel ye to my will. Appear!
 *[A star is seen at the darker end of the gallery: it is*
    *stationary; and a voice is heard singing.*

### FIRST SPIRIT

Mortal! to thy bidding bow'd,
From my mansion in the cloud,
Which the breath of twilight builds,
And the summer's sunset gilds
With the azure and vermilion
Which is mix'd for my pavilion;
Though thy quest may be forbidden,
On a star-beam I have ridden,
To thine adjuration bow'd;
Mortal—be thy wish avow'd!

### *Voice of the* SECOND SPIRIT

Mont Blanc is the monarch of mountains;
   They crown'd him long ago
On a throne of rocks, in a robe of clouds,
   With a diadem of snow.
Around his waist are forests braced,
   The Avalanche in his hand;
But ere it fall, that thundering ball
   Must pause for my command.
The Glacier's cold and restless mass
   Moves onward day by day;
But I am he who bids it pass,
   Or with its ice delay.
I am the spirit of the place,
   Could make the mountain bow
And quiver to his cavern'd base—
   And what with me wouldst *Thou?*

### *Voice of the* THIRD SPIRIT

In the blue depth of the waters,
   Where the wave hath no strife,
Where the wind is a stranger,
   And the sea-snake hath life,
Where the Mermaid is decking
   Her green hair with shells;
Like the storm on the surface

Came the sound of thy spells;
O'er my calm Hall of Coral
  The deep echo roll'd—
To the Spirit of Ocean
  Thy wishes unfold!

### Fourth Spirit

Where the slumbering earthquake
  Lies pillow'd on fire,
And the lakes of bitumen
  Rise boilingly higher;
Where the roots of the Andes
  Strike deep in the earth,
As their summits to heaven
  Shoot soaringly forth;
I have quitted my birthplace,
  Thy bidding to bide—
Thy spell hath subdued me,
  Thy will be my guide!

### Fifth Spirit

I am the Rider of the wind,
  The Stirrer of the storm;
The hurricane I left behind
  Is yet with lightning warm;
To speed to thee, o'er shore and sea
  I swept upon the blast:
The fleet I met sail'd well, and yet
  'Twill sink ere night be past.

### Sixth Spirit

My dwelling is the shadow of the night,
Why doth thy magic torture me with light?

### Seventh Spirit

The star which rules thy destiny
Was ruled, ere earth began, by me:
It was a world as fresh and fair
As e'er revolved round sun in air;

Its course was free and regular,
Space bosom'd not a lovelier star.
The hour arrived—and it became
A wandering mass of shapeless flame,
A pathless comet, and a curse,
The menace of the universe;
Still rolling on with innate force,
Without a sphere, without a course,
A bright deformity on high,
The monster of the upper sky!
And thou! beneath its influence born—
Thou worm! whom I obey and scorn—
Forced by a power (which is not thine,
And lent thee but to make thee mine)
For this brief moment to descend,
Where these weak spirits round thee bend
And parley with a thing like thee—
What wouldst thou, Child of Clay, with me?


*The* SEVEN SPIRITS

Earth, ocean, air, night, mountains, winds, thy star,
    Are at thy beck and bidding, Child of Clay!
Before thee at thy quest their spirits are—
    What wouldst thou with us, son of mortals—say?


MAN. Forgetfulness—
FIRST SPIRIT.                    Of what—of whom—and why?
MAN. Of that which is within me; read it there—
Ye know it, and I cannot utter it.
SPIRIT. We can but give thee that which we possess:
Ask of us subjects, sovereignty, the power
O'er earth, the whole, or portion, or a sign
Which shall control the elements, whereof
We are the dominators,—each and all,
These shall be thine.
MAN.                    Oblivion, self-oblivion—
Can ye not wring from out the hidden realms
Ye offer so profusely what I ask?
SPIRIT. It is not in our essence, in our skill;

But—thou mayst die.

MAN.      Will death bestow it on me?

SPIRIT. We are immortal, and do not forget;
We are eternal; and to us the past
Is as the future, present. Art thou answer'd?

MAN. Ye mock me—but the power which brought
  ye here
Hath made you mine. Slaves, scoff not at my will!
The mind, the spirit, the Promethean spark,
The lightning of my being, is as bright,
Pervading, and far darting as your own,
And shall not yield to yours, though coop'd in clay!
Answer, or I will teach you what I am.

SPIRIT. We answer as we answer'd; our reply
Is even in thine own words.

MAN.      Why say ye so?

SPIRIT. If, as thou say'st, thine essence be as ours,
We have replied in telling thee, the thing
Mortals call death hath nought to do with us.

MAN. I then have call'd ye from your realms in vain;
Ye cannot, or ye will not, aid me.

SPIRIT.      Say;
What we possess we offer; it is thine:
Bethink ere thou dismiss us, ask again—
Kingdom, and sway, and strength, and length of days—

MAN. Accursèd! What have I to do with days?
They are too long already.—Hence—begone!

SPIRIT. Yet pause: being here, our will would do thee
  service;
Bethink thee, is there then no other gift
Which ye can make not worthless in thine eyes?

MAN. No, none: yet stay—one moment, ere we part—
I would behold ye face to face. I hear
Your voices, sweet and melancholy sounds,
As music on the waters; and I see
The steady aspect of a clear large star;
But nothing more. Approach me as ye are,
Or one, or all, in your accustom'd forms.

SPIRIT. We have no forms, beyond the elements
Of which we are the mind and principle:

But choose a form—in that we will appear.

MAN. I have no choice; there is no form on earth
Hideous or beautiful to me. Let him,
Who is most powerful of ye, take such aspect
As unto him may seem most fitting—Come!

SEVENTH SPIRIT (*appearing in the shape of a beautiful
        female figure*). Behold!

MAN.                          Oh God! if it be thus, and *thou*
Art not a madness and a mockery,
I yet might be most happy. I will clasp thee,
And we again will be—            [*The figure vanishes.*
                    My heart is crush'd!
                        [MANFRED *falls senseless.*


(*A Voice is heard in the Incantation which follows.*)

        When the moon is on the wave,
            And the glow-worm in the grass,
        And the meteor on the grave,
            And the wisp on the morass;
        When the falling stars are shooting,
        And the answer'd owls are hooting,
        And the silent leaves are still
        In the shadow of the hill,
        Shall my soul be upon thine,
        With a power and with a sign.

        Though thy slumber may be deep,
        Yet thy spirit shall not sleep;
        There are shades which will not vanish,
        There are thoughts thou canst not banish;
        By a power to thee unknown,
        Thou canst never be alone;
        Thou art wrapt as with a shroud,
        Thou art gather'd in a cloud;
        And for ever shalt thou dwell
        In the spirit of this spell.

        Though thou seest me not pass by,
        Thou shalt feel me with thine eye
        As a thing that, though unseen,

Must be near thee, and hath been;
And when in that secret dread
Thou hast turn'd around thy head,
Thou shalt marvel I am not
As thy shadow on the spot,
And the power which thou dost feel
Shall be what thou must conceal.

And a magic voice and verse
Hath baptized thee with a curse;
And a spirit of the air
Hath begirt thee with a snare;
In the wind there is a voice
Shall forbid thee to rejoice;
And to thee shall Night deny
All the quiet of her sky;
And the day shall have a sun,
Which shall make thee wish it done.

From thy false tears I did distil
An essence which hath strength to kill;
From thy own heart I then did wring
The black blood in its blackest spring;
From thy own smile I snatch'd the snake,
For there it coil'd as in a brake;
From thy own lip I drew the charm
Which gave all these their chiefest harm;
In proving every poison known,
I found the strongest was thine own.

By thy cold breast and serpent smile,
By thy unfathom'd gulfs of guile,
By that most seeming virtuous eye,
By thy shut soul's hypocrisy;
By the perfection of thine art
Which pass'd for human thine own heart;
By thy delight in others' pain,
And by thy brotherhood of Cain,
I call upon thee! and compel
Thyself to be thy proper Hell!

And on thy head I pour the vial
Which doth devote thee to this trial;
Nor to slumber, nor to die,
Shall be in thy destiny;
Though thy death shall still seem near
To thy wish, but as a fear;
Lo! the spell now works around thee,
And the clankless chain hath bound thee;
O'er thy heart and brain together
Hath the word been pass'd—now wither!


SCENE II.—*The Mountain of the Jungfrau.*—*Time, Morning.*
MANFRED *alone upon the Cliffs.*

MAN. The spirits I have raised abandon me,
The spells which I have studied baffle me,
The remedy I reck'd of tortured me;
I lean no more on super-human aid,
It hath no power upon the past, and for
The future, till the past be gulf'd in darkness,
It is not of my search.—My mother Earth!
And thou fresh breaking Day, and you, ye Mountains,
Why are ye beautiful? I cannot love ye.
And thou, the bright eye of the universe,
That openest over all, and unto all
Art a delight—thou shin'st not on my heart.
And you, ye crags, upon whose extreme edge
I stand, and on the torrent's brink beneath
Behold the tall pines dwindled as to shrubs
In dizziness of distance; when a leap,
A stir, a motion, even a breath, would bring
My breast upon its rocky bosom's bed
To rest for ever—wherefore do I pause?
I feel the impulse—yet I do not plunge;
I see the peril—yet do not recede;
And my brain reels—and yet my foot is firm.
There is a power upon me which withholds,
And makes it my fatality to live;
If it be life to wear within myself
This barrenness of spirit, and to be

My own soul's sepulchre, for I have ceased
To justify my deeds unto myself—
The last infirmity of evil.   Ay,
Thou wingèd and cloud-cleaving minister,
                    [*An eagle passes.*
Whose happy flight is highest into heaven,
Well may'st thou swoop so near me—I should be
Thy prey, and gorge thine eaglets; thou art gone
Where the eye cannot follow thee; but thine?
Yet pierces downward, onward, or above,
With a pervading vision.—Beautiful!
How beautiful is all this visible world!
How glorious in its action and itself!
But we, who name ourselves its sovereigns, we,
Half dust, half deity, alike unfit
To sink or soar, with our mix'd essence make
A conflict of its elements, and breathe
The breath of degradation and of pride,
Contending with low wants and lofty will,
Till our mortality predominates,
And men are—what they name not to themselves,
And trust not to each other.   Hark! the note,
          [*The Shepherd's pipe in the distance is heard.*
The natural music of the mountain reed
(For here the patriarchal days are not
A pastoral fable) pipes in the liberal air,
Mix'd with the sweet bells of the sauntering herd;
My soul would drink those echoes.—Oh, that I were
The viewless spirit of a lovely sound,
A living voice, a breathing harmony,
A bodiless enjoyment—born and dying
With the blest tone which made me!


                *Enter from below a* CHAMOIS HUNTER
    CHAMOIS HUNTER.                         Even so
This way the chamois leapt: her nimble feet
Have baffled me; my gains to-day will scarce
Repay my break-neck travail.—What is here?
Who seems not of my trade, and yet hath reach'd

A height which none even of our mountaineers,
Save our best hunters, may attain: his garb
Is goodly, his mien manly, and his air
Proud as a freeborn peasant's, at this distance—
I will approach him nearer.

    MAN. (*not perceiving the other*). To be thus—
Grey-hair'd with anguish, like these blasted pines,
Wrecks of a single winter, barkless, branchless,
A blighted trunk upon a cursèd root,
Which but supplies a feeling to decay—
And to be thus, eternally but thus,
Having been otherwise!  Now furrow'd o'er
With wrinkles, plough'd by moments, not by years
And hours—all tortured into ages—hours
Which I outlive!—Ye toppling crags of ice!
Ye avalanches, whom a breath draws down
In mountainous o'erwhelming, come and crush me!
I hear ye momently above, beneath,
Crash with a frequent conflict; but ye pass,
And only fall on things that still would live;
On the young flourishing forest, or the hut
And hamlet of the harmless villager.

    C. HUN. The mists begin to rise from up the valley;
I'll warn him to descend, or he may chance
To lose at once his way and life together.

    MAN. The mists boil up around the glaciers; clouds
Rise curling fast beneath me, white and sulphury,
Like foam from the roused ocean of deep Hell,
Whose every wave breaks on a living shore
Heap'd with the damn'd like pebbles.—I am giddy.

    C. HUN. I must approach him cautiously; if near,
A sudden step will startle him, and he
Seems tottering already.

    MAN.                              Mountains have fallen,
Leaving a gap in the clouds, and with the shock
Rocking their Alpine brethren; filling up
The ripe green valleys with destruction's splinters;
Damming the rivers with a sudden dash,
Which crush'd the waters into mist and made
Their fountains find another channel—thus,

Thus, in its old age, did Mount Rosenberg—
Why stood I not beneath it?

    C. HUN.                                     Friend! have a care,
Your next step may be fatal!—for the love
Of him who made you, stand not on that brink!

    MAN. (*not hearing him*). Such would have been
        for me a fitting tomb;
My bones had then been quiet in their depth;
They had not then been strewn upon the rocks
For the wind's pastime—as thus—thus they shall be—
In this one plunge.—Farewell, ye opening heavens!
Look not upon me thus reproachfully—
Ye were not meant for me—Earth! take these atoms!

    [As MANFRED *is in act to spring from the cliff, the*
        CHAMOIS HUNTER *seizes and retains him with*
        *a sudden grasp.*

    C. HUN. Hold, madman!—though aweary of thy life,
Stain not our pure vales with thy guilty blood!
Away with me—I will not quit my hold.

    MAN. I am most sick at heart—nay, grasp me not—
I am all feebleness—the mountains whirl
Spinning around me—I grow blind—What art thou?

    C. HUN. I'll answer that anon.—Away with me!
The clouds grow thicker—there—now lean on me—
Place your foot here—here, take this staff, and cling
A moment to that shrub—now give me your hand,
And hold fast by my girdle—softly—well—
The Chalet will be gain'd within an hour.
Come on, we'll quickly find a surer footing,
And something like a pathway, which the torrent
Hath wash'd since winter.—Come, 'tis bravely done;
You should have been a hunter.—Follow me.

    [*As they descend the rocks with difficulty, the scene*
                              *closes.*

## ACT II

SCENE I.—*A Cottage amongst the Bernese Alps*

MANFRED *and the* CHAMOIS HUNTER

C. HUN. No, no, yet pause, thou must not yet go
    forth:
Thy mind and body are alike unfit
To trust each other, for some hours, at least;
When thou art better, I will be thy guide—
But whither?
    MAN.        It imports not; I do know
My route full well and need no further guidance.
    C. HUN. Thy garb and gait bespeak thee of high
    lineage—
One of the many chiefs, whose castled crags
Look o'er the lower valleys—which of these
May call thee lord? I only know their portals;
My way of life leads me but rarely down
To bask by the huge hearths of those old halls,
Carousing with the vassals; but the paths,
Which step from out our mountains to their doors,
I know from childhood—which of these is thine?
    MAN. No matter.
    C. HUN.        Well, sir, pardon me the question,
And be of better cheer. Come, taste my wine;
'Tis of an ancient vintage; many a day
'T has thaw'd my veins among our glaciers, now
Let it do thus for thine. Come, pledge me fairly.
    MAN. Away, away! there's blood upon the brim!
Will it then never—never sink in the earth?
    C. HUN. What dost thou mean? thy senses wander
    from thee.
    MAN. I say 'tis blood—my blood! the pure warm
    stream
Which ran in the veins of my fathers, and in ours
When we were in our youth, and had one heart,
And loved each other as we should not love,
And this was shed: but still it rises up,
Colouring the clouds, that shut me out from heaven,

Where thou art not—and I shall never be.

    C. Hun. Man of strange words, and some half-
        maddening sin,
Which makes thee people vacancy, whate'er
Thy dread and sufferance be, there's comfort yet—
The aid of holy men, and heavenly patience—

    Man. Patience and patience! Hence—that word
        was made
For brutes of burthen, not for birds of prey;
Preach it to mortals of a dust like thine,—
I am not of thine order.

    C. Hun.             Thanks to heaven!
I would not be of thine for the free fame
Of William Tell; but whatsoe'er thine ill,
It must be borne, and these wild starts are useless.

    Man. Do I not bear it?—Look on me—I live.

    C. Hun. This is convulsion, and no healthful life.

    Man. I tell thee, man! I have lived many years,
Many long years, but they are nothing now
To those which I must number: ages—ages—
Space and eternity—and consciousness,
With the fierce thirst of death—and still unslaked!

    C. Hun. Why, on thy brow the seal of middle age
Hath scarce been set; I am thine elder far.

    Man. Think'st thou existence doth depend on time?
It doth; but actions are our epochs: mine
Have made my days and nights imperishable,
Endless, and all alike, as sands on the shore,
Innumerable atoms; and one desert,
Barren and cold, on which the wild waves break,
But nothing rests, save carcasses and wrecks,
Rocks, and the salt-surf weeds of bitterness.

    C. Hun. Alas! he's mad—but yet I must not leave
        him.

    Man. I would I were, for then the things I see
Would be but a distemper'd dream.

    C. Hun.                 What is it
That thou dost see, or think thou look'st upon?

    Man. Myself, and thee—a peasant of the Alps,
Thy humble virtues, hospitable home,

And spirit patient, pious, proud and free;
Thy self-respect, grafted on innocent thoughts;
Thy days of health, and nights of sleep; thy toils,
By danger dignified, yet guiltless; hopes
Of cheerful old age and a quiet grave,
With cross and garland over its green turf,
And thy grandchildren's love for epitaph;
This do I see—and then I look within—
It matters not—my soul was scorch'd already!

   C. Hun. And wouldst thou then exchange thy lot for
      mine?

   Man. No, friend! I would not wrong thee nor
      exchange
My lot with living being: I can bear—
However wretchedly, 'tis still to bear—
In life what others could not brook to dream,
But perish in their slumber.

   C. Hun.           And with this—
This cautious feeling for another's pain,
Canst thou be black with evil?—say not so.
Can one of gentle thoughts have wreak'd revenge
Upon his enemies?

   Man.        Oh! no, no, no!
My injuries came down on those who loved me—
On those whom I best loved: I never quell'd
An enemy, save in my just defence—
But my embrace was fatal.

   C. Hun.           Heaven give thee rest!
And penitence restore thee to thyself;
My prayers shall be for thee.

   Man.         I need them not,
But can endure thy pity. I depart—
'Tis time—farewell!—Here's gold, and thanks for thee;
No words—it is thy due. Follow me not;
I know my path—the mountain peril's past:
And once again, I charge thee, follow not!

                        [*Exit* Manfred.

SCENE II.—*A lower Valley in the Alps.—A Cataract*

*Enter* MANFRED

It is not noon; the sunbow's rays still arch
The torrent with the many hues of heaven,
And roll the sheeted silver's waving column
O'er the crag's headlong perpendicular,
And fling its lines of foaming light along,
And to and fro, like the pale courser's tail,
The Giant steed, to be bestrode by Death,
As told in the Apocalypse.　No eyes
But mine now drink this sight of loveliness;
I should be sole in this sweet solitude,
And with the Spirit of the place divide
The homage of these waters.—I will call her.

    [MANFRED *takes some of the water into the palm of
        his hand, and flings it in the air, muttering the
        adjuration.　After a pause, the* WITCH OF THE
        ALPS *rises beneath the arch of the sunbow of the
        torrent.*

Beautiful Spirit! with thy hair of light
And dazzling eyes of glory, in whose form
The charms of earth's least mortal daughters grow
To an unearthly stature, in an essence
Of purer elements; while the hues of youth
(Carnation'd like a sleeping infant's cheek
Rock'd by the beating of her mother's heart,
Or the rose-tints, which summer's twilight leaves
Upon the lofty glacier's virgin snow,
The blush of earth embracing with her heaven)
Tinge thy celestial aspect, and make tame
The beauties of the sunbow which bends o'er thee.
Beautiful Spirit! in thy calm clear brow,
Wherein is glass'd serenity of soul,
Which of itself shows immortality,
I read that thou wilt pardon to a Son
Of Earth, whom the abstruser powers permit
At times to commune with them—if that he
Avail him of his spells—to call thee thus,
And gaze on thee a moment.

WITCH.                         Son of Earth!
I know thee, and the powers which give thee power;
I know thee for a man of many thoughts,
And deeds of good and ill, extreme in both,
Fatal and fated in thy sufferings.
I have expected this—what wouldst thou with me?
   MAN. To look upon thy beauty—nothing further.
The face of the earth hath madden'd me, and I
Take refuge in her mysteries, and pierce
To the abodes of those who govern her—
But they can nothing aid me. I have sought
From them what they could not bestow, and now
I search no further.
   WITCH.                What could be the quest
Which is not in the power of the most powerful,
The rulers of the invisible?
   MAN.                         A boon;
But why should I repeat it? 'twere in vain.
   WITCH. I know not that; let thy lips utter it.
   MAN. Well, though it torture me, 'tis but the same;
My pang shall find a voice. From my youth upwards
My spirit walk'd not with the souls of men,
Nor look'd upon the earth with human eyes;
The thirst of their ambition was not mine,
The aim of their existence was not mine;
My joys, my griefs, my passions, and my powers,
Made me a stranger; though I wore the form,
I had no sympathy with breathing flesh,
Nor midst the creatures of clay that girded me
Was there but one who—but of her anon.
I said, with men, and with the thoughts of men,
I held but slight communion; but instead,
My joy was in the Wilderness, to breathe
The difficult air of the iced mountain's top,
Where the birds dare not build, nor insect's wing
Flit o'er the herbless granite; or to plunge
Into the torrent, and to roll along
On the swift whirl of the new breaking wave
Of river-stream, or ocean, in their flow.
In these my early strength exulted; or

To follow through the night the moving moon,
The stars and their development; or catch
The dazzling lightnings till my eyes grew dim;
Or to look, list'ning, on the scatter'd leaves,
While Autumn winds were at their evening song.
These were my pastimes, and to be alone;
For if the beings, of whom I was one,—
Hating to be so,—cross'd me in my path,
I felt myself degraded back to them,
And was all clay again.  And then I dived,
In my lone wanderings, to the caves of death,
Searching its cause in its effect; and drew
From wither'd bones, and skulls, and heap'd up dust,
Conclusions most forbidden.  Then I pass'd
The nights of years in sciences, untaught
Save in the old time; and with time and toil,
And terrible ordeal, and such penance
As in itself hath power upon the air
And spirits that do compass air and earth,
Space, and the peopled infinite, I made
Mine eyes familiar with Eternity,
Such as, before me, did the Magi, and
He who from out their fountain dwellings raised
Eros and Anteros, at Gadara,
As I do thee;—and with my knowledge grew
The thirst of knowledge, and the power and joy
Of this most bright intelligence, until—
  WITCH. Proceed.
  MAN.                Oh, I but thus prolong'd my words,
Boasting these idle attributes, because
As I approach the core of my heart's grief—
But to my task.  I have not named to thee
Father or mother, mistress, friend, or being,
With whom I wore the chain of human ties;
If I had such, they seem'd not such to me—
Yet there was one—
  WITCH.          Spare not thyself—proceed.
  MAN. She was like me in lineaments—her eyes,
Her hair, her features, all, to the very tone
Even of her voice, they said were like to mine;

But soften'd all, and temper'd into beauty;
She had the same lone thoughts and wanderings,
The quest of hidden knowledge, and a mind
To comprehend the universe; nor these
Alone, but with them gentler powers than mine,
Pity, and smiles, and tears—which I had not;
And tenderness—but that I had for her;
Humility—and that I never had.
Her faults were mine—her virtues were her own—
I loved her, and destroy'd her!

 WITCH.     With thy hand?

 MAN. Not with my hand, but heart—which broke her
  heart;
It gazed on mine, and wither'd. I have shed
Blood, but not hers—and yet her blood was shed—
I saw, and could not stanch it.

 WITCH.    And for this
A being of the race thou dost despise,
The order which thine own would rise above,
Mingling with us and ours, thou dost forego
The gifts of our great knowledge, and shrink'st back
To recreant mortality—Away!

 MAN. Daughter of Air! I tell thee, since that hour—
But words are breath—look on me in my sleep,
Or watch my watchings—Come and sit by me!
My solitude is solitude no more,
But peopled with the Furies;—I have gnash'd
My teeth in darkness till returning morn,
Then cursed myself till sunset;—I have pray'd
For madness as a blessing—'tis denied me.
I have affronted death, but in the war
Of elements the waters shrunk from me,
And fatal things pass'd harmless—the cold hand
Of an all-pitiless demon held me back,
Back by a single hair, which would not break.
In fantasy, imagination, all
The affluence of my soul—which one day was
A Crœsus in creation—I plunged deep,
But, like an ebbing wave, it dash'd me back
Into the gulf of my unfathom'd thought.

I plunged amidst mankind.—Forgetfulness
I sought in all, save where 't is to be found,
And that I have to learn—my sciences,
My long pursued and superhuman art,
Is mortal here; I dwell in my despair—
And live—and live for ever.
  WITCH.      It may be
That I can aid thee.
  MAN.     To do this thy power
Must wake the dead, or lay me low with them.
Do so—in any shape—in any hour—
With any torture—so it be the last.
  WITCH. That is not in my province; but if thou
Wilt swear obedience to my will, and do
My bidding, it may help thee to thy wishes.
  MAN. I will not swear—Obey! and whom? the spirits
Whose presence I command, and be the slave
Of those who served me—Never!
  WITCH.      Is this all?
Hast thou no gentler answer?—Yet bethink thee,
And pause ere thou rejectest.
  MAN.      I have said it.
  WITCH. Enough!—I may retire then—say!
  MAN.          Retire!
         [*The* WITCH *disappears.*
  MAN. (*alone*). We are all the fools of time and terror:
    Days
Steal on us and steal from us; yet we live,
Loathing our life, and dreading still to die.
In all the days of this detested yoke—
This vital weight upon the struggling heart,
Which sinks with sorrow, or beats quick with pain,
Or joy that ends in agony or faintness—
In all the days of past and future, for
In life there is no present, we can number
How few, how less than few, wherein the soul
Forbears to pant for death, and yet draws back
As from a stream in winter, though the chill
Be but a moment's.  I have one resource
Still in my science—I can call the dead,

And ask them what it is we dread to be:
The sternest answer can but be the Grave,
And that is nothing;—if they answer not—
The buried Prophet answered to the Hag
Of Endor; and the Spartan Monarch drew
From the Byzantine maid's unsleeping spirit
An answer and his destiny—he slew
That which he loved, unknowing what he slew,
And died unpardon'd—though he call'd in aid
The Phyxian Jove, and in Phigalia roused
The Arcadian Evocators to compel
The indignant shadow to depose her wrath,
Or fix her term of vengeance—she replied
In words of dubious import, but fulfill'd.
If I had never lived, that which I love
Had still been living; had I never loved,
That which I love would still be beautiful—
Happy and giving happiness.   What is she?
What is she now?—a sufferer for my sins—
A thing I dare not think upon—or nothing.
Within few hours I shall not call in vain—
Yet in this hour I dread the thing I dare:
Until this hour I never shrunk to gaze
On spirit, good or evil—now I tremble,
And feel a strange cold thaw upon my heart.
But I can act even what I most abhor,
And champion human fears.—The night approaches.
                                    [*Exit.*


SCENE III.—*The Summit of the Jungfrau Mountain.*

*Enter* FIRST DESTINY

The moon is rising broad, and round, and bright;
And here on snows, where never human foot
Of common mortal trod, we nightly tread,
And leave no traces; o'er the savage sea,
The glassy ocean of the mountain ice,
We skim its rugged breakers, which put on
The aspect of a tumbling tempest's foam,
Frozen in a moment—a dead whirlpool's image.

And this most steep fantastic pinnacle,
The fretwork of some earthquake—where the clouds
Pause to repose themselves in passing by—
Is sacred to our revels, or our vigils.
Here do I wait my sisters, on our way
To the Hall of Arimanes, for to-night
Is our great festival—'t is strange they come not.

### A Voice without, singing

The Captive Usurper,
   Hurl'd down from the throne,
Lay buried in torpor,
   Forgotten and lone;
I broke through his slumbers,
   I shiver'd his chain,
I leagued him with numbers—
   He 's Tyrant again!
With the blood of a million he 'll answer my care,
With a nation's destruction—his flight and despair.

### Second Voice, without

The ship sail'd on, the ship sail'd fast,
But I left not a sail, and I left not a mast;
There is not a plank of the hull or the deck,
And there is not a wretch to lament o'er his wreck;
Save one, whom I held, as he swam, by the hair,
And he was a subject well worthy my care;
A traitor on land, and a pirate at sea—
But I saved him to wreak further havoc for me!

### First Destiny, answering

The city lies sleeping;
   The morn, to deplore it,
May dawn on it weeping:
   Sullenly, slowly,
The black plague flew o'er it,—
   Thousands lie lowly;
Tens of thousands shall perish—

> The living shall fly from
> The sick they should cherish:
>   But nothing can vanquish
> The touch that they die from.
>   Sorrow and anguish,
> And evil and dread,
>   Envelope a nation—
> The blest are the dead,
> Who see not the sight
>   Of their own desolation;
> This work of a night—

This wreck of a realm—this deed of my doing—
For ages I've done, and shall still be renewing!

*Enter the* SECOND *and* THIRD DESTINIES

### *The Three*

> Our hands contain the hearts of men,
>   Our footsteps are their graves;
> We only give to take again
>   The spirits of our slaves!

FIRST DES. Welcome! Where's Nemesis?
SECOND DES.                         At some great work;
But what I know not, for my hands were full.
    THIRD DES. Behold she cometh.

### *Enter* NEMESIS

FIRST DES.                  Say, where hast thou been?
My sisters and thyself are slow to-night.
    NEM. I was detain'd repairing shatter'd thrones,
Marrying fools, restoring dynasties,
Avenging men upon their enemies,
And making them repent their own revenge;
Goading the wise to madness; from the dull
Shaping out oracles to rule the world
Afresh, for they were waxing out of date,
And mortals dared to ponder for themselves,

To weigh kings in the balance, and to speak
Of freedom, the forbidden fruit.—Away!
We have outstay'd the hour—mount we our clouds!

                                             [*Exeunt.*

Scene IV.—*The Hall of* Arimanes—Arimanes *on his Throne, a
        Globe of Fire, surrounded by the Spirits.*

### *Hymn of the* Spirits

Hail to our Master!—Prince of Earth and Air!
  Who walks the clouds and waters—in his hand
The sceptre of the elements which tear
  Themselves to chaos at his high command!
He breatheth—and a tempest shakes the sea;
  He speaketh—and the clouds reply in thunder;
He gazeth—from his glance the sunbeams flee;
  He moveth—earthquakes rend the world asunder.
Beneath his footsteps the volcanoes rise;
  His shadow is the Pestilence; his path
The comets herald through the crackling skies;
  And planets turn to ashes at his wrath.
To him War offers daily sacrifice;
  To him Death pays his tribute; Life is his,
With all its infinite of agonies—
  And his the spirit of whatever is!

### *Enter the* Destinies *and* Nemesis

First Des. Glory to Arimanes! on the earth
His power increaseth—both my sisters did
His bidding, nor did I neglect my duty!
  Second Des. Glory to Arimanes! we who bow
The necks of men, bow down before his throne!
  Third Des. Glory to Arimanes! we await
His nod!
  Nem.      Sovereign of Sovereigns! we are thine,
And all that liveth, more or less, is ours,
And most things wholly so; still to increase
Our power, increasing thine, demands our care,
And we are vigilant.—Thy late commands
Have been fulfilled to the utmost.

*Enter* MANFRED

A SPIRIT.                              What is here?
A mortal!—Thou most rash and fatal wretch,
Bow down and worship!
    SECOND SPIRIT.              I do know the man—
A Magian of great power and fearful skill!
    THIRD SPIRIT. Bow down and worship, slave! What,
        know'st thou not
Thine and our Sovereign?—Tremble, and obey!
    ALL THE SPIRITS. Prostrate thyself, and thy con-
        demnèd clay,
Child of the Earth! or dread the worst.
    MAN.                              I know it;
And yet ye see I kneel not.
    FOURTH SPIRIT.              'Twill be taught thee.
    MAN. 'Tis taught already;—many a night on the earth,
On the bare ground, have I bow'd down my face,
And strew'd my head with ashes; I have known
The fulness of humiliation, for
I sunk before my vain despair, and knelt
To my own desolation.
    FIFTH SPIRIT.              Dost thou dare
Refuse to Arimanes on his throne
What the whole earth accords, beholding not
The terror of his Glory?—Crouch! I say.
    MAN. Bid *him* bow down to that which is above him,
The overruling Infinite, the Maker
Who made him not for worship—let him kneel,
And we will kneel together.
    THE SPIRITS.              Crush the worm!
Tear him in pieces!—
    FIRST DES.              Hence! Avaunt!—he's mine.
Prince of the Powers invisible! This man
Is of no common order, as his port
And presence here denote. His sufferings
Have been of an immortal nature, like
Our own; his knowledge and his powers and will,
As far as is compatible with clay,
Which clogs the ethereal essence, have been such

As clay hath seldom borne; his aspirations
Have been beyond the dwellers of the earth,
And they have only taught him what we know—
That knowledge is not happiness, and science
But an exchange of ignorance for that
Which is another kind of ignorance.
This is not all; the passions, attributes
Of earth and heaven, from which no power, nor being,
Nor breath from the worm upwards is exempt,
Have pierced his heart; and in their consequence
Made him a thing, which I, who pity not,
Yet pardon those who pity.  He is mine,
And thine, it may be;—be it so, or not,
No other Spirit in this region hath
A soul like his—or power upon his soul.

   NEM. What doth he here then?
   FIRST DES.                          Let him answer that.
   MAN. Ye know what I have known; and without
      power
I could not be amongst ye: but there are
Powers deeper still beyond—I come in quest
Of such, to answer unto what I seek.
   NEM. What wouldst thou?
   MAN.                          Thou canst not reply to me.
Call up the dead—my question is for them.
   NEM. Great Arimanes, doth thy will avouch
The wishes of this mortal?
   ARI.                          Yea.
   NEM.                                    Whom wouldst thou
Uncharnel?
   MAN.       One without a tomb—call up Astarte.


NEMESIS

Shadow! or Spirit!
  Whatever thou art
Which still doth inherit
  The whole or a part
Of the form of thy birth,
Of the mould of thy clay

Which return'd to the earth,—
    Re-appear to the day!
Bear what thou borest,
    The heart and the form,
And the aspect thou worest
    Redeem from the worm.
Appear!—Appear!—Appear!
Who sent thee there requires thee here!

[*The phantom of* ASTARTE *rises and stands in the midst*

MAN. Can this be death? there's bloom upon her cheek;
But now I see it is no living hue,
But a strange hectic—like the unnatural red
Which Autumn plants upon the perish'd leaf.
It is the same! Oh, God! that I should dread
To look upon the same—Astarte!—No,
I cannot speak to her—but bid her speak—
Forgive me or condemn me.


NEMESIS

By the power which hath broken
    The grave which enthrall'd thee,
Speak to him who hath spoken,
    Or those who have call'd thee!


MAN.                              She is silent,
And in that silence I am more than answer'd.
    NEM. My power extends no further, Prince of Air!
It rests with thee alone—command her voice.
    ARI. Spirit—obey this sceptre!
    NEM.                          Silent still!
She is not of our order, but belongs
To the other powers. Mortal! thy quest is vain,
And we are baffled also.
    MAN.                    Hear me, hear me—
Astarte! my belovèd! speak to me:
I have so much endured, so much endure—
Look on me! the grave hath not changed thee more
Than I am changed for thee. Thou lovèdst me

Too much, as I loved thee: we were not made
To torture thus each other, though it were
The deadliest sin to love as we have loved.
Say that thou loath'st me not, that I do bear
This punishment for both, that thou wilt be
One of the blessèd, and that I shall die;
For hitherto all hateful things conspire
To bind me in existence—in a life
Which makes me shrink from immortality—
A future like the past.  I cannot rest.
I know not what I ask, nor what I seek;
I feel but what thou art—and what I am;
And I would hear yet once before I perish
The voice which was my music—Speak to me!
For I have call'd on thee in the still night,
Startled the slumbering birds from the hush'd boughs,
And woke the mountain wolves, and made the caves
Acquainted with thy vainly echo'd name,
Which answer'd me—many things answer'd me—
Spirits and men—but thou wert silent all.
Yet speak to me! I have outwatch'd the stars,
And gazed o'er heaven in vain in search of thee,
Speak to me!  I have wander'd o'er the earth,
And never found thy likeness—Speak to me!
Look on the fiends around—they feel for me:
I fear them not, and feel for thee alone.
Speak to me! though it be in wrath;—but say—
I reck not what—but let me hear thee once—
This once—once more!

    Phantom of Astarte.  Manfred!
    Man.                  Say on, say on—
I live but in the sound—it is thy voice!
    Phan. Manfred!  To-morrow ends thine earthly ills.
Farewell!
    Man. Yet one word more—am I forgiven?
    Phan. Farewell!
    Man.        Say, shall we meet again?
    Phan.                 Farewell!
    Man. One word for mercy!  Say, thou lovest me.
    Phan. Manfred!  [*The Spirit of* Astarte *disappears.*

NEM.                 She's gone, and will not be recall'd;
Her words will be fulfill'd.  Return to the earth.
    A SPIRIT. He is convulsed—This is to be a mortal
And seek the things beyond mortality.
    ANOTHER SPIRIT.  Yet, see, he mastereth himself, and
        makes
His torture tributary to his will.
Had he been one of us, he would have made
An awful spirit.
    NEM.                Hast thou further question
Of our great sovereign, or his worshippers?
    MAN. None.
    NEM.              Then for a time farewell.
    MAN. We meet then!  Where?  On the earth?—
Even as thou wilt: and for the grace accorded
I now depart a debtor.  Fare ye well!
                                        [*Exit* MANFRED.
        (*Scene closes.*)


                    ACT III

    SCENE I.—*A Hall in the Castle of* MANFRED

            MANFRED *and* HERMAN

    MAN. What is the hour?
    HER.                      It wants but one till sunset,
And promises a lovely twilight.
    MAN.                        Say,
Are all things so disposed of in the tower
As I directed?
    HER.          All, my lord, are ready:
Here is the key and casket.
    MAN.                      It is well:
Thou may'st retire.                    [*Exit* HERMAN.
    MAN. (*alone*).      There is a calm upon me—
Inexplicable stillness! which till now
Did not belong to what I knew of life.
If that I did not know philosophy
To be of all our vanities the motliest,
The merest word that ever fool'd the ear

From out the schoolman's jargon, I should deem
The golden secret, the sought "Kalon," found,
And seated in my soul.  It will not last,
But it is well to have known it, though but once:
It hath enlarged my thoughts with a new sense,
And I within my tablets would note down
That there is such a feeling.  Who is there?


*Re-enter* HERMAN

HER. My lord, the abbot of St. Maurice craves
To greet your presence.


*Enter the* ABBOT OF ST. MAURICE

ABBOT.                     Peace be with Count Manfred!
MAN. Thanks, holy father! welcome to these walls;
Thy presence honours them, and blesseth those
Who dwell within them.
    ABBOT.                 Would it were so, Count!—
But I would fain confer with thee alone.
    MAN. Herman, retire.—What would my reverend
        guest?
    ABBOT. Thus, without prelude:—Age and zeal, my
        office,
And good intent, must plead my privilege;
Our near, though not acquainted neighbourhood,
May also be my herald.  Rumours strange,
And of unholy nature, are abroad,
And busy with thy name; a noble name
For centuries: may he who bears it now
Transmit it unimpair'd!
    MAN.                 Proceed, I listen.
    ABBOT. 'Tis said thou holdest converse with the things
Which are forbidden to the search of man;
That with the dwellers of the dark abodes,
The many evil and unheavenly spirits
Which walk the valley of the shade of death,
Thou communest.  I know that with mankind,
Thy fellows in creation, thou dost rarely
Exchange thy thoughts, and that thy solitude

Is as an anchorite's, were it but holy.

MAN. And what are they who do avouch these things?

ABBOT. My pious brethren, the scared peasantry,
Even thy own vassals, who do look on thee
With most unquiet eyes. Thy life's in peril.

MAN. Take it.

ABBOT. I come to save, and not destroy.
I would not pry into thy secret soul;
But if these things be sooth, there still is time
For penitence and pity: reconcile thee
With the true church, and through the church to heaven.

MAN. I hear thee. This is my reply: whate'er
I may have been, or am, doth rest between
Heaven and myself; I shall not choose a mortal
To be my mediator. Have I sinn'd
Against your ordinances? prove and punish!

ABBOT. My son! I did not speak of punishment,
But penitence and pardon; with thyself
The choice of such remains—and for the last,
Our institutions and our strong belief
Have given me power to smooth the path from sin
To higher hope and better thoughts; the first
I leave to heaven,—" Vengeance is mine alone!"
So saith the Lord, and with all humbleness
His servant echoes back the awful word.

MAN. Old man! there is no power in holy men,
Nor charm in prayer, nor purifying form
Of penitence, nor outward look, nor fast,
Nor agony, nor, greater than all these,
The innate tortures of that deep despair,
Which is remorse without the fear of hell
But all in all sufficient to itself
Would make a hell of heaven,—can exorcise
From out the unbounded spirit the quick sense
Of its own sins, wrongs, sufferance, and revenge
Upon itself; there is no future pang
Can deal that justice on the self-condemn'd
He deals on his own soul.

ABBOT. All this is well;
For this will pass away, and be succeeded

By an auspicious hope, which shall look up
With calm assurance to that blessed place
Which all who seek may win, whatever be
Their earthly errors, so they be atoned:
And the commencement of atonement is
The sense of its necessity.—Say on—
And all our church can teach thee shall be taught;
And all we can absolve thee shall be pardon'd.

MAN. When Rome's sixth emperor was near his last,
The victim of a self-inflicted wound,
To shun the torments of a public death
From senates once his slaves, a certain soldier,
With show of loyal pity, would have stanch'd
The gushing throat with his officious robe;
The dying Roman thrust him back, and said—
Some empire still in his expiring glance—
"It is too late, is this fidelity?"

ABBOT. And what of this?
MAN.           I answer with the Roman,
"It is too late!"

ABBOT.      It never can be so,
To reconcile thyself with thy own soul,
And thy own soul with heaven. Hast thou no hope?
'Tis strange—even those who do despair above,
Yet shape themselves some fantasy on earth,
To which frail twig they cling like drowning men.

MAN. Ay—father! I have had those earthly visions
And noble aspirations in my youth,
To make my own the mind of other men,
The enlightener of nations; and to rise
I knew not whither—it might be to fall;
But fall, even as the mountain-cataract,
Which, having leapt from its more dazzling height,
Even in the foaming strength of its abyss
(Which casts up misty columns that become
Clouds raining from the reascended skies)
Lies low but mighty still.—But this is past,
My thoughts mistook themselves.

ABBOT.           And wherefore so?
MAN. I could not tame my nature down; for he

Must serve who fain would sway—and soothe, and sue,
And watch all time, and pry into all place,
And be a living lie, who would become
A mighty thing amongst the mean, and such
The mass are; I disdain'd to mingle with
A herd, though to be leader—and of wolves.
The lion is alone, and so am I.

 ABBOT. And why not live and act with other men?

 MAN. Because my nature was averse from life;
And yet not cruel; for I would not make,
But find a desolation.  Like the wind,
The red-hot breath of the most lone Simoom,
Which dwells but in the desert and sweeps o'er
The barren sands which bear no shrubs to blast,
And revels o'er their wild and arid waves,
And seeketh not, so that it is not sought,
But being met is deadly,—such hath been
The course of my existence; but there came
Things in my path which are no more.

 ABBOT.       Alas!
I 'gin to fear that thou art past all aid
From me and from my calling; yet so young,
I still would—

 MAN.   Look on me! there is an order
Of mortals on the earth, who do become
Old in their youth, and die ere middle age,
Without the violence of warlike death;
Some perishing of pleasure, some of study,
Some worn with toil, some of mere weariness,
Some of disease, and some insanity,
And some of wither'd or of broken hearts;
For this last is a malady which slays
More than are number'd in the lists of Fate,
Taking all shapes and bearing many names.
Look upon me! for even of all these things
Have I partaken; and of all these things,
One were enough; then wonder not that I
Am what I am, but that I ever was,
Or having been, that I am still on earth.

 ABBOT. Yet, hear me still—

MAN. Old man! I do respect
Thine order, and revere thine years; I deem
Thy purpose pious, but it is in vain.
Think me not churlish; I would spare thyself,
Far more than me, in shunning at this time
All further colloquy; and so—farewell.

[*Exit* MANFRED.

ABBOT. This should have been a noble creature: he
Hath all the energy which would have made
A goodly frame of glorious elements,
Had they been wisely mingled; as it is,
It is an awful chaos—light and darkness,
And mind and dust, and passions and pure thoughts,
Mix'd, and contending without end or order,
All dormant or destructive. He will perish,
And yet he must not; I will try once more,
For such are worth redemption; and my duty
Is to dare all things for a righteous end.
I'll follow him—but cautiously, though surely.

[*Exit* ABBOT.


SCENE II.—*Another Chamber.*

MANFRED *and* HERMAN

HER. My lord, you bade me wait on you at sunset:
He sinks beyond the mountain.
MAN. Doth he so?
I will look on him.

[MANFRED *advances to the Window of the Hall.*
Glorious Orb! the idol
Of early nature, and the vigorous race
Of undiseased mankind, the giant sons
Of the embrace of angels with a sex
More beautiful than they, which did draw down
The erring spirits who can ne'er return;—
Most glorious orb! that wert a worship, ere
The mystery of thy making was reveal'd!
Thou earliest minister of the Almighty,
Which gladden'd, on their mountain tops, the hearts
Of the Chaldean shepherds, till they pour'd

Themselves in orisons! Thou material God!
And representative of the Unknown,
Who chose thee for his shadow! Thou chief star!
Centre of many stars! which mak'st our earth
Endurable, and temperest the hues
And hearts of all who walk within thy rays!
Sire of the seasons! Monarch of the climes,
And those who dwell in them! for near or far,
Our inborn spirits have a tint of thee,
Even as our outward aspects;—thou dost rise
And shine, and set in glory. Fare thee well!
I ne'er shall see thee more. As my first glance
Of love and wonder was for thee, then take
My latest look: thou wilt not beam on one
To whom the gifts of life and warmth have been
Of a more fatal nature. He is gone;
I follow.                        [*Exit* MANFRED.

SCENE III.—*The Mountains.—The Castle of* MANFRED *at some distance.—A Terrace before a Tower.—Time, Twilight.*

HERMAN, MANUEL, *and other Dependants of* MANFRED

    HER. 'Tis strange enough; night after night, for
        years,
He hath pursued long vigils in this tower,
Without a witness. I have been within it,—
So have we all been oft-times; but from it,
Or its contents, it were impossible
To draw conclusions absolute of aught
His studies tend to. To be sure, there is
One chamber where none enter: I would give
The fee of what I have to come these three years,
To pore upon its mysteries.
    MANUEL.             'Twere dangerous;
Content thyself with what thou knowest already.
    HER. Ah, Manuel! thou art elderly and wise,
And couldst say much; thou hast dwelt within the
        castle—
How many years is 't?

MANUEL.                    Ere Count Manfred's birth,
I served his father, whom he nought resembles.

HER. There be more sons in like predicament.
But wherein do they differ?

MANUEL.                              I speak not
Of features or of form, but mind and habits;
Count Sigismund was proud, but gay and free—
A warrior and a reveller; he dwelt not
With books and solitude, nor made the night
A gloomy vigil, but a festal time,
Merrier than day; he did not walk the rocks
And forests like a wolf, nor turn aside
From men and their delights.

HER.                              Beshrew the hour,
But those were jocund times! I would that such
Would visit the old walls again; they look
As if they had forgotten them.

MANUEL.                              These walls
Must change their chieftain first. Oh! I have seen
Some strange things in them, Herman.

HER.                                    Come, be friendly;
Relate me some to while away our watch:
I've heard thee darkly speak of an event
Which happen'd hereabouts, by this same tower.

MANUEL. That was a night indeed! I do remember
'T was twilight, as it may be now, and such
Another evening; yon red cloud, which rests
On Eigher's pinnacle, so rested then,—
So like that it might be the same; the wind
Was faint and gusty, and the mountain snows
Began to glitter with the climbing moon.
Count Manfred was, as now, within his tower,—
How occupied, we knew not, but with him
The sole companion of his wanderings
And watchings—her, whom of all earthly things
That lived, the only thing he seem'd to love,—
As he, indeed, by blood was bound to do
The Lady Astarte, his—

                         Hush! who comes here?

*Enter the* ABBOT

ABBOT. Where is your master?
HER.                              Yonder in the tower.
ABBOT. I must speak with him.
MANUEL.                          'Tis impossible;
He is most private, and must not be thus
Intruded on.
    ABBOT.         Upon myself I take
The forfeit of my fault, if fault there be—
But I must see him.
    HER.                Thou hast seen him once
This eve already.
    ABBOT.            Herman! I command thee,
Knock, and apprize the Count of my approach.
    HER. We dare not.
    ABBOT.                  Then it seems I must be herald
Of my own purpose.
    MANUEL.            Reverend father, stop—
I pray you pause.
    ABBOT.        Why so?
    MANUEL.                But step this way,
And I will tell you further.            [*Exeunt.*


SCENE IV.—*Interior of the Tower*

MANFRED, *alone*

The stars are forth, the moon above the tops
Of the snow-shining mountains.—Beautiful!
I linger yet with Nature, for the night
Hath been to me a more familiar face
Than that of man; and in her starry shade
Of dim and solitary loveliness,
I learn'd the language of another world.
I do remember me, that in my youth,
When I was wandering,—upon such a night
I stood within the Coliseum's wall
Midst the chief relics of almighty Rome.
The trees which grew along the broken arches

Waved dark in the blue midnight, and the stars
Shone through the rents of ruin; from afar
The watch-dog bay'd beyond the Tiber; and
More near from out the Cæsars' palace came
The owl's long cry, and, interruptedly,
Of distant sentinels the fitful song
Begun and died upon the gentle wind.
Some cypresses beyond the time-worn breach
Appear'd to skirt the horizon, yet they stood
Within a bowshot. Where the Cæsars dwelt,
And dwell the tuneless birds of night, amidst
A grove which springs through levell'd battlements
And twines its roots with the imperial hearths,
Ivy usurps the laurel's place of growth;—
But the gladiators' bloody Circus stands,
A noble wreck in ruinous perfection!
While Cæsar's chambers and the Augustan halls
Grovel on earth in indistinct decay.
And thou didst shine, thou rolling moon, upon
All this, and cast a wide and tender light,
Which soften'd down the hoar austerity
Of rugged desolation, and fill'd up,
As 't were anew, the gaps of centuries;
Leaving that beautiful which still was so,
And making that which was not, till the place
Became religion, and the heart ran o'er
With silent worship of the great of old,—
The dead, but sceptred sovereigns, who still rule
Our spirits from their urns.—
                          'T was such a night!
'T is strange that I recall it at this time;
But I have found our thoughts take wildest flight
Even at the moment when they should array
Themselves in pensive order.

*Enter the* ABBOT

ABBOT.                         My good lord!
I crave a second grace for this approach;
But yet let not my humble zeal offend

By its abruptness—all it hath of ill
Recoils on me; its good in the effect
May light upon your head—could I say *heart*—
Could I touch *that,* with words or prayers, I should
Recall a noble spirit which hath wander'd
But is not yet all lost.
    MAN.               Thou know'st me not;
My days are number'd, and my deeds recorded:
Retire, or 't will be dangerous—Away!
    ABBOT. Thou dost not mean to menace me?
    MAN.                       Not I;
I simply tell thee peril is at hand,
And would preserve thee.
    ABBOT.           What dost thou mean?
    MAN.                   Look there!
What dost thou see?
    ABBOT.         Nothing.
    MAN.              Look there, I say,
And steadfastly;—now tell me what thou seest.
    ABBOT. That which should shake me—but I fear it
    not:
I see a dusk and awful figure rise,
Like an infernal god, from out the earth;
His face wrapt in a mantle, and his form
Robed as with angry clouds: he stands between
Thyself and me—but I do fear him not.
    MAN. Thou hast no cause; he shall not harm thee, but
His sight may shock thine old limbs into palsy.
I say to thee—Retire!
    ABBOT.         And I reply,
Never—till I have battled with this fiend:—
What doth he here?
    MAN. Why—ay—what doth he here?
I did not send for him,—he is unbidden.
    ABBOT. Alas! lost mortal! what with guests like
    these
Hast thou to do? I tremble for thy sake:
Why doth he gaze on thee, and thou on him?
Ah! he unveils his aspect: on his brow
The thunder-scars are graven; from his eye

Glares forth the immortality of hell—
Avaunt!—

    MAN.       Pronounce—what is thy mission?

    SPIRIT.                       Come!

    ABBOT. What art thou, unknown being? answer!—
      speak!

    SPIRIT. The genius of this mortal.—Come! 't is time.

    MAN. I am prepared for all things, but deny
The power which summons me. Who sent thee here?

    SPIRIT. Thou 'lt know anon—Come! Come!

    MAN.                   I have commanded
Things of an essence greater far than thine,
And striven with thy masters. Get thee hence!

    SPIRIT. Mortal! thine hour is come—Away! I say.

    MAN. I knew, and know my hour is come, but not
To render up my soul to such as thee:
Away! I 'll die as I have lived—alone.

    SPIRIT. Then I must summon up my brethren.—Rise!
                                    [*Other Spirits rise up.*

    ABBOT. Avaunt! ye evil ones!—Avaunt! I say,—
Ye have no power where piety hath power,
And I do charge ye in the name—

    SPIRIT.                  Old man!
We know ourselves, our mission, and thine order;
Waste not thy holy words on idle uses,
It were in vain: this man is forfeited.
Once more I summon him—Away! away!

    MAN. I do defy ye,—though I feel my soul
Is ebbing from me, yet I do defy ye;
Nor will I hence, while I have earthly breath
To breathe my scorn upon ye—earthly strength
To wrestle, though with spirits; what ye take
Shall be ta'en limb by limb.

    SPIRIT.               Reluctant mortal!
Is this the Magian who would so pervade
The world invisible, and make himself
Almost our equal?—Can it be that thou
Art thus in love with life? the very life
Which made thee wretched!

    MAN.               Thou false fiend, thou liest!

My life is in its last hour,—*that* I know,
Nor would redeem a moment of that hour.
I do not combat against death, but thee
And thy surrounding angels; my past power
Was purchased by no compact with thy crew,
But by superior science, penance, daring,
And length of watching, strength of mind, and skill
In knowledge of our fathers when the earth
Saw men and spirits walking side by side
And gave ye no supremacy: I stand
Upon my strength—I do defy—deny—
Spurn back, and scorn ye!—

    Spirit.                    But thy many crimes
Have made thee—

    Man.   What are they to such as thee?
Must crimes be punish'd but by other crimes,
And greater criminals?—Back to thy hell!
Thou hast no power upon me, *that* I feel;
Thou never shalt possess me, *that* I know:
What I have done is done; I bear within
A torture which could nothing gain from thine.
The mind which is immortal makes itself
Requital for its good or evil thoughts,
Is its own origin of ill and end,
And its own place and time; its innate sense,
When stripp'd of this mortality, derives
No colour from the fleeting things without,
But is absorb'd in sufferance or in joy,
Born from the knowledge of its own desert.
*Thou* didst not tempt me, and thou couldst not tempt me;
I have not been thy dupe nor am thy prey,
But was my own destroyer, and will be
My own hereafter.—Back, ye baffled fiends!
The hand of death is on me—but not yours!

                              *[The Demons disappear.*

    Abbot. Alas! how pale thou art—thy lips are white—
And thy breast heaves—and in thy gasping throat
The accents rattle. Give thy prayers to Heaven—
Pray—albeit but in thought,—but die not thus.

    Man. 'T is over—my dull eyes can fix thee not;

But all things swim around me, and the earth
Heaves as it were beneath me.  Fare thee well—
Give me thy hand.
   ABBOT.          Cold—cold—even to the heart—
But yet one prayer—Alas! how fares it with thee?
  MAN. Old man! 't is not so difficult to die.

                             [MANFRED *expires.*
  ABBOT. He's gone, his soul hath ta'en its earthless
      flight;
Whither?  I dread to think; but he is gone.

THE PUBLISHERS OF THE HAR-
VARD CLASSICS · DR. ELIOT'S
FIVE-FOOT SHELF OF BOOKS · ARE
PLEASED TO ANNOUNCE THE
PUBLICATION OF

## THE JUNIOR CLASSICS
### A LIBRARY FOR BOYS AND GIRLS

"The Junior Classics constitute a set
of books whose contents will delight
children and at the same time
satisfy the legitimate ethical require-
ments of those who have the children's
best interests at heart."

CHARLES W. ELIOT

THE COLLIER PRESS · NEW YORK
P · F · COLLIER & SON